THE TRIALS OF MASCULINITY

ANGUS McLAREN

THE TRIALS OF MASCULINITY
Policing Sexual Boundaries
1870–1930

THE UNIVERSITY OF CHICAGO PRESS
Chicago & London

Angus McLaren is professor of history at the University of Victoria. He is the author of several books including: *A Prescription for Murder: The Victorian Serial Killings of Dr. Thomas Neill Cream* (University of Chicago Press, 1993); *Our Own Master Race: Eugenics in Canada* (McClelland & Stewart, 1990); and *A History of Contraception* (Blackwell, 1990).

The University of Chicago Press, Chicago 60637
The University of Chicago Press, Ltd., London

© 1997 by The University of Chicago
All rights reserved. Published 1997

Printed in the United States of America

06 05 04 03 02 01 00 99 98 97   5 4 3 2 1

ISBN (cloth): 0-226-50067-5

Library of Congress Cataloging-in-Publication Data

McLaren, Angus.
    The trials of masculinity : policing sexual boundaries, 1870–1930
/ Angus McLaren.
        p.   cm.—(Chicago series on sexuality, history, and society)
    Includes bibliographical references and index.
    ISBN 0-226-50067-5 (cloth : acid-free paper)
    1. Men—History—Sources.   2. Masculinity (Psychology)—History—
    Sources.   3. Sex role—History—Sources.   I. Title.   II. Series.
HQ1090.M397   1997
305.31'09—dc21   96-29523
                                                              CIP

Contents

ACKNOWLEDGMENTS

IN THE COURSE OF THE NINETEENTH CENTURY, MANY MEN made a point of becoming bigger and fatter to advertise their wealth and power. Even genius, claimed Théophile Gautier, manifested itself in a man's girth. It was taken as high praise to state that Balzac had a barrel-like body, that Rossini resembled a hippopotamus, that Lablache was elephantine. The cult of corpulence had worshipers on both sides of the Atlantic. When in 1908 William Howard Taft was elected president of the United States, he weighed in at 332 pounds. At the turn of the century, as E. L. Doctorow noted in *Ragtime,* "the consumption of food was a sacrament of success. A man who carried a great stomach before him was thought to be in his prime." Perhaps because I have a slight build myself, I long wondered how it could be that such bloated behemoths were once taken as paragons of masculinity. And who were these big men most trying to intimidate, women or lesser men?

These sorts of apparently inconsequential questions started me on an exploration of evolving models of manhood. Regretfully I found that to come to a satisfying understanding of how concepts of normal and deviant masculinity were worked out in the past I had to abandon the entertainments provided by nineteenth-century saloons and chop-houses for the more restrained theatrics that courts and consulting rooms offered. I had, however, very good company. Those who contributed to making this book possible include Judith Allen, Peter Bailey, Leonard Berlanstein, Vern Bullough, William Bynum, Alain Corbin, Christine Delphy, Karen Dubinsky, John Duder, Richard Evans, Marvin Glasser, John Gillis, Annalee Golz, Lesley Hall, John Fout, Anita Fellman, Christopher Friedrichs, Ginger Frost, Philippa Levine, Arlene Tigar McLaren, John McLaren, Francis Ronsin, Martine Segalen, Mary Lynn Stewart, and Cornelie Usborne. Useful feedback on portions of the work was provided by participants at a "Gender and Crime" conference held at the Roehampton Institute, a "History of the Body" conference sponsored by the Society for the Social History of Medicine at University College London, a history workshop at the University of British Columbia, and by the audiences at a series of lectures given at Indiana University. Portions of chapters 4 and 6 appeared in *Medical History* and the *Journal of Social History;* I am grateful to the Trustee, the Wellcome Trust, and the editors and publishers for permission to reprint this material. I owe special thanks to Brian Dippie and Robert Nye, who read the entire manuscript and offered trenchant criticism. Sara Smith did even more. In addition to savaging a first draft, she peppered me with a steady stream of references and citations.

I would also like to express my gratitude to the Social Sciences and Humanities Research Council of Canada, whose generosity made possible the numerous research trips that this project required. At home at the University of Victoria, I received essential support from both the secretaries and my colleagues in the History Department and the librarians at McPherson Library. Susan Johnston was an incredibly insightful and industrious research assistant. When I was on the road, the staffs of the Wellcome Institute for the History of Medicine, the British Library, the Bibliothèque Nationale, the Public Archives of British Columbia, and the Woodward Medical Library at the University of British Columbia were, as always, enormously helpful. John Fout prodded me into launching this study and Douglas Mitchell, Matthew Howard, and David Blair made completing it a pleasure.

In Victoria June Bull did a wonderful job in rescuing me from the various catastrophes caused by a reliance on an ancient—that is to say, five-year-old—computer. In Paris, when the said laptop finally crashed, Christine Delphy kindly offered the use of her own machine. Arlene and Jesse kept the project on an even keel; Arlene by continually impressing upon me the necessity of appreciating the insights of feminist scholarship; Jesse by demonstrating how inherently fascinating the passage to young manhood is.

A READING OF THE *Oxford English Dictionary*'S ENTRIES under the subject "man" serves as a forceful reminder of how central sex and gender norms were to power and cultural categories at the turn of the century. To have a "man-to-man talk," we are told, was to speak directly; "to be one's own man" was to be in full possession of one's faculties; to "play the man" was to act courageously; to be "the man" was to be the one in charge. These were more than simple figures of speech. Around 1930 a man who killed "like a man" was applauded by spectators and set free in one courtroom, while in another the judge sentenced the accused, whose only crime had been to dress like a woman, to a prison term of eighteen months' hard labor. Such cases dramatically demonstrated the importance early twentieth-century society assigned to the question of sexual identity. Western culture had, of course, always stressed male and female differences. But in relatively recent times, gender had become privileged, often eclipsing one's rank, status, profession, race, or religion as the key determinant of personality.[1]

The body, Pierre Bourdieu reminds us, carries the "fundamental principles of the arbitrary content of the culture." For "nothing seems more ineffable, more incommunicable, more inimitable, and, therefore, more precious, than the values given [the] body, the process whereby male and female bodies are split is mystified."[2] This study seeks to reveal how the process of construction of what many in the West now assume to be natural, timeless male and female genders took place between the eighteenth and the twentieth centuries. The book focuses particularly on the period between 1870 and 1930, when extreme claims for sexual incommensurability were made. There is much good evidence, as a number of historians have demonstrated, that new scientific norms of male and female sexuality were propounded in the late nineteenth century by sexologists and psychiatrists because social transformations (such as the changing nature of men's work, the rise of the white collar service sector, the reduction of the birth rate, and women's entry into higher education and the professions) appeared in the eyes of anxious observers to have undermined the explanatory powers of older notions of masculinity and femininity.[3]

Many of the scholars who first examined the emergence of the late-nineteenth-century preoccupation with sex and gender presented it as a positive, progressive refashioning of our thinking about human sexuality.[4] Michel Foucault countered such optimism, arguing that the freshly created sexual categories and gender norms of the nineteenth century underlay yet another system of power. The professionals in medicine, criminology, pedagogy, and the law, he asserted, took over the regulatory and punitive functions of the absolutist state and elaborated new mechanisms of constraint. The experts' ultimate goal was to organize power over the social body through the agency of human bodies.[5] In essence, male power was revived and now buttressed by biologism. Authors who have followed up on many of Foucault's insights while seeking to avoid the notion of a simple conflict between the forces of freedom and oppression include Thomas Laqueur, Lawrence Birken, and Cynthia Eagle Russett with their important studies of models of sexuality; Ruth Harris, Judith Walkowitz, and Caroll Smith-Rosenberg who investigated the policing of femininity; Jeffrey Weeks, who analyzed the construction of homosexuality; and Robert Nye, E. Anthony Rotundo, Lesley Hall, and Kevin White, who dealt particularly with the refashioning of notions of heterosexuality.[6]

This book has as its focus the turn-of-the-century mapping of the boundaries of masculinity.[7] The goal is to show that the norms of male heterosexuality were not innate, but socially and culturally constructed. The intent is to shatter the illusion of permanence and naturalness with which experts endowed late-nineteenth-century gender relations. We do so by revealing the ways in which new boundaries of normal male and female behavior were freshly established by doctors, sexologists, magistrates, and sex reformers between 1870 and 1930. The focus is primarily on how such experts exploited the stereotype of a virile, heterosexual, and aggressive masculinity. They did not so much "create" the stereotype; it would be more accurate to say that they selected and declared preeminent one particular model of masculinity from an existing range of male gender roles.

An examination of these professionals' preoccupations helps us to see that men were gendered subjects and that masculinity had a variety of changing forms. The approach adopted here is to ask why some sex roles were naturalized and others disqualified, why there were inclusions and exclusions. This tack allows a historicizing of a range of purportedly value-free psychological, sexological, and psychoanalytic concepts. It allows the neurasthenic male to be seen as the product of definite historical type of society, the exhibitionist or serial killer as the creation of a specific culture.[8]

Socially, I examine notions of masculinity in both the working class and middle class. The same authorities, in condemning laborers' brawls as irrational outbursts while turning a blind eye to gentlemen's duels, were implicitly acknowledging that "the typologies designating honorable and dishonourable masculinity were highly class specific."[9] What is of special interest is Joan Scott's point that interclass references to sexuality "seem to be part of a more complicated process of 'class construction' in which definitions of the middle class involve notions of sexual self-control and . . . depend on negative examples or 'social others.' In this case the social 'other' is the working class; its 'otherness' is indicated by representing it as woman."[10] Geographically I deal primarily with developments in England and France, but I also draw on sexological discussions in central Europe and changing norms of manhood in North America. The study purposely tends to a "geographical eclecticism." Too many studies of sexuality have, as Theodore Zeldin has pointed out, unthinkingly embraced the notion of national stereotypes—that nineteenth-century Englishmen were given to flogging, Italians to crimes of passion, Germans to sadism, and Frenchmen to dueling and philandering.[11] I am suggesting not that strong national traditions did not exist but that a preoccupation with them can blind us to more important sex and gender traditions and conventions that the nations of western Europe and North America shared. Non-Western societies, however, obviously did have different understandings of masculinity. To pursue that question would be to broach an enormous topic. In this brief study, we have to restrict ourselves to no more than the odd passing reference to the important relationships of race and gender.[12]

Because so many excellent studies of the creation of models of modern femininity have been produced, I devote most of my attention to the policing of masculinity. Women's role has long been regarded as problematical and therefore worthy of investigation and regulation. Men, in contrast, have been regarded as unchanging and therefore their sexuality has not warranted examination. Freud's famous question "What do women want?" has garnered a good deal of indignant attention. Few have observed that he did not ask "What do men want?" the assumption being that everyone knew.

Women will not be ignored in the following chapters since masculinity was always defined in contrast to femininity, the one concept having no meaning in isolation from the other. This book seeks to complement, not eclipse the study of femininity; its premise is that it is essential that the relational aspects of gender not be lost sight of. Accordingly, in the course of the book, we will look at a would-be gentleman trying to marry his way out of hard work, but also at his female counterpart; trace the careers of both the bounder and the barmaid; and examine the ways in which both the gentleman and the lady employed images of appropriate gender roles to avoid entanglements with the law.

A large though recent literature on the emergence in the late nineteenth century of the homosexual identity also exists. While homosexuality is not the focus of this study, any account of the concept of nineteenth-century "normal" heterosexual masculinity can only be understood in relationship to contemporary ideas concerning its "inversion"—homosexuality. A number of pioneering studies of the history of homosexuality have appeared in the last decade; this book in a sense serves as their complement.[13] It looks at the shifting definition of normality, at the lines that were drawn and redrawn to separate the deviant from the normal, the male from the female. Gay history is helping us to understand how these lines were made, blurred, and reimposed, but a more self-conscious understanding of "normal" maleness and heterosexuality also has to be provided.

Setting the goals of the book was one thing; determining the methodology was another. What I wanted to do was to find ways of revealing and testing the process by which concepts of masculinity were propounded. Freud once said that the hysteric can be compared to the criminal. The criminal has a secret that he tries to guard; the hysteric has a secret of which he is himself unaware. It is this secret that the determined psychoanalyst, like the ruthless juge d'instruction, has the task of extracting from his unwilling interlocutor. I too found that for my purposes an exploitation of both the medical and legal discourses on sexuality worked well. I began by examining much of the medical and psychological writing of the time and then turned to trial records. Ironically, the same age that gendered abstract qualities such as "strength" and "independence" as male declared its all-male court system to be objective and gender free.[14] Nevertheless, I found that trial records were an invaluable means of gauging the public impact of the concepts of normal and abnormal sexuality. Few sources so strongly distinguished between the sexes.

This study is about two specific sorts of "trials" of masculinity. The first were the formal courtroom dramas where great importance was placed upon determining whether or not the accused had acted in a "manly" fashion. Mikhail Bakhtin has suggested that the law court is a site for the production of meaning inasmuch as trials have always fulfilled a critical role in linking the law to general culture.[15] In following up this insight, the first portion of this project might be likened to the works of Guido Ruggiero.[16] I too appreciate the enormous value of legal records while trying to be sensitive to the fact that trials tended to reify boundaries, artificially and neatly divide the normal from the abnormal.

I rely heavily on legal documentation because my central working hypothesis—much like Sander Gilman's—is that understanding how previous generations conceived of the "normal" is often most dramatically demonstrated by analyzing their treatment of the "other."[17] The prosecution of sex crimes "forced the issue" in interesting ways for in the courtroom society had to make clear where the boundaries lay between normal and deviant behavior. It could be said that my "hard cases" are not representative, reflect only extremes of behavior, and rely on sensational evidence and as such cannot tell us about "ordinary" men. But these trials also offer the differing interpretations contemporaries made of the evidence introduced and thus reveal not one but several competing discourses—of doctors, lawyers, journalists, politicians, radicals, laymen.

Since this study exploits a number of criminal cases, it necessarily deals with the subject of male violence. Criminologists, while knowing that men are far more likely than women to commit violent crimes, surprisingly see no need to investigate masculinity.[18] Even some of the more recent historical studies of masculinity are amazingly silent on the issue of force.[19] Yet anthropologists tell us that the more violent the society the more it is male dominated.[20] It is tempting to argue that if female sexuality was policed in the nineteenth century, male sexuality was as well. But it would be simplistic to suggest that the result was some sort of symmetry. Roper and Tosh make the point that masculinity is always "shaped around male power" and "relative to femininity." In other words males can always have recourse to violence; such actions enjoy cultural legitimacy. The "policing" of masculinity in the nineteenth century was not only repressive; as will be seen, it included the sanctioning of certain forms of male violence, thereby acknowledging that gender relationships were also power relationships. If many of the men in the following chapters were "losers," the fate of the few scapegoats or sacrificial lambs should not blind us to the fact that the power of most of the male flock was enhanced.

The second sorts of "trials" of masculinity examined in this book are those in which doctors played a key role. Psychiatrists and sexologists, employing biological and psychological arguments that stressed sexual in-

commensurability, emerged in the last century declaring themselves to be
the experts best equipped to understand and buttress essential gender differences. To answer the question of when and why medicine took over as
arbiter of the perversions, the latter portion of the study is devoted to the
historical construction of the male sex pervert.[21] In a sense the term "male
pervert" is redundant. Sexologists, until Freud, although they catalogued
female forms of deviancy such as nymphomania and lesbianism, defined
the perverse in such a way that only the male could be a "real" pervert.
Ostensibly society policed such misfits to protect women and children from
sexual danger, but it was never that simple. First, "policing" included, as
Foucault suggests, the development of various forms of regulation including therapy. Second, the construction of new sex roles involved shifts in
real power.

The study in examining both medical and legal regulation follows a trail
blazed by Michel Foucault and is inspired by a modest measure of post-
modernism. The project is not trying to simply contrast the "what ought
to be" of the medical and prescriptive texts, with the "what was" of the
courtroom. Rather, a more complex picture is sought. On the one hand, I
am suggesting that there was an intriguing "real" material power in the
medical discourses. On the other hand, several chapters should lead one to
be cynical about the supposed "realness" of the criminal court transcripts.
The "text-like" and constructed nature of their deliberations were often
only too obvious. Courts were theaters.[22] André Gide, who sat on a jury in
1912, was fascinated by the impact that the accused's "performance"
could have on the proceedings.[23] To understand the roles that were either
appropriated by or attributed to prisoners, we will necessarily have to draw
at times on the standard cast of male characters portrayed in popular contemporary plays and novels.

In short this study—in particular the chapter on medical confidentiality—allows us to see law and medicine meeting and the difficulties of separating prescriptive literature from positive science. In wider terms the book
seeks to point up the value of exploiting a range of discourses rather than
hiving off for examination simply one set of records and regulatory systems. There was not one right and one wrong discourse. There were multiple discourses, each of which has to be appreciated to understand the
complexity with which gender expectations were woven. Power was not
unified but dispersed, not coherent but broken up into different social
"fields of force."[24]

It is accordingly too stark a question to ask who won and who lost. The
cast of characters in this study include—in addition to the frequently cited

sexologists, psychologists, magistrates, and public moralists—murderers, sadists, transvestites, abortionists, exhibitionists, fraud artists, and sex radicals. My central argument is that the boundaries of masculine comportment, normal sexual behavior, and male gender identity were constructed and maintained by law, medicine, politics, and popular ritual.[25] When respectable society stigmatized what it took to be dangerous forms of male sexual behavior, it was not primarily preoccupied with protecting potential female victims. The first effect of the new models of heterosexuality was to shore up the power of "normal" men. This exploration of a discourse in which experts lamented the passivity of perverts while sanctioning aggressive male sexuality accordingly promises to deepen our understanding of both the realities and perceptions of early-twentieth-century gender relations.

The study of masculinity or rather various masculinities that evolved over time is an immense undertaking that scholars have only just begun. It would take a team of researchers to master simply the enormous literature produced by the European sexologists. The modest ambition of this book is to provide a number of case studies to illuminate the key forces that were at work in the changing constructions of appropriate male sexual behavior. It seeks to map out the cultural grid of conflicting and overlapping accounts of what it meant to be a man. We will be tracing both the rapidity of the emergence of the ideology of "hegemonic masculinity" and the slowness and unevenness of imposing such new gender norms.

The book's argument proceeds in synchronic rather than chronological order, with the various narratives pertaining to criminality and perversion circling around the central question of masculinity. Part One of the study begins with the question of why in the western world at the turn of the century the issue of sexual identity took on such great importance. What was a "real man" or "real woman"? These were not timeless notions, but tied to the particular social and ideological preoccupations. Part Two shifts from the prescriptive literature, which said how men should behave, to the actual boundaries of sexuality imposed by the law. A number of cases will be presented to reveal the contested process by which masculinity was shaped. The law was actively involved in the construction of male and female roles, though the boundaries themselves were flexible, bending under class, gender, and ethnic pressures. Indeed, the four chapters show that even fictional representations of how males were supposed to act had a direct impact on the fate of men involved in legal entanglements resulting from courtship, seduction, abortion, and finally murder.[26]

By exploiting the legal wranglings of a matrimonial agency whose case

I stumbled upon, I show in chapter 2 how lower-class men tried to ape upper-class models to represent themselves as eligible marriage partners. Class concerns required that the presumptuousness of marginal males be punished by their superiors. Humor and laughter figured centrally in this as in other cases as a weapon employed by elite males to ward off threats that struck close to home. To move the analysis from courtship to seduction, I employ in chapter 3 bigamy and abortion trial records. The treatment of male bigamists is examined to determine why remarriage was deemed by the respectable to be more morally dangerous than adultery. And abortion laws are explored because, though they are usually believed to have penalized only women, a series of English cases in the 1890s reveals the extent to which men who did not play the appropriate masculine role were at risk. These latter trials dealing with the inducement of miscarriage are of particular interest in that they precipitated the first public defense—by men—of abortion in English.

Gender and comportment were intimately related in the 1890s. In chapter 4 I turn to the records of the nineteenth century's most famous trial pertaining to the issue of professional confidentiality to show how an appreciation of the way "ladies" and "gentleman" were supposed to behave could be exploited by daring individuals for the subversive purpose of turning attention away from what were in effect immoral and illegal practices. The ultimate form of the policing of male gender roles was the use of deadly force by either the individual or the state. Chapter 5 provides an analysis of several hundred homicides carried out by "normal" Canadian men in the first two decades of this century. The purpose is to show that, if it was a question of defending one's "manhood," society might even permit an individual the right to kill. Sexuality and danger were linked. Whether or not one acted "like a man" was a matter of life or death; a murderer had few better defenses than to claim that his victim was a homosexual or the seducer of his wife.

The men discussed in Part Two who fell foul of the law were chastised for not living up to the hegemonic model of masculinity, but they were not condemned by society as perverts. They were declared bad not mad. What they did, though wrong, was held to be understandable. In Part Three I move the discussion of masculinity beyond the margins of "normal" male behavior. We tend to think of Victorian women's sexuality being constrained. Transgressive male bodies, in contrast, have received little attention from historians. But at the turn of the century, the "pervert" was constructed; sexual practices (as Weeks and others have noted) once considered moral choices became regarded by the bourgeoisie as symptoms of biological or psychological flaws. Following Arnold Davidson's suggestive comments, I demonstrate how the creation of new labels—sadist, masochist, exhibitionist, homosexual—marginalized some males in the community while empowering others.[27]

What constituted normal and abnormal sexuality at the turn of the century? We set the scene with an analysis in chapter 6 of both the early scientific studies of sexuality such as those produced by Sigmund Freud and the popular sex manuals like those of "Dr. Jaf" to gauge how widespread were both the new, vulgarized notions of the sexologists and older sexual beliefs. New knowledge but also new worries were introduced to the public by such writings. In such books readers were familiarized with the dangers posed by sexual perversions. When and why the pervert was created is examined in the following three chapters.

School birchings and prison floggings had many respectable defenders in the late nineteenth century who would have been outraged by suggestions that such acts had any sexual coloring. Where does the sadist, a creation of the late nineteenth century, fit into the social construction of masculinity? The question posed in chapter 7 is if in constructing the sadist—the man who in pursuit of sexual pleasure inflicted an "irrational" amount of pain—sexologists were, in a back-handed fashion also legitimating the "reasonable" amount of pain the normal man might inflict. The exhibitionist was also a "creation" of the nineteenth-century medical experts. In chapter 8 an analysis of why exhibitionism, like voyeurism, was by definition said to be only a male complaint provides us with some insights into the restrictions placed on exposure of the male body. The exhibitionist threatened women, but one is struck by the fact the experts did not label the obviously far more dangerous rapist as a "pervert." The rapist was "normal" to the extent that he sought actual intercourse; the exhibitionist, because he did not, was deviant. The latter, by his ridiculous actions, endangered new nineteenth-century notions of the self-controlled male.

The final affront to masculinity was posed by the man who wanted to be a woman. The questions of why such desires were medicalized and pathologized and why it was considered more dangerous for a man to put on women's clothing than for a woman to put on men's are grappled with in chapter 9. Transvestism obviously built on an understanding of differences of gender and sexuality but called these very same categories into question. An examination of a number of trials of transvestites that drew the attention of the British Society for the Study of Sex Psychology tells us much about both shifting attitudes toward homosexuality and the medicalization of deviancy.

This book ranges from an analysis of how common male murderers could hope, by foregrounding their masculinity, to get away with their crimes to a discussion of why male transvestites denied their maleness. The goal is to demystify any notion of sexual essentialism by showing how concepts of masculinity were created, maintained, and policed. The study's central argument is that "dominant" forms of masculinity were constituted out of a set of "negative" varieties that appeared in everyday discourse and practice; that in a certain sense it was easier for society to note the bad examples rather than the exemplars of the manly ideal. The legal, medical, and psychological experts, in describing deviant males, were defining in negative terms "normal" men, though at times these experts could be detected projecting onto the "other" their own repressed desires.[28] The book will trace shifts both in gender identities and in those who policed their boundaries. In reviewing the turn-of-the-century construction of such sexual identities, we are reminded that, although the discourses on sexuality were male-dominated, men were also subject to them. Yet norms and community expectations were never carved in stone; the skillful could find ways of turning them to their advantage. The very concept of what it was to be a "man" was open to question. By examining the motives that lay behind the construction of a new range of sexual identities, we are provided with a clearer notion of the social and cultural anxieties of the age. Doctors and magistrates, in discussing what were purportedly issues of sex and gender, never succeeded in disentangling private acts from public preoccupations. Then as now, as one observer has aptly noted, "it is not sexuality which haunts society, but society which haunts the body's sexuality."[29]

PART ONE

MASCULINITIES

BRIAN DIPPIE, IN *THE VANISHING AMERICAN*,[1] HAS PROVIDED a brilliant account of the pervasive belief held by many late-nineteenth-century North Americans that the indigenous population was dying out. The native peoples of the New World, claimed several generations of investigators, simply could not survive the ravages of drink, disease, and the general pressures exerted by modern society. Some lamented the disappearance of the "Red Man," but with hindsight one can see that there was a good deal of wish fulfillment in such prophecies. It would not be necessary to take active means to eliminate cultures that stood in the way of progress; in the pitiless Darwinian world, they were in the process of eliminating themselves.

That whites should have convinced themselves of the all-but-certain disappearance of a "lesser race" seems hardly surprising. Harder to explain is that in the same decades observers such as Teddy Roosevelt were raising the specter of Western cultures committing "race suicide." Healthy, decent, white men in both western Europe and North America were, if one were to believe the sensationalist titles of a flood of lectures, books, and pamphlets, members of an endangered species. In France, F. A. Vuillermet challenged his readers to "be men." In Britain, General Frederick Maurice claimed that the army faced the difficulty of "Where to get Men." Daniel Carter Beard, creator of the American Boy Scouts, gloomily entitled his autobiography, *Hardly a Man Is Now Alive.*

What such writers meant, of course, was not that there was any shortage of males in the Western world. They were arguing that the problem was that there were too many men of the "wrong type." William James alerted his readers to the strategy employed by those who sought to increase their own power by denigrating other men as unfit. "Call a man a 'cad' and you've settled his social status. Call him a 'degenerate,' and you've grouped him with the most loathsome specimens of the race."[2]

James did not explain why, at the fin-de-siècle, such name calling should have reached such a crescendo. To understand the processes by which concepts of both healthy and diseased masculinity were created and the functions they served, we will begin in chapter 1 by examining closely the social and cultural preoccupations of the pessimistic.

ONE

DEVIANTS

IN THE COURSE OF THE 1912 LONDON SESSIONS, THE chairman of the court sentenced thirty men to be not only imprisoned but flogged. In western Europe's most liberal nation, what sorts of criminals would warrant such barbaric treatment? Eleven were whipped for soliciting and six for living on the earnings of prostitutes, five for indecent exposure, one for showing obscene pictures, three for being "incorrigible rogues," two for damage to a workhouse, one for assaulting a workhouse official, and one for failing to support his wife and family.[1] These men's backs were bloodied as a direct result of the late-nineteenth-century campaign to reintroduce corporal punishment. Respectable society, in declaring that male prostitutes, pimps, vagrants, and exhibitionists deserved a scourging that even male murderers and rapists were spared was not only attempting to draw a clear line between the criminal and noncriminal worlds; it was also responding to the idea that certain types of men had forfeited the right to be treated as human beings. The danger posed by male violence and sexual deviancy, according to self-declared "normal men," had become such a threat and its wickedness so exceeded common criminality that it warranted extraordinary penalties. An examination of this "moral panic," which journalists and parliamentarians whipped up out of the notion that women and children were being preyed on by untold numbers of brutes and perverts, provides an excellent point of entry into the nineteenth-century discussion of the crisis in masculinity. The recourse to flogging was a peculiarly Anglo-Saxon response, but as will be demonstrated in what follows, large numbers of commentators in both Europe and North America were equally shrill in their condemnation of the threats posed to healthy society by male deviants.

Corporal punishment—that is the administration of the lash, cat, or birch—had long been applied to criminals across the Western world, male and female, young and old.[2] In the seventeenth and eighteenth centuries it was a common punishment for misdemeanors, but in the nineteenth century prison sentences increasingly replaced the recourse to executions, transportations, and floggings. The new penitentiaries provided concrete evidence of progressives' optimistic belief in enlightened custodians' abilities to reform the felon and to make punishments fit both the crime and the specific age and gender specifications of the criminal.[3] Accordingly, from the 1820s onward, flogging in Britain was restricted to men; a new sensitivity to gender made it unthinkable that women be subjected to such pain. And even the men so chastised after 1832 had their punishments carried out in private.[4]

Britain was not alone in carrying out such reforms. In the course of the nineteenth century, resort to all forms of corporal punishment declined across Europe. In England humiliating corporal punishments such as birchings were increasingly thought fit only for boys and by 1848 were little used for adults.[5] The Punishment Bill, introduced in 1859, sought to retain the use of corporal punishment only for the violators of Treason Act of 1842. In Scotland the last flogging sentence was handed down in 1833; recourse to it was absolutely forbidden in 1862. Progressive thinkers imagined that floggings would soon be looked upon as a relic of the barbarian past. But in the latter half of the nineteenth century, the use of the lash was reintroduced in England and Wales. The return to such a brutal practice was rationalized by its proponents on the grounds that "normal punishments" were not felt to be adequate retribution for some crimes. Presumably hardened politicians, magistrates, and policemen were declaring that in dealing with some assaults they were overcome by feelings of revulsion. These crimes were not, as one might have anticipated, those that resulted in the greatest shedding of blood but, as the verdicts handed down at the 1912 London Sessions demonstrated, a hodgepodge of sordid misdemeanors that offended a new sense of bourgeois sexual decorum.

Radzinowicz and Hall, who produced the most thorough legal analysis of the resurgence of corporal punishment in late-nineteenth-century England, noted that those subjected to flogging came from what could be regarded as disparate categories: male prostitutes, pimps, transvestites, and vagrants. Since the authors did not attempt a gender analysis of the campaign, they did not note what all these criminals had so strikingly in common—a failure to live up to newly created standards of masculinity. The significance of the corporal punishment campaign is its revelation that at the turn of the century a few men in positions of power declared marginalized men—sexual perverts and vagrants—to be in some ways worse than the most violent of criminals and so deserving of the most humiliating of punishments. Though such fears were no doubt sincerely felt by some, they were simply exploited by others. In both cases the results were the same, the creation of the masculine "other" or outsider.

The resurgence of flogging was initially due to the "garroting" panic of 1862 caused by short-lived rash of London street robberies that the press played up.[6] Choking, suffocating, or strangling to commit a robbery was held to be so unmanly and so prevalent a deed as to require the special punishment specified in the Garroting Act. The high point for flogging for those convicted of robbery with violence occurred in 1894, when sixty men were flogged; such punishments thereafter sharply declined; only 130 were so chastised between 1900 and 1913.[7] Many members of the law-abiding public no doubt felt better when they read of the fate that awaited such felons, but no statistical proof of the effectiveness of flogging as a deterrent was ever advanced.[8]

In the latter decades of the nineteenth century, fears of robbery waned and the campaign to extend flogging to moral crimes was pursued. Attempts were made in 1853, 1856, and 1857 to have the "cat" applied to those convicted of assaults on women and children. Many judges claimed that the lash was needed when a crime involved a man's "baseness, depravity or cowardly abuse of strength."[9] Yet in the United Kingdom, four wife-beating bills were defeated. The key counter argument, advanced by the more cautious magistrates, was that such a penalty would make it even harder than it already was to get a conviction.[10]

In the United States in 1885, a bill was introduced in Massachusetts to punish wife beating with the whipping post. Lucy Stone, the early women's rights advocate, organized support in its favor.[11] It passed in the House but lost in the Senate. Whipping, authorized by the original 1790 act of Congress as a punishment for crimes, had been abolished in 1839.[12] With the Civil War, it was ended in the American army and in the navy as no longer a suitable form of discipline for "freemen."[13] Yet some states retained it; especially for dealing with boys. The Republicans led the campaign between 1876 and 1906 for its reintroduction as part of a general desire to legislate on morality. In New York and Chicago, attempts were made to have child molesters, perpetrators of incest, and habitual criminals flogged. The campaigns linked up the interests of those involved in child rescue, temperance, social purity, and women's rights, who called on the state to step in as a moral father and punish the "brutish son-in-law."[14]

In England the attempt to have rape punished by flogging was narrowly defeated in 1864, but the outcry that followed W. T. Stead's exposé of child prostitution in "The Maiden Tribute of Modern Babylon" led to the 1885 Criminal Law Amendment Act, which raised the age of consent to sixteen, made procuration of women and children a criminal offense punished by a term not exceeding two years and introduced flogging as a penalty for youths under sixteen convicted of assaulting a girl under thirteen.[15] In the late 1880s and 1890s, grand juries, Quarter Sessions, magistrates, and town councils continued to call for the extension of corporal punishment to a wide range of sexual offenses.[16] Conservative MPs in particular pushed for action against "abominable crimes," by which they hinted at bestiality and sodomy.[17]

Such a goal was to an extent achieved, not by producing new laws but by extending the provisions of the existing Vagrancy Act. Under the Vagrancy Act of 1744, "incorrigible rogues" were to be whipped in public before being returned to their place of settlement. The revised Act of 1824, which retained whipping as a provision for those convicted a second time, was aimed at miserable down-and-outers not brutal criminals. Its flogging provisions were used infrequently though never abandoned.[18] In 1904, for example, five old men were whipped for merely begging and sleeping rough. Such scandals enraged labor supporters, revealing as they did that the chief effect of the vagrancy act was to criminalize poverty.

The originality of the amended Vagrancy Act of 1898 was that it held that those summarily convicted of male sexual deviancy—such as pimps, male prostitutes, and exhibitionists—would be punished in the same manner as vagrants.[19] Such an amalgamation might at first hand appear bizarre, but tramps were thought by many to pose both a social and sexual threat. In the United States, according to the Reverend Frank Charles Laubach, it was so common for a boy to be "enslaved by a tramp for immoral purposes" that the latter went by the well-known appellation of "jocker." The term "punk," which in the eighteenth century was used to refer to rotten wood or something equally worthless, at the end of the nineteenth century designated a passive male homosexual, in particular a tramp's young companion. Some minor criminals were likable, conceded Laubach, but "The pervert is far on toward insanity, and is usually loathsome."[20]

The English 1898 vagrancy act, in allowing magistrates to deal summarily with a range of men charged with minor sex crimes, deprived the latter of the rights accorded more serious criminals. If they were found guilty under the Vagrancy Act of indecent assault, living on the earnings of prostitutes, or "masquerading in female attire," they were convicted as

"incorrigible rogues." Flogging was allowed as a punishment for such immoral acts; in particular for "solicitation by a male person for immoral
purposes."[21] Judge A. J. Lawrie at London Sessions passed a number of
such punishments against male prostitutes and male transvestites. The
cruel irony of the situation was that homosexual acts, though condemned
by the law, were not themselves punishable by flogging, but solicitation
was.

Men driven by exhibitionistic tendencies were similarly flogged. The
Leeds Mercury of 10 April 1914 reported that a man, convicted six or
seven times previously for the same offense of exposing himself, had just
been given twelve strokes.[22] Flogging was used "in cases of indecent exposure and similar offences," but these were, according to many observers,
really cases of disease or imbecility.[23] Doctors agreed that the compulsion
was related to mental imbalance and the Home Office was in fact aware
that the exhibitionist was not as serious a threat as the man who committed
an indecent assault, yet the Home Secretary continued to regard flogging
as an appropriate form of punishment for the former.[24] It was not ended
until 1948.[25]

Those who exposed themselves or assaulted girls were, thought a
progressive-minded observer like Joseph Collinson of the Humanitarian
League, "miserable specimens of humanity, all of them to be pitied, and
some of them fit subjects for a lunatic asylum."[26] But in fact they did not
even receive the treatment meted out to common criminals. Under modern
law flogging was not allowed for serious sexual crimes, and those so tried
usually had the privilege of trial by jury. This did not hold if—as in the
case of exhibitionists or male prostitutes—they were tried under the Vagrancy Act.[27] Moreover, until the creation of the Court of Criminal Appeal
in 1908, the accused had no right to appeal their sentences. Though crimes
of violence such as rape and indecent assault were punished with long
prison terms, minor male moral offenses were treated as if they were in
some sense worse.

The corporal punishment crusade peaked with the White Slave Panic of
1912.[28] In a sensationalist campaign journalists and politicians succeeded
in convincing the general public that English women were at risk of being
drugged or seduced into prostitution by hoards of foreign procurers.[29] The
1898 Vagrancy Act had already included whippings for "souteneurs," but
alarmist talk about women being shanghaied into the sex trade was revived
in 1911 by people such as Lord Aberdeen, who in a talk to the National
Vigilance Association called for the whipping of procurers.[30] In 1912 the

Liberal government with the support of all parties passed the Criminal Law Amendment Act—better known as the White Slave Traffic Bill—which mandated the flogging of men summarily convicted of being pimps. In both the House of Commons and Lords, references were even made to branding, crucifying, and exterminating such miscreants.[31] As it was, no maximum number of strokes was fixed for their floggings; unlike as in the provisions of the Garroters Act, the number was left to the discretion of the courts.[32] The government thus left the public with the impression that the safety of society was more endangered by the pimp than by the strangler.[33]

It clearly salved the British conscience to believe that women were forced into prostitution by bullies rather than by sheer economic necessity. In fact it was rare to find cases of procurement. Only eight a year had been brought to court during the period 1900–1909. Under the stimulus of the White Slave Panic, the number jumped to seventy-three in 1913, then fell to forty-one in 1914, and by 1929 was finally back to five or six a year.[34] Some zealots wanted to go still farther in tracking down those who violated the standards of male decency. A Duty and Discipline Society was formed to advance the use of the cat, rod, and birch. The British Anti-Mormon League, reported the *Daily Sketch,* sought the flogging of Mormon elders.[35] William Tallack, of the John Howard Society, called for use of the lash against anarchists who had "scattered death and misery amongst peaceable citizens by means of dynamite or similar explosives."[36] Dr. H. C. Miller sought the flogging of male drunkards. The yellow press could always be relied upon to demand the extension of flogging to young men frequenting Hyde Park for immoral purposes or for perpetrators of incest. Yet once the 1912 act was passed, the moral panic subsided. Although in 1913 the five thousand telephone "girls" in London were warned by their superiors to look out for drugged chocolates, the outbreak of World War I turned the reading public's attention from questions of seduction to far more serious issues.[37]

Explaining the success of the corporal punishment campaign initially poses a challenge, countering as it does the generally accepted account of nineteenth-century criminals being subjected to ever more "humane," rational, and reformist punishments. "It is not easy," the authors of the fullest account of the British flogging craze state, "to put the advocates and opponents of flogging into neat categories."[38] Predictably most conservatives supported such actions, though some did not. Less predictable was the support given flogging by Liberals and "progressives" including John Stuart Mill and Harriet Martineau. Although he considered almost any punishment preferable to flogging, Mill stated, "In the case, however, of certain grave moral delinquencies, chiefly those which are either of a cowardly or brutal character, corporal punishment in that or some equivalent form may be admissible."[39] Even members of the John Howard Society, many opponents of capital punishment, and the supporters of the reformatory movement, though critical of the cruelty of the prison system, backed the call for the lash, the latter group because it would at least keep boys out of prison.

On the rational level, the proponents of flogging argued that prisons—expensive and enslaving—did not always work; that liberal reformers had gone too far in coddling prisoners; that by providing them with food, lodging, and training, the soft-hearted positively encouraged the crimes of ruffians, evil-doers, and hoodlums; and finally that society needed to be effectively protected.[40] Simeon Baldwin, the leading American advocate of the whip—and later governor of Rhode Island—provided a report on the subject for the American Bar Association in 1886. Baldwin argued that flogging was less costly than imprisonment and the charity needed to succor the felon's family should he be jailed.[41] Other proponents of flogging presented it as a rational response to moral outrages and likened its opponents in their sentimentalism to the antivivisectionist faddists opposed to the advance of scientific medicine.

But the real impact of the argument of the proponents of corporal punishment lay in what might be called the "irrational" side of their argument, their sensationalist portrayals of the victims and perpetrators of violence: "the particular class of cruel and brutal men who are apt to despise other influences, and from whom it is necessary that their ordinary victims, weak women and tender children, shall be more effectually protected."[42] The sensationalist device exploited by Henry Labouchère, the Liberal M.P., in his newspaper *Truth*, was to publish weekly accounts comparing the severe punishments leveled against those convicted of property crimes and the lax ones against those convicted of brutal crimes. Typical examples were the Warwickshire man who assaulted a seven-year-old girl and was fined ten shillings while another who stole four shirts received three years, and the Gloucestershire man who repeatedly made indecent assaults on a married woman and received six weeks in jail while one who stole nails got five years penal servitude. "Apparently very little importance is attached to a child's purity, or a woman's honor," an outraged Labouchère lamented.[43] Society had to protect itself likewise, declared William Tallack, secretary of the John Howard Society, against "a ruffian who has violated young children or brutally maimed weak women."[44]

Sexual fears dominated such melodramatic arguments. If any woman "fell," claimed the campaigners, it was due to the machinations of such ruffians, never by her own volition. The lash promised to cow such brutes and so end forever the social blight of prostitution. "But so long as British, American and Continental law permits, as hitherto, the nastiest and vilest of human kind to derive a profitable trade from the ruin of female virtue and the causation of cruelest misery to myriads of pitiable creatures, so long will prostitution flourish."[45] The use of the image of the child victim was an even more effective ploy. So Tallack climaxed a long list of horrible assaults committed on women with a chilling assertion: "There is a crime still meaner than that to which I have alluded, that a man can commit towards the weaker sex. It is when he lures a child into dishonor."[46]

The corporal punishment campaigners played off the image of the saintly child or woman victim against a stylized villain. They continually harped on the notion that the ruffian's greatest failing was his lack of manliness. Those subjected to the lash were described not as men but as "human dogs," "despicable miscreants," "inhuman foes," "monsters," "cowards and bullies." In the words of one politician, these were the cruel and cowardly, "compared with whom the ordinary thief is a paragon of virtue." Such brutes had forfeited any right to be treated as humans and had to be subjected, as were animals, to the whip. "It is absurd to talk about 'degrading' them by this infliction. THEY HAVE ALREADY DEGRADED THEMSELVES TO THE UTTERMOST. Any process of treatment which either checks their crimes, or brings them to some sense of wholesome fear or shame, is at once an ELEVATION and a MERCY."[47]

Not surprisingly, such proponents of flogging played on racial fears, attributing sexual assaults on white women and children to the classic outsiders, the "Negroes and Jews," the "sleek, soft-living degenerates," and "diseased creatures" who haunted city centers.[48] The role of the pimp or procurer, claimed Arthur Lee, the leading parliamentary supporter of the White Slave bill, was something that no healthy Englishman could embrace. "A very large proportion of them, I am glad to say, are not Englishmen. I regret that some are, but if the hon. Members could see not merely foreigners, not merely debased Englishmen, but dozens of negroes in the West End of London running white English girls on the streets, they could see at whom we wish to get."[49]

Such talk was also responsible for the success of the whipping campaign in the United States. With the White Caps active in Indiana and the Ku Klux Klan in the South, some American proponents of flogging presented themselves as humanitarians, arguing that the option of flogging blacks might be turned to by whites as an alternative to lynching.[50] But the proponents also claimed that black men enjoyed imprisonment, offering as it did food and lodging. More disturbingly, prison held out the appeal to black men of being the one place in America where they might find something approximating racial equality. "They find there [in the prison] the only ground where they can mingle with their white fellow citizens on terms of social equality. But they are sensitive to physical pain. A flogging they dread just as a boy dreads a whipping from his father, because it hurts."[51] The American debate over flogging—which was successfully introduced in Maryland in 1882, Delaware in 1901, and Oregon 1905—was thus a symptom of a new racism that focused on the dangerous black freedman.[52] The British also employed flogging to keep down a subject race; the use of the rattan cane was a common means of punishment in India throughout the nineteenth century. In 1878 alone 75,223 such whippings were administered.[53] Few punishments better symbolized the attempts of the "mother country" to infantilize restive and unruly natives.

A few proponents of corporal punishment were so concerned by the issue of protecting the race from dangerous men that they took the next logical step and embraced the notion of sterilizing or castrating vagrants and sexual deviants. Simeon Baldwin, citing the support of various doctors and the Women's Christian Temperance Union, argued that castration was a suitable punishment for sodomy and rape.

> It is what many sociologists are gravely considering as a possible and permissible mode of preventing the propagation of a degenerate class of imbeciles or paupers. It is what, in fact, is being actually done in a quiet way by not a few of the medical profession who are in charge of almshouses and other public institutions in which are feeble minded children, the progeny of a worthless stock. Their castration is sometimes deemed an appropriate remedy to which to resort to prevent their falling into vices or disorders, to which their nature makes it difficult for them to offer any effectual resistance; and none the less appropriate, because it will end the line of a family which is misusing the earth.[54]

In England William Harbutt Dawson, who had given evidence before the 1904 Departmental Committee of Inquiry on the poor law reform, likewise hinted only sterilization would end the multiplication of the idle, the professional loafers, and the social parasites who lived by begging, blackmailing, and pillaging and enjoyed only the "parody" of a family life.[55] French proponents of sterilization hailed this "American" form of chastisement— it was first enacted in Indiana in 1907—as a defense weapon that could be used against men who lacked any sense of morality and personal dignity.[56]

How is one to interpret the corporal punishment campaign? Class and race preoccupations were clearly involved in the success of the movement in both America and England. Viewed in the context of the 1890s depression and rising worker militancy, the surging flogging crusade, in exploiting the specter of increased numbers of habitual criminals, tramps, and perverts, who only feared the lash, marked a clear resurgence of social conservatism. The class bias of the laws was obvious. Tories were aware that they were accused of indulging "in the congenial task of flogging the working man."[57] In the debate over flogging procurers, one hostile M. P. pointed out that it was ridiculous to claim that the law applied to both the rich and poor. "How could it be possible for a poor woman to be keeping a man who had millions of money? The thing is utterly absurd, and what we are legislating for, and what we are providing punishment for, is a special set of criminals who happen to be poor men, while there is absolutely no possible chance of your securing convictions against wealthy persons employed in this trade." Another pointed out that the law was now going to force a poor man to prove he was not living on the avails of prostitution just as it had previously forced poor women to prove they were not prostitutes.[58]

The way in which class, race, and gender preoccupations overlapped was made especially clear when, in the House of Commons debate over the White Slave Act, attempts were made to declare intercourse with any feeble-minded woman statutory rape. That the intent was not so much to protect women from male lust as to spare society the need for caring for the resulting "unfit" offspring was indicated when the question was asked how one defined "feeble-mindedness." An imbecile was, Dr. Chapple answered crisply, obviously any woman living on charity who had more than one illegitimate child.[59]

At first glance the reintroduction of flogging might be taken as a sign of a sensitivity to the turn-of-the-century growing feminist agitation in favor of equal rights. Protection of women and children was certainly used as a banner by the proponents of corporal punishment, but many were in fact extreme social conservatives and accordingly opposed to women's emancipation. Some of their opponents were nevertheless taken in by their rhetoric. Lawson Tait, in a talk to the Humanitarian League, attributed the call for the lash to a "clique of old-fashioned woman suffragists."[60] Suffragists were not adverse to taking advantage of the white slavery agitation, but

Mrs. Pankhurst, their most radical leader, pointed out the hypocrisy of the proponents of the lash: they claimed to be opposed to prostitution, but they only wanted pimps to be whipped, not the prostitutes' customers.[61]

Opponents of the lash, in an effort to point out the illogicalities of the arguments in favor of flogging, asked why those who presented themselves as defenders of children did not ask for the flogging of women; after all, they committed many of the attacks on the young. And others wondered why only men were to be punished for procuring when many brothels were run by women.[62] More seriously the Humanitarian League pointed out that the Liberal government, seeking to ward off suffragist demands, was exploiting the flogging craze in order to silence, not respond to, the spokespersons of women's rights: "They will not give women the vote, which would be in accordance with Liberal principles, but they try to console them by whipping White Slave traffickers, which is in violation with those principles. As the Parliamentary correspondent of the *Daily News* shrewdly remarked: 'Any one who has watched the treatment of this sort of Bill can hardly avoid the conclusion that the defeat of the weakening amendments is the direct result of the franchise movement.'"[63] Indeed some of the proponents of the whip blatantly revealed their antifeminist colors. Ernest Vizetelley in the *Daily Telegraph* recommended that the birch be used on militant suffragettes. Mr. Justice Day expressed his regret that he could not flog women.[64] Proponents of flogging saw themselves as chivalrously coming to the rescue of ladies in distress; they were not about to let women help themselves.

The White Slave Traffic Act of 1912 was a highly emotional response to the fear that, without the help of special laws, British women could not be kept "pure." The moral-purity supporters of flogging clung to the notions of an older, simpler world in which helpless females naturally turned to men for protection. The dangerous city, with its foreigners, drugs, cinemas, and automobiles, was the arena in which—to use the words of the Archbishop of Canterbury—"silly" and "credulous" but innocent women were most at risk.[65] Those women who insisted on leading more independent lives were regarded by the proponents of flogging as part of the problem. Protecting youths and women meant more effectively controlling them. Teresa Billington-Greig, an active suffragist, was enraged that the implicit message of the "neuropaths and prudes" who sowed the seeds of the White Slave Panic was that women could do nothing to help themselves; they had to rely on the protection of males. As a woman who had run away from home at seventeen, she was indignant that fear mongers slandered both men and women in claiming that every missing girl had been kidnapped.

"It is positively nauseating that we should have cases and statistics of girls missing from home quoted with solemn tone and finger pointing to the brothel, as though there and only there could they be."[66]

The idea that women were at risk once they ventured forth from the home was hardly new. The key insight offered by a gendered analysis of the flogging campaign is that it conjured up the specter of new villains—tribes of male deviants who posed new dangers to the weak and innocent. Women were always women, but some men were failing the challenge to "be a man." Churchmen, defending "Christian manliness" maintained that the "dignity of British manhood" could only be asserted by the whip.[67] Enthusiastic supporters of the lash, such as Colonel Lockwood, declared they were at war not with a man but an animal, one whose "man-like instincts have vanished," who has lost "all ideas of honor and all ideas of anything which makes a man a man."[68] Lyttelton asserted that procurers were "men who have not the nature of man."[69] Such overheated rhetoric was no doubt colored by contemporary literary accounts that played up the frightening prospects of the dangers posed by an unleashing of the dark side of the male psyche. Robert Louis Stevenson's *Strange Case of Dr. Jekyll and Mr. Hyde* had presented the "ape-like" and "dwarfish" Hyde as a being marked by "complete moral insensibility." Oscar Wilde's *Portrait of Dorian Gray,* another classic man's story all about men, likewise concluded with the portrait, which in mirroring only the influences of the passions, had become a "monstrous and loathsome thing."[70] Similarly the authors of modern horror tales, such as *Dracula* (1897) and detective stories, which had recently emerged as an important new literary genre, enjoyed great success inasmuch as they projected elite males' sexual fears and anxieties onto the "other."[71]

This exaggerated hatred that "normal" men so vociferously declared they had of the "abnormal" had disturbing sexual undertones, which those in the campaign against flogging could not help but notice.[72] Opposition was led by the Humanitarian League under its secretary Joseph Collinson with the support of such intellectuals as Edward Carpenter, Henry Salt, and George Bernard Shaw.[73] That many of these same men were interested in sex reform was no accident.[74] They suspected that the corporal punishment campaign was largely fueled by conservative males' fears, not of the threat that male deviants posed women and children but the threat they posed "normal" men. And these threats in turn could be detected to be at least in part the repressed desires of the respectable projected onto the "other."[75]

Thomas de Quincey earlier in the century had pointed to the sexual nature of the flogger's motivation when he declared that flogging was to males what rape was to females. After noting that John Donne had defended a noble woman's preference for death to the dishonor of rape, Quincey asserted that "with regard to the other sex, corporal punishment is its peculiar and *sexual* degradation; and, if ever the distinction of Donne can be applied safely to any case, it will be to the case of him who chooses to die rather than to submit to that ignominy."[76] The lust to inflict pain and see blood flow was palpable in many of the pronouncements of the flogging lobby. "The man who gratifies his own passions at the expense of a cruel and humiliating insult inflicted on another is himself shamefully and painfully humiliated," declared James Fitzjames Stephen, clearly oblivious of the fact that as a defender of the whip he was describing himself.[77] One colonel was not embarrassed to cry out in debate, "I want to see the marks of good British muscle on their backs!"[78] Another M. P. said he was willing to do the whipping himself. An opposing M. P. warned that such outbursts revealed an unsavory sadistic bent that warranted examination. He had himself witnessed a flogging and recalled that the warder who had first shrank from the blood he shed soon "seemed to be taken with a blood lust, and could hardly stop himself from inflicting the punishment."[79] But, in this pre-Freudian age, the self-declared opponents of sexual deviancy were happy to continue to acknowledge their morbid desires with startling candor.

George Bernard Shaw, in a lecture of 24 March 1898 on "Flagellomania," pointed out that flogging was a form of debauchery, a mania based "on a sensual instinct" and a "special disorder of the imagination."[80] He returned to the issue in a 1912 article, spelling out the fact that those in favor of the lash ignored or pretended not to know that the desire to flog or be flogged was a vice. But raids on brothels always uncovered whipping paraphernalia. Theresa Berkeley's famous establishment was reported in 1899 to house a special "horse." Newspapers such as the *News of the World* frequently reported prostitutes' use of birches on willing clients.[81] Yet sexual ignorance should not be fully discounted. Some newspaper proprietors were so dense, according to Salt, that in 1909 they printed a long series of letters to the editor on the birching of girls, not realizing that they were being exploited by those with a prurient interest in indecency. The correspondence was only dropped when a perceptive colleague alerted the editor.

Salt, like Shaw, dwelt on the irony that the lash was defended by the purifiers of morals and traced the "psychopathic side" of the question from Jean-Jacques Rousseau's *Confessions* through to the contemporary analyses of sadism and masochism provided by Ellis, Bloch, and Moll. Salt was not opposed to voluntary and harmless sexual practices but attacked enforced flogging, which he asserted, was "the grossest and most sensual" form of physical violence. The campaign against the white slave trade would, Shaw agreed, create yet another rush of men to the brothels to demand the services that they read about in the newspapers. "The Act," he concluded, "is a final triumph of the vice it pretends to repress."[82] Salt concurred: "the good people who think they can put down vice by having recourse to the implements of the brothel are unintentionally doing more to promote immorality than to repress it."[83]

The flogging campaigners attempted to divide men into two camps—the good and the bad. They owed their success to the feeling many in respectable society had at the turn of the century that the numbers of the latter were increasing and they were inexorably entering a new and dangerously sexualized world. An English M. P., who in 1912 asked himself what had resulted from all the attempts made in the past several decades to control vice, replied. "An increase, I am sorry to say, of juvenile depravity, of incest, and sodomy. The painted boy has made his appearance in the London streets. He was not known a generation ago."[84] This was nonsense. Yet even if the knowledgeable had pointed out that such youths had haunted Drury Lane and Covent Garden a century earlier, it would have had little effect. The success of the flogging campaign demonstrated that in the Anglo-Saxon world such threats were thought to have so suddenly and so seriously risen that the "normal" had to turn to the whip to beat them back.

$\int$

THE FLOGGING CAMPAIGN WAS A PECULIARLY ANGLO-SAXON RESPONSE TO the purported threat male vagrants and perverts posed the respectable, but viewed in the larger cultural context of the late nineteenth century, it can also be seen as a symptom of a more general shoring up of the definition of "normal" masculinity.[85] The modern sense of what it meant "to be a man," which was hammered out in the latter decades of the nineteenth century, was indeed based not so much on positive assertions as on the castigation of those males declared to be "unmanly." As the White Slave Panic demonstrated, it was easier for journalists and politicians to decry what they took to be a lack of "manliness" than to agree on the specifics of true masculinity. And well beyond Britain's shore, those preoccupied by manliness carried out a similar process of constructing images of dangerous male outsiders.

To serve as contrast to healthy masculinity, late-nineteenth-century propagandists created a number of stock countertypes. First came the procurer or pimp, the favorite target of the British corporal punishment lobby. In the United States, the Mann Act was passed to target such individuals.[86] The continental regulationist states, such as France and Germany, which controlled and policed prostitution could not, for obvious reasons, become quite as aroused by such a character.[87] Nevertheless, under the pressure of morality leagues and fears of venereal disease, they joined the campaign against "white slavery," salving their conscience by implying that vice was the responsibility of the "other."[88]

Moreover in France a panic over the activities of gangs of young working-class petty criminals—dubbed by the popular press "Apaches" because their cruelty supposedly mirrored that of the Indians subdued by the United States military in the 1880s—complemented the English white slave agitation.[89] The stereotype of the urban lout can be found in Dr. Lejeune's sensational work *Faut-il fouetter les Apaches?* (1910). London had its hooligans, Rome its teppisti, and Paris, Lejeune warned, had its Apaches.[90] The Apache's lack of manliness was made apparent by his use of knives, his cruelty, his cowardly attacks on the defenseless, and most all by his sexual exploitation of women. He was a degenerate who bore the stigmata of venereal disease, alcoholism, and an "almost feminine" slightness of build.[91] Defenders of the lash in France, such as the contributors to the popular journal *Le Matin,* argued that its success in England and the United States and Denmark's returned to the "bastonnade" in 1905 showed that the dangerous young males could, if dealt with severely, be subdued.[92]

Alexandre Lacassagne, professor of criminal anthropology at Lyon, was France's most eminent proponent of the whip. The guillotine was used less frequently, and prisons, he argued, had increasingly lost their power to inspire fear, particularly in that abnormal 5 percent of the school population that was produced by alcoholic parents. Ant colonies sanely sacrificed their useless members; in modern human societies the soft-hearted insisted deviants be spared. Lacassagne concluded that France, faced with thirty thousand precocious, drunken louts who only respected the whip, had no option but to turn to the "manière forte" of corporal punishment.[93]

The second stock male countertype was the vagrant. The vagrant was the man who, like the woman, purportedly did not work. The images of the feckless vagrant, the lying gypsy, the homeless tramp, and the thoughtless nomad, ran completely counter to bourgeois moralizing on the uplifting nature of work and thrift. These wanderers appeared as increasingly frightening and sinister figures in an ever more settled urban landscape. Moreover the vague definitions given vagabondage had the effect of blurring the line between crime and unemployment. Observers, in referring to itinerant workers as "tribes" of savages and riffraff, exploited the fears that "honest workmen" could be somehow dragged back down the evolutionary scale by association with such degenerates.

Cesare Lombroso, the Italian criminologist who presented the tramp as a biological throwback, an atavistic being, set the initial terms of the late-nineteenth-century discussion of vagrancy.[94] In America the hobo initially enjoyed a more romantic image, yet even there the tenor of the times could be detected in Josiah Flynt's opening statement in *Tramping with Tramps* (1899) that he was inspired to look at "human parasites" and "criminals" on the road after observing his laboratory colleagues' investigation of vermin.[95] Unmanliness apparently could be contagious. His countryman the Reverend Frank Charles Laubach declared that real men worked; vagrancy was the refuge of "cowards" given to drugs, drink, gambling, and sexual immorality. The proximity of such men injured and defiled honest laborers.[96] Accordingly turn-of-the-century labor unrest was attributed by American conservatives to the influence of anarchistic foreign trash whereas American populists believed that the country was being divided between tramps and millionaires.

In France the "chemineaux," in particular Italian beggars, were likewise called the enemy of the peasants.[97] Gypsies were singled out by the apprehensive as thieves.[98] Magistrates worried that with the ending of the "livret" or workers passbook in 1890 it would be harder to keep the poor under surveillance. Urban workers needed identification papers to obtain jobs, but tramps did not. Jailing offered no remedy, so it was claimed, as vagrants actually wanted, at least during the winter months, to be imprisoned.[99] Judge Émile Fourquet, the leading French expert on "les vagabonds criminels," raised the specter of a nomadic army of four hundred thousand men, the "roulans" who, despite work opportunities that could put "luxuries" within the reach of the industrious, prowled the countryside.[100] The appeal of the road, with its dissipations and distractions, inevitably led to demoralization. Citing as an example the career of Vacher, the serial sex killer, Fourquet attributed a purported late-nineteenth-century surge in murders, thefts, rapes, and assaults on children to tramps.[101] Vagrancy was presented by such experts as a psychological, rather than a economic problem. Tramps, like swindlers, according to the German psychiatrist Emile Kraeplin, suffered from a disorder marked by a hyperactivity of the imagination, an inaccuracy of memory, and an instability of the emotions.[102]

The third stock male countertype was the pervert. In subjecting a number of male sex criminals—pimps, transvestites, male prostitutes, exhibitionists, and purveyors of pornographic material—to the lash, the English were responding to a widespread fear of male sexual deviancy. Such sick individuals, claimed the anxious, posed the greatest threats to the virtue of both young men and young women. Attention was thus deflected away from the male heterosexual whose rapes and assaults were implicitly "normalized."[103] The fact that by the 1890s some common criminals were seeking to justify their assaults by claiming their victims were homosexuals shows how quickly this new ranking of asocial behavior was popularized.

European experts in sexuality, while acknowledging the different mores of ancient Greeks and Eastern cultures, asserted that healthy male sexuality had, with the advance of Western culture, become resolutely heterosexual. Accordingly evidence of any erosion of the natural gender boundaries was attributed to the "decadence" of the upper classes or the "degeneration" of the lower. Paolo Mantegazza, the Italian sexologist, employing the popular notion that ontogeny recapitulated phylogeny, argued that the gender differences necessarily increased with age and civilization. But with old age there was some unavoidable slippage; elderly men, for example, with their embarrassing temper tantrums and unseemly flightiness, acted more and more like their female counterparts.[104] Dandyism and homosexuality were cited by others as evidence that even the younger male could slip into femininity. In central Europe Otto Weininger lamented the appearance of masculine women and feminine men; in Vienna Karl Kraus condemned his age as one of confusion and bisexuality.

Popular notions of the possibility of evolution "going backward" were constantly exploited by those seeking to explain the apparently sudden emergence of deviancy. Henry Maudsley, the pioneering English psychiatrist, noted that many talked of evolution, but degeneration was as natural and as much an ongoing process. Just as some new chemical products were only made possible by decomposition of compounds,

> so new products of an asocial or antisocial kind are formed in the retrograde metamorphosis of the human kind; wherefore it is that we meet with not only degenerate varieties of the kind, such as idiots and lunatics, but also with a great many forms and varieties of degradation in persons who are neither idiots nor lunatics. . . .

> The ingenuity of vice which he [man] has achieved in that respect
> has reached the limit of its variety only in the limits of the physical
> capacities of his bodily mechanism; so that, these having been now
> exhausted, happily no one, howsoever great his practical genius,
> will be able to invent a new vice of that sort.[105]

Man used his reason to multiply and gratify selfish, animal passions, which animals did not. So man, according to Maudsley, would not return to his origins as a monkey but descend to the rank of a slavering idiot.

The emergence of the homosexual—the term was only coined in the 1860s—was both the cause and the effect of the growing fear of the male "other."[106] Until the latter half of the nineteenth century, the public was told by experts that male lust was "natural" and unchangeable. There was no such thing as the homosexual, although there were men who performed perverse acts.[107] The last sodomite to be burned alive in France perished in 1783. The nineteenth century saw a shift away from a concern for particular sexual acts and toward the notion of particular "types" of male deviants.[108] In Paris police officials such as Tardieu, Carlier, and Macé created and popularized the image of the homosexual as the spawn of degenerative forces, atavistic urges, and congenital defects.[109] The extent of such beliefs can be gauged by Friedrich Engels' response when Karl Marx sent him a call for homosexual rights that had been written in 1869 by Karl Heinrich Ulrichs: "The Pederasts are starting to take stock and to find that they constitute a power in the state. As yet, an organization is missing even though secretly it exists already. . . . it is lucky that we ourselves are too old to witness the victory of their cause and to pay the price with our own bodies."[110]

In England Labouchère's amendment to the Criminal Law Amendment Act of 1885, added in the first place to protect the young of both sexes from predatory older men, had the chief effect of hitting male same-sex relations.[111] The legislation created the deviants it policed. Suddenly parents of sons were alerted by legislators that the new sexual types of the pederast and invert posed a serious sexual danger. W. T. Stead, the muckraking journalist, noted pointedly at the time of Oscar Wilde's 1895 trial that the virtue of the young male was now declared sacrosanct; the young female was still fair game. "If Oscar Wilde, instead of indulging in dirty tricks with boys and men, had ruined the lives of half a dozen simpletons of girls, or had broken up the home of his friend's wife, no one would have laid a finger on him."[112]

Late-nineteenth-century social observers of youth worried more about boys than about girls. Young women, it was assumed, simply had to be prepared for marriage whereas young men had to be trained for more important and complex roles in the worlds of labor, the military, and politics.[113] Psychologists such as G. Stanley Hall—who coined the term adolescent—raised the alarm that boys were put at risk in urban environment just when they were most impressionable.[114] Such new preoccupations with protecting young men fueled the late-nineteenth-century campaigns against smoking, dancing, drinking, lurid dime novels, and what one observer called the "gangrene of pornography."[115] Moral entrepreneurs such as René Beranger in France and Anthony Comstock in the United States created repressive leagues calling for censorship.[116] In France pornography was particularly seen as fueling the threats of national degeneration and depopulation.[117] If one was to believe such propagandists, young men on the continent were exposed outside lycées and at "fêtes patronales," cafés, concerts, and theaters to a constant barrage of temptations and seductions. Salacious material came in the forms of cards, photographs, newspapers, books, stereoscopes, and cinematographes. Boys were offered, in publications that carried advertisements for "moyens anticonceptionnels" and abortifacients, the purchase of everything from lewd slides to fully inflatable rubber women.[118] Immorality led to debauchery; overexcitation to sadism, heterosexual excesses finally to homosexuality. Pornography was declared to be even more dangerous than antimilitaristic propaganda to new nations; the debauched not only failed to reproduce, they became rebels or "Apaches" who drifted into criminality. For the republic to survive, claimed the moral purists, let alone prove its moral superiority to other regimes, it was necessary to silence those seeking to drag young men down into immorality.[119]

The last threat to the ideal of masculinity to which the flogging craze drew attention was not the unmanly man but the unwomanly woman. In England, as noted above, some of the proponents of flogging suggested that suffragettes be subjected to the lash. Such anger was evidence of the feelings that many men harbored at the turn of the century, the sense that if there were a crisis in masculinity it was primarily due to the fact that women were unilaterally redefining themselves and thereby the relations of both sexes. On the continent from the 1870s onward, a host of male writers, playing on strong misogynistic cultural themes, launched a backlash against the modest advances women had made in work and education. In France Alexandre Dumas, Émile Zola and Octave Mirbeau added their new misogynistic musings to the older theories of feminine subordination that had been earlier worked out by Jules Michelet, Auguste Comte, and Pierre-Joseph Proudhon. Such writers presented men as the truly dispossessed sex and vulgarly labeled Victor Marguerite, Jules Bois, and Léopold Lacour, whom they judged to be traitorously sympathetic to women's plight, "les vaginards."[120]

Misogyny seemed to advance with women's emancipation. Freud reported from Vienna that it was common to find that a man "only develops full potency when he is with a debased sexual object."[121] This would have made no sense to a confirmed bachelor like Henry Maudsley, who asked what could be more unworthy of a man—a rational being—than to be transported by the touch "of another being less rational than himself."[122] In central Europe, as Jacques Le Rider has pointed out, the misogyny of Schopenhauer, Nietszche, and Weininger reached unparalleled heights.[123] There women were commonly compared by their denigrators in academic circles to Jews, blacks, and native American Indians. A book like Paul Julius Moebius's *Sur l'imbecilité physiologique de la femme* (1900) was a best seller. Moebius, who asserted that women were more instinctual, egotistical, and degenerate than males, called for a new masculine culture that would herald the "emancipation of men." This phrase was the actual title of a book—Norbert Grabowsky's *Die Bestimmung des Menschen*—published in 1897.[124]

Even in America the "new woman" was often presented by her foes as an androgyne or lesbian. She was regarded in colleges neither as a man nor as a traditional woman.[125] Male professional psychiatrists and psychologists, in shifting the definition of female deviance from rejection of motherhood to rejection of men, increasingly classed independent women as something akin to an intermediate sex.[126] Such concerns would find a place in the American novel, where the theme of the well-meaning man leaving the confusing world of women for the simpler homosocial world of men was already well established.[127]

It made sense for those attacking the "new women" to believe that once upon a time the meanings of both masculinity and femininity had been clear, unquestioned, and natural as opposed to the confused state in which they were now found. The gender debate had a centuries-long pedigree, but a particular constellation of political, social, and cultural forces in the late nineteenth century made the discussion of appropriate male and female roles an especially sensitive issue. In the increasingly democratic world of citizens, the old status divisions that had once separated all subjects into graded ranks were eroded. Indeed as both political and industrial revolutions seemed to sweep away the artificial barriers separating peoples, the only "natural" ways in which to categorize individuals appeared to be according to age and gender. The fears voiced by a line of the most "progressive" thinkers from Rousseau through to Proudhon and beyond that the sexes might be confused—that women would encroach on male prerogatives—was but one indicator of the new political importance accorded masculinity.[128] In the self-consciously scientific, positivistic world of the nineteenth century, biological arguments about "real" differences played an ever greater role in justifying social hierarchies and one's sex necessarily became more important, a "privileged" sign of social identification.

"Manly," which in the eighteenth century was primarily used to mean the opposite of the boyish or childish, was in the Victorian age increasingly employed as the antonym of the feminine or effeminate. The nineteenth-century bourgeoisie were so concerned that the "naturally" different genders of men and women not be confused that they demarcated as sharply as possible the lines splitting the female from the male world; the home from the workplace, the private from the public.[129] Seen in this context, the bourgeoisie's stress on the virile nature of work and labor can more easily be understood. Middle-class propagandists such as Cobden and Bright declared that to take the idle aristocrat, fop, or roué as a male role model was a thing of the past. Manliness was now demonstrated by one's industry and competence not by chance.[130] Following the argument of the natural separation of spheres, men worked and women did not—or at least not outside of the home. Trade unionists in turn defended the notion of the male "bread-winner" wage on the grounds that only it would allow working-class men the income required to keep their women folk at home. The songs of the German socialist movement had titles like "Brothers Embrace the League," "Now Stand Together, Man to Man," and "Man of Labor, Awaken and Recognize your Strength." In England, as elsewhere, working men, to prove their virility, shunned domestic work: "If, on occasion, they had to lend a hand . . . they locked the doors first so that the neighbours would not see. Those husbands who were caught in the act of scrubbing a floor, washing, or cooking were apt to be called derisive names such as 'mop rag' or 'diddy man.'"[131]

The nineteenth-century reading public was led from the stress on Christian manliness that marked the fictional works of Charles Kingsley and Thomas Hughes to Henty and H. Rider Haggard's depiction of robust heroes driven by brutal energy and dominating wills.[132] To be a man required effort and labor that was not required of women. One did not goad on a female by force of will to "be a woman"; she was born one. Exertion and activity was required to "be a man."[133] In effect the public accepted implicitly the notion that manliness was a constructed identity because a male had to "prove" repeatedly at work and at play that he was a "man." But with technological advances such arguments increasingly rang hollow; much of urban men's work no longer posed the sorts of challenges that once weeded out the indolent and weak from the industrious and brawny. By the end of the century, an army of white bloused women workers emerged as teachers, secretaries, telephone operators, and nurses. Lower-middle-class men, who occupied similar positions, took the brunt of public sarcasm as those whose only ambition was to achieve security. In France Barrès mocked functionaries as "demi-mâles," while in Britain laborers cruelly joked about the fellow who "was born a man but died a clerk."[134]

Pierre de Coubertin responded to such concerns by attempting to turn France to athleticism. In 1888 the Ligue nationale de l'éducation physique won the support of such public figures as Marcellin Berthelot, Georges Clemenceau, Louis Pasteur, and Jules Verne, and in 1895 Coubertin created the International Olympic Committee.[135] In the United States, Theodore Roosevelt publicly embraced the strenuous life, exalting the need for

> the rougher, manlier virtues, and above all the virtue of personal courage, physical as well as moral. If we wish to do good work for our country we must be unselfish, disinterested . . . but in addition we must be vigorous in mind and body, able to hold our own in rough conflict with our fellows, able to suffer punishment without flinching, and at need, to repay it in kind with full interest. A peaceful and commercial civilization is always in danger of suffering the loss of the virile fighting qualities without which no nation, however cultured, however refined, however thrifty and prosperous, can ever amount to anything.[136]

Bernarr A. MacFadden struck the same chord, promising male office workers that physical education could save both their minds and bodies.[137] In England Robert Baden-Powell, alarmed that urbanization was producing men who were "stunted, narrow-chested, easily wearied; yet voluble, excitable, with little ballast, stamina, or endurance," launched the scouting movement.[138] Bodily vigor, such activists asserted, was an indicator of moral vigor; physical and moral strength were equated. Attempts were even made to masculinize religion. Christ, Billy Sunday informed his 1890s

American congregations, was "no dough-faced, lick-spittle proposition. Jesus was the greatest scrapper that ever lived."[139] More serious thinkers believed that more than muscles was needed to make a man. A French Catholic writer, F. A. Vuillermet, began *Soyez des hommes: à la conquète de la virilité* (1909) with the dramatic assertion, "There are no more men!" For him real virility had been undermined by the forces of materialism and irreligion.[140] Arthur Lautrec, in *La Fin du monde prochainement* attributed the sorry state of current morality to the "invasion" of France by Jews, socialism, Free Masonry, and the "culte de la femme."[141]

What is one to make of this sense of manhood under siege? The importance of the flogging craze in England is that it draws our attention to the ways in which, by conjuring up a cast of characters against which a real man had to battle, masculinity was reconstituted. Masculinity was at the turn of the century obviously going through a period of deconstruction and reconstruction. The context was one in which the older disciplinary mechanisms employed by elite males to control women, workers, and young people—essentially those of the church, family, shop, and farm—were breaking down and being replaced by teachers, policemen, and doctors. These professionals disciplined the deviants they themselves were in the process of inventing or discovering. For example, in France the myth of the menace posed the race by male subnormals who would inevitably drift into vagabondage and crime was created by the first generation of educators who carried out culturally biased forms of school testing.[142] Similarly the number of men who committed sexual offenses against females appeared to rise in England once the Children's Act of 1908 allowed an indecent assault upon a young person to be tried summarily.[143]

Save for a few perceptive gadflies such as George Bernard Shaw, most contemporaries found it difficult to place the apparent emergence of disturbing, new forms of male sexuality in social perspective. Defenders of bourgeois society assumed that those on the margins—homosexuals, Jews, vagrants—were lacking in manliness. And taking it as a given that everything that was rational, productive, and orderly was necessarily an aspect of manliness, they bewailed as a symptom of emasculation whatever succeeding social or economic threat currently preoccupied them. Accordingly France's declining birth rate, Britain's loss of industrial supremacy, and Germany's labor unrest were in each case attributed to waning virility. Pessimistic Americans believed that with the end of frontiering they would meet the same fate. Viewed in this light, the diplomatic rhetoric of the turn of the century becomes more understandable. "Much of the language of compensatory bellicosity was in fact sexual. The virtues of strength, military preparedness, courage, hardness, aggression, vitality, comradeship, productivity, and so forth were all virtues associated with masculinity."[144]

And yet at the level of individual cases the idea of manliness remained very flexible, reflecting the observer's class, race, and cultural preoccupations. In the same years that the American tramp was turned into a fearful figure, the American cowboy—yet another itinerant, unskilled laborer—emerged as a model male.[145] Men who claimed to be alarmed at the threat posed by homosexuality forced on their sons not only westerns but the books of H. Rider Haggard and Jules Verne with their suspiciously all-male casts of purported bachelors.[146] The very same readers who were appalled at the idea that social degenerative forces could return European men to the level of the apes were thrilled by Edgar Rice Burroughs's Tarzan stories.[147] And a moralist like Dr. Lejeune, who declared himself revolted by the senseless crimes committed by the Apaches of Paris, was not ashamed to admit that the case of a man killing his wife in a fit of jealousy—"a crime of passion"—was something he could understand.

The turn of the century campaign for the reintroduction of flogging signaled that unmanly behavior had come to be regarded by many as posing a serious danger to respectable society. As a way of further testing and exposing such gender expectations in what follows we will turn to a variety of other court cases that cover a wide range of male conduct. Western culture created, maintained and policed concepts of masculinity in countless ways. The notion that there were two distinct and opposite sexes was so well inculcated that what it meant to be a man was rarely problematized; maleness was rendered almost invisible. The trials that involved those perceived to be rogue or deviant males are accordingly invaluable sources because they made explicit, as contemporaries such as Dr. Lejeune vaguely perceived, the vital though often changing nuances of the injunction "be a man."

PART TWO

LEGAL DISCOURSES: MEN, MELODRAMA, AND CRIMINALITY

To TRACE THE WAYS IN WHICH THE COURTS PARTICIPATED IN the policing of masculinity, we analyze in the following section a series of trials in which the question of the manliness of the defendant figured centrally. The issues that precipitated these courtroom dramas have been purposely chosen from a wide range of cases: from the relatively inconsequential—the losing of a few pounds as a result of a failed courtship—to the most serious—murder and manslaughter. Judges and juries, given that they dealt with such vital issues as an individual's life, liberty, and property, sought to impress upon the community that their findings were based not on prejudice but on the facts of the case and the dictates of the law. Yet in case after case, as soon as the elusive but vital question of gender reared its head, the court found itself forced to square appeals to the potent, albeit intangible, concept of "manhood" with references to matters of "fact."

The mixing of fact and fantasy, which played such an obvious role in the White Slavery Panic, could be expected to be encountered whenever the issue of "manliness" emerged in legal confrontations. In the theatrical environment of the turn of the century courtroom, defendants and plaintiffs inevitably found themselves assuming the role of one of the standard characters in the play of masculinity. These roles tended to follow the conventions of the Victorian melodrama—one was either a hero or villain. The melodrama, it will be recalled, emerged in early-nineteenth-century Europe as a popular theatrical form that reflected, in an overheated fashion, concerns for the class and sexual exploitation of the lower orders. In such breathless classics as *London by Night* (1844), *The Poor of New York* (1857), and *Under the Gaslight* (1867), the audience was told that beneath the orderly appearances of everyday life lurked some dangerous secret, which the heartless villain would try to turn to his advantage.[1] The blackguard's usual intent was to have his way with some unwilling woman; the closer the heroine came to succumbing to the assaults on her virtue, the greater the tension of the play. Only in the last act did the virtuous hero, by some stroke of luck, rescue the innocent female victim from the long anticipated rape or seduction.[2]

Melodrama, despite its formulaic absurdities and exaggerations, created a cast of stock characters who would live in the public's imagination well into the twentieth century. The simple, stark moral claims such characters made gave them enormous appeal. Since the courts were believed to deal with issues of right and wrong, it was not surprising that the public that followed their proceedings used notions drawn from the melodrama to make sense out of an increasingly complex world.[3] Such an apportioning of roles worked perfectly in the White Slave Panic. The social purity activists could be easily taken—and certainly saw themselves—as audacious heroes, the prostitutes as passive victims, and the pimps as villains. In many criminal trials and in most civil disputes, however, the power relations of the accused and plaintiff would not from the outset be as asymmetrical. In such cases there would ensue from the very start a struggle over the question of who had the right to appropriate the role of "hero" and thereby relegate their antagonist to the position of "villain." And if the participants in the trial did not immediately make such identifications, the popular press could usually be counted on to make them on behalf of its readership. In knowing that the accused had acted like a "gentleman" or a "cad," a "decent fellow" or a "bounder," the newspaper public had a fairly good idea of the trial's final outcome. As the following four chapters demonstrate, an individual's manliness, which played a vital role in the outcome of such contests, was not simply a "fact." It was something that a man in court, by turning to his purposes the melodramatic narrative of sexual danger, had to prove.

TWO

FOOLS

ON 11 NOVEMBER 1895, THE OPERATORS OF THE WORLD'S
Great Marriage Association (Limited) of London and its magazine, the
Matrimonial Herald, were charged at the Bow Street Magistrate's Court
with fraud. In the course of the long court process, which dragged on until
March of the following year, it came out that the accused had, by offering
to arrange advantageous marriages, bilked countless men and women of
large sums of money. The curious trial proceedings are, like most reports
of successful conspiracy frauds, inherently interesting, but for the historian
of nineteenth-century gender and sexuality, the most striking aspect of the
affair is the light that it casts on Victorians' views of men and marriage.

Matrimony, the assumption holds, has been chiefly a woman's concern.
According to the tired old joke, a man chases a woman until he is caught.
Women seek marriage; men avoid it. Yet until the latter half of the nineteenth century, middle- and upper-class males were quite candid about
both their interests in marriage and the amounts of wealth that made a
woman an especially suitable matrimonial prospect. Writing to his sister in
1862, a young Canadian ended his glowing account of his intended bride's
accomplishments with the not untypical observation "and best of all [she]
is possessed of property, and has no hangers on. Now there is something
for you to reflect on." Only in the 1890s could the middle classes "be heard
to denounce this materialistic hunt as unworthy of an idealized union,
which should be a blending of hearts rather than a transfer of funds."[1] And
even then some retorted that the current attacks on the "marriage market"
were mere cant.[2]

What occurred at the lower levels of the social hierarchy? Stories of the
occasional predatory middle-class male fortune hunter from whose advances heiresses had to be protected have been told, but little has been
said of the ways in which lower-middle- and working-class men perceived
marriage as possibly offering an economic "opportunity."[3] A review of the

39

Matrimonial Herald trial serves the useful purpose of reminding us that in Victorian England it was assumed that men of all social classes would make such calculations.[4] The victims in this case came to grief, so the readers of the popular press were told, not because they sought to make reasonably advantageous matches, but because in their greed they reached too far. For their miscalculations they were doubly punished; first by fraudulent businessmen who took their money and then by better situated middle-class males who both in and out of court cruelly enjoyed what they took to be a hilarious account of how simple-minded lower-class men, in seeking to use the marriage market to move beyond their appointed station in life, had come a cropper.

The declared goal of the *Matrimonial Herald and Fashionable Marriage Gazette,* which ran from 1884 to 1895, was to provide "HIGH CLASS MATCHES," but its readers were assured that no request for assistance was considered too modest.[5] The pages of the *Herald* contained little beyond advertisements for men and women seeking partners. Such queries could be placed in its columns at a cost of four shillings for fifty words; letters in response were sent care of the editor. The *Herald* and the association claimed that their advertisements appeared in local papers throughout the United Kingdom and that responses were received from around the world. The association guaranteed that absolute discretion was assured by its large staff, which worked with "celerity and facility."

Matrimonial advertisements had been placed in newspapers by individuals from the eighteenth century onward.[6] Commercial agencies were active by the mid nineteenth century and were from the beginning suspected of fraud. In 1934 George Orwell wrote to a friend that he had just purchased a year's issue of an unidentified 1851 weekly paper.

> They ran among other things a matrimonial agency, and the correspondence relating to this is well worth reading. "Flora is twenty-one, tall, with rich chestnut hair and a silvery laugh, and makes excellent pastry. She would like to enter into correspondence with a professional gentleman between the ages of twenty and thirty, preferably with auburn whiskers and of the Established Church." The interesting thing to me is that these people, since they try to get married through a matrimonial agency, have evidently failed many times elsewhere, and yet as soon as they advertise in this paper, they get half a dozen offers. The women's descriptions of themselves are always most flattering, and I must say that some of the cases make me distinctly suspicious—for of course that was the great age of fortune hunting.[7]

The actual work of tending to the enormous correspondence elicited by the *Herald* was carried out at the World's Great Marriage Association, located at 103 New Oxford Street. Those who preferred not to advertise openly could work through its management and arrange contacts by "private overture." A fee of five shillings was charged for a consultation and additional sums were levied for introductions. The owners affirmed that, by a "lavish outlay of capital" and through the intercession of the agency's many "ambassadors" who moved in society, countless happy unions were created. Indeed the *Herald* asserted that the association produced matches that worked as well and indeed were often happier than those that resulted from "promiscuous meetings." By 1895 the *Herald* was boasting that in responding to the demands of its clients with "an enormous and ungrudged expense" it was leading the contemporary movement toward "rational marriage." Its staff, so it claimed, numbered fifty; its successful clients included on the one hand thousands of young, beautiful, rich women with estates and residences and on the other the representatives of the "sterner sex" who ranged from peers and professionals down to common waiters. A "Pamphlet of Extracts" of the testimonials produced by satisfied customers, declared the *Herald,* was available on request.[8]

The *Herald*'s activities, though known to many, were broadcast to the entire nation when its owners appeared at a preliminary hearing at Bow Street before Mr. Lushington on 11 November 1895 charged with conspiracy to defraud. In the dock sat Mortimer Daniel Skates (alias Daniel Mortimer), proprietor of the World's Great Marriage Association; his brother John Charles Skates (alias Charles Barrington); his father-in-law John Abrahams (alias Daniel Mortimer alias John Charles Skates alias Charles Barrington); the Skates's nephew Norman Golding Hannah, secretary of the association; and Anthony Maddows, editor of the *Matrimonial Herald.*

Acting on numerous complaints, the police had descended on the offices of the association—which proved to consist of eleven clerks, all but one who were shareholders—at Oxford Street and Mecklenburgh Square, seizing books, registers, and thousands of letters and photographs. When Detective Sergeant McCarthy read the warrant, the Skateses protested that at least one of the complainants had already been given his money back. The police responded that this restitution had only been provided after the complaint had been lodged and proceedings begun.[9] It soon came out that for the previous several years Scotland Yard had received reports that the agency placed bogus advertisements in newspapers to draw in victims from whom it extracted registration fees, fees to become a member, and after-marriage subscriptions, all the time having no intention, or at least failing, to provide the contacts it promised.[10] But it was only now that witnesses were willing to lay charges.[11] After a lengthy preliminary hearing, the defendants were on 29 January 1896 committed to trial, which took place in March in the Recorder's Court of the Old Bailey.[12]

How had the frauds been perpetrated? Clients, most of whom appeared to be men, were lured into contacting the World's Great Marriage Association through advertisements in local papers purportedly placed by wealthy individuals seeking spouses.[13] Men who responded were told by return mail that they could be best served by joining the association; normally such a membership cost £10 10s. but given the large number of eligible ladies on the register, the fee would be reduced to £5 5s., or even as low as 12s. 6d. On receipt of fees, more dummy descriptions of wealthy young women were sent out. Once the men were well involved in their romantic correspondences with these prize catches, the association informed them that if they married they would have to pay the agency an additional fee of 2½ percent of the woman's estate, but if they paid in advance a £12 10s. "free associate membership fee," all additional duties would be waived. Presumably men who were convinced they were about to successfully snag an heiress felt it was a small price to pay. But once the association was assured that it had obtained all the men's available money, the mysterious wealthy women who had been used as bait to draw in the male clients suddenly went abroad or regretfully broke off the correspondence.

The association was shrewd enough to realize that it could not simply take its clients' money and run. It remained in business for more than ten years because it provided, in addition to its fictitious heiresses, some bona fide introductions. When its male clients had been clearly milked of all the money they were willing to hazard, the agency began to send them the names and addresses of real women that it had on its register, and contacts were actually made. But these women, much to the disappointment of the fortune hunters, turned out not to be heiresses but domestic servants or poor governesses who had themselves sent off their meager savings to the association in hopes of marrying one of the rich gentlemen whose advertisements appeared in the *Herald*. The sad irony was that the duped male and female clients of the association had much in common: they shared the same modest social class backgrounds, their hopes for upward mobility via marriage had led to their entrapment, and when they met their prospective partners the expectations of both were cruelly disappointed.

No doubt some marriages did result from the agency's activities. Mr. Lushington, the presiding magistrate at the preliminary hearing, mentioned

having received letters from such people.[14] But in giving their clients introductions to real individuals, the association was primarily concerned with
providing itself with a legal cover. Even so, there were countless disgruntled
clients; when John Charles Skates was arrested, he had on his person nineteen letters complaining of "delusive advertising" and one demanding a
refund.[15] But clients obviously had to think twice before complaining to
the police. After all they had been given some bona fide introductions, and
if it came to a court case they would be obliged to declare to the world
their own gullibility and sordid calculations.

Because of its careful planning, the association had a long and prosperous career. So complicated were its machinations—the accused not only
posed as fictitious clients but impersonated each other, hence the many
alias—that it took weeks for the crown to work out exactly what had been
done and to whom. The police found on the association's premises a series
of thirteen index books containing the names of thirty thousand men and
women. An advertisement book listed the many dummy notices placed in
provincial newspapers. Some were especially successful. Three hundred
and fifty-six letters were received in reply to an advertisement signed "Ce-
cil" and 163 were addressed to a "Mrs. Huntley." The owner of the Lamb's
Conduit Street stationer's shop, which served until 1895 as the association's
letter drop, said he received 100 to 150 letters a day addressed to the "editor" or "negotiator."[16] In the first ten months of 1895 the receipts of the
association's registration department totaled £3,375; those of the "free
marriage department" £2,095. John Charles Skates, as managing director,
skimmed off the handsome salary of one thousand pounds a year.[17]

ſ

WHAT DOES THIS FRAUD REVEAL ABOUT VICTORIAN CONCEPTS OF
masculinity? The successful fraud artist necessarily has to know more than
most about the desires, ambitions, and "great expectations" of the gullible.
The obvious interest of this case is that through its analysis we can see
what confidence men knew of both the fantasies and the realities of-late
nineteenth-century matrimony. Let us begin with the fantasies on which
the Skateses and their associates played. In perusing the trumped up advertisements, one is first provided with what the editors of the *Herald* assumed
would look to their readers like prize catches. Typical men's advertisements read:

> A builder, clearing over £2000 a year, would like to correspond
> with a dark handsome young lady, of good family, with a view to

> marriage. Advertiser is forty-five, of kind disposition, but is very shrewd in business. If correspondent can play the piano, so much the better.
>
> A merchant in the West Indies, making about £3000 a year, on account of his sister, who has for some years acted as his house-keeper, being about to marry, wishes with a view to matrimony, to make the acquaintance of a refined, cultured, prepossessing young lady.

The purported eligible males were presented as kindly, prosperous, and mature. Why had such eminently marriageable men not already been picked off? In explaining their recourse to advertising, they were given a variety of stock answers; not infrequently it was that they had been recently widowed or only lately had returned from India. These fictional bachelors further fitted the romantic contemporary male stereotype of the rugged, successful male. The repeated assertion of their being "kind" seems to have been a code word for "I will not assert the right, which as a man I have, to chastise physically my spouse." They appeared to be largely indifferent to their potential spouse's financial situation yet had set ideas about the physical attractions she should possess; most men hoped she would be young but "domesticated," and many went on to describe the color of hair and shape of figure they preferred.

The advertisements purportedly written by female clients, though they frequently expressed a preference for a partner with taste and a position in life, were, in contrast to the men's, strikingly undemanding.[18]

> Caroline, twenty-three, a blonde, thoroughly accomplished, pre-possessing, with good, well-developed figure, and possessing a private income of £300 per annum, would be pleased to hear from a gentleman residing in the neighborhood of Leeds, who must not exceed the age of thirty-five.
>
> An orphan young lady of large means, who having just lost her aged parents, whom she had devotedly attended in their dying days, was anxious to assuage her grief by meeting with a gentle-man, bachelor or widower, with the same marital object to follow.[19]

"Prepossessing" perfectly described the model Victorian female. Whereas a man did not suffer from being initially difficult or gruff, a woman was supposed to make an agreeable first impression and be obviously attractive. Such young beauties had just, so it was commonly claimed, entered the marriage market. Some were provided with assertions that, having recently been orphaned or having quarreled with their family, they now suddenly had to think of matrimony. Others blushingly confessed that, dutifully caring for invalid relatives, they had hitherto virtuously put off marriage.

The descriptions provided by the *Herald*'s advertisements drew directly from the ideal Victorian male and female stereotypes of powerful men and demure women. The advertisers appear to have stepped from the pages of cheap novels or from the stages of popular melodramas. But as patently artificial and repetitive as they may appear today, at the time they successfully served the Skateses and their associates as brilliant lures with which to hook thousands of enterprising, if naive, men and women. Of course, most readers of such advertisements recognized them for what they were and turned the page. But many reread them, hesitant though hopeful, wondering if this was not the opportunity they had been waiting for. What struggling young clerk making do on a yearly salary of £80 did not dream of meeting a "Caroline" with her well-developed figure and £300 per annum?[20]

The *Herald*'s enterprising proprietors exploited not only such dreams but the gap that separated sparkling fantasy from drab reality. Assuming that their readership included many males who, because of some slight correctable problem with their appearance, had not yet been romantically successful, they offered a variety of invaluable products and services. In addition to carrying notices of where one might contract a quiet wedding, the *Herald* ran advertisements for obesity medicines, cures for the deaf, hair dyes, male corsets, shoe elevators, Restauro Tonics, and electropathic belts guaranteed to provide life and vigor. Alex Ross, a particularly prolific inventor, used the *Herald* to boast of the efficacy of Spanish Fly to grow hair, a "Skin Tightener," a "Nose Machine," and for 10s. 6d. "Ross's Ear Machine, for placing the ears close to the head."[21] If the commercial advertisements in the *Herald* conjured up the depressing picture of a mass male readership of short, deaf, balding, white-haired, overweight, impotent, jug-eared men, it is only fair to note that its notices for Arsenic Wafers (to improve the complexion), abortifacient solutions, and discrete adoption services suggested that its female readers were also far from perfect.

SO MUCH FOR THE FANTASIES. IT IS WHEN WE TURN FROM THE *HERALD* to the trial accounts of its proprietors that we are given a sense of the brutal realities men had to face when attempting to penetrate the Victorian marriage market.

The accused really had no defense. Thomas Henry Gurrin, a handwriting expert called by the crown, declared that the letters purportedly signed by a variety of female advertisers were all written by the same individual.[22] The defense's weak response was to admit that some ladies' names had been falsified, but only in order to protect such women until the men interested in them had their backgrounds checked. Even one of the victims, Bason, acknowledged that he assumed that some ladies would use a *nom-de-plume*. But at the trial, the defense was finally forced to concede that many letters were in fact written by the proprietors and to fall back on the argument that only those who wanted to be duped could have been taken in since there was no attempt at disguising the handwriting.

The defense's second line of argument, which it first announced at the preliminary hearing in January 1896, was that it would, if forced, subpoena large numbers of wealthy men and women who had married through the agency. The fact that some clients successfully married, so counsel claimed, provided the association with a reasonable belief that others would too. As it would obviously take some time to track down the witnesses who would establish the character of the defendants, the defense called for an adjournment. But Lushington, the presiding magistrate, was not taken in by the argument that the association's character could be demonstrated by showing that *some* of its services had not been fraudulent. He insisted that the defense only call witnesses pertaining to the actual cases complained of; evidence drawn from other cases would not be admissible.[23] To prove that the advertisements were not fraudulent, the defense called at the preliminary hearing one woman, whose name was not released, who testified that she had in fact corresponded with two of the complainants. She was still looking for a husband worth a £1,000 a year and admitted to having written to over a hundred men.[24] Her testimony did not counter the complaints of the other plaintiffs, and at the trial the defense chose to call neither her nor any other witness.

When the case was heard at the Old Bailey, the counsels retained by the proprietors of the World's Great Marriage Association realized that they only had one hope of mounting an effective defense. That hope lay in appealing to the social superiority of the judge and the all-male jury by attacking the complainants as socially marginal characters who, stupidly believing in the impossible, did not deserve the protection of the law. Presumably the proprietors of the association had long harbored the idea of such an argument because when arrested John Charles Skates immediately exclaimed, "We get a lot of these outsiders that pay us a pound or two and expect us to find them a wife with a fortune in a week or two." [25]

The crown was for its part very much aware of the problem posed by witnesses in such fraud cases being too embarrassed to come forward. Many who knew they had been taken advantage of would under no circumstances enter the witness box to be made the butts of the defense counsels. Nevertheless, at the preliminary hearing and the final trial, a dozen witnesses appeared for the crown, all telling much the same story of victimization.

The defense's strategy was not to deny the facts of the case but simply to pour ridicule on those who related them. In doing so it was appealing to the common Victorian assumption that like should marry like, that any reasonable man seeking marriage would confine his ambitions to those of a similar social status. "A fool and his money are soon parted" ran the common saw. The defense's goal was to portray the complainants as just such fools whom the law could never hope to protect.

The defense first ridiculed the witnesses for believing they could marry above themselves. The treatment meted out to Alfred Jordan, Brighton tobacconist and self-proclaimed three-time English champion draughts player, was typical. He had replied to an advertisement in the *People* and was sent the *Herald*.[26] He stipulated that he sought a lady who, in addition to having £200 a year, should be "about twenty years of age, with brown eyes, dark hair, height about 5 ft. 6 in., good-looking, good teeth and complexion, able to see and hear without artificial aid, spinster, middle class, must be English and belong to the Church of England, and must be domestic, musical, well-educated, fond of tennis and games of skill and able to swim, should take an interest in sociology, temperance, dress reform, hygiene, &c, and if she would be able to interest herself in draughts, cricket, or billiards so much the better." [27]

Jordan was to his joy put in touch with "Alice May," a twenty-two-year-old brown-eyed heiress, who was taken by his photograph and declared herself to be "especially interested in his position in the world of draughts." [28] But once Jordan paid his money, the young woman, though "made" for him (in more ways than one) broke off the correspondence. At the trial Lockwood, for the defense, laughingly wondered if Jordan really believed that the sort of a paragon that he sought could have actually existed. Playing up the notion that Jordan must have been fantasizing, the defense further asked the embarrassing question if it were not true that Jordan had even gone so far as to request a woman with "filbert nails."

Similar grillings were given the other complainants. When the defense

asked Adolph Gruenfeld, a Wigmore Street tailor's cutter, who sought a
lady with £300 to £400 a year, how he could claim to be worth £200 a
year, Gruenfeld could not answer.[29] Charles Otto, an electrician of Vincent
Square, Westminster, paid a fee of £2 12s. 6d. and asked for a wife with
an income of about £1000 a year. Defense counsel smirkingly inquired why
Otto, who only earned £3 a week at Siemens Brothers, had the temerity of
expecting to wed a heiress or at least buy one for £2 12s. 6d. Flustered,
Otto protested that he read of such cases in the papers and believed them
to be true.[30] William G. Pitcher, who saw his first advertisement in the *Nor-
folk News,* claimed to have an income of £40 a year but when pressed
admitted to living with his brother-in-law and having no income. "And did
you," asked defense counsel Warburton with feigned astonishment, "really
think that you—22 years of age, earning nothing, and with £40 capital
only—could get a wife?"[31] Pitcher replied that he believed he could. Robert
Brocket, a Scottish forester who sought a wife with an income of £500 a
year, similarly admitted to earning the paltry sum of 18 shillings a week.[32]
And finally the defense extorted from Henry Sutton the confession that
although he demanded a woman worth at least £100 a year he did not tell
his correspondents that he was earning a mere ten shillings a week and
board, an admission that elicited loud guffaws in court.

The presumptuousness of working and lower-middle-
class men seeking to wed wealthy women, the defense then turned its attack on the complainants' crassness. Here were men who thought they
could stipulate what sort of woman they would marry. Counsel pointed
out that Otto had the poor taste of requesting a "spinster, orphan preferred" as one might order a meal in a restaurant. "Mr. Warburton—'Oh,
so you did not wish for a mother-in-law?—No.'"[33] A letter was read in
court that Jordan wrote to the association stating, "I don't expect to get
exactly what I want, but you may take it as a general rule that the bigger
the income the less particular about looks, etc., I shall be, and *vice versa.*"[34]
And the defense, in noting that John Charles George, a house decorator of
Mexborough, Yorkshire, joined the association in August but was asking
for his money back in October, commented that he seemed to think a marriage could be arranged immediately.[35] All this evidence, the defense argued, revealed the complainants to be unsympathetic bumbling boors for
whom few could feel much pity.

The presumptuousness and crudity of the witnesses was all the more
galling, implied the defense, when one saw that men, who had the mis-
placed notion of marrying beautiful young women, were themselves so

lacking in personal charm. Defense counsel pointedly asked Joseph Avery, an elderly man who had been married twice before, "Does it not strike you that you with £130 to £150 a year, a widower—well, not in the first bloom of youth—and with four children, were not a very great catch?"[36] Avery had no answer.

Henry Sutton, a Bow clerk, described himself in his letters as having a "slim, military appearance." The press did not say what Sutton actually looked like, but his self-appraisal was so far off the mark that when it was read at the preliminary hearing it elicited a burst of laughter.[37] Defense counsel Warburton, knowing he was on to a good thing, inquired about Sutton's other attempts at courtship.

> Am I to understand that these negotiations were not success-
> ful?—They were not successful.
> In spite of your military appearance? (Laughter.)

George Bason, a short, bald Northampton machinist earning £80 a year answered an advertisement in the *Weekly Times and Echo* and was thus entrapped by the *Herald*. He also, defense counsel clearly implied, was no Adonis.

> By Mr. Cook.—You sent your photo to Miss Burford at her re-
> quest?—Yes.
> And it was after receiving it that she ceased to write you?—Yes.
> (Laughter.)[38]

At the preliminary hearing, defense counsel further suggested that Bason lied about his age and received no response to the question of whether he really believed his self-description of "44 look younger." Poor Bason became so distraught by the mocking cross-examination that he fainted and had to be carried from the court. Upon his return the heartless defense counsel insisted that one of his letters be read in court, which included the line "I know that some ladies don't like too mutch [*sic*] loving, but the lady must expect it from me." The intent was obviously to expose the witness's lack of education. The defense's overall argument was that such men were so lacking in social graces and physical attractiveness that no one, not even the proprietors of the World's Great Marriage Association, could be held guilty for not finding them suitable mates.

The defense went further, bringing up the fact that the men had been introduced to women of a similar station in life, whom they had spurned. Warburton pointed out that a London witness—who would not have testified without a subpoena and was allowed to give evidence without making his name public—had been put in touch with many women.[39] "One lady he met had a £100 a year, and if he had married her he would have had nothing to complain of as regards the association. The ladies introduced to him were of his own social standing and one or two were fairly good-looking."[40] But what the witness stubbornly pursued was a woman with at least £200 a year. A second man, whose identity at the preliminary hearing was also not disclosed, had been looking for a woman with £500 per annum and complained he had been introduced to women with only £40 to £70 a year.[41] To spotlight Jordan's self-serving calculations, the defense noted that he had not told "Alice May" he was corresponding with fifty-one other women at the same time. And Jordan was forced to admit that twenty ladies were interested in him but he judged that all were, because of their lack of means, unsuitable.[42] Gruenfeld was vague but obviously for the same reasons found that the two women he actually met were not satisfactory.[43] When Warburton asked Pitcher what was wrong with the women, mostly domestic servants, to whom he had been introduced, Pitcher—who himself had only £40 capital—replied that they had no money.

> Might not they have saved at least £40?—Yes.
> And could you not have started in a humble way with £80?—
> That was not what I expected. I expected at least a thousand
>   or two.[44]

And finally the defense pointed out that Sutton had been put in touch with a Miss Adams, whom he had spurned, judging her nest egg of £170 insufficient to support his attempts to launch a musical career. The witness clumsily replied that he needed money—"his intention was to practice the flute as much as possible (laughter)."[45]

Outbursts of laughter repeatedly punctuated the preliminary hearing and trial proceedings. The courtroom spectators found it screamingly amusing that lower-class men who had entertained ideas of marrying above themselves had come to grief. Such men had to learn to accept their appointed place in life. Reiterating this lesson Lockwood cruelly mocked Bason by reading the self-description offered by one of the women to whom he was introduced.

> "Tall, well-educated, domesticated, grocery and off-licence" What
> more could you want than that? (Renewed laughter.)[46]

The defense concluded—after having accused the complainants of being presumptuous, crass, unattractive, and hard to please fantasists—by pointing out that almost all of them in providing their own self-descriptions had lied. To take only one example, Daniel Driver, an Irish law student, complained of having been led to believe he was courting a J.P.'s daughter worth £800 a year. In his cross-examination the defense called attention to the fact that if Driver was complaining of fraud, he was a fraud himself. It was elicited from the witness—much to the noisy amusement of the jury—that Driver described himself, not as a law student but as a lawyer. "Please moderate your hilarity, gentlemen," interjected the Recorder in an attempt to stifle the outbursts of laughter. "This is, after all, a serious case."[47] But the defense was maintaining that it was not a serious case; it was a joke. Who could seriously believe that for £5 one could obtain an heiress worth a thousand?

As humiliating as the attacks on the plaintiffs might have been, in the end it made no difference in law. The judge, in summing up, noted that the case had occasioned a good deal of hilarity and that the defense had shrewdly attempted to laugh the case out of court. It was now his task to remind the jury that "although there had been a large amount of laughter at the outset it remained a very serious case indeed."[48] He summed up strongly on behalf of the prosecution pointing out that some of the advertisements and the names employed by the association were obviously bogus and therefore fraud had undoubtedly occurred. After forty minutes the jury found the Skateses and Abrahams guilty of conspiring and obtaining money by false pretenses. The judge, in castigating the accused for having preyed on "simple-minded and gullible people," sentenced John Charles Skates, as ringleader, to five years penal servitude and Mortimer Daniel Skates and the seventy-year-old Abrahams to three years. Hannah—over whom the jury disagreed—was put back to the next session; Maddows was discharged.

GEORGE ORWELL WAS ONE OF THE FIRST SCHOLARS TO RECOGNIZE THE invaluable insights into popular culture offered by publications like the *Matrimonial Herald*. "Papers like the *Exchange and Mart*, for instance, or *Cage-Birds*, or the *Oracle*, or *Prediction*, or the *Matrimonial Times*, only exist because there is a definite demand for them, and they reflect the minds of their readers as a great national daily with a circulation of millions cannot possibly do."[49] Outbursts of laughter resulted when, thanks to the testi-

mony that came out in court, the thoughts dancing in the minds of a particular portion of the male readership of the *Matrimonial Herald* was made
known to the general public. Few trials took place in the gloomy confines
of London's Central Criminal Court that the audience found so amusing.
And jokes, as Robert Darnton has recently reminded us, usually do not
travel well; if we hope to fully understand what was thought to be so funny
in this conspiracy case, we have to understand the age in which it took
place.[50]

The case revolved around gender expectations but also tells us a good
deal about social mores. First it brings home to us the newly recognized
powers of the late-nineteenth-century press. The characters presented in
most of the *Herald*'s advertisements appear so stereotyped—the active,
powerful male and the attractive, passive female—that it is hard to imagine
that anyone could have believed in their reality. This was, of course, the
argument advanced by the paper's legal counsel; the plaintiffs must have
known it was all a joke. But thousands clearly either believed or half-
believed what they read. Everyone knew that such advertisements might
not reveal the whole truth, but some thought that they were not entirely
fraudulent. And no doubt some readers, eager to participate in the fantasy,
probably did not care if the advertisements were true or not.

Was the *Herald,* which did not inform but did at least entertain, all that
much different from the rest of the tabloid press? It was obviously a product of the age of "New Journalism," in which mass-circulation papers relied, not simply on "facts," but increasingly on by-lines, headlines, pictures,
interviews and most important of all, the letters in their correspondence
columns. Who wrote these letters? Even respectable papers in the last decades of the nineteenth century whipped up debate and increased their circulations by having journalists write their own controversial letters to the
editor with the intent of luring enraged readers into responding. And a
muckraking journalist like W. T. Stead, who purchased a young girl to pub-
licize the scandal of child prostitution, provided the most dramatic demonstration of how newspapers could create as well as report the news.[51] In
such an increasingly ambiguous culture, how did one know what the
"truth" was? The self-appointed task of some newspapers seemed to be to
make the world more rather than less mysterious. Viewed in this context,
the *Matrimonial Herald* could be seen as taking to its logical extreme newspapers' temptation to blur the line separating facts from fictions.

In revealing that thirty thousand clients had turned to the World's Great
Marriage Association, this case also demonstrated the fact that many Vic-

torians found themselves in an increasingly anonymous world in which one might have to rely upon professional go-betweens in arranging what once had been intimate family matters. Appealing to the sensitivities of the propertied, the defense shrewdly argued that if matrimonial agencies were made illegal so too should the firms that provided registers of servants. The implication was that the respectable middle class might laugh at the idea of a business providing spouses but that it too more and more relied on similar businesses when it came to the crucial question of engaging staff.[52]

The defense noted that on the continent matrimonial businesses flourished but acknowledged that in England there was a prejudice against such undertakings. In fact occasional scandals across Europe and North America revealed the seamy side of such affairs. In New York in the 1850s, reporters exposed the fraudulent dealings of matrimonial agents, some of whom also presented themselves as astrologers, phrenologists, clairvoyants, and purveyors of patent medicines.[53] In London in 1890, seventy-year-old Leslie Fraser Duncan, proprietor and editor of the *Matrimonial News*, was condemned in the press as an "elderly Lothario" for attempting to seduce a twenty-year-old client. The woman's successful breach-of-promise suit resulted in an award of ten thousand pounds in damages.[54] From Germany and France as well came occasional reports of agencies involved in "l'escroquerie au mariage."[55] M. Geray was sentenced in Paris to five years in prison in 1877 and two additional years in 1886 for managing from the misleadingly named "Loyal Office" a fraudulent marriage agency.[56] Auguste Bebel, the German socialist leader who was well known for his interest in evolving gender relationships, reported that the nefarious activities of such businesses had also been disclosed in central Europe.[57]

Nevertheless in England the *Matrimonial Post and Fashionable Marriage Advertiser*, founded in 1860, was still going strong well into the mid twentieth century, and was to be rivaled from 1904 on by the almost equally long lived *Matrimonial Times*.[58] Unfortunately we know very little about the extent of their activities because they avoided entanglements with the law. Historians are in debt to the Skateses inasmuch as in forcing the police to respond to their disreputable undertakings they allow us a glimpse of the ambitions and aspirations of some who relied on such firms.

The second significant aspect of the case is that it tells us a good deal about the linkages of class and courtship. The propertied, who laughed at the plaintiffs, customarily failed to understand the courting customs of the lower classes. The latter were condemned by their betters at times for hasty marriages and unthinking sensuality and at other times for acting out of

cold calculation.[59] In this case the plaintiffs' goals, although they were regarded as ridiculous by the well-off public, were not all that bizarre.
Middle-class males were supposed to postpone marriage until they had established themselves professionally; for some members of the lower-middle
and working class it was often the reverse; early marriage and the economic
aid of a spouse made the establishment of an independent household possible.[60]

And were the unions of the upper classes free of such calculations? "A
wedding has been arranged" was a favorite phrase commonly employed by
newspapers when announcing a forthcoming society marriage. Although a
middle-class man's dignity required him to feign indifference to the money
his wife could bring to the marriage, such monetary support was considered essential. The dowry, asserted one contemporary humorist, could best
be defined as an "export tax" paid by the father of the bride.[61] Although
a French reformer such as Léon Blum forthrightly condemned mercenary
marriages, a British psychiatrist like Henry Maudsley and an Italian sexologist like Paulo Mantegazza were more representative of bourgeois thinking in insisting that both marriages of love and interest could turn out
equally well.[62]

If the Skateses' attorneys had been more forthcoming in their defense
of marriage brokers, they might have said that in England what created
scandal was not so much the question of whether marriages were arranged
but how they were arranged. English and European middle- and upper-
class parents, although they were beginning to ease the close supervision
of their marriageable children through such institutions as chaperonage,
continued to arrange their marriages by the tried and true methods of informal surveillance of school and social contacts.[63] Priding themselves on
the success of their private, informal stratagems, the middle and upper
classes could only view public, commercial undertakings with distaste. To
have to fall back on such crude tactics obviously indicated that one laugh-
ably lacked both savoir faire and access to the best circles of society. Henry
Leach—a sixty-year-old Bradford painter and house decorator who was
looking for a slightly younger, wealthy woman and who maintained to
the end his belief in the necessity of such marriage agencies—was for this
reason regarded by the court as hopelessly comic. "He still thought that
an association of this kind was one of the great wants of the people.
(Laughter.)"[64]

The third and most important aspect of the case is what it reveals about
gender. The trial tells us a good deal about lower-class men and women's

marriage strategies, but particularly men's. Why were only men involved in the prosecution? No doubt many women lost money to the association, but the shame they experienced deterred them from appearing in court. John Charles Skates tried to fend off the police who descended upon the Association's offices by appealing to their chivalry: "This is a monstrous thing. This is a respectable business; we have thousands of ladies upon our books."[65] Mr. Lushington mentioned during the preliminary proceedings that he had received "letters upon letters" from people who had corresponded with the agency and did not want their names mentioned.[66] Presumably they included some women. But most of the evidence suggests that men were the association's most likely victims. Men had more money to invest in such schemes, they had greater freedom and endured less surveillance in their courtships, and they were not as restrained by a sense of decorum from plunging into such enterprises. The same reasons would appear to hold true a century later. Many dating services of the 1990s allow women to participate free, but charge men because males' interest in such services so exceeds females'.[67]

The case also reminds us that the male world was split not only between the working and the middle classes but between the married and the unmarried. Although in nineteenth-century male culture bachelorhood was praised and the loss of freedoms attendant upon marriage ritually lamented, the man who remained celibate could be regarded by his peers as not having attained full adult status.[68] The plight of the spinster was often bewailed by the press, but the old bachelor who failed to marry her was, at the best of times, subjected to gentle ridicule.[69] The French, in employing the terms *célibataire* and *vieux garçon*, made even clearer his anomalous position. Indeed in France pronatalists like Bertillon advanced the overrepresentation of single males in asylums, prisons, and hospitals as proof of the actual social dangers posed by the bachelor.[70] Durkheim concurred, warning the unmarried male that he was twice as likely as the married man to commit suicide.[71]

The most striking aspect of this trial, however, was its theatricality. The public attending nineteenth-century court contests expected to be told a story that followed a familiar script with the stereotypical passive female victim, brave hero, and nasty villain. The melodrama and the sensationalist novel had a major influence in providing the nineteenth-century public with such a set of representations with which to make sense of changing realities. But if the melodrama had such an influence, why, in this case of poor men being defrauded by disreputable scoundrels, did the public decide that it was viewing not a tragedy but a comedy? The answer is that the success of a man in court depended, as we noted earlier, on the extent to which he was able to appropriate the role of hero. The Skateses clearly could not assume such a role because their guilt was obvious. But the plaintiffs, because of their stupidity and mendacity, were debarred as well. At times they were almost relegated to the feminine role of passive victim. But the public remembered at some unconscious level that most melodramas included the character of the "poor innocent" or "le pauvre niais," who, when the tension grew too great, was brought on for comic relief.[72] It was this role of the "fool" that the plaintiffs found themselves playing. Lower-middle-class males, sabotaged by their mix of pretensions and insecurities, may well be the archetypal "fools" of modernity. If the victims of this fraud had been women, they could have embraced the role of victim and the case would have been played out in court as tragedy; since they were men, it had to be played out as farce.

Of course middle-class males were always prepared to laugh at the foibles of lower-class men. The readers of popular detective stories were constantly invited to share in both the upper-class hero's hatred for the immorality of the villain and his amusement at the inherent ineptitude of the lower orders, personified by the bumbling bobby or confused Cockney.[73] In this particular case, however, the popular press also joined in the laughter. Peter Bailey has recently reminded us that "knowingness" was a central theme of music hall comedy. Working-class audiences wanted to laugh at fools and be assured that they were not among their number. The "swell" who successfully and mockingly appropriated the dress and manners of gentility would be applauded while the inept and impoverished clerk who unsuccessfully tried to pass himself off as a "gent" was hooted with derision. The plaintiffs in the *Matrimonial Herald* trial, having been exposed for putting on airs (after the fashion of the music-hall would-be gentleman, "Burlington Bertie from Bow"), let themselves in for exactly the sort of mocking ridicule the working-class reserved for those whom the community had decided had too high an opinion of themselves.[74]

The trial was used in a variety of ways by a variety of actors to police both male courtship and notions of masculinity. In a recent study, Judith Walkowitz demonstrated how a series of sensational media stories produced in the last decades of the nineteenth century "both highlighted and managed the boundary disputes paradigmatic of metropolitan life."[75] Walkowitz dealt primarily with the ways in which the concern with the "prostitution problem" was employed to restrict respectable women's freedoms.

The pummeling that the male witnesses in the *Herald* case received at the hands of the defense counsels—gleefully retold in the press—served a similar sort of purpose.

A new masculine identity was in the process of being constructed in the late nineteenth century. To be a respectable man, one ideally had to enjoy a degree of economic independence. Such independence was in fact increasingly difficult if not impossible for the working man to achieve, but he could at least aim at winning a "breadwinner's" wage, which made him the proud sole support of his wife and children.[76] They were declared by the middle class to be "dependents," and their access to the labor market restricted by the enactment of compulsory education and protective labor legislation. Women and children had in the past made essential contributions to the working-class's family economy, but now households that relied too heavily on their income were no longer considered entirely respectable.[77] The plaintiffs in the *Matrimonial Herald* trial, revealed to be men who intended to live off their wives, were accordingly savaged for having attempted to violate newly established but already sacrosanct gender roles.

That one of the plaintiffs should have fainted—like a woman—was almost too perfect inasmuch as the defense's contention was that none of them had acted like real men. Such a blurring of gender was to be expected since it was popularly believed that the extended continence demanded of the unmarried was unhealthy, making women masculine and men effeminate.[78] There were thus obvious sexual implications in the chortles to which the plaintiffs were subjected. In the music halls, not far from the Central Criminal Courts where this trial took place, male impersonators such as Nellie Power won gales of laughter by exploiting the notion that fraudulent gents were not only social shams, they were less than men.

> And he wears a penny flower in his coat, lah di dah!
> And a penny paper collar around his throat, lah di dah!
> In his hand a penny stick
> In his mouth a penny pick.
> And a penny in his pocket, la di dah![79]

Social historians have noted that, "like marriage in other hierarchically arranged societies, Victorian marriage served important strategic functions: it helped define levels of society, maintain class positions, and locate an individual's place in the social structure."[80] It was not, of course, a crime for a man of modest means to try to court a woman of a higher social status, but any who harbored such ideas must have had second thoughts when reading the *Matrimonial Herald* trial reports. The men involved were not to be remembered for having courageously played a part in putting to an end an enormous fraud conspiracy. The brief moment of fame these humble fellows enjoyed consisted of being made the butt of several barristers' wit. The Skateses were found guilty; so in a way were the plaintiffs. Their crime was to have attempted to marry above themselves. Their punishment was to be made a laughing stock, covered with scorn and derision, and told in no uncertain terms to give up dreams of easy upward mobility. Until the nineteenth century, it had been the tradition in parts of rural England and western Europe to subject such upstarts to the public mockery of a charivari or rough music. By the 1890s the courts and press were fulfilling this role in declaring that wealthy women were strictly the preserve of men of the same social class; poachers would be severely dealt with. A man who was caught trying to broach class barriers risked having both his motives and his masculinity questioned.

THREE

CADS

Turn of the century society had at its disposal an impressive range of epithets with which to characterize the man deemed guilty of immoral behavior. The "lady killer" (*tombeur des femmes*) was credited with a dangerous power of fascination over women. "To womanize" meant, in the sixteenth century, to emasculate, but by the late nineteenth had taken on its modern sense, to consort illicitly with women, and the "womanizer" (*coureur des jupons*) was accordingly the man who was said to look upon all women as fair game. The term "rake" (*roué* or *débauché*), used to designate the man of loose habits and immoral character, was originally applied to dissipated men of fashion and never completely lost its upper-class associations. The "bounder" or "cad" (*butor* or *goujat*) was, however, like the fellows considered in the previous chapter, clearly an "outsider" and no gentleman. In 1790 a "cad" was a horse omnibus conductor who picked up passengers for his own profit; by Victorian times the term conjured up implications of immorality as well as working-class dishonesty.[1] Further down the class scale, one could locate the scoundrel (*crapule* or *vaurien*) and blackguard (*canaille*). Far more examples could be provided, but these suffice to give some sense of the richness of the vocabulary respectable turn-of-the-century society applied to male villainy.

One is not only impressed by the range of labels; one is also struck by the fact that today all these terms sound terribly dated. The triumph in the late twentieth century of the belief that women are not passive beings who have to be "protected" from men presumably explains why it is now hard to think of any polite word commonly employed to designate the man who takes sexual advantage of a woman. Yet the powerful resonance that words like *cad* or *bounder* had at the turn of the century was made repeatedly evident in court case after court case. Judges and juries explicitly asserted that it was their task to defend both the law and a largely unwritten code of legal chivalry according to which virtuous women were to be protected from evil men. The question of whose interests were best served by such chivalry warrants attention.

As way of an answer in this chapter we turn to two archetypal nine-teenth-century scoundrels—the bigamist and the man implicated in the abortion of a single woman. Though the discussion of bigamy is drawn from a series of nineteenth-century French trials and that of abortion from one sensational English case, both reveal that the courts and the popular press, maintaining the popular stereotypes of the innocent female victim and the malicious male villain, played up the notion that if only all men adhered to honorable standards of manliness women would be safe. Though the self-congratulatory tone of such declarations was obvious, many of those who made them were no doubt well intentioned. Neverthe-less the chief effect of these assertions was to attribute the sexual dangers prevalent in modern society to the moral failings of a few wretches and to deflect attention from the social conditions in which bigamous marriages and dangerous abortions occurred.

$$\int$$

IN JANUARY 1886 THE PARISIAN PRESS DEVOTED AN ENORMOUS AMOUNT of attention to the trial of Louis-Prosper Lecouty, the "bigamist of Alfort-ville." Five years earlier this twenty-nine year old jewelry broker had mar-ried Emma Marie, a young dressmaker. In 1883, having become bored by his marriage, Lecouty met and set out to seduce sixteen-year-old Blanche Levanneur, whose family resided in Alfortville. He pilfered from his em-ployer and his clients in order to shower her with gifts; her parents—igno-rant of his marital status—finally consented to her marriage. Although still residing with his first wife, Lecouty had marriage banns read at Maisons-Alfort and rented a wedding outfit, telling his wife he was going to attend a friend's nuptials. No sooner had his second marriage been solemnized than his legitimate wife discovered the subterfuge. Lecouty was jailed, pro-testing that he had acted out of passion. Though his first wife begged for the court's clemency, he was sentenced to five years in prison.[2]

This was the sort of bigamy case, a melodramatic mixture of sordid calculations, passion, and betrayal, that caught the nineteenth-century bourgeois reading public's attention. Bigamists were the archetypal nine-teenth-century cads. Given the stiff prison terms imposed on them, one is given the impression that there were few nonviolent crimes viewed by the respectable as so loathsome. Bigamy was vile and harmful, the public was repeatedly informed, because it best represented the despotism of males and the submission of females. Every bigamy trial could therefore be construed as yet another demonstration of respectable men's intent to prevent the seduction and abandonment of innocence women by immoral males. In reality most bigamy cases, though they culminated in the punishment of men, were turned by elites males to purpose of legitimating their right to police the morality of their social inferiors.

Who were the bigamists? The story of Lecouty, the dashing young man moved by a crazed passion to attempt to maintain two households simultaneously, which so fascinated the Parisian reading public, was, as is made clear by a perusal of the *Gazette des Tribunaux,* hardly typical. Most bigamists were, it is true, men. They tended, however, not to be terribly young. A sampling of cases indicates that the average culprit was not a dashing young Lothario. Of course to be a bigamist a man would have to have been married at least twice, which normally meant that the youngest would be in their mid twenties. Most men charged were in fact in their thirties, forties, or fifties. Few crimes were so heavily weighted toward the middle aged. Nor were there many crimes in which 100 per cent of the perpetrators were married. Moreover bigamists' first marriages were rarely as short as Lecouty's, and many of their second marriages were quite lengthy.

Lecouty was also different in being, in social terms, a cut or two above most bigamists. Men charged with bigamy included the odd merchant or officer, but most occupied much humbler situations—they included railway workers, canal men, house painters, shoe makers, cooks, waiters, and hair dressers. Their first and second spouses were rarely heiresses and were more likely drawn from the ranks of maids, seamstresses, market women, and laundresses. Bigamy was primarily a working-class crime. Why? Bourgeois observers attributed it to the lusts and vices of lower class males—the cads and bounders who preyed on unwitting women. Commentators generally overlooked the social context in which such ménages were set up. A reading of bigamy cases reminds us of the transient nature of much male, nineteenth-century laboring life, of which settled, propertied, middle-class men had little understanding. The demands of work that required a spouse being away from home for long stretches of time could fracture a marriage. Workmen, because they were more geographically mobile than women, had the opportunity to be bigamous. Jules Brélaz, a locomotive engineer, married in 1874 and again in 1882.[3] A Belgian railway worker, tried in 1889, who told his second wife that his first was simply an old mistress, reminds one of the character Pecqueux, the railway fireman in Zola's *La Bête humaine,* who had women in both Le Havre and Paris.[4] Sylvain Derou moved from the Creuse to Paris and then from Paris to Algeria, leaving a wife behind each time.[5] A man lodged in the Mazas prison in 1886 married for the first time in France, the second time in Romania, and a third time again in France.[6] Joseph Vial, a cook, first took a wife in Italy, but when he came to work in the spa town of Vichy wed a "femme de chambre."[7] More exotic and upper class was the Mexican officer who, as a result of being captured by the French during their support of emperor Maximilien's Mexican expedition, was brought back as prisoner of war to Tours, where in 1864 he bigamously married the "épicier" with whom he lodged.[8] On occasion geographic mobility was simply used as a cover. One Rouselle, a grocer who left his wife and children in Paris's fourteenth arrondissement, let it be know he had gone to America. In fact he only moved as far as the nearby suburb of Bois-Colombes, where he set up a new household with a widow.[9]

Evidence of the disruptions caused working-class lives by France's political turmoil also emerged in the bigamy trials. In 1848 Bastien left his village to go off to support the revolution in Paris; as a result of ending up on the losing side, he was sentenced to eight years in the "bagne," forget about his first wife, and on his release remarried.[10] A similar story came out in the trial of an old fédéré Louis-Victor Marty, a fifty-five-year-old shoe-maker, whose case came to court in 1877. Both he and his wife, Françoise Gaçoin, having married in 1868, had thrown themselves into defending the Paris Commune of 1871 against the troops sent to crush the short-lived experiment in socialism. Françoise was seized while defending a barricade on the rue Monge. Marty was stationed at the Panthéon and prudently went underground when the Versailles troops invaded the capital. Françoise was taken in chains to Versailles and in 1872 sentenced by a Council of War to five years penal servitude in the prison at Chartres. Marty, wishing to remarry, claimed that she had been shot and with the financial aid offered by the sisters of Saint Vincent de Paul and the Société de Saint François Régis wedded for a second time. Only in 1875 did the truth about his first wife's fate emerge.[11]

Working-class men had the opportunity to commit bigamy; what were their motives? Bourgeois moralists portrayed them as crude sensualists or cunning fortune hunters. The defenses that the men presented in court obviously have to be taken with a grain of salt, but to be fair it must be noted that some might have been confused as to what constituted legal marriage. Joseph Vial claimed, for example, that his first marriage was not legal since he had not received his parents' consent. Some of the accused were obviously not too bright. Ramé, an "ouvrier terrassier," was fairly dim-witted, and Taupier, a thirty-seven-year-old red-headed fellow, much amused spectators by dutifully replying to every question put to him by the president of the court—even the most incriminating—with the expression, "Oui, Monsieur le Président." And if some did not understand what made a marriage, others were uncertain about how divorce, only reintroduced in 1884, was regulated. Taupier asserted that he had reason to think that he had been divorced.[12] Similarly it was claimed in court that a businessman charged "la femme Duhamel" 100 francs for a paper that she believed granted her a legal separation.[13] In 1886 David Hertzfeld, when appearing before the Paris assizes, argued that thirteen years before he had married according to Jewish rites and therefore assumed that he had the right to repudiate ritually his first wife.[14]

A review of possible extenuating circumstances is not to be taken as a denial that some men were drawn by mercenary motives to marry bigamously. All agreed that Sylvain Derou was a drunk, thief, and bigamist of detestable habits. Monsieur Simon, another dissipated character, deserted his wife of thirty-two years to marry a twenty-year-old woman with a dowry of ten thousand francs. He told the latter that they should be discrete and lodge under a false name because he was being stalked by an old mistress, but his mother-in-law's suspicions were raised, and he was eventually arrested.[15] Alcide Crouzière, a thirty-two-year-old painter-decorator described in the press as a good-looking fellow, had purportedly duped many. A professional confidence man, he called himself a baron and member of the Académie française. For buying jewels on credit and pawning them, he had already been condemned four times for abuse of confidence. Ten days after his marriage in February 1892 he was arrested in Saint-Lunaire (Ille-et-Vilaine). Evidence was produced that in 1885 he had married at Teste (Gironde) one Marie Condom, whom he deserted in 1891. He claimed that she told him she had obtained a divorce and that he had simply married his second wife to legitimate the child she was expecting. Both women declared in court that they were still in love with him.[16]

Men could commit bigamy more readily than women because they could move more easily both socially and geographically. Women emerged from the majority of the press reports represented simply as seduced and abandoned victims. Yet some wives did desert their husbands. Such a situation was reported in the case of Paul-Antoine Henry, a nasty and jealous man, whose wife went off to Russia in 1873 with her employer, a "grande couturière." Eleven years later he married for a second time; his first wife found out and lodged a complaint. Despite his claiming that he thought she was dead and his second wife's pleas that she loved him, he was sentenced to three years in prison.[17] More typical was the case of Brélaz, who left his first wife in 1874 and in 1882 married a seamstress. Ten years later, having sired five children, he was tried for bigamy. His first wife had only discovered his second marriage because she sought proof of his death so that she could marry a baker.[18] Likewise the wife of Mastien, who had deserted her in 1848, wanted to remarry and in trying to obtain his death certificate unintentionally unearthed his new ménage. The figures available on separations show that women were, if anything, more intent than men on getting out of unsuccessful marriages. In the third quarter of the nineteenth century, 85 percent of requests for judicial separations came from wives.[19] It follows that women were presumably as likely as men to want to remarry, but because they tended to remain in their home community and had to keep up their reputations, they could not flout the rules of matrimony as easily as their absent spouses.

According to the moralists' scenario, the bigamist was almost by definition the man, and the victim the woman, but the press did report the trials of some female bigamists. In 1868 Amélie Arnoult, a laundress, married a monsieur Thomas. She left him for a fellow by the name of Hamet in 1872, depositing her two children in an orphanage. Nineteen years later, in order to regularize her situation, she used her sister's birth certificate to pretend that she was widowed so that she and Hamet could be married at the mairie of Paris's eighteenth arrondissement. Unfortunately witnesses came forward to testify that Thomas was still alive; Amélie was sentenced to three years in prison and a hundred franc fine.[20]

Women, according to the press, were less sensual than men and therefore less prone to pursue a second spouse. Ignored were the more obvious, practical reasons noted above why they would be less likely than men to commit bigamy, and one is not surprised to find that the court records suggest that they made up less than a quarter of those charged. It could be the case, however, that the judicial figures did not provide a true reflection of reality inasmuch as men were more likely than women to be prosecuted for bigamy. Abandoned wives were sometimes driven to file charges since they and their children needed the economic support of a man. A deserted husband rarely had any economic incentive to track down a wayward wife. It is unlikely that women were happier than men with their wedded lot. A proportion of women stayed in unhappy marriages or tried to maintain them out of sheer economic necessity.[21] Yet as far as the press was concerned, the scale of female bigamy was really of no great importance. Male journalists simply did not find female bigamists very interesting and knew their readers were unlikely to be enthralled by the mundane, unromantic calculations of impoverished wives and mothers.

The bourgeois press ridiculed and derided the men involved in bigamy trials as "le volage" (the flighty or inconstant spouse), "le fêtard" (the merry maker), and "le fricoteur" (the womanizer), but notes of voyeuristic male envy can often be detected in these accounts. Such was the case in the press's description of Israel Bernard who, with two households on either side of Paris, was presented as trying to eat at two troughs at the same time. He had originally abjured his faith to marry a mademoiselle Chassang and later exchanged vows with a mademoiselle Fourny. For a time he astonished his wives with his hectic days, which started at five in the morning and took him from Montrouge to Batignolles. The ingenious fashion by which he tried to maintain both ménages, when it came out in court, obviously piqued the imagination of the newspaper reading public. Unfortunately an inquisitive mother-in-law proved his undoing. His career finally ended in a cell in the Mazas prison in 1897.[22] In the English-speaking world, a similar voyeuristic bourgeois fascination with the taking of more than one wife underlay the interest held by the Mormons and articles with titles like "The Most Successful Bigamist on Record."[23]

What most interested the public was the male bigamists' initial sordid seduction and then the story's melodramatic dénouement. How was the man caught? In theory, since bigamy was a serious crime, the community should have denounced the culprit. In practice the onus of filing a charge was usually placed on the aggrieved spouse. The customary scenario was for the first wife to lodge a complaint while the second wife, who had everything to lose if her husband was found guilty, stuck by her man. Sometimes, however, both wives acted in concert.[24] Occasionally a grown child of a first marriage, a jilted mistress, or a mother-in-law began the prosecution. In the latter half of the nineteenth century, it was conservatively estimated that about two bigamous marriages a month were performed in the department of the Seine.[25] Four or five went to trial in all of France each year. Between 1885 and 1894, there were sixty-seven charges laid and fifty-two condemnations, that is to say a fairly high conviction rate of about 78 percent.[26] The law considered the children of the second marriage to be innocent victims, and, as long as there was proof that one parent (presumably the mother) had acted in good faith, they were legitimated and enjoyed rights of succession. Second marriages were automatically nullified by the court, but if in the meantime the first spouse died the second marriage could be maintained, the intent again being to legitimate resulting children.[27] Sentences for the men found guilty ranged from two to eight years imprisonment, with the average being about four years. A monsieur Hermant who married near Toulouse, remarried in Paris, and then returned to his first spouse and confessed, received a light two-year term.[28] The heaviest punishments—eight-year prison terms—were imposed on men who had been involved in the Commune and the Revolution of 1848, which suggests that the courts were using the law on bigamy to do more than simply protect the family.

Why did the law treat bigamists so harshly? In 1920 a soldier who had been taken prisoner in 1914 and then upon his release at the end of the war had married bigamously appeared in court. His lawyer, while admitting that his client might have acted out of ignorance, insisted that he was no fortune hunter and had no criminal intention. His deed was more ridiculous than odious. Moreover, why, the lawyer asked, was bigamy a crime when adultery was not and divorce was now freely available?[29] Laws against bigamy were first passed by the emperor Augustus with the avowed purpose of shoring up the Roman family. In Christian Europe bigamy was lumped in with the most odious of crimes.[30] In England it was made a felony for the first time in 1604; though the law was initially fairly lenient, it later treated the crime as a capital offense. The fate that awaited the main character in Natalie Zemon Davis's *The Return of Martin Guerre* reminds us that the Catholic church in the early modern period was very much concerned by breach of promise and bigamy cases.[31] The Council of Trent sought to prevent clandestine marriages by insisting that weddings be publicized and the blessing of marriage be made obligatory. Bigamy was regarded by churchmen as worse than adultery since it was longer lasting. Moreover the bigamist, like the heretic, profaned the sacraments. In the sixteenth century, the death penalty was frequently imposed on bigamists; others were whipped and banished. The last case in France of bigamy being punished by death occurred in 1626; a 1658 edict formally ended this extreme form of punishment.[32] Thereafter a convicted man was customarily condemned to appear for three days before the public in an iron collar hung with a distaff for each of his wives; a convicted woman had to wear a straw hat for each of her husbands. In England the guilty were branded on the hand. In France, after their public penance, they were either banished or, if men, sent to the galleys, while the women were locked up in convents. Despite such harsh penalties, it is highly likely that the number of bigamous marriages was quite large.[33]

Although it is impossible to tabulate the exact number, the ease with which men could desert their families and the absence of divorce leads one to expect that the rate of bigamy until the late nineteenth century had to have been high. The fact that few cases were reported suggests that only when a bigamous marriage was offensive to the community did it create a public scandal that then led to a trial.[34] Neighborhood sympathy and an individual's discretion were more important than the law. Even in the nineteenth century, marriages continued in the first instance to be policed by the family. Ramé waited until his parents were dead and then abandoned his laundress wife and married another.[35] Paul-Antoine Henry also took the passing of his father and mother as the signal that it was safe to remarry. Alcide Crouzière claimed his parents were dead, but to the delight of the court his father—an old revolutionary who had been proscribed for opposing Napoleon III's seizure of power in 1851—turned up to testify.[36]

Following the French Revolution, the penal code of 25 September 1791 decriminalized adultery, and in 1792 divorce was established—though it was only to last until 1815.[37] With the general movement toward the liberalizing of the criminal law, it comes as a surprise to discover that Article 33 of the 1791 code called for bigamy to continue to be punished by harsh prison terms of up to twelve years. Under Article 310 of Napoleon's 1810 Criminal Code, the penalty was only reduced to between eight and ten years. Christian moralists had called for stiff penalties because they regarded bigamy as both a violation of the sacrament of marriage and a sort of "continuous adultery." In a liberal, bourgeois world, some of this moralizing was maintained, but the irreligious nature of bigamy was no longer regarded as its primary danger. Lawmen asserted that France now was an individualistic society made up of free individuals held together by freely entered contracts. In such a context, bigamy had to be considered as the worst sort of fraud inasmuch as it was a dastardly violation of a contract, indeed the community's most important contract—marriage—that established families, which were the natural building blocks of society.[38]

Yet if marriage was a contract, it was an unusual one—given the absence of divorce in France between 1815 and 1884—in that it was indissoluble. Bourgeois males, rather than acknowledging that the pressures imposed on the lower classes sometimes led to bigamy, insisted that it was bigamy that created disorder in working-class communities. In giving rise to public scandal, bigamy was, in the words of public commentators, a "social crime." Bigamy was a manifestation of the worst sort of deceit and deception; in sowing confusion in families it undermined social order. Working-class males, so their betters agreed, had to be trained to accept and respect the sort of clear contracts employed by the middle classes.[39]

What these sorts of assertions failed to take into account was that there were practical reasons why bourgeois and working-class males would have different views on marriage and the establishment of households.[40] Common law marriage, or "concubinage" as its detractors called it, was common in poorer neighborhoods.[41] It is true that it could lead to confusion that the unscrupulous could exploit. Jean-Baptiste Lainé, for example, claimed that his first wife was only his concubine when he married a second time.[42] In the 1890s it was estimated that there were about forty thousand "unions libres" in the city of Paris alone. Workers often lacked the time and money to assemble the dossier required to marry. Catholic charities like the Société de Saint François Régis had as their mission the goal of trying to convince workers living in common law relationships of the moral advantages of legal marriage. The Société was first established to help soldiers under the First Empire. By 1850 it had financially assisted forty-two thousand couples. The charity recognized the difficulties posed workers by existing marriage laws that required birth certificates, death certificates, and the consent of parents.[43] Several bigamists, such as Jean-Baptiste Dufour, turned to this very charity for aid when committing their "crime." Many other men married bigamously women with whom they had been living for years. The irony was that if they had continued to live "in sin," they would have gone unmolested. By trying to formalize a domestic arrangement and assure the legitimacy of their children, they became criminals.

Members of the working class also had their own ideas about what terminated one marriage and allowed another. Bigamy in the nineteenth century was, as one historian has noted, a working-class fact of life.[44] Members of the lower classes took permanent separation, traditionally a seven-year silence, as an indication of the moral ending of a marital relationship. For example, in England in 1807, a Somerset rector when asked by a woman if he would have her banns read, replied that he had been told she had a living husband. "She said it was all false what folks said about his being alive; that he went to the East Indies as a soldier upwards of seven years ago, and had never been heard of since."[45] In Britain the lower classes also employed the "sale of wives" as a form of popular divorce.[46] What the courts represented as bigamous marriages might have resulted from amicable separations, but by law such informal arrangements, though they suited the individuals involved, could not be permitted. Bastien was caught eighteen years after his first marriage and given a five-year sentence. Lainé was arrested twenty-nine years after his first marriage. A decade of a second happy marriage was taken into account by the jury, which wanted to show its leniency in the case of Brélaz. A bigamy trial could accordingly destroy simultaneously two households. Alfred Bloquel, for example, a coiffeur from Passy, had been deserted by his first wife in 1872 when he was in jail. He was happily married in 1886 to a Céleste Evrard, who ran a fruit stall. Fourteen years after the ending of his first marriage, a vindictive ex-mistress informed the police that he was already married, investigations were carried out, and the authorities found his first wife living peacefully in Rouen with another man.[47] Divorce in France was not available until 1884.[48] And even divorce, which had its own legal costs and complications, could not be expected to eliminate workers' recourse to bigamy.

Prosecutors in bigamy cases repeatedly stressed the need to defend the family, the cornerstone of society. It was therefore a somewhat curious situation that men who were seeking to create a family, to formalize a relationship and legitimate their children should be locked away for up to eight years. The bigamy law, purportedly designed to protect families, would in practice often be used to break them up. It should be remembered, however, that the same logic was followed under nineteenth-century divorce law in both England and France, which held that a spouse found guilty of adultery was not to be allowed to marry his or her lover. The notion that vice was not to be rewarded was more important to moralists than assuring the happiness of a new family. A similar moralism was manifested by the Catholic charities that sought to encourage the working-class to enter formal marriages. Priests actually condemned the stable common law partnerships of workers—which sometimes had resulted in grandchildren—as more sinful, since longer lasting, than short-term promiscuity.

The class and moral preoccupations of the defenders of the law on bigamy were clear. For our purposes the most interesting aspect of the discussion of bigamy is the light it sheds on nineteenth-century notions of masculinity. Bigamy, claimed middle-class lawmen, was an evil inasmuch it was naked demonstration of the despotism of males and the submission of females. The courts argued that the most common case usually consisted of a man's base desire, by the employment of odious lies, to seize the modest economies of some poor girl. The crime was considered so noxious that married women, normally only allowed to launch a prosecution after they received their husband's permission, were in the case of bigamy granted exceptional freedoms.[49] Following a similar logic, children, who were generally harangued to respect their parents in all things, were in bigamy cases permitted some latitude. A child of a first marriage was allowed to launch a suit of nullity against his father's new marriage in order to ensure that he obtained his rightful inheritance.[50] By so arming women and children against their husbands and fathers, the state could be seen as striking a blow against patriarchy. In reality upper-class men, who controlled the judicial system, were employing the law against lower-class males. Bigamous males no doubt frequently took advantage of less powerful females. The criminal code was employed, however, not so much to speak to the needs of such women but rather to bring the lower classes within the pale of the law, to impose on them the moral standards of their social superiors.

Most of the discussion of bigamy consisted of bourgeois males lamenting the lower moral standards of the working-class man, but they were not beyond finding amusement in some poor fellow's entanglement with the law. Bigamy trials, according to the *Petit Parisien,* usually elicited a mixture of tears and laughter. The tears were obviously shed by the members of the family or families devastated by the court's findings. The laughter came from the middle-class observers. Such hilarity burst forth in the trial of Jean-Baptiste Dufour, described as a fifty-year-old "Lovelace." He had married in Bône (Algeria) in 1853, in Le Havre in 1868, and in Algiers in 1871. A large audience came out to see the 1874 trial at Le Havre of the "polygamist." A wig-maker recently widowed with whom he worked reported that he had proposed to her. "Question—You would have consented to marry him? Answer—(confidently) Oh, yes sir, after the nine months [of mourning] (general hilarity)."[51] Amusement in more typical trials was provided by what the court reporters presented as the parade of sheepish or contrite husbands and the generous or foolish wives willing to take back their straying spouses. When the second husband of a woman tried for bigamy died, the reporter of the usually staid *Gazette des Tribunaux* quipped that one husband was lost but another found. One can think of few other occasions in which women in mourning were made the butt of bad jokes.[52] Journalists covering the trials of the working class felt that sensitivity was not required because passion was rarely the cause of bigamy; working-class men were understood to be moved by baser instincts. Bourgeois males found the idea of a man like Alfred Bloquel living off his wife particularly disgusting.[53] Even Lecouty was ridiculed by the judge for claiming to be rich though having to rent clothes for his wedding. Bigamy was undoubtedly a form of fraud that was often employed by men to victimize women. But as in the case of the trial of the owners of the World's Great Marriage Association, the courts, when dealing with bigamy, seized the opportunity to denigrate the morality and manliness of the working classes and exalt the superiority of bourgeois norms of masculinity.

ſ

THE POLICING OF MEN INVOLVED IN THE ABORTION OF SINGLE WOMEN was turned to similar purposes. In March 1896 an English judge pronounced the death sentence on John Hindson, a forty-three-old commercial traveler who had helped a woman friend procure the inducement of miscarriage from which she ultimately died. It comes as something of a shock to realize that less than a century ago those who assisted women seeking to end a pregnancy could be subjected to the harshest sentences English courts had at hand. In 1803 the inducement of miscarriage had for the first time been made a statutory criminal offense in the United Kingdom, abortion being the one operation specifically prohibited by statute. In the course of the nineteenth century, the law was repeatedly amended for the purposes of simplifying its enforcement, and by the time of the 1861 Offenses Against the Person Act an abortion conviction could result in a maximum penalty of life imprisonment. It could be argued, however, that the law had little real impact. A number of historians have concluded that, given the increased social pressures on families to restrict fertility in the late nineteenth century, abortion rates actually soared. If few abortions were reported, it was because many members of the law and medical professions felt there was little to be gained in prosecuting desperate women who sought by dangerous means to end their pregnancies.[54]

The general picture painted by historians of the late-nineteenth-century abortion law is that it targeted women but was infrequently employed; that it faced much popular opposition but that serious calls for its reform or repeal had to wait until the twentieth century. The interest offered by a review of the Hindson case is that it forces us to revise to some extent such views. First, the prosecution of John Hindson provides evidence that the abortion law was used to police the morality of men as well as that of women. Second, Hindson was charged with murder. This serves as a reminder that abortion attempts were most likely to come to the authorities' attention when something went seriously wrong but that in such cases the law could respond with ferocious vigor. English courts repeatedly levied death sentences after induced miscarriages resulted in unintended mortal consequences. Third, the Hindson trial precipitated an unprecedented discussion of both abortion law and the morality of abortion itself. In the context of this debate, the first public defense of abortion by men was published in an English journal, preceding the writings of Stella Browne by twenty years and the activities of the Abortion Law Reform Society by more than forty. A review of the Hindson case is accordingly of obvious interest, promising as it does to reveal who became implicated in criminal abortions, how the law against them was enforced, and why calls were made for its reform. Despite the purported concern for the "unborn child" brandished by the opponents of abortion, this case makes it clear that the abortion law was not just about reproduction but employed to police gender. As such abortion laws played an unexpected role in defining masculinity.

Hindson's troubles began in October 1895 when Sarah Eden, a fifty-seven-year-old Aston midwife, was indicted for the death of both Rebecca Simister, a neighbor, and that of Mabel Gordon, a young woman who had worked as a barmaid and bookkeeper at the Albion Hotel in Leeds. On 12 September a doctor had informed Gordon that she was pregnant. The young woman began taking large quantities of patent medicines to induce a miscarriage, but they did no good. She then turned to John Millar Hindson for assistance. All the evidence suggests that he had impregnated her. Hindson, a married, forty-three-year-old commercial traveler of Torry Street, Hull, was depicted in the press as apparently the archetypal sleazy traveling salesman who had a woman friend in every town. Subsequent police investigations revealed that he was on "intimate terms" with Isabella Pirie in Aberdeen, Matilda Manning in Birmingham, and Mabel Gordon in Leeds. Isabella Pirie was at one time engaged to Hindson for eight weeks and believed, as presumably did the other women, that he was single. Hindson was obviously not a "gentleman" as the term was understood at the time, but he did not abandon the pregnant Mabel Gordon. He wrote Isabella Pirie in Aberdeen that Mabel Gordon had been betrayed by some man and that she had therefore turned to him "to keep her." He then set about arranging a complicated plan by which the barmaid could save both her reputation and his own. Hindson went to Birmingham, from where he wrote Pirie that he had found a place where an abortion "could be brought off all right."[55] He concluded by sending Pirie love and kisses and the request she destroy his letter. To Pirie's suspicious question, "Why you?" Hindson reiterated that he was not responsible for Gordon's pregnancy and was just being a good friend.

Hindson asked Pirie to pose as a relative of Gordon's and send a telegram to Leeds saying Gordon had to return to Aberdeen. This would allow Gordon to get away from her employer for a week or so and have her abortion in secret.[56] This Pirie did. On 15 October Mabel Gordon showed to the Albion Hotel housekeeper the telegram saying she had to return home to Aberdeen. The ruse permitted her to travel secretly to Birmingham. It was not by chance that Hindson had arranged for Mabel Gordon to go to Birmingham to stay with Matilda Manning. Hindson had known Manning for six years and when in the Birmingham area lodged at her home. He was on extremely good terms with her, addressing her in letters as "My darling Tillie" and concluding them—like the letters he wrote to Isabella Pirie—with "love and kisses." Hindson initially did not tell Mabel Gordon of his relationship with Matilda Manning but eventually had to.

Mabel Gordon arrived at New Street Station, Birmingham at 11:20 on 16 October. Gordon, according to Manning, claimed that she had been seduced by a Leeds bookmaker. The next day Manning took Gordon to nearby Aston to meet the local midwife—the same Sarah Eden who attended Rebecca Simister. Eden provided an abortion for which a fee of five pounds was charged. Gordon returned to board at Matilda Manning's, where on 18 October she fell ill, but it seems that Hindson was informed by post that the operation was a success. On 22 October he wrote Isabella Pirie to report that everything had gone off as planned. But a few days later Gordon, much enfeebled, returned by train to Leeds, where she died of blood poisoning on 26 October.[57]

The midwife Sarah Eden accordingly found herself in December charged with the murder of Rebecca Simister and indicted along with Matilda Manning for the manslaughter death of Mabel Gordon. The lesser charge was levied in the case of Gordon's death because the Leeds coroner's jury was of the opinion that the young woman might have lived had she received better medical care.[58] Sarah Eden was tried for the murder of Rebecca Simister before Mr. Justice John Day in the Shire Hall, Warwick, at the Warwick Assizes of the Midland Circuit, on 10 December 1895.[59] The trial took only a few hours. The defense argued that no evidence was advanced by the prosecution to connect Eden directly to the operation of 23 October that Simister underwent. Doctors further testified that Simister could have possibly induced her own miscarriage. But Mr. Justice Day summed up strongly against Eden, and after a mere four minutes the jury returned with the verdict that Eden was guilty of willful murder.

The reporter for the *Daily News* claimed that the jury's finding shocked most of the spectators, but Mr. Justice Day congratulated it on its acumen, insisting that no other verdict was possible. Day, turning to the prisoner, who had been rendered half-unconscious by the unexpected verdict, sanctimoniously warned her that she should not look to his intercession, but rather seek mercy where it was only truly found: "at the feet of the Savior

who if approached with true sorrow and contrition, would receive her."[60]
He then sentenced Sarah Eden, a trembling woman of fifty-seven, to death.
Eden collapsed and was carried away in a faint.

Mr. Justice Day was not finished. Having dealt with Eden, he now presided over the trial of Matilda Manning, the thirty-eight-year-old dressmaker who had been indicted for the manslaughter of Mabel Gordon.
Manning, as was noted, had taken Gordon along to meet Sarah Eden. Eden
had been indicted with Manning for Gordon's death, but since Eden had
already been convicted of Rebecca Simister's murder, Eden was not tried
with Manning on the second count. The crown's case against Matilda Manning was weak. Manning stuck to her story that she had nothing to do with
Mabel Gordon's abortion and honestly believed that Gordon had come to
Birmingham simply to arrange for her confinement. Manning's trial ended
in an abrupt and most unexpected manner but not because of either the
clumsiness of the crown counsel or the skill of Manning's barrister. The
first witness called was John Millar Hindson, the man who had arranged
for Gordon to go to Matilda Manning's to seek an abortion. Not appreciating the dangerous situation in which he found himself, Hindson shocked
the court by testifying in a cool, nonchalant manner about Gordon's efforts
to free herself of her pregnancy. Despite Mr. Justice Day's muttered warning that he need not give self-incriminating evidence, Hindson moreover
freely admitted that he wrote letters on Mabel Gordon's behalf to the accused. When asked why he destroyed other possibly incriminating letters
from women friends, he flippantly replied: "I always do."[61]

Hindson's cross-examination had no sooner begun than a juryman, perhaps taken aback by the witness's candor, collapsed in a fit. The trial was
halted and a conference of the counsels held. The prosecution decided to
drop its weak circumstantial case against Manning. Mr. Justice Day grudgingly concluded that "considering her position" he would give the woman
a light sentence and she was released with a caution. But once Manning's
trial was concluded, Day, outraged by what he had heard of Hindson's promiscuous private life and now out for blood, ordered the police to arrest
the commercial traveler for the murder of Mabel Gordon. Hindson was
seized as he tried to leave the Shire Hall.[62] He was naturally shocked at
being charged with a murder that took place miles away from where he
had been. "I was never near the place," he protested to the police, "and I
can prove it."[63]

The unexpected turn of events was played up by the press. The *Daily
Chronicle,* under the headline "The Warwick Sensation," reported that

John Millar Hindson, a family man, was charged with procuring the abortion services of Matilda Manning and Sarah Eden and with the murder of Mabel Gordon.[64] Hindson was formally charged 23 December; in March 1896 a Grand Jury issued a true bill against him for Gordon's death, and he was committed for trial on the charge of willful murder.[65] He was tried at the Warwick Assizes before Mr. Justice James Mathew on 8 March 1896. The *Birmingham Daily Gazette* gave a discreet version of the trial, noting that the subject had already been dealt with "and it was not necessary, and certainly not desirable, to discuss the details of a very painful case."[66] A full account was made available by other, less prudish newspapers. They reported that Eden and Manning testified to Hindson acting for them and Mabel Gordon as a go-between. Sarah Eden's testimony drew "much interest" as she was the woman who a few months earlier had been condemned to death. She spoke very quietly, for which she was admonished, again insisting that she had done nothing illegal to Gordon who, Eden reported, had confessed to spending three to four pounds on abortifacient pills before coming to Birmingham. As regards Hindson, Eden asserted that she did not know him and had never met him.

Dr. Green, the medical witness, testified that there was evidence that suggested Mabel Gordon might have miscarried before. Regarding her death he reported that an instrument had been used on her but the drugs she took and the jostling railway trip back from Birmingham to Leeds in her weakened condition could have played a contributing part in precipitating her final collapse. The defense pointed out that, whatever the cause of Gordon's death, there was no evidence of Hindson's being directly involved in either murder or an illegal operation. Sarah Eden, who operated on Gordon, did not even know him; he had been a hundred miles away when the operation actually took place.[67]

The judge obviously viewed Hindson as Mabel Gordon's seducer, asking why he went to such extremes in offering to help the young woman. But Hindson could not, by law, provide a direct answer. Mr. Justice Mathew noted that the accused in criminal cases was not in fact allowed to testify on his or her behalf. A bill allowing the accused so to testify had just passed the Lords and had been sent on to the Commons. Mathew, presumably regretting not hearing what Hindson might have to say, declared that it was a badly needed reform, which would help judges in determining appropriate punishments.[68] Although Mathew seemed to want to appear to be fair, he nevertheless summed up strongly against the prisoner. After a brief fifteen minutes, the jury returned with the verdict of guilty, though the foreman, stating "we are all sorry for him," passed on the jury's recommendation for mercy. "Without a pause of any sort," noted the press, "the judge passed the sentence of death."[69]

§

THESE ARE THE "FACTS" OF THESE CASES AS THEY WERE PRESENTED IN the trials. What do they tell us about nineteenth-century abortion law and its relation to the policing of masculinity? Presumably the main intent of the courts in enforcing the law was to prevent women from inducing their miscarriages. On reflection one can see that this goal was only achieved in an indirect fashion. Women who sought abortions were rarely prosecuted. For a doctor, even one violently opposed to such practices, to bring to the notice of the authorities a patient's successful induction of miscarriage was also very unusual. And most newspapers, including many which decried any attempt at fertility control, carried advertisements for a wide range of the sort of reputed abortifacients that Mabel Gordon had consumed. A single issue of the *Penny Illustrated Paper* of 30 April 1892, for example, puffed "Dr. Mackay's Marvelous Remedies," "A Blessing to Ladies," "The French Remedy," "Madame Leno's Remedy," "Kelsey's Widow Welches Female Pills," "Nurse Bayley's World Renowned Specific," and the "Ladies' Mission-The Great Infallible Remedy."[70]

Abortion, through a crime, was widespread, and the law against it both difficult to apply and half-heartedly enforced. Juries simply would neither indict nor convict a woman who induced her own miscarriage, the assumption being that she had suffered enough. It was the abortionist, not the woman who aborted, who was inevitably charged. And even then prosecutions under the Offenses Against the Person Act of 1861 usually took place when a woman had died. In short the law was primarily concerned, not so much with who had abortions but with who provided them. There were, of course, some in the community who lamented the laxity with which abortion was treated. Such views were clearly expressed by Mr. Justice Day, who asserted that it was necessary to impose the harshest possible penalties to deter an act that led, so he claimed, to many deaths. Women were so tempted to commit this crime, the judge observed, that it had to be severely punished when proved. He went on to confess that he even felt some "satisfaction" in pronouncing the death sentence on Sarah Eden, inasmuch as it would deter others.[71] The punishment, Day hoped, would act as a warning to those "who practised for hire this wicked trade."[72] The *Birmingham Daily Gazette* rejoiced in such severity, complaining that the "unlawful operation" was a crime of "deplorable frequency." The newspaper shared

Day's view that since so many abortions went undetected "severe and exemplary punishment is necessary."[73] The thought never crossed the minds of either Mr. Justice Day or his supporters that the fact that so many women were tempted to commit such a crime implied that there might be something wrong not with women but with the law.

Abortion trials pitted men against women. Although one of the rationales at the beginning of the nineteenth century for making the providing of abortion a statutory crime was to protect women from dangerous practitioners, it remained a crime that women mostly committed and men alone punished. The trial of Sarah Eden provided a clear demonstration of this alignment of power and gender. The judge, police, and jury were, of course, all males, as were most of the spectators. Indeed in some abortion cases, the evidence relating to women's reproductive organs was thought so unsavory that the judge ordered all "ladies" to leave the court.[74] An occasional doctor was implicated, but the abortionists tried were, like Sarah Eden, usually older neighborhood women who acted sometimes in pursuit of monetary gain; sometimes out of kindness. They included in 1890 thirty-five-year-old Dinah Clapp, midwife; in 1891 Elizabeth Berry and Dorothy Davis, midwives; in 1892 Lizzie Ann Mitchell, herbalist; in 1893 Mary Ann Baker, dressmaker and Annie Stewart, midwife; in 1899 sixty-seven-year-old Jane White, midwife; in 1900 forty-eight-year-old Ernestine Katz, midwife.[75] Almost inevitably these female practitioners had to face the hostile testimony of male doctors who, though alarmed by the dangers illegal operations posed, were especially concerned to use the law against abortion to eliminate competing medical services.

But the Hindson trial also points out the patriarchal nature of the law—that is, its use by powerful men to control not just women but other, marginal men. The attempt by Sarah Simister, a married woman, to use abortion to limit family size did not seize the Victorian reading public's imagination. The policing of her sexuality was assumed to be the responsibility of her husband. In the nineteenth century, the mention of abortion was far more likely to conjure up the image of a Mabel Gordon, a seduced, single young woman seeking to protect her honor. In such cases the abortion law was obviously used by the courts to police female sexuality by making intercourse out of wedlock dangerous. As the Hindson case revealed, the law was also employed to police the sexuality of males involved in such extra- or premarital relationships. The husbands of women like Simister, who aborted, even when such men clearly acted as accessories, were rarely prosecuted. Unmarried males often were.[76]

Hindson simply did not understand why he was being prosecuted. He

wrote to the press protesting his sentence, claiming that he had not been
on immoral terms with Mabel Gordon and that the Leeds coroner's jury
had established the paternity of her child. More importantly he asked how
it was possible for him to be found guilty of a greater crime than either
Eden or Manning.[77] He did not realize that he had been sentenced to death
not just because of an abortion death but because of its link to his promiscuity. Mr. Justice Mathew noted with distaste that what the trial had revealed was "the remarkable influence some men had over women."[78] The
newspaper press portrayed Hindson as a licentious, calculating character,
a married man but with unbridled passions. "One of those loose-living,
self-indulgent, reckless characters," reported the *Birmingham Daily Gazette,* whose sole aim was to corrupt women.[79] The *Birmingham Daily
Mail* described him as "a thoroughly loathsome fellow, a Lothario without
scruple, a scoundrel without a shred of conscience." The morals of this
"low, libidinous blackguard" had led to the noose.[80] The *Yorkshire Evening Post,* while speculating that Hindson's death sentence would be ultimately commuted, concluded with self-satisfaction that as "a heartless sensualist, he will be rightfully punished with a 'lifer.'"[81]

What no one said but few could have ignored was that if Hindson had
simply walked away from Gordon after he found out that she was pregnant
he would be a free man. He was in prison not because he seduced her but
because he helped her obtain an abortion from which she died. The not-
so-hidden message the court was giving to men was that the sexual exploitation of barmaids could be winked at; a man only put himself seriously at
legal risk if in addition he involved himself in assisting such a woman to
induce a miscarriage. And as Hindson's name was blackened, Mabel Gordon's reputation was conversely rescued. We know very little about her, but
at first glance this transformation appears rather surprising. It might be
remembered that the barmaid was in the nineteenth century the archetypal
male sexual fantasy figure, credited by her oglers with having a looser
moral code than most women.[82] Moreover evidence had actually been
heard in court that Gordon might have aborted on a previous occasion.
Nevertheless the logic held that if Hindson were to be portrayed as villain,
Gordon would have to emerge as his innocent victim.

What was the public reaction to these trials? In the 1890s only a handful
of murderers in England were executed each year.[83] The passing of two
death sentences in the course of four months in two abortion trials not
surprisingly precipitated a good deal of heated discussion. In one case a
midwife had been begged by a friend to provoke a miscarriage; in the other
the prisoner had assisted a female friend in distress and been a hundred

miles away when she died. Did either warrant the death penalty? Treating abortion deaths as murder obviously bothered many in the community. In Hindson's case the connection was especially tenuous. But severity did have its defenders. The *Birmingham Daily Gazette,* without openly mentioning abortion, argued that the "law" was hard, but on reflection one could see that such a law was "necessary." A crime that resulted in death had to be treated the same as murder.[84] The *Birmingham Daily Mail* similarly felt obliged to remind its readers that, according to Lord Bramwell, aiding another, even with her consent, to abort if it led to death was murder.[85] At the Liverpool Winter Assizes in 1858, Bramwell had held in the Stadtmühler case that if a person for an unlawful purpose used dangerous instruments or medicine to induce miscarriage and death ensued, this was willful murder.[86] But Stadtmühler, unlike Hindson, was actually present and assisted at an abortion.

Much of the public discussion necessarily centered on Mr. Justice Day, who, the *Birmingham Daily Gazette* admiringly noted, had in the past built up a reputation as a scourge of criminality. Day (1826–1908) began his legal career as a successful and highly paid barrister. In 1882, at the age of fifty-six, he was made a judge. He was not ashamed of his old-fashioned views and, according to his son, was a pointed critic of contemporary enthusiasms for European criminal anthropology and "pseudo-scientific sentimentalism." "It must have been early in his judicial career that Mr. Justice Day decided that he woud [*sic*] do most good by devoting his main energies to enforcing the moral law, and to deterring criminals from further offenses against God and society by means of severe sentences including, when possible, the use of the lash."[87] But Day, so his son claimed, having terrorized poor wretches with the prospect of corporal punishment, often ultimately reduced the harsh sentences that he had imposed.

In 1886 Mr. Justice Day clinched his reputation as one who enjoyed administering a "law of terror." At that year's November Assizes in Liverpool, intent on impressing the local citizenry with the dignity of the law, he sentenced twenty young robbers to twenty to thirty strokes of the cat. And to ensure that the memory of the degradation remained fresh, Day ordered that the last applications of the lash were to be inflicted just before the unfortunates finished their prison sentences. On a later occasion he regretted not being able to have flogged another gang of young thieves knowing, as he claimed, that youths cared only for their skins.[88] In fourteen years Day inflicted 3,766 strokes of the lash on 137 prisoners. "Show your back to your dissolute friends when you come out," was his customary advice to such criminals. The lip-smacking pleasure with which the judge imposed such sentences was bound to elicit criticisms. Was that the way a gentleman behaved? The chief constable of Liverpool remembered Day as a careful judge, "though undoubtedly a very severe one."[89] Even Day's son had to admit, with a large measure of understatement, that his father "was not gifted Newman-like, with a true apprehension of the feelings of others."[90] Day's infatuation with flogging and his lack of judicial calmness was attributed by his contemporaries to the ferocious brand of Roman Catholicism that he embraced. John Morley, the Liberal M. P., on 30 July 1888 read to the House of Commons a letter from Judge Adams, one of the Belfast Commissioners, who described Day as "a man of the seventeenth century in his views, a Catholic as strong as Torquemada, a Tory of the old high-flyer and non-juror type."[91]

Sarah Eden could not have come before a less sympathetic judge. Day was especially prejudiced in sex cases.[92] His religious beliefs no doubt explained his expressed hatred of abortion and the general opinion was that the severity of Eden's treatment was clearly due to Day's preoccupations. The *Daily News,* which on earlier occasions had attacked Day as a brute, protested that Eden's death sentence was against justice and nature; it was a "miserable subject of judicial error" that had to be remedied quickly. The newspaper assumed that the Home Office had been alerted, "because, in the matter of capital sentences Mr. Justice Day notoriously needs constant watchfulness. He has a gloomy passion for severity, which makes it necessary to be ready to save him from himself, as well as to save culprits from the consequences of his peculiar conceptions of his duty."[93] The *Daily Chronicle* concurred that it would be a scandal and a crime if Sarah Eden were executed. "We do not believe that one Englishman in a hundred would consent to regard her offense as one of willful murder, or to punish her deed, gravely culpable as it was, with the last dread sentence of the law. Least of all can such a penalty be properly carried out at the instance of a judge holding the views of punishment which have been most unhappily illustrated on scores of occasions by Mr. Justice Day."[94] In short, in attacking Day as a "brute," the liberal press was assuming the role of chivalrous protector of women. Even the *Birmingham Daily Gazette,* an avid supporter of law and order, asked that "womanhood" be given mercy. On legal grounds Eden had been correctly found guilty, but perhaps, the newspaper suggested, she ignorantly sought to do good. Hopefully the judge would say something. But in fact Day refused to recommend mercy; that, he declared, was to be decided by higher authorities.[95]

Sir James Charles Mathew (1830–1908), Hindson's judge, did not enjoy Day's reputation for severity. Mathew was an ardent radical, known for his facile and humorous sallies. But as a devout Roman Catholic, he had as little time for sex crimes as Day.[96] Hearing the jury's guilty verdict, he immediately passed Hindson's death sentence. But traditionally murder had to entail "malice aforethought." Hindson, the liberal press protested, was clearly not guilty of "willful murder"; to suggest that he intended Gordon's death was absurd.

So much for the journalists' critiques of the courts. What of the public discussion of abortion? Most English newspapers lamented the severity of the abortion law as it manifested itself in the Eden and Hindson cases; few had the courage to embark on any detailed investigation of why there was a demand for abortion. Of the leading dailies, the *Daily News* went furthest in asking if inducement of miscarriage might not be, in certain circumstances, legitimate. "Mrs. Eden, at the earnest solicitation of a married woman who had reason to dread the agony of a confinement, consented to perform an illegal operation. . . . She had no corrupt motive; she acted only from a feeling of pity and perhaps on some confused idea of the similarity of her ministrations to those in which the life of a child unborn is sometimes freely and blamelessly sacrificed to save the life of a mother."[97] The writer was expressing what many no doubt felt. The act of a promiscuous single woman trying to hide evidence of her sexual transgressions was not the same thing as an ill mother seeking to terminate a seventh pregnancy. In applying the law on abortion, the courts had to take into account the character of the individuals involved. But this is as far as the leading dailies would go.

For an actual defense of abortion, one has to turn to an article written by Alexander Cohen entitled "The Case for Mrs. Eden," which appeared in an obscure journal called *The Torch of Anarchy*. Cohen's defense of abortion, because of its daring originality, deserves quotation in full.

> Justice Day, the well-known worshipper of the "cat" has made himself notorious once more. At the last Warwick Assizes, this highly respectable old flogger managed, by his summing up, so to direct twelve imbecile jurymen that they returned a verdict of *willful murder* against Sarah Eden, a charwoman, who by an "illegal operation" was alleged to have caused the death of a woman, a certain Mrs. Sinister [*sic*].
>
> We do not intend to dwell on the sentence of Death pronounced by Day. But we are anxious to know what is the meaning of these prosecutions, and in the name of what "principle" they are instituted.
>
> Here is the case. A poor wretched woman, who neglected to

prevent, at the right moment, the conception of her child, obtained the services of another woman to procure abortion, in order to spare herself the anguish of child-bearing, and at the same time to save the prospective baby the pain of living. The operation is carried out, and the woman dies.

Now if at any time there existed a right of property, then most indisputably it is that which a woman has over her unborn child. And it would be just as reasonable to hang a surgeon who, by amputating a broken limb, causes the death of his patient, as to condemn to death a Sarah Eden, under whose more or less experienced hands a woman dies after undergoing a so-called illegal abortion.

But let us look at the question from another point of view: the most important one. Why should not women, even when they are not in a weak state of health, as Mrs. Sinister [*sic*] is said to have been, and do not dread the physical pain of child-birth, abort, if they choose to do so. How, in such a case, can the interference of judges, as representatives of Society—that rotten abstraction— be justified?

For the question is not whether a woman dies or not in consequence of the operation. If she does not, she and the "operator" are nevertheless prosecuted and condemned, if the thing becomes known.

Women *must* procreate, women *must* be prolific, women may *not* extirpate or destroy the fruit of their womb. So says the law, and so say the brainless idiots who abide by and worship it.

We say: The bringing forth of children, so long as the "joy of living" cannot reasonably be expected to be their fate, is a *crime,*— the greatest we are able to conceive. How much better would it not have been had the scores of cursed children we meet in the streets, livid, bloodless, and thin, so many indictments against their reckless procreators, if their coming into existence had been prevented, of if they had been taken, as soon as they came to the darkness of the light, by the heels, and their brains been dashed out against the wall?

Wretched women:—be sterile, close your wombs, abort![98]

Despite its rhetorical excesses, this was a remarkable document. Its author, Alexander Cohen, a Dutch anarchist who had lived much of his life in France, earned a living translating into French the works of such German writers as Hugo von Hoffmansthal, Gerhardt Hauptman, and Eduard Dekker. Cohen was deported from France and tried in absentia at the August 1894 *procès de trente* after an outbreak of anarchist bombing attacks led the French government to pass laws that allowed it to try conspirators.[99] Cohen found in the London of the 1890s a lively anarchist culture, dominated by European exiles.[100] The *Torch,* which declared itself a journal of "Anarchist-Communism," was owned and operated by three young people in their twenties, Olivia, Arthur, and Helen Rossetti, the nieces and nephew of Dante Gabriel Rossetti, the pre-Raphaelite painter.[101] The *Torch* paraded an advanced sex-radicalism. It attacked as "the goody-goody old cats" the prudes who attempted to close the Empire, a popular music hall,[102] castigated the police for harassing prostitutes,[103] and leapt to the defense of Edith Lanchester, a young woman who had been committed to an asylum by her parents when she sought to live unmarried with a socialist.[104]

The *Torch* stressed that it was necessary to understand, if not condone, the desperate acts of women who, given existing social mores, were endangered by their own fertility. The journal defended Minnie Wells and Amy Gregory, who were sentenced to death for having committed infanticide.[105] Wells, a twenty-three-year-old laundry worker from Reigate, was delivered of twins in May 1894; evicted from her home and impoverished, she drowned her two babies in June.[106] In March 1895 the *Torch* similarly presented Amy Gregory, who had strangled her child, as a victim of society. Was it any surprise, it asked, that Gregory, a twenty-three-year-old laundress who having given birth in the workhouse, starving, turned out of her house and unemployed, should have killed her baby daughter to protect her from a life of pain?[107] Such discussions provided a remarkable example of leftist men, whom the respectable press customarily depicted as scoundrels and blackguards, appropriating the discourse on chivalry.[108] Mr. Justice Day was the cad; anarchists, they asserted, were the true "gentlemen" in alone defending poor, persecuted women. This example of "anarchist gallantry" reminds one that men on the left, even when condemning the economic and political aspects of bourgeois society, prided themselves on their strict adherence to a masculine code of honor.[109]

Most of the *Torch*'s articles on sex issues were the product of Fersenheim, a Berliner who wrote under the name of F. S. Paul. He followed a familiar leftist line in attacking bourgeois marriage as a crass commercial transaction but also chided other anarchist males for not recognizing women's sexual needs. He sounded a new note for the left in England in defending birth control.[110] Paul, in an article entitled "Malthusianism," though admitting a large family was still probably an economic advantage to the working-class household, declared that anarchists had no objections on moral grounds to the "use of preventive appliances."[111] Paul provided the *Torch*'s defense of Hindson. Hindson, according to Paul, instead of denying his guilt, should have forthrightly declared: "Every woman has an inalienable right to do with her body whatever she likes; to give herself to whomsoever she lists." Hindson would, of course, have been crazy to have made such a statement in court, and for Paul to make such a suggestion indicates that he had little understanding of English mores. Nevertheless there is no gainsaying the fact that Paul was willing to state what no English writer would. Hindson, he observed, "made arrangements which, if successful, would allow her [Gordon] to face the future with a light heart. And for this he is to die! . . . What a farce, what a tragedy; to have to spend a lifetime behind iron bars for the crime of having befriended an unfortunate woman!"[112]

In Britain the *Torch* went far further in its sex radicalism than any other leftist journal. The nineteenth-century British socialist movement was fairly prudish, in part due to the fact that fertility control was associated with the conservative doctrines of Malthus.[113] Accordingly the raising of the sex issue was regarded by many on the left not only as immoral but impolitic. The broaching of the abortion question reflected an emerging consciousness of the symbolic and political importance of sexuality among a handful of leftists, but did not mark a major turning point. Once the *Torch* ceased publication in 1896 and Alexander Cohen returned to the continent, radical discussions of sex issues by the English left flagged.[114]

Nevertheless, following the flurry of newspaper discussions, Eden and Hindson's death sentences were commuted. Eden's sentence roused great public interest.[115] The *Daily News* reported receiving innumerable letters protesting her trial's outcome. A petition on her behalf ultimately garnered thirty thousand signatures.[116] The Home Secretary announced the commutation of Sarah Eden's death sentence in late 1895; instead she was subjected to life imprisonment. The *Birmingham Daily Gazette* praised the Home Office for its leniency; the *Birmingham Daily Post* grudgingly admitted that the commutation was needed but insisted that everyone should agree that crime had to be beaten back. The *Daily News,* in referring to the "terrible sentence," stated that it could not believe that the final word had been said, and a new petition was launched calling for the reduction of Eden's prison term.[117]

As regards Hindson, the press had noted at the outset that his death sentence would "not arouse the emotional sympathy which entered so largely into the case of Mrs. Eden."[118] In other words the discourse of male chivalry could not be turned to protect him. Indeed his trial was described by conservative newspapers as having revealed a "nauseous tragedy."[119] Nevertheless, in mid-March of 1896, the Home Office, in response to a petition, replied that Hindson's death sentence had also been respited with a view to its commutation.[120] Hindson still protested that, not having been allowed to speak in court, his side of the story had not been heard. And he continued to ask how he could be guilty of the murder of a woman he had only tried to help.[121]

Why were Eden and Hindson reprieved? Although the articles by Cohen and Paul are of obvious historical significance, the Home Office was, if aware of them, obviously not to be swayed by the writings of a few anarchists. Were the newspaper reports and petitions influential? Perhaps, but at the end of the day the Home Office acted to strengthen the law not undermine it. Eden's reprieve was hardly unexpected. Given gender concerns in late Victorian England, it was unusual for a woman to be executed for even ordinary murder. In 1895 sixteen men and three women were found guilty of murder. Eleven of the men and none of the women were executed.[122] More to the point, no one had been executed for an abortion-related death in England since 1875 when Alfred Thomas Heap was hanged in Kirkdale Gaol, Liverpool. Heap, a midwife's husband, fatally injured a woman when using a spindle to precipitate her miscarriage. He had been previously convicted and sentenced to five years imprisonment for a similar offense. Nevertheless the public regarded his 1875 death sentence as excessive. The jury protested to Baron Pollock, the presiding judge, that if it had known its recommendation for mercy would be ignored it would not have found Heap guilty of willful murder but have brought in a manslaughter conviction.[123] Nevertheless Heap hanged.

Mr. Justice Phillimore in the Wark case spelled out the law as it pertained to abortion deaths as follows.[124]

> If the unfortunate woman caused her own miscarriage, then, so far as she was concerned, it was in law a case of suicide or *felo de se*. If the prisoner were her accomplice in that, if he were present aiding and abetting an illegal operation which caused her death, though he did not actually use the instrument, he was equally responsible for her death. If he were there, or encouraged or assisted her by getting a room, he would be what the law called a principal in the second degree. If he merely urged or counselled, and was not himself present at the illegal operation, he would be what the law called an accessory before the fact, and would still be guilty of murder.[125]

This theory of "constructive murder" might have made sense to judges, but the public found it unsatisfactory. Following the Heap trial, although the death sentence was mandatory when the woman died, those convicted of murder resulting from a procured abortion were given reprieves by the Home Office.[126]

For our purposes the Eden and Hindson trials are of interest for several reasons. They serve as useful reminders that the law on abortion, although rarely used, could lead to the imposition of savage punishments, that it hit men as well as women, and by 1895 was subject to attack. As utopian as the anarchist contributors to *The Torch* might have been, they did at least recognize the truth that any law against abortion—which pitted men against women, the wealthy against the poor—was unjust and unworkable. The respectable newspapers avoided such social analyses and sought to individualize the tragic consequences of the administration of the law by, for example, blaming Sarah Eden's fate on the heartlessness of that old reactionary Mr. Justice Day. Injustices occurred but they were due, the press reassured the public, to personal rather than to structural faults. Yet despite such comforting interpretations, many female readers must have been led to the troubling conclusion, which few could or would yet voice, that the laws pertaining to reproduction systematically penalized women and that every judge presiding over an abortion trial was free to administer a law of terror.

But these trials also tell us a good deal about men, and in particular, about late-nineteenth-century notions of the male sexual predator and his relationship to the model female. Mabel Gordon died because of the law on abortion not because of any action of Hindson. He was made a scapegoat because he forced his actions on the notice of the court. Yet the court did not really know what to do with him, caught between its rhetoric and its reason. Hindson's crime, as the press repeatedly stressed, was that he had acted like a cad or bounder, but did that warrant the death penalty?

∬

APPLYING PUNISHMENT ACCORDING TO A CULPRIT'S CHARACTER AND morals was by no means new. The traditional summary legislation for dealing with the loose, idle, and disorderly led to people being imprisoned for what they were rather than for what they did. The interest held by the violent castigations of the seducer that came out in bigamy and abortion trials stems from the fact that they were a relatively recent development, suggesting an evolution in nineteenth-century notions of masculinity. Tales of mythic Don Juan figures had long been a staple of Western culture. Eighteenth-century novelists like Richardson, Laclos, Crebillon, and Restif de la Bretonne plotted the machinations of the seducer in excruciating and often admiring detail.[127] Nineteenth-century bourgeois society resolutely turned its back on such themes. Or one might more accurately note, as has Tony Tanner, that the Victorian writer could only justify the portrayal of sexual transgressions by moralistically portraying their necessarily tragic consequences.[128]

One might protest that there is no proof that nineteenth-century men were any less promiscuous than their eighteenth-century forebears, but that is not the issue. Representations of sexual relations changed even if actual behavior did not. Unwed mothers were regarded with less compassion.[129] Cuckolds were not to be laughed at; the seducer was no longer a figure of fun. In part because those who embraced the new ideal of companionate marriage based on affective relationships necessarily viewed with distaste those discussions of extramarital sex that once had been sources of popular amusement.[130] In part because the Don Juan figure, who devoted his energy to amorous conquests rather than to social accomplishments, was increasingly castigated by serious middle-class men as a "feminine" type. Accordingly "don juanisme" was to attract the attention of Gregorio Marañon, Spain's foremost sexologist, who was interested in the indecisiveness of the seducer's sexuality.[131] The new masculine hero of a materialistic age was supposed to seek worldly success. Even young romantic adventurers, portrayed in the novels of Stendhal and Balzac, while they pursued women, had as their real goal social mobility.[132] Accordingly, to be labeled a seducer, a Lothario, as Hindson and many of the bigamists were, could have serious consequences at the end of the nineteenth century. This was an age in which in Britain Ellice Hopkins' White Cross Movement was asserting that if there were no seducers there would be no prostitutes, while in France seduction was in addition held responsible for a host of social ills including poverty, still births, abortion, and infanticide.[133]

But these trials also alert us to the fact that masculinity was the subject of more than one discourse. Due to the popularity of the melodramatic narrative of sexual danger, the dominant discourse on masculinity successfully presented Mabel Gordon as the passive female victim and Hindson as the libertine.[134] Yet the debates elicited by the abortion cases revealed that there were counterdiscourses at work as well. Who was acting like a true gentleman? The man who assisted a pregnant woman in finding an abortionist? The judge who sentenced to death an elderly midwife? The anarchist who defended a poor woman's right to control her own body? The very fact that such questions were even raised demonstrates that although there was a hegemonic discourse on masculinity it did not go undisputed.

FOUR

GENTLEMEN

IF THE WORD *BOUNDER* HAS TODAY A CURIOUSLY ARCHAIC ring, so too has the term *gentleman*. Yet it was only in the 1800s that the appellation of gentleman took on its special significance. It says something of both the newness and the social importance of the concept that the nineteenth-century French, though they spoke of "un homme bien élevé" or "bien né," had no exact equivalent and so simply adopted the English expression, referring, for example, to "un vrai gentleman."[1] Alexis de Tocqueville was struck by the fact that in France under the Old Regime "gentilhomme" was employed when referring to a member of the restricted, landed, social caste, whereas in America he found that respectable men of every class considered themselves "gentlemen."[2] That is to say, they believed that the public esteem enjoyed by a man in a modern nation was no longer directly determined by his birth. A society that assumed social fluidity necessarily held that the morality that a man exhibited in his daily dealings could override even the disadvantages of humble social standing. And contrarily, a man, no matter how rich, could be condemned by the public should he fail "to act like a gentleman." What this exactly entailed could never be fully spelled out, but the very vagueness of the gentlemanly ethic enhanced its attractiveness as a bonding credo for men who, despite the pressures of an increasingly individualistic world, saw themselves striving to maintain certain ideals of honesty and generosity. This ethic, in purportedly symbolizing a new standard of morality to which most men, both rich and poor, could adhere, helped to serve as a means of accommodation for the white, male citizens of new acquisitive and competitive societies. In America and England in particular, character, courtesy, and cultivation were declared by public commentators to be replacing birth and wealth as the hallmarks of the "natural gentleman." Middle- and lower-middle-class men, though often continuing to dream of aristocratic connections and obsessed by status anxieties, were at the same time won to the appeals voiced by novelists and clergymen, politicians and professionals to embrace the populist and fraternal cult of the gentleman.[3] Even working-class men were not immune. Gladstone, the English prime minister, made a point of always addressing his laboring audiences as "gentlemen" in order to imbue them with the flattering notion that their concerns were taken seriously by the leadership of the Liberal party.[4]

Given the pervasive adulation of gentlemanly or chivalrous behavior, a hostile, public confrontation between a "lady" and a "gentleman"—something that in theory should never occur—was bound to create a sensation. The situation would be all the more explosive if the contest also involved the men who staffed the professions of law and medicine, epitomizing as they did, by their concern for the trust placed in them by their clients or patients, the archetypal virtues of the "scholar and gentleman." For these reasons in this chapter we focus on a late-nineteenth-century trial that not only dramatically demonstrated the powerful moral attributions given by the public to the terms lady and gentleman, but also revealed how law and medicine—two key systems of gender regulation—could, because of professional rivalries, on occasion clash.

∬

THE SENSATIONAL KITSON V. PLAYFAIR TRIAL OF 1896 WAS LONG TAKEN to be Britain's most publicized test of "privileged communication." This celebrated case centered on a doctor's defense of his right to betray a female patient's confidences.[5] For our purposes the most important aspect of the trial is that it shows how class and gender preoccupations shaped the practices of both law and medicine. The legal wrangles in Kitson v. Playfair took such surprising twists and turns precisely because gender preoccupations were used to counter both the letter of the law and the scientific pronouncements of the London medical elite. The trial and the responses made to it both inside and outside of the medical profession are also of interest in that they cast a revealing light on late-nineteenth-century doctors' confused understanding of exactly what confidentiality meant, a confusion exacerbated rather than clarified by court rulings. The case demonstrates how the medical profession found, to its discomfort, that in having as one of its representatives a man who failed to act like a gentleman, it left itself open to attack by its old rival, the legal profession.

The Kitson v. Playfair trial was on one level a domestic dispute. The Kitson family fortune was established in the mid nineteenth century by a Leeds iron founder who sired three sons and one daughter. In 1864 Emily

Kitson, the only daughter, married Dr. William Smoult Playfair, a well-known obstetrician, who was on his way to becoming the royal accoucheur. Sir James Kitson (1835–1911), the eldest son, led an active public life as Lord Mayor of Leeds (1896–97), president of the National Liberal Association (1883–1890), and Liberal member of Parliament representing Colne Valley (1892–1907). Although a radical he consented to concluding his career as the first Baron Airedale and left an estate worth one million pounds.[6] Hawthorn, the second son, looked after the family businesses in Yorkshire, which centered on the locomotive works at Hunslett. Arthur, the youngest, filled the role of family ne'er-do-well, his life "undoubtedly marked by irregularities of conduct."[7] Ostensibly acting as his father's overseas agent, he went off to Australia to make his fortune. There in 1881 he married an English woman, Linda Douglas. She gave birth to two daughters in quick succession; the pregnancies precipitated a good deal of illness followed by a series of weakening miscarriages.

In October 1892 Linda Kitson and her children returned to England while Arthur, still trying to strike it rich and apparently pursued by creditors, set off from Port Darwin on a series of mysterious trips in the Pacific, including stops in Hong Kong and Hawaii. Upon Linda Kitson's arrival in England, Sir James and Hawthorn Kitson decided to make over to her and her children the allowance of some five hundred pounds a year that they had hitherto sent to her husband in Australia. The family had apparently decided that Arthur had led the life of a remittance man long enough and was now to be left to sink or swim on his own. Linda Kitson settled in a house in Kensington and, her health still failing, consulted Dr. Muzio Williams.[8] As an obstetrical problem seemed to be the source of her discomfort, Williams suggested that Dr. Playfair, her brother-in-law, be called in as a consultant. She was initially reluctant but in January 1894 agreed.

William Smoult Playfair (1836–1903) was perhaps the best known obstetrician in Britain. He had received his M.D. from Edinburgh in 1856, served briefly in India, and was appointed professor of obstetrics at King's College Hospital in 1872. He enjoyed a reputation as a well-known society physician, especially for women's complaints, having introduced to England the "rest cure" popularized in the United States by Weir Mitchell. In the 1890s Playfair—as royal accoucheur and respected patron of the arts— was at the peak of his career. He had recently turned down a knighthood in the confident expectation of ultimately receiving a baronetcy.[9]

Dr. Playfair's personal success unfortunately made it difficult for him to sympathize with the misfortunes of others. When he saw Linda Kitson on

16 January, he noted nothing exceptional arising from his brief examination. But in addition to her physical problems, Linda Kitson was plagued by worries about her absent husband's financial problems. "Let him starve," was Playfair's cold response. "It would be the best thing that could happen to him." [10]

Playfair attended the still ailing Linda Kitson again on 24 February. It was now revealed that she had not menstruated since December. She was put under chloroform by Playfair with Williams present, and her cervix dilated (so the court was later crudely informed) to the size of a five shilling piece. According to her later testimony she became partially conscious in the midst of the examination and heard Playfair saying, "I don't know what else it can be. I know very little about her. She must have been up to some hanky panky." [11] Williams protested that he could not believe this as she had been so candid. Both doctors later denied that any such words had been uttered. Their recollection was that Linda Kitson awoke to ask them what they were accusing her of when they had as yet accused her of nothing. [12]

What was said did not really matter. The point was that both men, who had begun the operation in the belief that they were dealing with an intra-uterine cancerous growth, discovered that Linda Kitson had recently had either a natural miscarriage or abortion, which they had to clean up. [13] This meant that she must have had sexual intercourse within the previous three months, and given the fact that she had not seen her husband for something like a year and a half, it could only be concluded that she was an adulteress. Presumably no discovery made by the royal accoucheur could have been more mortifying than stumbling upon evidence of his sister-in-law's promiscuity. [14]

Playfair had the placental material that he removed from Linda Kitson examined at King's College Hospital by his cousin, Dr. Hugh Playfair, who confirmed his suspicions. Playfair immediately determined that he could not allow his unchaste sister-in-law to socialize further with his wife and grown-up daughters, and he had Dr. Williams inform her of his decision. Linda Kitson frantically wrote to Playfair saying she could not communicate with him through Williams and begged for a personal interview. To his implication that she had been made pregnant by an adulterous relationship, she responded with the guarded assurance: "I can say as to whatever it is you are thinking, that none but the right one is the cause. My heart is breaking. There is only one can clear me, but not yet." [15] What she appeared to be implying was that yes she had been made pregnant, but her husband, who was responsible, could not for the moment reveal that he had secretly been in England.

Playfair, ever the prig, coolly replied that she should use her illness as an excuse to leave London. If she did not, he would be duty-bound to inform his wife of the facts. "No one who respects himself, his wife and his family can suppose for a moment that I can allow social relations between you and my family to go on as they were when I know you have had a miscarriage."[16] There ensued a protracted and confusing correspondence. Throughout it Linda Kitson, although never denying the "facts" of the case, pleaded for time to vindicate herself. She repeatedly implied that her husband could clear her name. Playfair never really believed her, but declared himself ready to be convinced. "If you are able to inform me that your husband has been in London I shall not only greatly commiserate you, but be very sorry for the suspicion which under the circumstances was inevitable."[17] But Linda Kitson never provided a straight answer; she would not say that which she insinuated. To do so would be to lie because, as she later admitted, her husband had in fact not been in England.

Playfair, not getting a clear answer and faced with the prospect of his family renewing their social ties with Linda Kitson, finally wrote to say he had no alternative but to inform his wife of the situation.[18] Linda Kitson now wrote to Emily Playfair begging her not to tell her brother, Sir James. Mrs. Playfair, like her husband, asked for assurances that Arthur had been in London, though she wondered how that could be since the family had received his telegrams from Australia.[19] No clear response again being made, Mrs. Playfair asked her husband to inform Sir James Kitson of the situation. Sir James immediately wrote Linda Kitson that all communication with the family had to cease, that her allowance was ended, but if she returned to Australia, he would provide a small maintenance.

In the meantime, all through the spring of 1894, Linda Kitson had been trying to contact her husband, Arthur. A letter finally reached him in Australia in June; by September he was back in London declaring himself ready to fight his own people. His first move was to claim, falsely, that he had, as his wife implied, returned secretly to England the previous December. Playfair was begrudgingly forced to apologize. "Your coming surreptitiously to London without informing the family has been the cause of all this annoyance. Your statement that you have been in London allows of the withdrawal of any imputation on your wife."[20] Kitson was not appeased, presumably because the family allowance was still not renewed. Taking this as evidence that the Playfair apology was worthless, Linda Kitson in February

1895 filed suit for libel and slander against Dr. and Mrs. Playfair. The case, which began on 21 March 1896, was tried before a special jury at the Queen's Bench presided over by Mr. Justice Henry Hawkins, better known as "Hanging" Hawkins, a devoted opponent of immorality.

The Playfairs' solicitor was the well-known Sir George Lewis and their leading counsel Sir Frank Lockwood, Q.C., the former solicitor-general who in 1895 had successfully led the prosecution against Oscar Wilde for acts of "gross indecency." Counsel presented the defendants with a choice. One course open to them was "to justify," that is, contend that the slander was true. Truth is an absolute defense against the charge of slander. But proving to the satisfaction of a jury that Linda Kitson had committed adultery—the only evidence being medical—was a daunting challenge, and Playfair's counsel was aware that if the distasteful attempt of making such a dishonorable charge failed, an irate jury could be counted on to assess punitively high damages.

The apparently safer course was to argue that, even if Dr. Playfair's story of Linda Kitson's adultery was false, in this particular situation it was a "privileged communication," that is to say a communication that because it only occurred within the immediate family, could not be held as either libelous or slanderous.[21] Playfair, on the advice of his legal advisers, took this latter course of pleading privilege. The defense's line of argument was that Playfair, with no malice intended, but only the protection of family honor in mind, had felt duty bound to tell his wife of what he thought was evidence of Linda Kitson's immorality, and Mrs. Playfair in turn told her brother.[22]

The defense had what appeared to be more than enough ammunition to ward off an unfavorable verdict. Despite the fact that Lockwood fought the case on the grounds of "privileged communication," he presented in court a good deal of evidence that substantiated Playfair's belief in Mrs. Kitson's adultery. Indeed the medical evidence was almost wholly on the side of the defendant. Only Dr. Herbert Spencer, professor of midwifery at University College London, testified on Linda Kitson's behalf.[23] He made the astounding statement that her miscarriage of February 1894 was possibly related to a legitimate conception that occurred in October 1892. But though Spencer asserted that eighteen months after its "cause" a condition such as Linda Kitson's could exist, he had to admit he had never seen such a case himself. John Bland Sutton, FRCS, replied for the defense that placental material could not be retained for over six months. And the defense backed up its attack on Spencer's preposterous argument by calling on London's leading obstetricians, who, in addition to W. S. Playfair and Hugh Playfair, included Dr. Francis Champney, lecturer at St. Bart's, and Sir William Priestly, consultant at King's College Hospital.[24] At times it appeared as though the entire membership of the Obstetrical Society of London was in court. With the exception of Spencer, they all supported Playfair's view that Linda Kitson had been made pregnant a few months before February 1894. Her counsel rightly objected to the lengthy, hostile medical testimony, but Mr. Justice Hawkins allowed it to continue. Dr. Spencer's opinion was clearly laughed out of court by Playfair's medical witnesses; what the jurors thought of it remained to be seen.

Lockwood's second line of defense was to call on Sir John Williams and Sir William Broadbent, seasoned experts in issues relating to British medical ethics, to support the contention that Playfair's violation of his patient's confidences was, given the particular situation, warranted.[25] The testimony of Broadbent, senior censor of the Board of the Royal College of Physicians, carried particular weight. Both doctors said that as professionals they could envisage doing the same as Playfair.[26]

Lockwood largely skirted the embarrassing question of why Linda Kitson prevaricated and why Arthur Kitson had initially lied about being in England in December 1893. He wanted to present Playfair as a gentleman who was not out to humiliate his relatives. In any event, he argued, such details were not directly relevant to the question of privilege. In his summation Lockwood returned to the defense's basic line of argument that Playfair had been honor-bound to warn his family of his sister-in-law's situation and such intimate conversations, being privileged, were not actionable. These arguments, supported as they were by the testimony of so many eminent "gentlemen and scholars," should presumably have been sufficient to impress any British court.

Mr. Lawson Walton, who led for the plaintiff, could have argued the case on strictly technical grounds. The rumors that Playfair told others besides his immediate family of his suspicions regarding Linda Kitson might have been used to undermine the defense of "privileged communication," and malice could have been inferred from the fact that Playfair was aware that his disclosures jeopardized Linda Kitson's annual allowance of five hundred pounds.[27] But Walton shrewdly appealed to the emotions rather than the intellect of the male jurors. The real question, he argued, was whether or not Playfair had conducted himself like a gentleman.

The trial was believed by the public to hinge on what in Victorian society could only be considered the riveting question of whether or not a middle-class woman's adultery had been exposed by a man who was both her physician and her brother-in-law. This is what made the affair so sensational. The defense thought it safer and more gentlemanly to avoid such a volatile issue and argue simply for privilege. This proved to be a mistake because it prevented the defense from responding directly to Walton's constant portrayal of his client as an innocent woman—a lady—fighting to protect her honor against the slurs of a cold-hearted physician whose base motives could only be guessed at.

Linda Kitson was the picture of the affronted female; attractive but wracked by anxiety, dressed elegantly but demurely in black, a white rose at her throat.[28] She wept; she swooned. The first day of the trial she almost fainted and had to be led by her husband into the open air. The judge asked her to sit while testifying. She spoke in a whisper; her water glass rattled against her teeth. When what the press described as the "ordeal" of her testifying was over, she was assisted from the box by her husband.[29] He too made a good impression as the poor relative fighting his wealthy and powerful family to protect the honor of his wife.

The fact that Linda Kitson had lied proved not to be an embarrassment. Walton skillfully attributed her toying with the truth to Playfair's instigation. "Mr. Arthur Kitson had not been in the country, and yet his wife must assure Dr. Playfair that he had been in England within the last three months or have her fair name blasted. Dr. Johnson, in the last century, said that if a murderer asked which way his victim had gone, falsehood was justifiable to turn him off the track."[30] The inconsistencies, the insinuations of Linda Kitson, which on the face of it were so damaging, were transformed by Walton to form an integral part of his portrayal of an honest, innocent, impressionable woman driven to distraction by a "moral inquisitor."[31] The court allowed her simply to apologize for having falsely and repeatedly implied that her husband was in London, and it was left at that. Linda Kitson in short made an excellent witness. Sir Frank Lockwood, sensing that the jury sympathized with a lady who had apparently suffered much, was afraid of subjecting her to an intense cross-examination for fear that it could only win her more support. In any event, since the defense had declared it would not attempt to justify Playfair's allegations, Mr. Justice Hawkins could not have been expected to tolerate much questioning along such lines.

But the most important witness for the plaintiff proved to be Dr. Playfair. Under cross-examination he was asked if he still retained "an opinion adverse to this lady's honor." Now it is of prime importance to remember that this question was not at issue. Playfair had the intelligence to recognize the impropriety of the query and asked the judge if he should answer. Hawkins made the mistake of saying he should, but the self-righteous Playfair made the even greater blunder of coldly and categorically replying to Walton that he continued to view Linda Kitson as dishonored. Playfair's public assertion that his sister-in-law was guilty of "unchastity" caused a sensation in the courtroom.[32] Lawson Walton had what he wanted and pounced. Why then, he asked indignantly, had Playfair not been "man enough" to fight out the issue in court instead of employing the cowardly defense of privilege? Playfair replied, honestly enough, that he had simply followed his counsel's advice. This could only appear as yet another mealy mouthed answer. Walton had succeeded in indelibly portraying Playfair as a cad.[33]

Walton proceeded to ask if Playfair was not impressed by Dr. Spencer's medical testimony or if in fact any contrary testimony could make him reassess his views. Playfair replied that none would. Though all of this had little to do with the question of privilege, it further fixed in the jury's mind an image of Playfair as a dogmatic moralist who could not be reasoned with.

Playfair's key assertion that it was his duty to protect his family's honor was similarly parried by Walton with the question of how the accusation of so serious a charge as the adultery of a sister-in-law could be based simply on the findings of forensic medicine.

> Mr. Lawson Walton: In coming to this conclusion do you reject
>   all but medical considerations, and reject all moral ones?
> Witness: When a woman has had a miscarriage—in the face of
>   an actual abortion I do reject them.[34]

Walton, skillfully playing on Playfair's penchant for asserting that his medical conclusions were infallible, had teased out the notion that medical practitioners believed they had a right to base moral judgments on evidence unavailable to others, a notion many nineteenth-century juries were known not to share.[35] The price of Playfair claiming the infallibility of his medical opinions, thundered Walton, had been the sacrifice of a lady's honor.[36] In summing up Walton at last returned to the question of privileged communication. He conceded that Playfair might have had the right to divulge information to his wife but denied that the right of privileged communication could be extended to defend the passing on of such information to Sir James Kitson.[37]

Mr. Justice Hawkins now had his say. He was not regarded in legal circles as particularly able, but that did not prevent him from playing an

active role in every trial over which he presided. Some justices were content
to take notes; Hawkins declared that it was his "duty to see that the jury
does not go wrong."[38] Walton could only have been happy that Hawkins
repeatedly allowed the cross-examination to wander off into the realm of
justification when it should have been rigidly restricted to question of privilege. His directions to the jury also pleased Walton because there was little
doubt where Hawkins's sympathies lay. He agreed with the plaintiff's counsel in opining that if Linda Kitson toyed with the truth it was because Playfair had put her in a tight corner. Hawkins was moreover clearly hostile to
the defense's use of privilege, which he construed as signifying a doctor's
right to betray his patient's confidences whenever he chose. But most telling
of all was Hawkins's spirited depiction of a doctor's informing on a woman
who had aborted as a "monstrous cruelty," an issue to which we will
return.[39]

    In his summation Hawkins instructed the jury that three questions had
to be answered; were the words complained of uttered by Playfair in good
faith? Were they uttered without malice? Were they uttered, not from a
mere sense of duty, but from some indirect motive? Hawkins reminded the
jurymen that whether or not Linda Kitson had been unchaste was not at
issue but that "if they found that she had played the wanton they could
take that into consideration in estimating the damages."[40] After three hours
the jury returned to find for the plaintiff on all three counts. The amount
awarded to Linda Kitson was twelve thousand pounds, reputedly the
largest settlement for libel and slander ever made in a British court.[41] The
Times reported that the verdict was greeted with loud applause in the court.
Reynold's Newspaper, a more popular periodical, noted applause, clap-
ping, and stamping of feet.[42]

∬

THE KITSON-PLAYFAIR TRIAL LONG ENJOYED THE REPUTATION OF HAVING
been particularly significant in refining the medico-legal definition of privileged communications. In fact it left doctors in an ethical muddle, which
is what makes the case so interesting. The trial and the discussions it precipitated revealed the complex ways in which notions of professional confidentiality were inextricably enmeshed in legal, class, and gender preoccupations. Law not medicine determined the boundaries of confidentiality.
Playfair was sued not for breaking confidence but for libel and slander. The
fact that he was a doctor was legally not essential to the plaintiff's case.
Linda Kitson could have sued anyone who had said the same thing as Playfair. The defense of a "privileged communication" raised by him was like-

wise not specifically related to his status as a doctor. He was simply asserting that what a husband told his wife was a privileged communication, and so too what a sister told a brother.

In summation Hawkins stated that doctors might have their own rules regarding confidentiality, but they could not impose them on others; in the end the courts would decide. A doctor was not bound to inform on a patient, he told the jury; it all depended on the judge. Hawkins refused himself to instruct the jury on whether or not a doctor who gratuitously revealed a patient's secret was making an illegitimate breach of confidence. So the general question was left unsettled, Hawkins leaving the issue of privileged communications as confused as ever. The *Daily News* chided him, pointing out that the issue of privilege was a matter of law that he should have decided on, leaving the question of malice—a fact—to the jury.[43]

The legal discussion of medical privilege began in Britain in 1776, when a surgeon initially refused to testify regarding the Duchess of Kingston's bigamy. Lord Mansfield eventually forced him to give evidence, ruling that doctors could be compelled in court to divulge their patient's confidences.[44] Though criminal acts were not privileged, barristers and solicitors could not be forced to testify; the legal profession, unlike the medical profession, enjoyed the right of privileged communications.[45] Absolute privilege was only granted anything that was said—even if false or malicious—in court, in Parliament, and between husband and wife. Qualified privilege pertained to every other situation. Words exchanged in doctors' consulting rooms were not specifically privileged; even confidences imparted to priests were only privileged by tradition. In a suit for breach of confidence and slander, the trial judge usually decided if the particular occasion privileged the communication of statements that otherwise, if willfully and knowingly defamatory, were actionable.[46]

In France article 378 of the 1810 Criminal Code made medical secrecy mandatory for midwives and pharmacists as well as for doctors.[47] In North America the state of New York in 1828, as part of a public health campaign, launched the first departure from the common-law rule in instituting a statute protecting the privilege of medical communications.[48] By the end of the century, sixteen other states had followed suit. Charles Meymott Tidy, in enviously noting the American legislation, expressed the hope in 1882 that in Britain the same results would be achieved by individual effort. "It seems a monstrous thing to require that secrets affecting the honour of families, and perhaps confided in a moment of weakness, should be dragged into the garish light of a law court, there to be discussed and made joke of by rude tongues and unsympathetic hearts."[49] Tidy expected that some doctors would sacrifice their liberty for honor and go to jail rather than betray their patients' secrets. John Glaister's more modest suggestion was that even if courts forced doctors to divulge information they should always protest in order to impress on the public the jealousy with which they protected their patients' secrets.[50] Contagious diseases by law had to be reported. Since scarlet fever, for example, was known to be on the list of such diseases, its reportage by a doctor was not considered a violation of medical secrecy. It was assumed that the patient, in coming to a doctor, implied his or her consent to such disclosure.[51]

In short the general drift of nineteenth-century British medical discussions of confidentiality was toward the need for greater secrecy. But when doctors were put on the spot, as they were in the trial in question, they frequently allowed their "moral" preoccupations to cloud their understanding of what secrecy entailed. The medical witnesses who appeared for both Playfair and Kitson certainly did not have a firm grasp of what medical confidentiality really meant. Or perhaps it would be more accurate to say that they wanted to present the medical profession as both the guardian of the patient's secrets and the defender of public morality. They did not understand that they could not always be both.

Dr. Spencer, who appeared for Linda Kitson, when asked by Lockwood to explain the rule of confidentiality, replied that it could only be broken to prevent one from being made an accessory to a crime. He would not, for instance, warn a woman that her fiancé suffered from venereal disease since such a marriage violated no law. And if a man, to avoid jury duty, falsely claimed to be ill, what would Spencer do? Spencer replied he would say the man was not ill. And in so doing, Lockwood pointed out, the doctor would be betraying his patient's confidence.[52] Going further, Mr. Justice Hawkins asked Sir John Williams, a leading obstetrician, who appeared for the defense:

> Suppose a medical man were called in to attend a woman, and in the course of his professional attendance he discovers that she has attempted to procure an abortion. That being a crime under the law, would it be his duty to go and tell the Public Prosecutor?
> Witness: The answer of the College of Physicians to that very question was "Yes."
> Mr. Justice Hawkins: Then all I can say is that it will make me very chary in the selection of my medical man.[53]

Williams was no doubt dumbfounded that a judge should upbraid him for stating that a crime should be reported, but Hawkins's distaste for such tale-telling was obviously shared by the general public. They grasped, as Williams did not, the difference between the spirit and the letter of the law. A gentleman was discreet.

The press gleefully noted the pathetic figures cut by the so-called experts in medical ethics. The case, according to one writer, had revealed that at the highest levels of the profession was found an "absolute ignorance of the rules of professional honour."[54] An editorialist in the *Daily News* referred to the "rather irregular evidence" of Sir John William and Sir William Broadbent in which they asserted that a doctor, in order to protect his wife, had the right to betray his patient. This was, the journalist, declared, an "alarming proposition."[55] Such chiding represented the traditional suspicion, bordering on disdain, that barristers and journalists had for expert witnesses. Playfair's claims to medical infallibility obviously did him no good whatsoever. Reporters relayed the clear message that the public viewed with hostility a doctor who asserted that his medical evidence could not be challenged but then refused to submit such evidence to the judgment of the court. "This unscientific dogmatism," the *Daily News* declared, "as often found in scientific men, is as dangerous as any political or theological prejudice."[56]

In columns headed "West End Scandal" and "Doctor and His Patient: A Society Scandal" the press heartily agreed with the judgment and the huge award for damages. A restrained *Times* editorial declared that the trial had been an unfortunate spectacle; the only satisfaction was that a lesson had been taught to the few rash members of the medical profession of the need for careful judgment, it being preferable to sin by silence than by "indiscreet and uncalled for babbling."[57] The *Evening News* trumpeted that the verdict "supplied the medical profession with twelve thousand reasons why a doctor should keep the secrets of his patients inviolate."[58] In 1896 judges, barristers, and journalists, not for the first nor the last time, had the great pleasure of lecturing doctors on where their chief loyalties should lie.

Turning from the legal to the medical responses to the Kitson v. Playfair trial, it can be imagined how distressing the medical profession found the case. It was not just a question of medical expertise being denigrated; of more importance to a profession that asserted that its honor and authority was based in part on its dignified treatment of patients was that a representative had been found to have failed to have acted like a gentleman.[59] British doctors responded in one of two ways. The first, represented by the *Lancet,* was to concede that mistakes had been made. "We feel it our painful duty to assent to the proposition that Dr. Playfair did not act as discreetly as he might have done. Was it wise to place such alternatives before Mrs. Kitson? . . . Whilst we recognize his perilous position, we believe that he should have sought other professional advice to prove his determination to act justly between man and man."[60] But this last line was misleading. After all, Playfair had been supported by the most eminent doctors in the land. How would further consultations have made any difference?

The *British Medical Journal* represented a more pugnacious response, demonstrating far more support for Playfair than had the *Lancet.* Playfair, declared the *BMJ,* had only acted, as any honorable man would, to protect his family and had been "mulcted" for doing so.[61] Turning to the journalistic sniping which medical witnesses had to endure, the *BMJ* ridiculed the notion, popularized by the press, that doctors needed to be reminded of the sacredness of confidentiality. It pointed out that doctors were forever caught in the middle; patients wanted their secrets kept, but at the same time the public wanted doctors to report cases of abortion and overlaying.[62] Doctors who used their discretion were praised by some judges and damned by others. On the one hand those who refused to provide a court with information could be charged with contempt while on the other those who revealed their patients' secrets could be sued for slander and libel.[63] The *BMJ* concluded that to spare physicians further humiliations a new, definite law on the subject was needed.[64]

The complexities of confidentiality were further aired in the letters to the editor column of the *Times.* A member of the Royal College of Surgeons reminded readers that medical "secrets" were not possible given the need for medical consultations. Some writers recognized that a doctor's privilege was no different from the general public's; others wanted a hard and fast rule.[65] Several correspondents took the occasion to call for an extension of the list of notifiable diseases.[66] Turning to specifics, "E.J.D." asked if the Playfair judgment meant that a doctor should not inform the customers and employers of a syphilitic milkman of the dangers they ran.[67] "Honorarium" replied that the doctor should tell the patient he was legally and morally required to seek treatment; the doctor would not be liable if he sought to protect the public since in so doing, unlike Playfair, he would not be attempting to serve his own interests.[68] A legally informed contributor concurred that "justification" provided adequate protection from any charge of violation of confidentiality.[69] "Medical Jurisprudence" took the high road in declaring that a doctor did not have the right to decide what to do with the information he received from his patients. Citing the Hippocratic Oath, he pointed out that the doctor's only duty was to cure and tartly concluded: "It is indeed pitiable if a body of learned gentlemen should have to be forced by punishment to hold their tongues."[70]

Turning to the social context in which the trial took place, the press's constant references to the "ladies" and "gentlemen" involved made it clear that class played a key role in coloring nineteenth-century notions of confidentiality. Where one was located in the social hierarchy determined how much privacy one might legitimately enjoy. French commentators at the time spoke of honor as a sort of property and its loss equivalent to "theft."[71] Playfair was damned with the epithet of "moral inquisitor." Why? This was the age of temperance agitation, sabbatarianism, regulation of prostitution, and the raising of the age of sexual consent. Poor Law and Charity Organization Society investigators prowled through working-class neighborhoods reprimanding the dissolute. Given the fact that the Victorians prided themselves on their moral rectitude, why should Playfair's activities not have been applauded rather than so roundly condemned? Part of the answer lay in whose morality was being policed. The Victorian concept of confidentiality was very much a bourgeois conceit inasmuch as it was presumed that doctors would alert masters of the illnesses of their servants and help charities sort out the able-bodied from the impotent.[72] Linda Kitson's case was obviously quite different in that one was dealing not with a servant or prostitute but with a middle-class woman. Strikingly enough the press declared that a lady's character— by which it meant a middle-class woman's character—should never be decided on medical evidence alone.[73]

The concept of "privileged communications" was rarely fought out in court. If one relies, as has been done in this chapter, on legal records, one will only hear about the violation of the confidences of the Linda Kitsons of this world. This, of course, does not mean that only middle-class women ran such risks; it means that only those with sufficient money to launch costly legal actions appeared in the record. Similarly, when we search for suits launched by males, we surprisingly find that they often pitted one doctor against another. In 1884 a Dr. Casson unsuccessfully sued a colleague for telling those whom Casson served as club-surgeon that his incompetence was responsible for a member's death. The judge ruled that the second doctor's communication to the club was privileged and the trial ended in a nonsuit.[74] In 1899 a doctor told his assistant that a colleague had been drunk and in "a bit of a fog" when attending a patient. The latter doctor went to court where he accepted an apology and forty shillings.[75] Such cases signified not that doctors were particularly prone to back-biting but that they were better placed to respond to slander than were their patients. Members of the lower classes were effectively prevented from launching such suits because they lacked both the money and, more importantly, society's recognition that their privacy should be respected.

Gender concerns played the most important role in this particular breach-of-confidence suit. Linda Kitson won much support by perfectly playing the role of the lady in distress. About the only antifeminist response to the trial surfaced in the pages of the Marxist journal *Justice,* the mouthpiece of H. M. Hyndman's Social Democratic Federation. Its chief contributor, the misogynist E. Belfort Bax, having spent all of 1895 berating supporters of women's emancipation—including Eleanor Marx Aveling—was not about to let the trial go by without one last swipe at females. Having noted that the verdict had met with general approval, the "Tattler" went on to reflect: "Without in the least attempting to condone the action of Dr Playfair, however, one is constrained to point out that he, after all, only told his wife, and that, as usual, it was a woman who was mainly responsible for the injury wrought to one of her sex."[76] He concluded that Linda Kitson could consider herself "fortunate in being a woman." No man would ever receive twelve thousand pounds for slander, which proved, despite the whining of some, how advantaged women were. Several female correspondents immediately replied that *Justice,* full as usual of coarse and trite antifeminist abuse, failed to note that the judge and jury were all men. Women wanted not special treatment but "fair play."[77]

Aside from *Justice* and the *British Medical Journal*—two unlikely bedfellows—the press was overwhelmingly on the side of Linda Kitson. A letter that appeared in the *Times* provided in a nutshell the public perception of the trial. "Now we have an Englishman of the very highest standing torturing a feeble and lonely woman by threats of revealing what he thought he had learned."[78] Here were combined all the clichés of the blackmail thriller, the sensationalist novel and the antivisectionist tract. Many of the stock characters and situations appeared as well—the cruel doctor (ironically named Playfair), the damsel in distress, the administering of chloroform, the violation first of the woman's body and then of her secrets.[79]

Walton played up such themes in presenting the trial as a woman's heroic attempt "to escape from a charge which reflected upon her honour." Although Playfair was the actual defendant, Linda Kitson never ceased to be regarded by the public as the victim. Even Lockwood had to acknowledge ruefully that it was hard for the jury to free their minds of the image of Linda Kitson as a pathetic, terrorized creature and Playfair as her inquisitor.[80]

It was noted earlier that Playfair's decision to fall back on the defense of privilege was an enormous blunder. Lockwood could not disentangle the question of privilege in the public's mind, indeed in the minds of the judge and jury, from the aspersions cast on Linda Kitson. Middle-class society resolutely condemned adultery, but was even more hostile to anyone who would be so "unmanly" as to blacken a lady's reputation and then refuse to back up his words. Walton repeatedly argued that Playfair had cunningly not sought to prove the charges of adultery because he knew it was impossible; claiming privilege was the coward's way out. He had acted like a cad.

In response Lockwood appealed to the jurors as "men of honour and men of the world" to put themselves in Playfair's place. What else could Playfair have honorably done? This was another grave miscalculation on the part of the defense; hypothetical situations inspire hypocrisy. Most men felt they could have done far better, been far more charitable. Indeed the response of the popular press was dominated by expressions of self-righteous male indignation. The *Weekly Yorkshire Post* doubted if there existed "twelve rational Englishmen, with hearts beneath their waistcoats, who are capable of taking the Playfair view of the case."[81]

The trial largely revolved around the way in which men were supposed to behave. Victorian society believed that men necessarily had power over women but were not to abuse it. Middle-class males were rarely prosecuted for coercing women; it was rarer still for a doctor to be tried for intimidating a patient. When such rare cases came to light, an example was often made of the unlucky culprit. Playfair was no doubt just such a sacrificial lamb, punished for not playing his part as the chivalrous gentleman. The implication drawn by the press was that such misdeeds were not systemic, not the result of any asymmetry in the power wielded by men and women, but the result of some individual quirk. Patriarchal power was thereby strengthened rather than undermined by such show trials, demonstrating as they did that males could be relied upon to police themselves.

So strong was the male chorus of support for Linda Kitson that it drowned out the few female expressions of solidarity. One might have expected feminists to have seized upon the Kitson trial as a classic case of male oppression, but as far as can be determined, the leaders of the women's movement avoided extensive comment. Dealing as it did with the adultery and miscarriage of a middle-class woman, the Kitson affair perhaps hit too close to home. The leaders of the women's movement tended to be more comfortable in displacing their concerns about sexuality onto the topic of working-class prostitution.[82]

Nineteenth-century feminists had noted that confidentiality was "gendered," most notably under the Contagious Diseases Act, when physicians were relied upon to inform authorities which street walkers were ill and accordingly were to be incarcerated by the police.[83] Male doctors kept the secrets of their male patients, however, even from their wives or fiancées. Doctors could, of course, be expected to protect each other. The most extreme case occurred when Dr. Pritchard, the infamous medical murderer, succeeded in poisoning his wife because a colleague believed it was against the "etiquette" of the profession to report his suspicions.[84] Dr. Spencer, who appeared for Linda Kitson, was presented by Lockwood with a more familiar scenario. A male patient suffering from venereal disease announces his intention to marry; would Spencer warn the woman and prevent such a dangerous union from being forged? Spencer replied that he would not.[85] Protecting men meant, by the same token, betraying women. The point has been made many times before that doctors often kept nineteenth-century middle-class women in ignorance of the workings of their own bodies and the threats posed them by others. The classic case would be that of the doctor not informing a woman that she suffered from a venereal complaint because to do so would reveal that her husband or her husband-to-be had been unfaithful.[86]

But doctors also protected some women's confidences. In the Kitson case, not deception but candor was the threat. Playfair played the role of the blackmailer—a stock bogeyman of the age—in inspiring fear by threatening to reveal rather than suppress the truth.[87] If the classic male medical secret was that one was suffering from venereal disease, the female equivalent was to have had an abortion. Keeping the secret of a woman who aborted was morally less problematical than keeping the secret of a man who had a venereal disease because she did not pose a medical danger to those around her while he did. But abortion was a crime and communications pertaining to criminal acts were not privileged, even for barristers and solicitors. The confidences of the victims of crimes such as rape were to be protected, not those of defendants. But abortion was a special case. The woman, although party to the crime, was viewed by the courts as also its "victim," and therefore her physician's testimony was usually ruled to be inadmissible.[88] When one nineteenth-century doctor, who pretended to be assisting a couple in procuring an abortion, betrayed them and appeared in court as both a medical expert and prosecution witness, the judge, instead of lauding the physician's civic mindedness, damned him for having acted as an agent provocateur.[89]

Mr. Justice Hawkins went so far as to declare in open court that if a woman aborted to save her character, her reputation, and her livelihood, he doubted "very, very, very much" the justification of a doctor running off to the police to say: "I have been attending a poor, young woman who has been trying to procure abortion with the assistance of her sister. She is now pretty well, and is getting better, and in the course of a few days she will be out again, but I think I ought to put you on to the woman."[90] That, Hawkins asserted, would be "a monstrous cruelty."[91]

Hawkins's words serve as a useful reminder of how the class and gender preoccupations of the gentlemanly ethic could lead even a judge to turn a blind eye to certain crimes. When Hawkins thought about abortion, he assumed, as did most of his contemporaries, that the woman in question would be poor, single, seduced, and abandoned. Since she was in effect a victim of her own crime and her actions jeopardized neither property nor gender relationships, his heart could go out to her. But how would the courts respond to a wealthy, married woman who sought an abortion as part of her struggle to free herself from a hated husband? Just such a case surfaced a few years after the Kitson v. Playfair trial. In 1901 Jessie M'Ewan, who was undergoing the travails of both a nasty marital breakup and an unwanted pregnancy, called in the Edinburgh surgeon P. H. Watson to examine her. Watson (1832–1907), an expert in gynecology and honorary surgeon in Scotland to Queen Victoria, was to be knighted for his services in 1903.[92] In his private notes, the moralizing Watson took the trouble to record both the background to the patient's marriage problems and his advice that Jessie M'Ewan be sent to a nursing home to await her delivery. "This view not pleasing to patient nor to her father (who has married a second wife), and it seems they are all bent upon inducing premature labour so as to free the patient of any permanent reminder of this marriage, and, if possible obtain a separation."[93] Watson showed these notes to the solicitors of Jessie M'Ewan's husband and when the couple sought a divorce in 1903 appeared as a witness on his behalf. Jessie M'Ewan sued Watson for breach of confidence and slander. The case was fought all the way to the House of Lords, where Halsbury gave the leading judgment that what Watson told Mr. M'Ewan's solicitors was not actionable because it was both true and privileged.[94] Jessie M'Ewan had to bear both the heavy legal costs and the humiliating public exposure of her private affairs.

There was no doubt that Dr. Watson had violated the confidence of his patient. Jessie M'Ewan lost her suit because she emerged not as a long suffering female but as an angry and rebellious wife. There is equally little doubt about Linda Kitson's adultery, but her skilled counsel simply conjured it away. The public was willing, in the case of this pretty, persecuted woman, to believe in the possibility of a sixteen-month pregnancy.[95] Claiming all the while that in her "lightheaded" way she did not know what she was doing, Linda Kitson, in perfectly portraying the role of the female martyr, got away with adultery, perhaps abortion, and twelve thousand pounds as well.[96]

The press and laity thought that the Kitson v. Playfair trial had played an important role in establishing a clearer definition of doctors' duties as regards confidentiality.[97] This was, as we have seen, not true. Despite the general belief that doctors followed some elaborate secret code of ethics, the reality was, noted one 1905 commentator, that "obedience to the dictates of medical ethics implies application to the ordinary chances of professional life of the rule that a man should do as he would be done by."[98]

At the June 1920 meeting of the British Medical Association, a resolution urged its members to fight to keep confidential what they learned in their consulting rooms. Doctors opposed to such views immediately made their voices heard. One asked rhetorically if the physician was to remain blithely silent and indifferent when he knew that a male patient suffering from venereal disease risked infecting his innocent family. "Does that resolution mean this—that we are, as a profession, to allow a bounder to live and his wife and child to die?"[99]

In conjuring up the image of the chivalrous physician gallantly protecting a wife from her brutish husband, those arguing in favor of a doctor's right to decide when and if to divulge information were turning to an old ploy. Who could fail to respond to the call to protect women and children? But if doctors were simply relied upon to use their discretion and good sense in such matters, was it likely that most would turn their knowledge to the purposes of protecting the weak from the strong, women from men, servants from their masters? Doctors were asking to be to be trusted to act as gentlemen.[100] Although today one might say it is far from clear what this might mean, at the turn of the century such an appeal had real resonance.

"The age of chivalry is gone: that of sophisters, economists and calcula-

tors has succeeded: and the glory of Europe is extinguished."[101] So claimed
Edmund Burke at the end of the eighteenth century. Yet a hundred years
later, men were, if anything, even more entranced by the notion of selfless
acts of loyalty and sacrifice. Many middle-class men dreamed of what one
commentator has called "a return to Camelot" and paraded their distrust
of "cleverness" by ranking character ahead of intellect. In an evermore in-
dustrialized and bureaucratized world, it seemed all the more important to
believe that the amateur could out-do the hardened professional.[102] Chivalry tended to be domesticated in Britain and America, where "muscular
Christians" successfully promoted sport as a suitable demonstration of
masculine aggression and hardihood. But even the enduring popularity of
dueling in turn-of-the-century France and Germany was only another example of the more general desire of important segments of the bourgeoisie
to demonstrate that heroism was not restricted to aristocratic males.[103]
Only a coward would direct such aggressiveness at the "weaker sex"; indeed a concern for the protection of the "ladies" figured centrally in appeals to chivalry. This was not just rhetoric. Oppressive patriarchal power
began to give way in the last decades of the nineteenth century as those
sympathetic to women's rights castigated examples of the sort of excessive
male violence that were exposed in divorce court proceedings.[104] Given this
context the disaster awaiting Dr. Playfair was almost predictable.

It was only decades later that a variety of social critics began to assert
that the employment of appeals to gentleman morality largely served the
interest of elite males as a way of defending existing sexual and social hierarchies. Harold Laski, in an insightful 1932 essay entitled "The Dangers
of Being a Gentleman," pointed out that the cult of the "gentleman" flourished in the same age as the poor law and the sexual double standard. Laski
alerted his readers to the social exclusiveness and anti-intellectualism,
the conservatism and hypocrisy that were inherent components of "gentlemanly" ethics.[105] To assume that the accolade of gentleman had any potency, that chivalry had to be an inherent part of social interaction, meant
that one took as a given, indeed as "natural," that society was divided on
class lines between the powerful and the weak, the propertied and the prop-
ertyless, the respectable and the rough, and on gender lines between "gentlemen" and "ladies."

The contemporary embarrassment experienced in employing such terms
as lady and gentleman means that it takes some effort to appreciate the
power that these words had a century ago. As this chapter has indicated,
such was their resonance that though they chiefly served to justify the au-

thority of established hierarchies they could at times be turned, by the calculating, to serve as a cover for immoral or illegal practices. But such strategies can hardly be considered subversive; on the contrary Linda Kitson won precisely because she accepted the rules and played the game of "ladies and gentlemen" more successfully than Dr. Playfair.

FIVE

MURDERERS

FORCEFULNESS CONTINUED TO BE HAILED BY CONTEMPOR-
aries in the late nineteenth and early twentieth centuries as a crucial aspect
of male gender identity, while its counterpart, acquiescence or passivity,
was attributed to the female. But at what point did the forceful man become the violent brute? When could a lack of forcefulness brand one an
effeminate coward? One way of answering such questions is by using court
records that chronicled the recourse to the most extreme form of violence—murder. Judges and juries faced with such acts had to say, on the
behalf of the community, how far legitimate force could be pushed.[1]

Gender preoccupations obviously colored such deliberations. Yet the
fact that every jury decision did not win public approbation forcefully reminds us that the criminal justice system did not simply rubber-stamp public prejudices. Trial verdicts involving men were obviously not based solely
on the community's interpretation of masculinity. Those who served the
courts had their own agendas; their chief preoccupation was to oppose
threats to the rule of law. Proof that the accused had resorted to vigilantism
could accordingly counter any sympathy he might have garnered by demonstrations of manly assertiveness. Legal practitioners were naturally intent on demonstrating that cases were decided not on the basis of simple
community pressure but on the evidence presented. But when one exam-
ines the "evidence" advanced in the most serious cases, one is struck by
the inclusion of both hard facts and vague gender expectations. At a 1910
murder trial, one defense witness stated that the accused had "always
treated him like a man," a second testified that at the time of the killing the
accused had asserted that "a man has to defend his home," and the accused
himself recollected that when served with a warrant he had asked the special constable "why he had not produced it like a man."[2] Contemporaries
concurred that evidence that one had or had not acted "like a man" was
frequently crucial to a court's deliberations.

In addition to revealing how degrees of tolerable violence were carefully calibrated by communities in the past, the documentation generated by murder trials provides unusually intimate portrayals of male interactions.[3] According to an old maxim, men, unlike women, "do not like to talk," but the most taciturn, when put on trial for their lives, became loquacious. Such material, though obviously having to be used with caution—often the thoughts and actions of working-class men being interpreted for and by middle- and upper-class lawmen—nevertheless provides a priceless source for the investigation of the meanings given manhood.

In tackling such issues, the following chapter differs considerably from the previous. In turning from breach of confidence cases to murder trials, we will be moving from the relatively mundane to the most serious of conflicts. We will moreover be examining the confrontations, not of men with women, but simply of men with other men. And these men, be they murderers or victims, will be, unlike those of the previous chapters, very much alike, almost all being working class. A secure income and membership in a respectable profession represented for middle-class men like Dr. Playfair an important aspect of their notion of manliness. Laborers necessarily defined masculinity differently.

Because so much has already been written about murder and the male code of honor in Europe and the southern United States, we will focus on a series of trials that took place, so to speak, on the periphery of the Western world—in British Columbia, Canada's westernmost province.[4] In so abruptly shifting scenes, a number of purposes are served. First, the courtroom melodramas focusing on murder present the most dramatic examples of the importance of the accused being presented as either hero or villain. Second, popular mythology holds that the frontier was particularly prone to violence. We decided to chronicle the treatment of murder in the Pacific Northwest because it provides an especially interesting example of a region marked by British legal traditions, European immigration and American cultural influences. If, in this case study, despite the dramatic change in locale, personae, and crime, we find the now predictable constants—courts being swayed by a familiar melodramatic script with its invocation of the rights and duties of "manhood"—we will have attained some idea of the extent of the masculine mystique's pervasivness in both time and space.

Let us begin with a not atypical British Columbian killing that took place in Cranbrook, a small interior town, which lies on the western edge of the Rocky Mountain Trench, fifty miles north of the Montana border. At the turn of the century, most of its male inhabitants worked either for the Canadian Pacific Railway, which made the town a divisional point with round house and accommodations for train crews, or in lumbering. On 15 September 1915, Hugh McGill, a CPR shop employee, beat to death Samuel Watson, a former CPR brakeman. The inquest jury found that Watson "met his death from a fractured skull caused by falling against a verandah post through a blow struck by the accused, McGill."[5] The chief of police attributed McGill's attack to the fact that the twenty-five-year-old Watson "had been paying too much attention to his [McGill's] wife." Apparently a number of people in Cranbrook knew that Watson and Nellie McGill either had or were having an affair. They had exchanged letters. One read at the inquest, addressed to Sam and signed "Your devoted lover Nellie," referred to a past sexual relationship.[6]

McGill, knowing that Watson was coming to visit, lay in wait on the verandah and lashed out at his rival as soon as he knocked on the door. If there was a fight, it was very much one-sided. The accused was left with marks on his knuckles, but none on his face. The verandah post and the ground on which the victim lay were covered in blood. How had Watson died? A medical witness testified at the preliminary hearing that though the victim had been drinking, falling from the verandah and hitting his head on a post could not alone have caused death. An examination of the deceased suggested that he had been hit about the head with a blunt object three or four times.

Once Watson was down in a pool of blood, McGill's first thought was not to summon medical aid, but to fetch his friend, Percy Adams, the chief of police. McGill, though excited, was clear-headed enough to be already framing his defense. "You remember the man I told you about last year? . . . Well I got him. Come and see where he is. I will show you where he is." Adams on seeing the body called for a doctor and arrested McGill. Told by the police that his victim had died and warned to watch what he was saying, McGill replied: "It was coming to him. It was in self defense."

The Cranbrook courthouse, where McGill's preliminary proceedings in September and his trial in October took place, was packed with his friends.[7] The crown counsel informed the attorney general's office that the accused enjoyed "a great deal of public sympathy."[8] Nevertheless the prosecution proceeded with the case, arguing that McGill had to pay a price for being the aggressor in a fight that ended in death. The defense countered that Watson—though warned—had refused to stay away from the McGill house, made threats, and on the fatal night struck first with a riding crop. McGill now claimed that he simply defended himself and in the ensuing melee Watson accidentally fell backward and hit his head. The spectators, by their applause for the defense summation, made their loyalties known.

The jury was out no more than thirty minutes before returning a verdict of not guilty. Why had McGill been acquitted? The short answer is because he acted in a way that the community considered appropriate for a man. Murder was a desperate act, but it was understood that in a given situation a man had the right to kill.

An analysis of British Columbian trial and inquest reports for the years 1900 to 1923 provides a fuller answer to the questions of how, where, and why men killed other men. The first section of this chapter will deal with the how and the where—that is, account for the number, location. and means of killings. Section two will focus on the trickier issue of why. There can be little doubt that because of the way gender concerns patterned the use of violence, it was more "normal" for men than for women to resort to deadly force. Beginning with the premise that certain forms of male violence were sanctioned by the courts, we will see what murder trials tell us about the social construction of masculinity. When could forcefulness be pushed so far as to justify a homicide? Was murder necessarily a cowardly act? Were there "manly" ways of killing? What in short—according to judges, policemen, jurymen, lawmen, and newspapermen—did it mean to be a man?

Despite the fact that British Columbia at the turn of the century could be considered in many ways a frontier society, its murder rate was not exceptionally high. Germany and England's rates were less than 1 per 100,000 while those in the United States ranged from 6 per 100,000 in the Northeast to 28 per 100,000 in the Southwest. British Columbia's rate, like southern Europe's, was about 5 per 100,000.[9] The overwhelming majority of British Columbian killers were, as in the McGill case, men. In western Canada as elsewhere, then as now, men were far more likely than women to have recourse to violence.[10] Moreover, in the early decades of this century, British Columbia, like other pioneering communities, experienced a serious sex ratio imbalance, men far outnumbering women.[11] Between 1900 and 1923, 270 men and only eighteen women were cited in murder cases. Males also dominated as victims. Two hundred and twenty-one men were killed, but only thirty-five women.

This disparity between male and female murder rates is confirmed by the figures drawn from inquest records on unsolved and untried murders. Of the 205 victims who died in suspicious circumstances, 164 were men and forty-one were women. The sex of the majority of the assailants (149) was unknown, but of the known assailants (who usually had avoided trial by escaping, dying in jail, or committing suicide) fifty-one were men and only four were women.[12]

In the years we have examined, 214 men were the victims of male murderers. As in the McGill case, men "normally" killed other men of the same class and ethnicity. The "typical murder" involved a male (likely drunk) killing an acquaintance, friend, or workmate. Murders were endogenous. To kill outside of one's class, gender, or ethnic group was highly unusual. Male assaults on women obviously played a part in the construction of the masculine role, but the difficulties faced by a man who attacked a woman in defining his manhood will not be traced here.[13] In what follows we attempt to understand the meanings given masculinity in early twentieth-century British Columbia by examining the murders of men carried out by white working-class males (many of them immigrants), the justifications they provided for their acts, and the responses made to them by the courts and the press. The murders carried out by aboriginal and Asian men will not be treated here except in passing, in part because different ethnic groups might well have had different views of masculinity, but primarily because the prejudicial treatment the courts accorded members of visible minorities deserves more extensive analysis. Killings of and by women will, for similar reasons, also be set to one side.

Where were men killed? Both McGill and his victim worked for the railway. A grand jury noted in 1904 that murder "may, perhaps, be attributed to the floating population following railway construction."[14] A commonplace, often repeated by the press, was that a mobile, male culture served as a natural breeding ground for violence. But the point usually missed by contemporary observers was that such communities were more stable than they often appeared to outsiders. Killers were rarely strangers; men were mainly murdered by those whom they knew—men with whom they lived, worked, and played. Setting aside the cases in which women were the victims and the murders committed by native peoples and Asians, the reports reveal that in 130 cases the relationship of the white male murderer to the male victim was:

Acquaintance	38.5%
Friend, neighbor, boarder	27.7%
Stranger	18.5%
Workmate, employee, employer	12.3%
Relative	3.0%

Most men worked together in what were largely single-sex industries. The peaceful workplace could suddenly become a murder site. Guns and knives—the most common instruments of death—were readily at hand in the bush, on homesteads, and on ranches, but fists, boots, and ordinary tools also sufficed as weapons. Miners were bludgeoned to death, fishermen knifed or drowned, loggers' skulls split by axes, soldiers shot. A typical scenario saw a Greek fisherman meet his fate in a boat in Plumper's Pass off Vancouver Island. According to the accused: "I told him to get out and not come into my boat but just the same he jumps in the boat all right and grabbed me by the throat from behind. I bent forward and I was drunk myself and he had me down; I had a knife in my hand; the knife I had was one we had for cutting bread, cleaning fish or anything, one we used on the boat, the knife was about as long as this sheet of paper. . . . I don't know how he got the cut; I was lying down and he was on top of me; I think he must have stept [sic] on it himself in the row."[15] Murders at the workplace usually saw laborers turning on each other, but firing an employee could provoke similar violence. A storehouseman at the Esquimalt Naval Yard, dismissed in 1903 for negligence, retaliated by emptying his pistol at his supervisor.[16] In 1912 it was the Canadian Northern Railway gang foreman Barney Mulligan who killed an irate worker, who made the mistake of screaming at him in the camp kitchen, "You old bull shitter, you are no good, you come outside and I'll fix you up for what you did yesterday, you Irish son of a bitch."[17] Mulligan, who had dismissed the worker the day before, then struck him.

Men not only worked together, many lived together.[18] Criminologists often draw a distinction between "domestic" murders involving men and their families and "public" murders involving mainly men. But in British Columbia in the early decades of the century, such clear cut distinctions could not always be made. Murder trial accounts of six Chinese workers sharing a shack in Steveston, six Italian laborers bunking together in a house in Vancouver, and three drunken prospectors holed up in a cabin at Summit Camp captured the suffocating atmosphere of men piled up together both day and night, getting on each others' nerves, enjoying little privacy, and having nowhere to escape. Men were crammed together on fish boats and railway bunk cars and in isolated cabins and shacks, forced to endure either each others' company in the shared accommodations of thin-walled rooming-houses or the inquisitiveness of the suspicious families with whom they boarded. Large numbers slept in the barracks provided for soldiers and sappers and the bunkhouses for loggers, railwaymen, and road gangs.[19] Privacy was not even found in bed. In 1915 two Ruthenian laborers working on the Canadian National Railway tunnel at Mile 127, having opposite shifts but sharing the same bunk, eventually came to blows.[20]

Some sense of how the day-to-day tensions of such claustrophobic situations could escalate into violence was conveyed in the diary of Frederick Trumper, who in 1907 shared a tiny cabin at Pouce Coupe with an increasingly cantankerous sixty-year-old trapper.

Oct. 15th   Had talk with Coleman on his grouchiness.
Oct. 27th   Coleman is on one of his cranky spells again.
Nov. 10th   Coleman is on a tear again.
Nov. 18th   Coleman is now talking of moving out.

Unfortunately for Trumper, Coleman did not leave; instead on November 25 Coleman came at him with a rifle, and in warding him off with a mallet, Trumper delivered a fatal blow.[21]

Laborers may not have had the same desires as the middle class for privacy, but some single men would have liked at the least the option of living on their own; given the lack of public facilities, it was rarely possible. The irony was that the vast expanses of "frontier" wilderness often offered newcomers less privacy or anonymity than the larger cities of either the East Coast or Europe.

Men not only worked and lived together, their leisure time activities, especially drinking and gambling, were mainly shared with other men.[22] For many, to be a man was to drink. "The deceased was a pretty good man," said an Italian of a compatriot, "he drank just enough to keep him in grand shape."[23] Alcohol played a precipitating role in about half the murders.

And where did murders—usually of friends and acquaintances—occur? If not at the workplace, shack, or campsite, then the likelihood was wherever liquor was available. The hotel bar or saloon was usually the village or town's most important all-male institution. Male leisure pursuits were pursued in public. Murders frequently followed drinking bouts—at the Victoria Hotel in Vernon (1901 and 1908), at the bar room of Starke's Hotel, Peterborough (1901), outside the Germania Saloon in Victoria (1902), at the St. Elmo's Hotel at Trail (1907), Kirby's Hotel in Keremeos (1907), the Palace Hotel in Vancouver (1908), the Manhattan Saloon in Nelson (1911), the Queen's Hotel in Kamloops (1913), the New Telkwa Hotel in Telkwa (1913, 1915), and the Empress Hotel in Prince George (1921). Bartenders, often the only sober bystanders at such encounters, consequently found themselves being called as witnesses at inquests and trials.[24]

The court records describe the extensive popular vocabulary employed to describe drinking to excess. One man's dying declaration began with the line, "I am dying. I got full the day after pay day and Ed Morella threw a rock at my head and no one saw him throw it."[25] Victims and murderers were said to be "full," "on a spree," "wobbly," "under the influence," "quarrelsome in his cups," "mad drunk," "fighting drunk," and "absolutely inebriated, good and drunk." Participants in such drinking sessions could not always be sure that what began as parties or celebrations and degenerated into quarrels, "friendly scuffles," and brawls might not end in murder. One prospector recalled that seven or eight bottles of whiskey were consumed by half a dozen men at a Cariboo country get-together. "I left and that was the last I know of it, except the howling and screeching and shooting all night long as there was lots of noise."[26] Despite the commotion he was genuinely surprised to discover the next morning that his friends and partners' party had culminated in bloodshed. So too was the acquaintance of two trappers who exchanged shots in 1911: "they were good friends except when they were drinking."[27]

Although A. W. Vowell, superintendent of Indian Affairs in British Columbia, placed the blame for the high number of native murders on the presence of liquor, no group seemed to be immune.[28] But the importance of drink was possibly exaggerated. Claiming to have been drunk and not remembering what had happened was a convenient excuse for those who could think of no other. James Dale blamed drink for his 1906 shooting up of the town of Carmi, which resulted in two deaths.[29] Likewise, Charles Egan claimed: "The first time I knew a man had been killed was the next day Tuesday. Prisoner told me I had killed a man. When I first heard it I got sick."[30] "I got full," claimed a third murderer, "and can't remember anything after."[31] "I was full at the time," lamented Albert McDougal, who had killed his brother. "I don't remember how this thing happened."[32] Such defenses were usually successful in at least reducing a charge from murder to manslaughter and were accordingly trotted out again and again— though a witness said of a gunner who in 1910 killed his captain at Victoria's Work Point barracks, "It is the dope that does it."[33] In 1908 the manufacture and sale of opium was banned in Canada but at least as late as 1914 was still freely available, even in jail.[34]

The most common type of murder resulted from friends' or workmates' arguments escalating, under the influence of drink, into a trading of insults and finally to violence. Something as trivial as a rivalry in banjo playing led Frederick Collins in 1901 to kill Arthur Dando, better known as the Banjo Kid.[35] Sometimes the tension between friends rose over the course of months if not years; on other occasions it flared up after a drink or two. Such killings were rarely premeditated. Seven January 1914 began with Serre Coval and Andrew Charnot, two Russians working on railway construction near Thompson's Crossing, celebrating Russian Orthodox Christmas; it ended with Coval shooting Charnot.[36] John Doherty's last words, said of a fellow hospital orderly in 1919, were, "It is all right, he is afraid to press the trigger."[37] John Casey, a soldier in a forestry battalion, when told in 1917 that he had killed a comrade, drunkenly retorted, "Oh, he's all right, he's only fooling."[38] But he was not. "Get up Ernie, you son of a bitch," bellowed Charles Neff at his best friend, whom he floored on 11 August 1913 with a welding hammer, "You are not dead."[39] But he was. Scrapping and fighting were customary means by which assertions of masculinity were made by men who could pride themselves on little more than their muscle power. If such brawls escalated and blood was shed, they became a sort of lottery; who murdered whom depended largely on chance. It was less a matter of chance in the cases of the one or two "psychopaths" who killed more than once. Rocco Farrante, an obviously insane Italian B.C. Electric Railway laborer, who was found not guilty of the shooting death of a friend in November 1915, the next month decapitated his roommate.[40] In 1918 John Walsh, who had previously served seven years in prison for manslaughter in his native New Brunswick, was sentenced to death for the murder of a fellow logger.[41]

When strangers were murdered, it was often the unintended consequence of planned but bungled robberies. In 1911 the owner of the Manhattan Saloon in Nelson and in 1912 the owner of a Vancouver liquor store were murdered during robbery attempts.[42] Mike Popovich's sudden prosperity in 1914 linked him to the robbery and murder of a Russian laborer near Endako.[43] In Vancouver three Scots' attempt to stick up a bootlegger ended in the latter's death in 1919,[44] two Irishmen killed a logger for his money in 1920,[45] and a deaf man's failure to understand two thieves' order to "stick 'em up" led to his death in 1921.[46] Finally two teenage muggers' "warning shot" killed a Victoria bank clerk in 1923.[47]

The police killed, of course, but as their deeds were not treated as murder, they will not be examined here. But lawmen were also numbered among those killed. At two in the morning of 29 August 1914, a disheveled Mickey McKillarney told a friend that "he had a shooting scrape and he thought he had croaked a bull." Lawmen stood out as the usual victims of the handful of murders carried out by professional criminals. William Haney, an American bank and train robber, in 1909 shot to death a special constable outside Ashcroft and successfully got away.[48] In 1912 Walter James killed a police guard on board the steamer *Okanagan* while attempting to escape custody, and constable Lewis J. Byers died in a shootout in Vancouver. The same year at the New Westminster Penitentiary, two convicts, in the course of a jail break, murdered a prison guard.[49] In 1913 Henry Wagner and William Julian (Americans who were purportedly old members of Butch Cassidy's gang) shot to death a special constable who had surprised them during a robbery at Union Bay.[50] In May of 1913 a constable was the victim of two Vancouver robbers evading a police search.[51] One of the most famous murders of a lawman occurred in 1914 in Vancouver, when following the Komagata Maru affair (which involved the authorities' forcible prevention of the landing of a boatload of Sikh immigrants), Mewa Singh gunned down immigration officer William Hopkinson in the city courthouse.[52] The second police killing of 1914 in Vancouver took place when Mickey McKillarney, the ex-convict noted above, shot a detective.[53] In June 1914 a police constable was killed in Kamloops by a person or persons unknown.[54] In 1917 Malcolm McLennan, Vancouver's chief of police, died in a shoot-out with Bob Tait, a small-time African-American drug dealer.[55] Fred Deal, another black man, in 1922 killed a Vancouver police officer while resisting arrest.[56]

But murders resulting from run-ins with the police and bungled robberies represented only a small fraction of all cases. Most killings were precipitated, as we have seen, by quarrels and arguments. A threat to one's livelihood—which jeopardized both a man's property and honor—could also result in a death. Such struggles might involve the control of scarce resources. In 1908 Vernon farmers fatally fought over irrigation water.[57] Long feuds between Cariboo ranchers over gates and grazing rights ended in bloodshed in 1920 and 1923.[58] Yet when conflicts over property led to violence, they were more likely to be over the ownership of such things as guns, watches, bottles of liquor, sacks of potatoes, and sides of beef, in which the struggle between men was as much if not more over power, honor, and self-respect than for the paltry goods in question. Generally speaking thefts were not important in precipitating deaths; men murdered to defend challenges to their manhood.[59]

We have seen where deaths occurred and have some idea of why men killed each other. Once arrested what arguments did they employ as justifications for their acts? What responses were made to them by the courts and the press? At this stage what had often been private confrontations were suddenly made public. In theory those who had not intended to kill or whose assault had been provoked should have had their charge reduced from murder to manslaughter. In practice those who had murdered in the course of a robbery or in a fight with a lawman could, no matter what their defense, expect to receive short shrift. The six white men who between 1900 and 1923 were tried for the murder of a law-enforcement officer were each found guilty and sentenced to death.[60] But when it came to more typical murders, questions of intent and provocation were of crucial legal importance; it was understood that in struggles over honor and in defense of one's family a good man might be forced to kill. Had the accused, the public wanted to know, been sufficiently provoked? This was a life-and-death question. If the accused did not know what "he had to say" he was no doubt soon informed by his counsel. Generally agreed-on notions of masculinity played a key role in the community determining whether or not the accused had acted like "a man" or like an effeminate sneak, whether he should go free or be punished, and if punished, whether lightly or severely. Such gender concerns were especially evident in sex-related murders, but played a part in the presentation of every conflict that pitted one man against another. The courts, aware of the dangers frontier life posed for men, were not unsympathetic even to such venerable gambits as that essayed by a Dutch pre-emptor (or homesteader) who shot his partner in 1915: "I did not know the gun was loaded."[61] But the guilt or innocence of the accused largely depended—when the issues of class and ethnicity were not of primary concern—on what the court thought of a man's character, the situation in which he claimed he had to defend himself, the fairness of the fight, and his respect for the law.

Courts carefully scrutinized the character of both the accused and the victim. How was a man's character determined? Though testimony that the accused was truthful, temperate, and law-abiding was diligently recorded, the courts seemed particularly taken by the notion that a man's morality could be judged by his attitude toward work. A bad worker, it was assumed, was a bad man. Such aspersions were often cast on the dead, who were not there to defend themselves. Arthur Dando, shot to death in 1901, was disparagingly described by the chief constable of Peterborough as "formerly a bugler in the North West Mounted Police, a young man of inferior character disliking work."[62] Another murder victim was reported to have been "a heavy, powerful fellow, who did no work, but lived by card playing and 'bootlegging' and was constantly looking for trouble."[63] An Italian laborer charged with murder in 1910 shrewdly claimed that he was provoked into fighting by a man who, lazily dropping his tools, had bragged, "We don't give a damn for the job and I don't care to work."[64] To be work-shy, it was understood, was unworthy of a real man; or at least of any man who was considered a member of the working class.

A good worker was assumed to be a good man. Witnesses were constantly asked to comment on the work ethic of the accused. A policeman was quizzed regarding a prisoner charged with a 1901 Victoria murder:

Q. You found him a quiet orderly man?
A. Yes.
Q. A hardworking fellow?
A. Yes.

In 1915 a judge recommended that a bridgeworker, whose single punch had caused the death of a drinking partner, be given a suspended sentence. Despite the fact that the accused had been previously fined for fighting, the judge concluded "character evidence shows [he is a] good workman."[65] A constable at a 1917 inquest who began his testimony with the assertion that the accused was "a hard worker" appeared to regret having to add "but [he] has a crazy streak in him."[66] To be able to present oneself as "steady and industrious" was vitally important for any man on trial. The press's description of the accused in a 1921 trial as "a young man of frank and clean cut features . . . hardworking and honest" was a clear signal of the community's belief in his innocence.[67]

The hardworking individual presumably would have neither the time nor inclination to go about picking fights. But the notion that a reasonable man could not simply walk away from every provocation with full self-respect provided the basis for the argument of self-defense. "I shot Frank Martin," declared the accused in a 1919 trial, "first because I was afraid of him for he was twice my size. Secondly, because he was a bully. Thirdly, because he had threatened me, and fourthly, because he was a pro-German, unscrupulous, and a menace to the crown and government."[68] The protestations of nationalist concern, presumably tacked on because the Great War had just ended, today ring jarringly false. A more believable presentation was made on behalf of Murdock Campbell, who beat to death a fellow Scots miner. Campbell, so his friends claimed, in leaving a drinking establishment, had tried his best to avoid a confrontation with a bully. "The abuse was enough to make some men get up and fight. The prisoner in getting up and going out was subjecting himself to the taunt of being a coward."[69] A reasonable man could only take so much; the victim in pursuing Campbell was at fault. Campbell was found not guilty. Charles Egan's supporters likewise testified that he had been goaded into attacking his friend William Shiells: "Shiells was using bad language calling him a son of a bitch and a cock sucker. He was trying to provoke Charlie to fight."[70]

If things came to blows, it was expected that you would "take your medicine like a man." Implicit in such an attitude was the egalitarian notion that in a physical confrontation every man, no matter how humble his rank or status, had the opportunity of proving his masculinity.[71] But a "fair fight" was one in which the odds were judged to be even. Frank Nicolas, who stabbed a fellow Greek fisherman, protested, "If I hadn't killed him, he would have killed me."[72] Guiseppe Bianca, a stone mason who knifed a bricklayer, similarly argued that he had only defended himself.[73] But in each case, the accused had a knife and his victim did not. Nicolas was sentenced to five years in prison and Bianca to seven.[74]

The male community often made clear its views of such murderous encounters. Most of the witnesses were men who may have egged on the participants and at the very least provided an audience that judged the morality of the melodrama played out before them. When James McGill des Rivières for no apparent reason in a drunken quarrel stabbed to death his friend Harry Rowand, his argument of self-defense was accepted. The *Greenwood Weekly Times* explained, "Public opinion here is strongly in favor of the prisoner."[75] These things happened. But when a sixty-six-year-old man shot a sixty-year-old Vernon friend for making fun of him, a witness noted that the accused "showed more anger and excitement than the matter would warrant, more than I have ever known in him."[76] Similar negative community sentiment was expressed in 1913 in the small Cariboo village of Freeport. The cigar store keeper reported that Mulvihill "said he heard I accused him of shooting Kelly. I told him I had not expressed my opinion . . . but all the boys thought so."[77] The courts responded to the community's condemnation and found the accused guilty.

There was little judicial sympathy for the man who, claiming he had no where else to turn, actually launched a premeditated attack. Such was the case when Frederick Collins, whose house had been broken into, declared, "I want to see a magistrate as I want some satisfaction. If I cannot get satisfaction from a magistrate, I have got means of satisfying myself."[78] He then killed the purported intruder. Similarly a Vernon farmer who killed a neighbor claimed he had no choice. "He said that the law did not protect him and he would have to protect himself."[79] The courts made clear by imposing heavy punishments that they did not approve of such preemptive forms of self-defense.

The accused who measured up to the model of the hard-working individual who tried to avoid violence and fought fairly when he had no other
recourse, even if he had caused a death, stood a good chance of walking
away from court a free man. His chances were further improved if it could
be successfully argued that his adversary's actions had threatened the accused's very "manhood."

Fear of physical violence was used to justify murder; so too was men's
fear of sexual violence. Early-twentieth-century British Columbia was very
much a male world, for some a "homosocial" world. Even in bed a man
could be attacked. An Italian worker asleep in a bunkhouse, who found
himself "picked up blanket and all" from his cot, in a rage shot to death
the camp bully and went free.[80] This particular case had no obvious sexual
overtones, but it is not surprising that references to homosexual acts should
occasionally emerge from the murder records. The way in which they were
treated tells us good deal about how far one could go in defending one's
heterosexual masculinity.

On 13 October 1901 in the canteen of the Work Point Barracks just
outside Victoria, Harold Gill, a twenty-year-old English sapper in the Royal
Engineers, shot and killed Garland Clinnick, a gunner in the Royal Garrison Artillery. It was an accident; Gill, a poor shot, had meant to kill gunner
Mahoney, who was sitting next to the unfortunate Clinnick. Gill's defense
was that he had been "goaded into desperation" by rumors spread by his
fellow soldiers of a homosexual relationship he had had with Mahoney.[81]

Gill and Mahoney, both being members of the garrison band, had participated the week before in celebrating the leaving for England of the
Royal Horse Artillery. After an all night drunken party at the St. George's
Inn, they had been seen asleep together on a couch with only their shirts
on. Gill was thereafter unmercifully teased. "Look out, this man belongs
to the band" and "Look out, here's Mahoney's pal" greeted the blushing
Gill wherever he went. A comrade who admitted participating in the gos-
siping and teasing later protested "nothing I told him would lead him to
believe that an unnatural offense had been committed against him." Nevertheless Gill broke down under his tormentors' relentless hazing and apparently believed that he had been sodomized. How do you prove that you are
a heterosexual? Gill, in order to reassert his manhood, sought to kill not
the persecuting troublemakers but the fellow victim of this gossip, his purported homosexual seducer, Mahoney. Gill, by attacking Mahoney (following the advice of one or two friends who clearly put him up to it),
thought he could thereby demonstrate beyond doubt that he was not a
homosexual.

This incident says something about how serious the charge of being a homosexual could be taken in an all-male environment.[82] Some in the garrison no doubt thought it was a joking matter, but others believed it could justify murder. Gill, described immediately after the shooting as "excited and hysterical," cried that he would "rather be dead than dishonored." His demeanor and rhetoric, implied observers, manifested the very gender inversion he claimed to fear and loath. He bitterly regretted killing Clinnick and had no qualms about making it abundantly clear that when he raised his carbine his intention had been to murder Mahoney. At the ensuing trial, Gill's defense attorney pursued the argument that Gill's tragic act was understandable, if not entirely forgivable, because "he had been or believed himself to be, the victim of a monstrous indignity at Mahoney's hands." Indeed, the defense argued, Mahoney was the real culprit, a man who lied about the events at the St. George's Inn, who sought "to conceal his guilt." Gill, who had suffered an "outrage to his manhood," had, his lawyer argued, simply acted in "a blind instant of passion." This brazen attempt to argue that a homosexual act was worse than murder did not work for the simple reason that there was no proof that such an act had ever taken place. Gill, found guilty of the manslaughter death of the "innocent" Clinnick, was sentenced to fifteen years imprisonment.[83]

The verdict did not mean that the seriousness of the "disgraceful acts" committed by homosexuals was in any way diminished in the eyes of the court. Sodomy was still a crime. Even some heterosexual acts were regarded by the bar as perverse. The judge at a 1906 murder trial refused to allow evidence to be admitted of the accused's "peculiar sexual desires" (for cunnilingus). Such evidence, his lordship said, would "tend to indicate insanity."[84] In the Gill case, one suspects that if the accused had, as he intended, killed Mahoney a much lighter punishment would have been imposed. With Mahoney not in court to defend himself, a skilled counsel might well have succeeded, given the taunts and sneers that the subject of homosexuality elicited, in blaming the victim for his own murder.

Just such a defense was called into play on 22 October 1907, when Edward Bowen, a young English laborer, shot and killed Paratreap Singh at the Spokane Rooming House in Vancouver. The two men had only met that day at the bar of the Alexander Hotel. After drinks the new-found friends returned to Singh's room, a shot was heard, and a white man was seen running away. A policeman tracked Bowen down a few streets over from Singh's rooming house. "And the boy said he shot the Hindoo. . . . And he said 'Will I show you the place where the Hindoo was?' . . . And he told me that he had shot the Hindoo, and that the Hindoo had tried to commit an indecent act."[85] A friend of the accused corroborated the story that the Hindoo "tried to bugger him [Bowen]." Was this the case, or had Bowen attempted to rob Singh of the two hundred dollars he was reputed to have? The press laid out the options in a headline reading, "Bowen's Honor or Hindu's Purse."

Ironically, for a trial that focused on masculine honor, the defense asserted that "a man has the same right as a woman and was justified in taking a life to protect his honor."[86] Bowen and his counsel believed that the community's revulsion against homosexuality was such that the claim of having been sexually attacked held out to the accused the best hope of getting away with murder.[87] But once again, as in the Gill case, the prosecution succeeded in showing that there was no evidence of a homosexual attack; indeed there was much to suggest that Bowen's story had been contrived to cover his crime. He was convicted of manslaughter and sentenced to ten years in prison. As in the Gill case, Bowen's conviction did not signify a downplaying of the dangers posed by homosexuality. The public was left to understand that a homosexual advance might justify recourse to murder; the problem was that the attorneys in both trials had failed to convince the juries of the reality of such attacks on their clients' honor.

Such questions of loss of "honor" more commonly figured in men's struggles over women. Some men tried to seize other men's property; some men tried to carry off those who in common parlance were referred to as other men's women.[88] Although by the twentieth century women had been granted property rights, the commonplace assumption still held that a man owned both his wife's earnings and the wife as well. Latter-day notions of chivalry, which held that if a man had a right to defend himself he had a duty to defend his woman, were repeatedly and successfully used to justify murder. Leo English, found not guilty of murder in 1901, employed just a variant of this defense when charged with the shooting death of his brother-in-law. English claimed to be protecting his sister from her husband, who was treating her badly. The victim, disliked in Vernon as a dangerous drunk, attacked English with a stick and English shot him. A witness, although accidentally wounded in the melee, backed up the accused with the claim, "If ever a man had justification English had, to shoot."[89]

More typical was the case of a husband asserting that he had been forced to kill to protect his wife. In 1904 Louis Gillier was found not guilty of the murder of a logger whom the Frenchman had shot twice with a shotgun. Gillier's story was that the gun had gone off accidentally while he was attempting to free his wife from the drunken embraces of the victim.[90]

In 1905 Ole Oleson's shotgun killing of George Holcroft led to a not guilty verdict after Oleson's wife testified that Holcroft "pulled my clothes to pieces and hit me in the breast."[91] In 1921 the same verdict was rendered for a similar case on Moresby Island in which a man forced his attentions on a friend's spouse. Such actions were, declared the press, "ample provocation for the desperate deed."[92] The inquest jury was so impressed by the testimony of a Vancouver man who shot to death his wife's ex-pimp that he was not even indicted. The fact that the victim was an African-American who broke into the accused's home and attacked him no doubt played a role in the mercy shown.[93]

What if, as in the case of adultery, the wife did not want to be protected from the other man?[94] If a love triangle led to murder, the husband was usually the murderer and the lover or wife the victim, but on occasion the male roles were reversed. Louis Paquette killed Alfred Legère in order to obtain his wife. Paquette, Olive Legère testified, "was telling me that he loved me. He has been telling me that for nearly three years. He told me he was going to shoot me the next time I went to Notch Hill." Paquette's story was that "his passion became unbearable and he made up his mind to kill the husband and wife and then kill himself."[95] This violation of the family resulted in a death sentence. Similarly, in 1913 Bruno Cutri, who, while attempting to run off with Maria Diatella, killed her brother-in-law, was sentenced to death.[96]

But on occasion there were special circumstances in which "the other man" was not convicted. In 1910 Harriet Carlson's abusive husband was strangled by someone who broke into their house. The evidence pointed to an ex lodger with whom she was friendly, but the prosecution could not produce enough evidence to convince the jury.[97] In 1912 twenty-year-old Harold McNaughton successfully avoided going to jail for the accidental beating death of his woman friend's husband. McNaughton apparently had acted in self-defense but was unwise enough to pay the young woman to leave town. Given such suspicious behavior, why was he treated so leniently? The fact that he was the son of a leading Vancouver socialite and one of the few members of British Columbia's middle class to face a murder charge probably had an effect.[98] One might also assume that his age had something to do with it since McNaughton was described in the press as "a West End youth." But class and age were linked. A middle-class twenty-year-old male was referred to as a "boy" or "youth," a working-class twenty-year-old as a man. And McNaughton's sixteen-year-old woman friend, the wife of an iron worker, was never referred to as a "girl."

When adultery led to murder, the most common resolution and the safest course as far as the accused was concerned was, as in the Hugh McGill case, for the husband to kill the lover. In 1906 Charles Johnson was found near the dead body of his lodger yelling, so a witness recalled, "he would learn somebody to come around to try to fuck his wife." Hilda Johnson testified that her husband had been drinking all night: "My husband came into the front room and then he come and sit on the edge of the bed and I was laying in the bed and then he said 'somebody will be killed tonight.' Then he said for me to get up in the middle of the floor and then he'll kill me and then I jumped over the foot of the bed. When he was sitting on the edge of the bed he had a gun and put two cartridges into it. . . . I called 'John bring the revolver, he'll kill us. . . .' In a minute or very quickly after John came into the room the shot went off." Johnson did not deny the fact that his gun caused the lodger's death, but he claimed that he had been having "trouble with my wife. . . . She said she had been sleeping with John." And that it was her who, in trying to grab his gun, caused it to discharge and kill the lodger.[99] The defense was successful.

An even more dramatic example of the lenient treatment accorded to an enraged husband was provided in a 1919 Prince George trial. The accused's statement was clear enough.

> I said to Mast I understand you are going to take my wife away and break up my family. He said it is none of your damned business if I am, and started to abuse me and call me names and came towards me with his fists clenched and said he would make me eat smoke before he had done with me. I knew there was a rifle in the blacksmith shop so I stepped inside and took up the gun, which was standing in the corner. When he saw me with the gun he ran towards the sleigh, as soon as I saw him running I threw up the rifle and shot at him. When I fired he dropped to the sleigh and started pulling at the blankets in the sleigh and, as I thought he was getting at his gun I fired again and then a third time; at the third shot he fell to the ground.[100]

Although he fired three bullets into his rival's back, the fact that the farmer immediately gave himself up was enough to convince the court of his good intentions; he was found not guilty. In such cases the wife would often be the star witness, but on at least one occasion the defense was successful in arguing that she could not, because of her status under the Canada Evidence Act, testify against her husband. He accordingly went free.[101]

All the evidence suggests that a husband who murdered to keep his woman stood a very good chance of getting away with it. But the British Columbia courts did not extend the right of surveillance of the wife—as might have been the case in other cultures—to the husband's friends or relatives.

In 1922 a Swiss immigrant ranching in the Kootenays, in order to "redeem one's woman's honor," shot to death the man bothering his wife. When he was declared not guilty, the local press noted that "while the letter of the law was lost sight of by the jury their verdict was a just one." The judge was not so sure and told the accused that it was "in some ways incomprehensible to me they have found you not guilty." [102] But why should the judge have been surprised? Although judges on more than one occasion warned that they did not want to see "southern justice"—that is, American vigilantism—become common in Canada, in practice the courts repeatedly gave credence to the notion that the "protection of the home" could justify murder.[103]

We can conclude, as we began, with the Hugh McGill case. In it the court made explicit its acceptance of a husband's right to use deadly force to ward off sexual competitors. McGill acted like a "real man" in defending the patriarchal family and his ownership of his wife by murdering the man to whom she was attracted. McGill's sanity was never questioned; his morals were never disparaged. Indeed the judge congratulated McGill on his acquittal and, in case anyone should have misread the jury's findings, reminded the court that the not guilty verdict served as "a salutary warning to any man who in future sets out with the purpose of destroying another man's home." [104]

PART TWO OF THIS STUDY HAS BEEN DEVOTED TO DETERMINING THE WAYS in which the courts contributed to the social construction of masculinity. In our earlier chapters we saw how the melodramatic scripts that set the bounder against the bar maid and the gentleman against the lady could be played out. In a murder trial it was also obviously crucially important for the defendant to avoid being presented as the cad or villain. The model male who emerges from the trial transcript and press reports was the honorable, hard-working, fair-fighting individual who was loath to take the law into his own hands. But as law-abiding as he was, the courts warned interlopers that judges and juries would back up his right to employ violence against those who attacked his honor or violated his home. This was, of course, not new. The same arguments had been made in previous centuries. That men in Europe and North America should have turned more readily than women to murder is hardly surprising and certainly does not require the assumption of any innate masculine aggressiveness. Men were supposed to be forceful; they were repeatedly instructed by the courts and the press that in some situations their recourse to violence would not only be condoned but applauded.

Researchers who have plotted the evolution of definitions of maleness tell us that in the late nineteenth and early twentieth centuries there was a perceptible shift away from the cult of rugged masculinity and toward a new model of "masculine domesticity."[105] But these findings, though suggestive, are based primarily on the prescriptive literature that laid out the duties of the middle-class, suburbanized male. Did the new middle-class ideals filter down to the working class? And is one talking about real changes in behavior or only in cultural stereotypes? A convincing account of the shifting boundaries of appropriate masculine behavior is unlikely to be attained as long as research is restricted to traditional literary sources. The sources examined in this chapter—the records generated by the criminal justice system—have as yet gone largely untapped but, dealing as they so often did with men's use of violence against other men, greatly enhance our understanding of popular notions of masculinity.

We have found little evidence in early-twentieth-century British Columbia of the purported transition from the cult of rugged masculinity to that of "masculine domesticity." A softer image of masculinity might well have been emerging in eastern advice manuals, but in western courts there was more evidence of continuity than of change. Much aggressive and violent male behavior was judged not to be deviant but normal. That was perhaps to be expected, given that the ranks of the accused were not filled by middle-class, suburbanized males. Moreover the erosion of sharp lines of gender differentiation, a development associated with the rise of secondary industry and the growth of the service sector, was unlikely to occur in a region where physical skill and strength were still very much in demand. Yet, as we noted, the province's murder rate was not as high as that of most parts of the United States and was at about the same level found in the countries of southern Europe. One is moreover struck by the fact that even the urban, middle-class judges and journalists of the province, in drawing the moral of what a "man" might be forced to do, rarely appeared to discriminate along class lines. Compared to law-abiding England, the Canadian west, in sustaining higher murder rates, could be construed as manifesting a "cultural lag," but it was very much in step with many parts of

Europe and North America in maintaining traditional notions of aggressive manliness. Viewed in the context of what we have already seen in earlier chapters, we come away with the impression that in the Western world between 1880 and 1920 the general societal expectations of how a "real man" should behave, when seriously threatened, had changed very little.

Part Two of this study has focused on what might be called "bad men"; in Part Three we will move on to look at "mad men." By way of concluding our examination of male murderers, it is worth reiterating that the majority were regarded by their peers as having acted rationally. Recourse to violence was, so men were told by the press and the courts, in some circumstances a legitimate means by which to defend one's reputation. To fail to do so would be a sign of deviancy. To be known as someone who skirted risks, avoided dangers and refused to contemplate the use of violence was to expose oneself to the charge of not being a "real man." Confrontational homicide was located not beyond, but within the boundaries of normal masculinity.

1. "The Cat-of-Nine Tails in a London Prison. A humiliating punishment to which England subjects its 'Apaches' and so assures public safety." *L'Illustration*, 3 September 1910. By permission of the British Library.

"WOMAN'S WRONGS."

BRUTAL HUSBAND. "AH! YOU 'D BETTER GO SNIVELLIN' TO THE 'OUSE O' COMMONS, *YOU* HAD! MUCH THEY 'RE LIKELY TO DO FOR YER! YAH! READ THAT!"

"MR. DISRAELI.—There can be but one feeling in the House on the subject of these dastardly attacks—not upon the weaker but the fairer sex. (*A laugh*.) I am sure the House shares the indignation of my hon. friend who will, I hope, consider he has secured the object he had in view by raising, the question. * * * Assuring my hon. friend that Her Majesty's Government will not lose sight of the question, I must ask him not to press his Motion further on the present occasion."—*Parliamentary Report, Monday, May* 18.

2. "Women's Wrongs." This cartoon, drawn to support Parliamentary attempts to enact laws for the flogging of wife-beaters, was accompanied by a poem that included the verse: "Knot well the nine tails, strand on strand,/For the brute on a woman that lifts his hand;/And sharpen the claws of the cat to tear/His back with the pain he made her bear" (*Punch*, 30 May 1874).

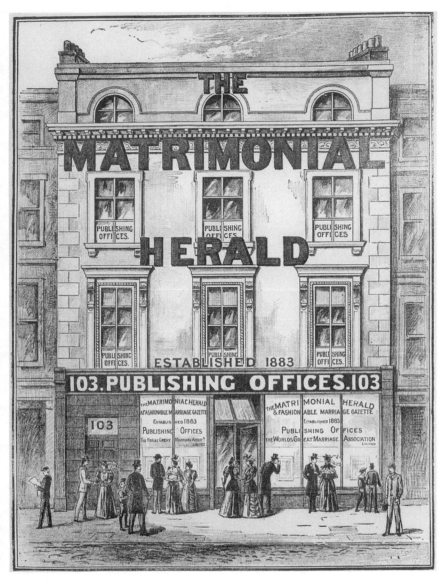

3. The publishing offices of the World's Great Marriage Association as presented in the *Matrimonial Herald*, 18 May 1895. By permission of the British Library.

4. Constance Thomas, the French abortionist, as portrayed by Théophile-Alexandre Steinlen. Thomas's court appearance—which occurred a few years before the Hindson trial—led to outbursts of expressions of public sympathy in France for women who were forced to resort to dangerous means to control their fertility. *Gil Blas Illustré,* 29 November 1891.

5. A portrait photograph of Dr. Thomas Smoult Playfair. *Lancet* 2 (1903): 573.

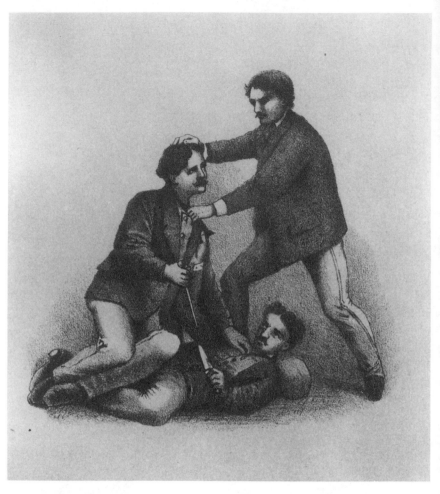

6. An Unfair fight. Purportedly a "Facsimile of a photograph of three murderers" from Cesare Lombroso, *L'Homme criminel* (Paris: Alcan, 1887).

7. A page of advertisements from a men's magazine for a range of goods and services—including cures for "nervous and physical debility," "surgical appliances," and a marriage agency—which sought to exploit an anxious male market. *Pick-Me-Up*, 26 October 1895.

8. A prison portrait of Joseph Vacher from Alexandre Lacassagne, *Vacher l'Éventreur et les crimes sadiques* (Lyon: Storck, 1899).

7ᵉ Affaire de Saint-Étienne-de-Boulogne. — Pierre Massot-Pellet

9. A police depiction of one of Vacher's victims from Alexandre Lacassagne, *Vacher l'Éventreur et les crimes sadiques* (Lyon: Storck, 1899).

10. "In Evening Dress." The portrayal of an exhibitionist. In this particular case the individual asserted that, because of the stress under which he labored, he was unaware of his nudity. *L'Intransigeant illustré,* 3 August 1893.

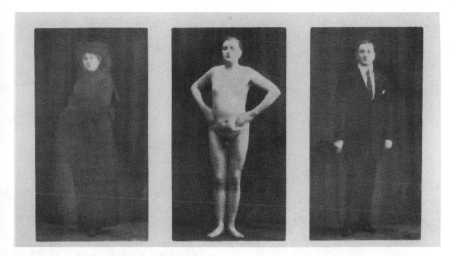

11. Magnus Hirschfeld, who coined the term transvestism, provided the following caption for these photographs. "Feminism in a Man. This case presents one of the frequent associations of androgyny, transvestism and homosexuality. Androgyny (picture 14) is particularly visible in the formation of the pelvis, chest and larynx, as well as in the facial expression, gestures and mimicry of the thirty-year-old patient. Picture 13 shows him as he appeared at the time of his military call-up. He is wearing mourning clothes because his mother has died; an indication of how seriously he takes his transvestism. Towards the female sex he displays complete indifference, whereas he is positively lustful as regards male persons." Magnus Hirschfeld, *Sexualpathologie* (Bonn: A. Marcus and E. Webers Verlag, 1921). By permission of the Wellcome Institute Library, London.

Photo by A. S. Rudland and Sons

GIANT GORILLA

Photo by Underwood and Underwood, N.Y

SOLDIER IN ACTIVITY

The physiognomy of the soldier compared with that of the brute illustrates well the fact that war is in truth a "Fling Back in Phylogeny."

12. Pictures produced by the surgeon-in-charge of the United States Ambulance Unit suggesting that the horrors of war brought out men's dangerous atavistic traits. George W. Crile, *A Mechanistic View of War and Peace* (London: Macmillan, 1915).

PART THREE

MEDICAL DISCOURSES:
WEAK MEN AND PERVERTS

A JUDGE, IN PORTRAYING A MAN AS A BULLY OR A CAD, A bounder or a scoundrel, was making clear to the community that the individual's guilt resided not so much in his breaking of any law as in his failure to live up to the unwritten code of manliness. In the last decade of the nineteenth century, authors of textbooks on legal medicine, sexology, and psychiatry in introducing to the public a new cast of male villains— the homosexual, the sadist, the exhibitionist, the transvestite—greatly expanded and modernized the vocabulary devoted to descriptions of the unmanly. The question of how and why certain male forms of sexual behavior became medicalized and pathologized is a complicated one, involving as it did not simply the policing of sexual acts but the surveillance of desires and emotions.

One striking indication of the attention paid to male emotionality cropped up in the late-nineteenth-century debate over flogging when, as we noted, each side accused the other of being "sentimental." The shedding of tears by grown men, a common trope of romantic theater and literature in the early 1800s, was by the 1890s regarded with embarrassment, if not disgust.[1] Educated men were supposed to restrict signs of emotion to appropriate occasions—the death of a loved one, the raising of the regimental flag. Darwin informed his readers that tears were largely given up by the civilized and more highly evolved; that is why idiots, women, and children were still prone to bouts of weeping while mature men reserved their energy for creative purposes, why soppy continentals were less restrained than the English.[2] In a society governed by pure reason, wrote Henri Bergson, one might laugh but no longer cry.[3] This repression of male emotionality did not signify that men's "naturalness" or "spontaneity" was suddenly lost; male tears had once been obligatory, but it was now understood that outbursts of male emotions were reserved for the private world. Men were taught to control their emotions just as women were instructed to indulge in theirs.[4]

The injunction against male tears was symptomatic of new nineteenth-century gender divisions in the creation of which medical science clearly played a crucial role. In early modern Europe, as Laqueur and others have noted, doctors' explanation of reproduction was based on a belief in the "one sex model" that implied that males and females had roughly similar sexual needs and feelings. Doctors began to draw radical distinctions between what were to be called the "opposite sexes" only from the seventeenth-century onwards. Indeed women began to be tellingly referred to as "the sex." A woman's sexuality—the fact that she had an uterus—was magnified in importance by natural scientists and philosophers and taken as an indication of both the private and public roles "nature" meant her to fulfill. Masculinity's linkage to sexuality was conversely much reduced. Men, unlike women, were no longer supposed to be bothered by sex. "Le mâle est mâle qu'en certains instants, la femelle est femelle toute sa vie, ou du moins toute sa jeunesse."[5] The general assumption made by observers like Rousseau and Michelet was that males were basically healthy and females unhealthy; that the male sex drive was unproblematic, the only concern being to keep it in check.[6] Marriage guides, admittedly providing imperfect reflections of marital practices, challenged middle-class men to prove themselves "athletes of continence." They in turn were to instruct their sons "as to a gentleman's duty of self-control and respect toward a lady, and as to the proper occasions for executing such self-control in the marital relation."[7]

In the latter half of the nineteenth century, male sexuality became problematized. It goes without saying that quacks based their lucrative practices on a successful exploitation of men's fears of disease; the question why doctors adopted a similarly alarmist view of male sexuality is examined in chapter 6. A nervous man could by force of will, the doctors asserted, hold himself back from the most dangerous sexual excesses; the pervert was likely lost forever. This medicalization of sexual deviancy—which we trace in chapters 7 to 9—advanced most quickly on the continent, where the tradition of magistrates calling on the aid of the "medical police" to deal with prostitution—regarded as a public health matter—was by the early nineteenth century already well established. Moreover doctors were happy to appear in European courtrooms that followed the Roman law system. As they were called on by judges as "experts" to assist the court in having a better understanding of difficult matters, they could anticipate being treated with respect.[8] Such was not at first the case in the Anglo-Saxon world. In the adversarial legal system, medical witnesses called by either the prosecution or defense could, as we noted in chapter 4, be subjected to harsh and often humiliating cross-examinations. Doctors in Britain and North America, though anxious to assist the authorities in maintaining public morality, were accordingly wary of legal encounters.

The courts' treatment of male sexual perversions does not at first glance appear to follow the melodramatic script that proved helpful in understanding the cases dealt with in part two of this study. The very fact that the stories told by male perverts "made no sense" was the reason why judges called on the help of medical men in the first place. Yet by placing doctors' construction of the sadist, the exhibitionist, and the transvestite in historical context, the enormous influence such cultural forms as the decadent novel, the charivari, and public shaming rituals had in framing the apparently new figure—the sex pervert—become immediately obvious. Mad men rather than bad men were now the purported targets of the authorities' sanctions, but doctors took the opportunity to turn the descriptions of the most idiosyncratic forms of behavior to the purposes of demarcating the boundaries of "normal" masculinity.

SIX

WEAKLINGS

IN AUGUST 1863 MONTAGUE AUGUSTUS CLARKE, A CAPTAIN in the Fiftieth Regiment stationed at Parkhurst, Scotland, perused the advertisement pages of his local paper. There he found notices for books on "marriage and its impediments" and the "vigour of youth regained," including Dr. Curtis's *Medical Guide to Marriage* and Dr. La'Mert's *Physiology of Marriage*, and a host of advertisements aimed at men for a variety of medications, including Dr. Brights' Speedy Cure, Dr. Watson's Self-Cure for Debility, Nervine Essence, Nerve Lozenges, Self-Cure for Spermatorrhoea, and the Silent Friend on Marriage. One advertisement in particular caught Clarke's eye. "Dr. Henery may be consulted in all cases of a private and confidential nature incidental to male or female. A cure effected in a few days. No charge unless cured. Hours from ten till two; Sundays before two. Particulars of the new discovery for six stamps—Address 52, Dorset-Street, Baker Street W."[1] Over the course of several months, Clarke consulted Henery, for whose services he paid one guinea per visit and from whom he purchased a tonic—which on later investigation proved to be nothing more than colored water—at £1 1s per bottle. Altogether Clarke saw Henery eleven times and paid out eighty-five pounds, roughly the equivalent in the 1860s of two years wages for an unskilled laborer.

Clarke took the medicine for four months and also followed Henery's advice regarding exercise and cold water bathing. The captain appeared to believe that the treatment worked and wrote Henery to say he felt stronger and was improving. But in July of 1864, when Clarke ceased his purchases, Dr. Henery attempted to blackmail him. And when Clarke refused to hand over 150 pounds, the doctor had an accomplice send his patient the following threatening letter.

> Now, supposing I were to inform you application will be made at
> the War-Office, with explanation of case, and if we were to do so
> you know what the consequences would be; or supposing I were

to inform you that I expect to be in your neighbourhood in Scotland next week, and that I don't intend leaving here, in the event
of your still persisting in your refusal to pay, without making it
known in the neighbourhood for what purposes I am here. I am in
no hurry, and will allow you time to reflect whether it will be better
to pay Dr Henery's legal and just claim or submit to exposure of
your filthy case.[2]

Clarke gave the letter to his attorney, the police were called, and on 26
November 1864 "Dr. Alfred Field Henery" (who proved to be William
Osterfield Wray) and William Anderson of 52 Dorset Street, Portman
Square, were tried before Mr. Baron Bramwell at the Central Criminal
Court.[3] At the trial it came out that the accused had for some time used
advertisements with such leading words as "manly vigour given" and cures
for "youthful indiscretion" to lure male clients who were worried about
their declining sexual powers. The accused insisted on acquiring the addresses of their patients, but it is not clear how many men they actually
blackmailed or threatened to libel. In any event, because of a technicality,
the libel charge filed against them in the Clarke case was ultimately
dropped; the conspiracy charge was upheld. On the 24 November they
were convicted and sentenced to two years hard labor.[4]

   The medical press played up the trial, the *Lancet* noting that many other
men lived in fear of such rogues. Indeed, in 1857 the police had revealed
that a Dr. Kahn, proprietor of an Anatomical Museum in Coventry Street,
had fraudulently obtained money from thousands of young men, including
many members of the clergy. At his trial one man reported that when he
asked for his money back Kahn replied, "If you dare ask for that, I shall
accuse you of masturbation." This testimony caused a sensation in the
court, the judge protesting, "Oh! even if it were true, it would be a monstrous thing for a medical man to assert."[5] The *British Medical Journal*
insisted that even the writers of melodramas and sensationalist novels had
never imagined villains as evil as Henery and Kahn.

> Novel-writers of the new sensation school have not been very scru-
> pulous in their resort to the catalogue of crimes; but they have
> found or invented no more odious character than that of a man
> who, possessing some fatal secret of another's life, uses it to extort
> money or gain other sinister ends. Not only is robbery commonly
> pushed to a ruinous extent, but the wretched victim is reduced to
> a condition of complete moral slavery, and subjected to increas-
> ing moral torture, which no corporal infliction can adequately rep-
> resent.[6]

Worse was to come. An inquest, held at the Chequers Inn, Higham, Kent, on James Miles, aged twenty-four, who had been found drowned on 19 January 1865, was told that in his pockets were handbills of Dr. de Rood of Tavistock Square and Dr. Smith of Burton Crescent. The local surgeon claimed, after looking at the papers, that "I have no doubt whatever they would cause a great depression of spirits, and tend to a person committing suicide. Persons suffering disease are highly susceptible of depression of mind. The papers are bills issued by quacks. It is not unusual for cases of suicide to arise from reading pamphlets similar to those produced."[7] The *Lancet* drew the lesson that by reading such advertisements that played up the dangers posed by "self-abuse," a poor, weak fellow fell "like so many others" into the way of death. Immense circulations were enjoyed by books that, asserted the editor, "contain every element of prurience, of vile suggestion, and of cunning terrorism."[8] There was no doubt that the trade was extensive. Quacks sent books to students, businessmen, army and navy officers, and members of the civil service. "What a frightful undercurrent of secret misery must be underlying the fabric of lower-class middle [*sic*] English life," the horrified editor of the *Lancet* lamented, "to make it worth the while of these wretched quacks to expend such enormous sums in advertising their abominable wares!"[9] So-called quacks had been denounced before, but these were the first serious salvos fired by regular physicians in what was to be a decades-long attack on the "irregulars" who catered to a market made up of males worried that masturbation, venereal disease, and sexual excesses threatened to render them impotent.[10]

Recent research has revealed that an analysis of obscene literature does not provide as many insights into the role sexual behavior played in evolving nineteenth-century definitions of masculinity as was anticipated. "Male sexuality, paradoxically, is one of the obscure areas in much pornography. Although early modern pornography was written by men for a presumably male audience, it focused almost single-mindedly on the depiction of female sexuality, as if male sexuality were too threatening to contemplate."[11] The medical literature on onanism has in contrast proven to be a fruitful source. It is not necessary to rehearse here the much-abused history of masturbation.[12] Suffice to say that though churchmen long condemned the sin of "pollution," they had not been preoccupied by its physical consequences. And early modern physicians for their part held that emissions were necessary to maintain health. With the appearance of *Onania* in early eighteenth-century England and the works of Tissot in France in the 1760s, however, the modern panic over the medical dangers posed by male "sexual excesses" was ignited.[13] In the nineteenth century, this market, exploited by the commercially minded—including Samuel La'Mert and J. L. Curtis in England, Dr. Brennus and Dr. Belliol in France, and Dr. Retau in Germany—no doubt expanded because in addition to anxious adolescents there must have been many among the increasing numbers of men who employed the withdrawal method of birth control (coitus interruptus or "conjugal onanism") to control family size—until the 1930s the most common form of contraception in the Western world—who wondered if such practices would have any deleterious side effects.[14]

Doctors were outraged by evidence that quacks turned to blackmail. But the medical profession was not satisfied by the bringing to justice of only one or two scoundrels like Henery and Kahn who had actually committed crimes. It wanted all quacks who exploited the sexual fears of gullible male patients silenced. Doctors offered a mixed message. On the one hand, the medical press called for the Medical Council to act to end displays of advertisements for "Vital Essences," "Elixirs of Life," and "Restoratives" that claimed to succor worn-out debauchees.[15] The *Lancet* insisted in particular that the government silence the "advertising scoundrels" whose activities were an outrage to morals and to the profession. Forty years later it was still warning that quacks were bilking or blackmailing a public worried about sexual weaknesses, genital disorders, and contraception.[16] Medical journals lamented that the newspaper press—the supposed guardian of public morals—was responsible for abetting such bounders. But on the other hand, the medical press asserted that a male patient's revelation of some sexual malfunctioning should not entail any shame or concealment. Yet the medical profession was not terribly willing to respond to the obvious demand for information on sexual matters. Many laymen pointed out that the reason the public turned to quacks was because doctors would often not answer their patients' questions.[17]

Most doctors in both Europe and North America were of the opinion that their profession, in the process of establishing itself, could only suffer if it became too involved with sexual issues, associated as they were in the public mind with midwifery, quackery, and prostitution.[18] Some no doubt remained true to the old notion that a man had to sow his wild oats, but they could no longer express such opinions in public. Others candidly admitted that in any event they knew no more than their patients when it came to dealing with sexual problems.[19] Most either avoided such issues or cloaked their ignorance in pessimistic moralizing.[20] But a small number began to treat male sexuality as a subject worthy of serious investigation. These doctors, who first turned to the problems posed by "weak and nervous men," were very much conscious of the need to distinguish themselves from irregular practitioners. Consequently they set out to make it clear to both their professional brethren and the general public that they were not—like quacks—about to pander to a male clientele of debauchees seeking easy relief from discomforts caused by sexual misdemeanors.[21] They did so by their gloomy prognostications and their prescribing of frequently painful and punitive therapies. Although they condemned irregulars for praying on the anxieties of their clients, doctors' portrayal of sexual malfunctioning tended if anything to be even bleaker. Indeed the genealogy of the grim appraisal of male sexuality can be traced directly from William Acton in the mid nineteenth century to Sigmund Freud in the early twentieth.[22]

Acton, who had helped in the prosecution of Kahn, was the best known mid-century British authority on the subject of male sexual disorders.[23] Youth needed sexual education, asserted Acton, to inoculate it against false knowledge. But the "education" he offered presented disease as a punishment for indiscretions, called for the dressing of boys in restraints to prevent their self-abuse, and warned men of the all-important need to harbor their "energy." Acton's complaint that otherwise intelligent gentlemen, when plagued by genital problems, threw themselves to disreputable harpies was made more understandable once one appreciated the therapies he offered. He subjected his male patients to galvanic treatments, doses of cantharides, and, if all else failed, painful cauterizations with a scalding caustic solution injected via a syringe forced up the urethra. Acton marveled that few ever asked for a second dose, apparently oblivious of the fact that the irrigation was so painful that the patient often could not walk for three to four days afterward.[24] The good doctor, in asserting that the sufferer's only true remedy lay in "self control," set a moralistic line of argument that subsequent generations of physicians, at least when dealing publicly with male sexual problems, closely followed.

In the United States, George Beard, who began speaking on the subject in 1868, declared that a variety of male genital weaknesses including debility, impotence, spermatorrhea, and prostate difficulties were all symptoms of tension.[25] Such tension was in turn the result of a complex mixture of stresses to which modern man was subjected by the march of progress. On the physical side, patients fell prey to addictions to evil habits, alcohol, and tobacco and on the psychological side to such tensions as those created by railway travel and the shock of bad news. Such combinations, Beard gloomily noted, could render some men hysterical.[26] He was the first to popularize the notion that the pressures of modern society were such that those men who could not stand up to them were turned into "weaklings."

Beard coined the term neurasthenia to refer to male sexual exhaustion.[27] Doctors, noted Beard, had in the past rarely asked for the sexual history of their male patients, so men suffering from stress were dismissed as hypochondriacs just as women often had been as hysterics. But now as gynecologists were uncovering women's real complaints, so too doctors who investigated men's distresses were also discovering worrying practices. The male's loss of "nervous force" was, according to Beard, what primarily led to irritability and nervousness. Nocturnal emissions and self abuse—if excessive—could cause loss of energy and ultimately impotence. "Prolonged" intercourse was hurtful too, but birth control encouraged the most damaging excesses. And of all the forms of unnatural coitus, withdrawal or the spilling of male seed was the worst.[28] As a warning to his male readers against squandering one's nervous force, Beard cited the frightening case of the "Mujerados," Pueblo Indians who were reportedly masturbated by their fellows until they lost all sexual desire and their organs shrank. They were thereafter dressed as women and played a religious role in the community.[29] When Beard spoke of "loss of manhood," he literally meant just that.

Aside from insisting that his patients give up their destructive habits, Beard offered a range of therapies including a meat diet to build up the patient's strength while his rebellious member was dealt with by electric therapies, sedatives, and cauterizations. Beard was particularly given to the dangers of the "redundant prepuce," which he suggested be dealt with by circumcision and/or "stretching." Beard also experimented with the use of placebos, which he found worked well with both functional and organic problems. Indeed he was very much a proponent of what he called "mental therapeutics," of appealing to work, travel, and marriage.[30] He, like Acton, believed that a man's real recovery was accomplished by force of will power. "Resolve," Beard advised his patients, "to become useful or famous."[31]

Such attacks on sexual excesses, particularly related to masturbation and coitus interruptus, became a commonplace of nineteenth-century medical literature. In France, Félix Roubaud declared that coitus interruptus was more debilitating for the male than normal coition.[32] In Canada, M. H. Utley, repeating Tissot's old line that one ounce of semen was the equal of forty ounces of blood, warned men of the danger of losing their "manhood."[33] In Austria, Victor G. Vecki suggested a range of cures for masturbation ranging from doses of nux vomica and cocaine to hydrotherapy, electrotherapy, and hypnotism.[34] Vecki's view that coitus interruptus was "a fruitful parent of all sorts of nervous and mental derangements" was shared by many.[35] In Britain, George Savage, in the midst of his 1907 Lumleian Lectures on "Insanity, Its Cause and Increase," solemnly declared, "I have no time to go into the question of sexual causes of insanity, but it would not be right if I did not express my opinion that the tendency to late marriages in men, the great limitation in the number of children, and the distaste of the mothers to nurse their children all have potent influence in producing mental instability."[36]

Freud, it is generally believed, stood out from his colleagues in attributing the exhaustion, weaknesses, and timidity of his male patients to psychological rather than somatic causes. Henry Campbell and Arthur Cooper, with their dire predictions about the dangers of masturbation, and F. W. Mott, with his warnings of the perils posed by the loss of the "highly phosphorized nucleo-proteids contained in the sperm," seem far removed from the measured introspection of Freud's better-known works. Yet as he made clear in *An Autobiographical Study,* his "momentous step" in starting out on his own path of discovery was made in linking the hysteria of his patients to their sexual lives.[37] In the 1890s he too came to the conclusion that there was a somatic side to every neurosis. Close observation moreover convinced him that a central form of sexual abnormality was the practice of coitus interruptus. It was this "abuse" that was the hidden cause of a multitude of nervous conditions.

> I thought that the anxiety from which the patients suffer should be looked on as a continuation of the anxiety felt during the sexual act—that is to say, that it was a *hysterical* symptom. Indeed, the connection between the anxiety neurosis and hysteria are obvious enough. Two things might give rise to the feelings of anxiety in coitus interruptus: in the woman, a fear of becoming pregnant, in the man the worry that his [preventive] device might fail. I then convinced myself from a number of cases that anxiety neurosis also appears where there was no question of these two factors, where it was basically of no importance to the people concerned whether they had a baby.[38]

An obvious question is if the couple were unconcerned whether they conceived a child, why were they practicing coitus interruptus? Freud appears to have overlooked this flaw in his logic, and in summing up the types of anxiety arising from sexual causes he accordingly listed after the abstinent and the virginal:

(4) Anxiety of women living in *coitus interruptus,* or, what is similar of women whose husbands suffer from ejaculatio praecox—of people, therefore, in whom physical stimulation is not satisfied.

(5) Anxiety of men practicing *coitus interruptus,* even more of men who excite themselves in various ways and do not employ their erection for coitus.[39]

To appreciate fully Freud's attitude toward coition, it has to be recalled that in his early writings he asserted, as did many of his contemporaries, that masturbation was itself a cause of nervous debility. Contraception either by coitus interruptus or by condom he presented in turn as little more than a subspecies of self-abuse. In Draft A of the "Aetiology of the Neuroses," written towards the end of 1892, he posed the question: "Is simple coitus reservatus (condom) a noxa [danger] at all?"[40] By "simple" he meant as unrelated to masturbation. In Draft B, written in February 1893, he answered in the affirmative. The source of "neurasthenia" or nervous exhaustion in youths was masturbation; in adults it was coitus interruptus or reservatus.

> This second noxa is onanismus conjugalis—incomplete coition in order to prevent conception. In the case of men all the methods of achieving this seem to fall into line: they operate with varying intensity according to the subject's disposition, but do not actually differ qualitatively. Even normal coition is not tolerated by those with a strong disposition or by chronic neurasthenics; and beyond this, intolerance of the condom, of extra-vaginal coition and of coitus interruptus take their toll. A healthy man will tolerate all of these for quite a long time, but even so not indefinitely. After a certain time he behaves like the disposed subject. His only advantage over the masturbator is the privilege of a longer latency or the fact that on every occasion he needs a provoking cause. Here coitus interruptus proves to be the main noxa and produces its characteristic effect even in nondisposed subjects.[41]

Reliance upon the withdrawal method required the male to control himself sufficiently that he climaxed only after exiting. The woman, however, would presumably be "left hanging," and her frustration would result in hysteria. Freud insisted that his investigation of the effects of coitus interruptus led to his major discovery that all forms of anxiety stemmed from a lack of sexual release.

In 1895 Freud expanded his account of the dangers of contraceptive practices.[42] Masturbation was the first danger or "noxa" that an individual faced in sexual life; coitus interruptus was the second. The former practice resulted in neurasthenia, which could in turn "dispose" one to anxiety neurosis if the later practice was adopted. Speaking specifically of anxiety neurosis, Freud asserted:

> There is no question but that it is acquired, and specially by men and women in marriage, during the second period of sexual noxae, through coitus interruptus. I do not believe that disposition owing to earlier neurasthenia is necessary for this; but where disposition is lacking, latency is longer. The causal formula is the same as in neurasthenia. The rare cases of anxiety neurosis outside marriage are met with especially in men. They turn out to be cases of congressus interruptus in which the man is strongly involved physically with women whose well-being is a matter of concern to him. This procedure in these conditions is a greater noxa for a man then coitus interruptus in marriage, for this is often corrected, as it were, by normal coitus outside marriage.[43]

It is striking that Freud should have linked masturbation and coitus interruptus. Presumably he was thinking that when solitary youths masturbate and married men enact coitus interruptus they both spill seed. Yet the motivations are obviously different, and they are such different practices; the first involves sexual self-excitement to ejaculation as quickly and conclusively as possible, the second involves withdrawal and restraint. Both might, for different reasons, produce anxiety—even guilt— but the one seems poor training for the other.

Freud acknowledged that his theory would be criticized. Some would say that "the number of people who practice coitus interruptus and the like is incomparably larger than the numbers who are afflicted with anxiety neurosis, and the great majority of the former tolerate this noxa very well."[44] When it was suggested that some men practiced coitus interruptus for years without any apparent ill effect, Freud replied:

> Those individuals who apparently tolerate coitus interruptus without harm, in fact become disposed by it to the disorders of anxiety neurosis, and they may break out at some time or other, either spontaneously or after a shock trauma which would not ordinarily suffice for this; just as, by the path of summation, a chronic alcoholic will in the end develop a cirrhosis or some other illness, or will, under the influence of fever, fall victim to a delirium.[45]

Freud's use of alcoholism as an analogy with sexual overindulgence reveals the extent to which he could fall back on the commonplaces of his age. As many historians have noted, the official morality of nineteenth-century Europe was heavily influenced by economic considerations in which over-expenditure, be it in money, alcohol, or sex, was presented as threatening the middle-class man with the dangers of monetary, physical, and psycho-logical bankruptcy. Freud did not escape this tendency.[46]

Freud was no doubt correct in holding that many must have found co-itus interruptus a frustrating practice. But what should not be forgotten is that he insisted that full satisfaction was only possible by penetration. Or-gasms achieved by any other means he condemned. The idea that normal intercourse might be spurned by patients who employed coitus interruptus and then proceeded by other means to reach climax could, claimed Freud, only lead to further problems. For the couple or the woman herself to fall back on some other means—such as clitoral stimulation—was in his eyes a retreat from maturity. In *"Civilized" Sexual Morality* (1908), he morosely chronicled the increased employment of such maneuvers.

> The sternness of the demands of civilization and the difficulty of the task of abstinence have combined to make avoidance of the union of the genitals of the two opposite sexes into the central point of abstinence and to favour other kinds of sexual activity, which, it might be said, are equivalent to semi-obedience. Since normal intercourse has been so relentlessly persecuted by moral-ity—and also, on account of the possibilities of infection, by hy-giene—what are known as perverse forms of intercourse between the two sexes, in which other parts of the body take over the role of the genitals, have undoubtedly increased in social importance. These activities cannot, however, be regarded as being harmless as analogous extensions [of the sexual aim] in love relationships. They are ethically objectionable, for they degrade the relationship of love between two human beings from a serious matter to a con-venient game, attended by no risks and no spiritual participation.[47]

The language is revealing: civilization made stern demands, normal sex was a "serious matter," nongenital variants were "ethically objectionable" be-cause they were "attended by no risks," by which he meant that conception could not occur. Indeed Freud was to go so far in defending "normal inter-course" that he was later to write in his *Introductory Lectures,* "We . . . describe a sexual activity as perverse if it has given up the aim of reproduc-tion and pursues the attainment of pleasure as an aim independent of it."[48]

Turn-of-the-century doctors did not, of course, speak with one voice on the subject of sexuality. A handful defended birth control. Some, like James Paget in England, pooh-poohed the dangers of masturbation.[49] F. R. Sturgis, professor of medicine at the City University of New York, who dedicated a 1902 study to the "sexual cripples of the United States," went so far as to joke about the "the homely pleasure of the hand."[50] But the majority of doctors thought it safer to adopt far more conservative positions. Freud, who differed in many ways from his colleagues, shared with most the pessimistic notion that men had to pay a price for their unfettered pursuit of sexual pleasure.

Male patient's voices are rarely heard in such discussions, but there is evidence that many men were not impressed by doctors' warnings about "sexual excesses." The contributors to the *Grande Dictionnaire du XIXe siècle* obviously found the subject of "impotence" a laughing matter, listing under the entry a string of amusing anecdotes.[51] And in London in 1857, the male spectators burst out laughing when the court heard that Dr. Kahn had terrorized a young man who thought he had spermatorrhoea with the assertion, "Your brains are passing out into your water, and you will die."[52] Likewise a German worker who was informed in the 1890s by a social superior that coitus interruptus was health-threatening retorted that if that was the case "everyone would be sick."[53]

Such men were, of course, unlikely to have read Freud or Beard. But thanks to the trial of Rex versus Descôtes, which took place in Montreal, Canada, on 23 December 1924, we are given some idea of how such new sexological ideas were vulgarized.[54] L. A. Descôtes, the proprietor of a book store at 290 Mont Royal Est, was charged with selling a number of obscene texts including *La Péderastie, La Virginité, La Prostitution, La Perversion Sexuelle,* and *La Folie érotique,* all the products of the pen of the prolific French author, "Dr. Jaf."[55] Judge Lacroix could imagine no circumstances in which the sale of such books could be defended and accordingly found the accused guilty as charged, sentencing Descôtes to the option of either immediately paying a fifty dollar fine or serving three months in prison.[56]

We have seen that the official nineteenth-century medical discussion of sexuality was dominated by pious moralizing. What was the message of the "obscene" books of "Dr. Jaf" and his ilk? The significance of such a literature is that it documents important changes but also reveals remarkable continuities in sexual beliefs. A perusal of these books suggests that the vulgarization of modern sexological knowledge, taking the forms that it did, was unlikely to have precipitated either men's descent into corruption as bewailed by judge Lacroix or the "flight into knowledge" toward "sexual enlightenment" some later historians have claimed to detect.[57]

"Dr. Jaf" was the pen name of the enterprising and productive Dr. Jean Fauconney, who also wrote dozens of books under the anagram "Dr. Caufeynon." Most appeared in a series published in Paris in the first decade of this century entitled the "Bibliothèque populaire des connaissances médicales." The Bibliothèque populaire boasted of presenting at the modest price of one franc per volume absolutely precise, scientific findings in a clear, simple language accessible to all.[58]

It is impossible to say how many read these books. One has to take with a large grain of salt the author's claim that by 1926 *Sécurité des deux sexes en amour* had sold eight hundred thousand copies. But we do know that these books were read widely not only in France but, as the Quebec case makes clear, throughout the francophone world. They were also translated into Spanish and English in the 1920s, and some volumes continued to appear in American editions as late as the 1950s.[59]

Although it would be hazardous to attempt to make any precise claims about the extent of Dr. Fauconney's readership, it is safe to say that at the very least his books provide some idea of what the adventurous male French reader of the early twentieth century in search of up-to-date sexual information would have been likely to find. Such a man might have heard of Forel or Freud, Havelock Ellis or Krafft-Ebing, but probably sought out the less academic, more accessible, and cheaper texts that the Bibliothèque populaire provided. Dr. Fauconney's success in selling so many books for so long presumably stemmed from his ability to know both what well-known medical authorities were saying and what ordinary readers wanted to hear.

What did these books contain? Some of the volumes were produced simply for the curious or voyeuristic. *L'Eunuchisme: Histoire générale de la castration,* although it did contain some pertinent information on ovariotomies and circumcision, could hardly be considered morally offensive.[60] The volume on *L'Hermaphrodisme,* which provided a surprisingly full treatment of the discussion of the subject from Montaigne in the sixteenth century to Tardieu in the nineteenth, was equally circumspect.[61] Preoccupying turn-of-the-century medical topics, which at first glance seemed to be only tangentially related to sexuality, also received Dr. Fauconney's attention in such volumes as *L'Hystérie, L'Hypnotisme,* and *Les Morphinomanes.* The good doctor even dedicated an entire book to *Les Tatouages,* revealing to the inquisitive the ways in which criminals, prostitutes, and homosexuals purportedly used body markings as secret codes.[62] But Dr. Fauconney focused primarily on the problems posed by heterosexuality, with the twenty titles in the Bibliothèque populaire moving (in alphabetical if illogical order) from *L'Avortement* via *La Syphilis* to *La Virginité*. Altogether, more than forty books dealing with various sexual problems appeared under the names of "Dr. Jaf" or "Dr. Caufeynon," many simply repeating and repackaging the same information and anecdotes in a variety of contexts.

What first strikes the contemporary reader is how "old" much of this "new" discussion of sexuality was. Most of Fauconney's books appeared in the first decade of the twentieth century, but the discussion of contemporary sexual issues was constantly being linked to the past by, for example, citations culled from Martial, Catullus, and Ambroise Paré. Fauconney, understanding that his readers wanted to know what previous generations had thought of sexuality, moreover produced full editions of the works of both the popular eighteenth-century writer Nicolas Venette and the medieval scholastic Albertus Magnus devoted to "conjugal duties."[63]

Dr. Fauconney's own books on the sexual issues preoccupying the belle époque consisted of a curious amalgam of both old and new information, a blend of traditional lore and scientific discovery. Dr. Lutaud's success in using syringes to carry out artificial inseminations was noted by Fauconney alongside traditional beliefs in the ability to determine the sex of the unborn child and the power of a mother's imagination.[64] For example, a white woman who was passionately in love with a black man, the reader was informed, would have a black baby whatever the color of her spouse.[65] Likewise the old argument that a woman in full possession of her senses could not be raped by one man—though those who were asleep, drugged, or hypnotized could—was retold.[66] Fauconney's discussion of the causes of hysteria ranged similarly from traditional notions of pent-up genital excitement to Morel's targeting, in the mid-nineteenth century, of the impact of heredity to Charcot's more recent announcement of the neurological basis of both male and female hysteria.[67] In short Dr. Fauconney's books were stuffed with a curious and comforting hodgepodge of citations drawn from both ancient and modern discussions of sexuality. The new sex manuals, like the old chapbooks and almanacs that contained ambiguous or contradictory information, often left the reader purposely free to pick and choose what he wanted to believe.[68]

The distinctly anticlerical tone found in many of the sex manuals enjoyed a venerable French lineage. The enemies of the Catholic church from at least the eighteenth century onward used the sex question as a stick with which to beat clerics. Dr. Fauconney followed this tradition in, for example, searching the church's penitentials for evidence of the vices of medieval monks.[69] Ambroise Paré's seventeenth-century reference to an abbé who died from sexual excesses was similarly cited by Dr. Fauconney when asserting that celibacy, which was propagated by the church, disastrously resulted in madness, an argument buttressed by citations drawn from the eighteenth-century *philosophes* Rousseau and Montesquieu.[70] Confessors were, as was to be expected, attacked in the sex manuals, as they had been in so many nineteenth-century republican tracts, for prying into families' private affairs. Dr. Fauconney attributed hysteria in particular to women's irrational fears being on occasion exacerbated and exploited by the alarming teachings of the church.[71] And if religion could lead to madness, madness could lead to religion. The religious delirium of women was, claimed Dr. Fauconney, in fact often simply a phenomenon precipitated by menstrual complications.[72]

The anticlericals' tactic of attributing the causes of those vices they found most objectionable to the influence of priests worked well for authors who wanted both to exploit an interest in sexuality and present themselves as moralists. Accordingly, the act of sodomy could be simultaneously described and condemned. Fauconney, in characterizing it as the greatest possible outrage which could be committed against women, reproached the church for popularizing by its teachings such unnatural acts. He claimed that in a work like "De Sodomia" by the Capuchin Father d'Ameno there was evidence that casuists argued that anal sex was acceptable as long as sperm was not ejaculated. In short the church doctors proved themselves on examination, the indignant author claimed, to be more immodest than lay lovers.[73]

Carrying the campaign against the church even further, Fauconney included in some of his books advertisements for a specialized "Collection Anti-cléricale" with such offerings as *La Bible amusante* and *La Vie de Jésus* by Léo Taxil as well as even more outrageous titles such as *Le moine incestueux, Le Couvent de Gomorrhe, Les Amours secrètes de Pie IX, La Belle dévote, Les débauches d'un confesseur,* and *Une Orgie au temps de Jésus.* The sex manuals, containing as they did so many gratuitous attacks on the priesthood, necessarily scandalized the faithful. But Dr. Fauconney, who aimed his writings at a wide male readership, obviously felt that such references were unlikely to endanger sales in France. They might even help.

Priests, in their skirts, though not viewed as real men, were frequently regarded by husbands as rivals in controlling the intimate matters of the
household. Given the fact that such suspicions could be traced back over
several centuries, many readers must have found that anticlerical slurs gave
the texts a cozily familiar if not a downright old-fashioned ring.

Dr. Fauconney's books were no doubt anticlerical. Were they immoral?
Clearly much of the Bibliothèque populaire aimed to titillate; such works
would include, for example, *Les Vénus impudiques: La Grande prostitution à travers les âges.*[74] But even this book, a dutifully thorough review of
the careers of grand courtesans from the ancient world to the Renaissance,
demanded a good deal from its readers. The purchaser drawn by the sensational title would likely be disappointed to find himself or herself plunged
into what at times read like an uninspired survey of European history. Similarly, readers attracted by a title like *La Prostitution — débauche — corruption* were no doubt frustrated to discover that they had purchased a fairly
dry historical account of the government regulation of vice.

Did such books offer men practical advice on how to flaunt the laws of
God and man? No, at least certainly not in the sense that they in any way
questioned the "normality" of heterosexuality. Same-sex relations were, as
will be noted below, resolutely condemned. But in discussing heterosexual
relations, did such books say anything, for example, about birth control,
which was being so intensely debated in France at the turn of the century?
Presumably many, with the thought in mind of limiting family size, purchased Drs. Jaf and Caufeyron's *Securité de deux sexes en amour.* But here
again the book proved to be less radical than one might have imagined. In
part one, entitled "Hygiène des sexes," the reader was categorically told
that the natural goal of intercourse was reproduction. The text, although
it noted that the church's condemnation of contraception—even when a
woman's health was at risk—was short-sighted, went on to note that "nature" also condemned "frauds."[75]

Today's reader would probably expect that a discussion of "security" in
a sex manual would entail an examination of methods of contraception.
But Dr. Fauconney's chief concern in this text was not with undesired pregnancies but with venereal disease. This preoccupation highlights the fact
that Dr. Fauconney wrote not simply with the heterosexual reader in mind,
but more particularly for the male heterosexual reader. For protection
against sexually transmitted diseases, the man was advised to use vaseline
before intercourse and calomel afterwards. But as part two—"La Sterilité
vaincue"—made clear, reproductive failure was also viewed as a problem.

The author attributed sterility to the traditional reason of lovers' too great desire. Patients—both men and women—were advised that love, sympathy, and affinity were required to ensure a successful conception. Some nineteenth-century scientific advice on timing was added, but unfortunately it was based on Pouchet's inaccurate calculation of the woman's ovulation cycle.[76]

For those in search of practical birth control information, the advertisements that appeared in the back pages of Fauconney's books were no doubt often more useful than the texts themselves.[77] In his *Amour et mariage en Orient,* which was mainly a discussion of polygamy, appeared advertisements for "préservatifs" and "éponges de sûreté." The latter when used by the woman with an aseptic douching water like "l'eau Cyrienne" was said to act as a contraceptive and alone could also be employed "pour protéger le linge aux époques menstruelles." A number of contraceptive sheaths with such evocative names as "Le Favori," "Le Nervi," and "Le Cygne" were also offered for sale.[78] The advertisements that appeared in the last pages of *L'Hystérie*—notices for pornographic novels and venereal disease cures crammed together cheek by jowl with those for cooking manuals—seemed directed at the sort of sophisticated French readership that some historians have come to believe was a mere stereotype.[79]

Turning from Dr. Fauconney's treatment of normal heterosexuality to his examination of what he deemed "perversions," one has a better sense of the limitations of such a literature. Judge Lacroix declared that these books describing sexual practices had the effect of inflaming lascivious desires. What has to be noted is that the volumes in the Bibliothèque populaire constantly harped on the notion that society was threatened by a lack not an excess of passions. Dr. Fauconney repeatedly expressed the fear that one was living in an enervated age. The decadence and degeneration of the urban middle classes he attributed to their debaucheries, the assumption being that the physically demanding life led by peasants and workers spared them such blights. Fauconney, asserting like so many contemporary medical authorities that sexual excesses were a cause rather than an effect of perversions, accordingly preached moderation. This medical moralism was made especially clear in the passages he devoted to the discussions of masturbation, prostitution, and homosexuality.

The message of the dangers posed by self-abuse was carried in Dr. Fauconney's *Aberrations, folies et crimes du sens génital,* which drew heavily on the horror stories found in the academic works of Lombroso, Tardieu, and Magnan. Masturbation—which the author claimed nurses taught to

nine-month-old babies—was castigated as the root of the madness of murderers like Gabrielle Bompard and abortionists like La Thomas.[80] Nevertheless, in *L'Onanisme chez l'homme* an unusually balanced account of
masturbation was provided. The author, after noting that the ancients were
untroubled by the vice, observed that only after the appearance of the
works of Tissot in the late eighteenth century were excitement, imagination, and heredity targeted as causes of self-abuse. Admitting that because
of "sympathy" excessive masturbation could be harmful to the whole
body, the book concluded by asserting that work and exercise were better
than the terror and mechanical restraints brandished by some nineteenth-
century doctors and that in any event boys almost always dropped such
habits once they discovered women.[81]

Dr. Fauconney presented those men who were weakened by self-abuse,
necessarily seeking forms of satisfaction less demanding than those found
in the marriage bed, as turning to commercial sex. The same moralizing tone that he employed in his treatment of masturbation was carried
over into his discussion of prostitution (much of it drawn from Parent-
Duchâtelet's classic 1830s account) in which the clients were described as
idle, overeducated, enervated young men and the prostitutes as slothful,
superstitious, sentimental young women. The extent of the trade Dr. Fauconney attributed to the evil of arranged marriages, which in creating disgust and boredom in the partners drove them to seek pleasures outside
the home.[82]

And the debauched clients of prostitutes, protested Dr. Fauconney, were
no longer content with traditional services.[83] Oral sex in particular was
becoming popular because of men's fear of venereal disease. Modern society, according to Fauconney, was overexcited and enervated by animal
foods, books, plays, sexual precocity, and the incessant contact with members of the opposite sex.[84] The sex acts that this environment spawned Fauconney described as "absolutely disgusting," but—with an eye on sales—
he described them nevertheless.[85]

Dr. Fauconney even tried his hand at writing a pornographic novel
about prostitution entitled *Scènes d'amour morbide (Observations psycho-
physiologiques)*. Containing as it did lewd photographs, it was obviously
more titillating than the books in the Bibliothèque populaire series, but it
was just as moralistic. Emma, the main character, followed a predictable
course, degenerating from the young innocent of the early chapters into the
debauched street walker of the novel's middle portions to a sordid death in
the concluding chapter at the hands of a gang of Parisian Apaches.[86]

The ultimate form of perversion, in Dr. Fauconney's eyes, was homosexuality. According to the doctor, it was the men who lacked even the energy to track down the women of the streets who finally turned for sexual satisfaction to other males.[87] Homosexuality he labeled the "turpitudes de vieillards," "la fin du vieux libertin à bout de ressources" who was vainly seeking new pleasures.[88] In *La Pédérastie,* the reader was informed that the practice of male same-sex relations—though not a crime in France as it was in Austria and Germany—had been determined by doctors such as Pouchet and Tardieu to be a failing, a sort of animality, that was spawned by the laxity of modern society.[89] Once embraced voluntarily by the morbid, it spread by a sort of moral contagion. The character flaws of its adherents—their lies, hypocrisy, gossip, and vanity—made them easy to detect.[90] That is, female characteristics were attributed by Dr. Fauconney to homosexuals and, following the same logic, male characteristics were attributed to lesbians. The pathology of women's same-sex relations was discussed by Dr. Fauconney in the context of the works of Moll, Krafft-Ebing, and Martineau. All homosexuals manifested moral failings, he asserted, but he also followed the older ideas of Lombroso in arguing that deviance was in addition revealed by physical stigmata.[91] Fauconney shared with his more respectable medical colleagues the belief that only one dimension—the gender of the object choice, rather than the act or the frequency—should be taken as the crucial indicator of male sexual orientation.[92]

Though Dr. Fauconney singled out homosexuality and prostitution as the chief expressions of the wave of lubricity outraging public decency at the turn of the century, in his books all excesses were presented as dangerous. The doctor, citing contemporary experts like Charcot and Krafft-Ebing, warned that self-abuse caused excessive sensitivity and jealousy, use of cantharides sapped vigor, nymphomania debased women, and other similar excesses resulted in epilepsy and madness. Thus the male reader who waded through the discussions of folly, nymphomania, satyriasis, and other vices in works like *L'Amour malade* and *La Folie érotique* was left with the stern warning ringing in his ears that sexual dissipation inevitably led to physical decay and decay led in turn to perversion.[93]

Dr. Fauconney's discussion of sexuality, like so many other purportedly "frank" accounts that appeared in the early twentieth century, was marked by an unmistakable moralism. Foucault has argued that the Victorians' attempt to deny the significance of sexuality had the unintended effect of inciting an interest in the subject.[94] Taking the books of Dr. Fauconney as examples, one is led to conclude that many early-twentieth-century sex manuals worked the other way round: although promising to titillate, their very explicitness and preoccupation with malfunctions may well have often fanned the flames of guilt and anxiety. In the eighteenth and early nineteenth centuries, those who wrote about sexuality, obsessed as they were by the threats posed by the traditional problems of sexual "excesses" such as nymphomania and satyriasis, assumed that the challenge was to provide advice on how to control or rein in the passions. In the later nineteenth and early twentieth centuries, the task taken up by the sexologists was just the opposite. Their concern, faced with declining birth rates that they attributed in part to the modern plagues of frigidity and impotency spread by an overcivilized society, was with the new problem of how to guarantee "arousal." Western culture had accordingly shifted from fearing lusts to fearing enervation, from a preoccupation with the oversexed male to a concern for the undersexed weakling.[95] Some have argued that psychiatric patients, in unconsciously learning to signal their distress by changing their symptoms from those of hysteria to those of fatigue, similarly demonstrated an understanding of what caught the attention of modern medicine.[96]

The course of civilized, urban life, which, it once had been hoped, would counter the complaints posed by the animal passions, was increasingly viewed as the cause rather than the cure of vice. The French, whose fertility rate had been more or less declining continuously since the 1860s while that of the Germans remained ominously high, were particularly prone to express such fears.[97] And eugenicists added to the gloomy prognostications of the pronatalists in warning that a careless approach to the crucial question of reproduction threatened the quality as well as the quantity of future generations.[98] We have worked our way through a great number of texts dealing with the perversions to see what they tell us about evolving notions of masculinity. What we found was that a reading of a nation's sex manuals tells us as much about a culture's view of its body politic as about the male body per se.[99] Doctors translated into medical language the fantasies of their age.[100]

An examination of the trials in which such books figured also reveal the growing powers enjoyed by the medical profession. The fact that Dr. Jaf's books were prosecuted while the regular medical texts he quarried went undisturbed, that the medical press condemned quacks who sold their patients nothing worse than sugared water while applauding doctors who subjected their male patients to painful and pointless cauterizations, serves as a forceful reminder of the success physicians achieved in appropriating the role of sex expert. With only the occasional protest, the public conceded to them the role of judging which male sex acts were "legitimate" and which were not. A new range of medical criteria accordingly had to be met to prove one's "manhood." It was hardly surprising that regular physicians should have "discovered" in the nineteenth century that apparently growing numbers of men were suffering from sexual malfunctions. The cynical might conclude that the discovery or invention of a somatic basis of nervousness was predictable because it justified physicians' colonization of a lucrative field previously monopolized by quacks. Rejuvenation treatments, for example, were very much in demand by wealthy male patients at the turn of the century.[101] The more sympathetic might argue that doctors simply failed to note that their pessimistic prognostications were based on an examination of a self-selected sample of overly anxious patients. Of course the bleak picture that many doctors painted no doubt created anxieties where they had previously not existed. Sexual moderation had long been preached in the Western world; now it was backed up with disease sanctions.[102]

A real man, doctors informed their readers, was forceful. "Nervousness," declared Professor Krafft-Ebing, Germany's leading sexologist, "is only the mildest expression of an inferior organization of the central nervous system tending towards degeneration in the anthropological, biological and clinical senses of the word."[103] When doctors referred to impotence as "loss of manhood," they meant just that. Traditionally cowardice was equated with impotency and virility with honor.[104] In a modernizing world, physicians continued to attribute any number of a man's social and psychological failings to sexual malfunctions. Men's nervousness and fear of honeymoon "fiascos" presumably could have only risen as they were repeatedly told that the pressures of modern life necessarily produced casualties. A culture that embraced Spencerian if not Darwinian notions of the "survival of the fittest" naturally enough regarded the purported rise in the number of the nervous to the inability of the inherently weak to stand up to the stresses and strains of rapid social change. The self-confident welcomed such pressures as they would necessarily sort out the weak from the strong.[105] Yet even healthy men, doctors warned, who did not carefully husband their physical and psychological resources might tumble into the ranks of the weak and nervous. Policing and judging what was excessive was a task appropriated by physicians. Whereas in the past "masculinity" was determined in large part by the explicit displays of the social, economic, and political power one wielded, now doctors were declaring it to be a more mysterious quality that only the trained professional could accurately judge.

$$\int$$

A YEAR BEFORE THE DESCÔTES TRIAL, HENRI MARTIN, AN OBLATE PRIEST, raised the warning that Quebec morality was threatened by the discussions of contraception and sexuality that were filtering into the province from both France and the United States. "Our judges," he predicted, "will know only too well how to deal vigorously with the wretches, convicted in the courts of such utterances." [106] He was proved right. Judge Lacroix was motivated by the belief that society was endangered by urban youths being oversexed, whereas Dr. Fauconney lamented the fact that sexual vigor was endangered by city life. This dialogue of the deaf alerts us to an important sea change in the discussion of Western sexuality that was taking place at the turn of the century, a shift from a concern with male "excesses" to a concern for male "arousal." It was in this context that the pervert was invented.

SEVEN

SADISTS

IN THE MID 1890S, JOSEPH VACHER, A DISCHARGED SOLDIER, committed a series of horrific sexual assaults and murders across rural France. Alexandre Lacassagne, the country's leading expert in legal medicine, concluded his review of these apparently inexplicable crimes with the assertion that Vacher was not insane; he was a sadist. "Certainly he is abnormal as regards the satisfaction of his sexual instinct. Vacher had spontaneously put into practice the theories of de Sade."[1] The questions raised by Lacassagne's revealing words lie at the heart of this chapter. Sex crimes were nothing new; why now call a man who committed them a sadist? What was sadism? How did the concept make the world more intelligible? In what ways did such a concept frame notions of "normal" masculinity?

The term sadism only entered the medical vocabulary sometime in the 1880s. One could accordingly argue that strictly speaking the marquis de Sade should not be described as a "sadist." The social construction of the sadist took place in the last decades of the nineteenth century—not the eighteenth—as part of the elaboration of the sexual identities of a host of male "perverts"—homosexuals, masochists, fetishists, and exhibitionists. The classification and definition of sexual pathologies represented in part a new medicalization of sexuality. In the works of sexologists who demanded detailed confessions from their clients erupted into print "the speaking pervert."[2] Before, such men were silenced or their mutterings ignored; now careful reports were kept of their incriminating statements. In classical times virtually the whole range of sexual practices had been categorized, but in the late nineteenth century certain sorts of sexual deviants were discovered or one might say "invented." What doctors now declared to be important was not so much what a man did as what a man was; having adopted an essentialist model, they shifted attention from "doing" to "being." We saw this same process in the debate over flogging when "vagrant" and "idle" ceased being adjectives and became nouns. Ian Hacking has argued that by this process, "a kind of person came into being at the same time as the kind itself was being invented. In some cases, that is, our classifications and our classes conspire to emerge hand in hand, each egging the other on."[3]

But sexology did not simply create its subjects. "Sadism" was as much a literary as a scientific construct. De Sade was himself a writer of fictions, many of whose themes were taken up by the decadent novelists of the 1880s before they were pursued by doctors. Accordingly, the increased use of the term sadism at the end of the century did not mean that there was any necessary increase in violent sexual acts nor any real growth in psychiatric knowledge. Reality was more likely copying art than art reality.[4] Why were both doctors and novelists at the end of the nineteenth century so morbidly obsessed with what they regarded as sexual perversity? In what follows it will be argued that their concerns were not sparked so much by the new threats purportedly posed to society by perverts, as by such disturbing social phenomena as the decline of fertility rates and the rise of the women's movement, which were taken as chilling evidence of the failure of the "normal" to embrace appropriate gender roles. In particular the emergence of the concept of sadism was a symptom of a late-nineteenth-century male identity crisis. Sadism, this chapter will suggest, was primarily used by public commentators to police male behavior and so played a not insignificant role in the construction of modern notions of normal masculinity. The apparent explanatory powers that social investigators attributed to the notion of sadism are accordingly only fully understandable when placed in the context of the literary, cultural, and political concerns of the fin-de-siècle.

∬

ON 1 SEPTEMBER 1895 AT BÉNONCES (AIN), ELEVEN-YEAR-OLD ALEXandre Leger was asked by a stranger to come into the woods to see something pretty. The boy refused. Later that day fifteen-year-old Jean-Marie Robin, noticing that the cattle had been allowed to wander into a clover field, set out to look for the village shepherd, sixteen-year-old Victor Portalier. Jean-Marie discovered in a ditch Victor's sexually-abused, butchered, and disemboweled body.[5] Two years later, on the afternoon of 4 August 1897, a stonecutter at Champuis (Rhône), responding to repeated cries for help, subdued and held for the gendarmes a lout who had attempted to molest a farm woman. The assailant, a vagrant by the name of Joseph Vacher, was on 7 September found guilty of assault and sentenced to three months in jail. As his description matched that of the suspected murderer of Victor Portalier, he was handed over to Émile Fourquet, a juge d'instruction, who had since 1895 been struck by the similarity of the description of the suspects in a number of rural murders with that of the tramp seen with Portalier. Vacher was quickly identified by witnesses to the outrage at Bénonces. But to the horror of his interrogators, Vacher also confessed to not only killing Portalier, but also to the murder and sexual violation of an additional seven females and three males.[6]

Vacher's first victim had been a twenty-one-year-old female worker in the Isère in May 1894; the second in November 1894 a thirteen-year-old farmer's daughter in the Var; the third in May 1895 a seventeen-year-old female day worker in the Côte d'Or; the fourth in August 1895 a fifty-eight-year-old widow in the Savoie. Vacher's fifth, sixth, and seventh victims, all killed in September 1895, were Victor Portalier in the Ain, a sixteen-year-old farmer's daughter in the Drôme, and a fourteen-year-old male shepherd in the Ardèche. A year later, in September 1896, Vacher claimed his eighth victim, a nineteen-year-old woman tending a flock in the Allier; his ninth in October 1896, a fourteen-year-old girl shepherd in the Haute-Loire; his tenth in May of 1897, a fourteen-year-old boy vagabond in the Rhône; and his eleventh and last in June 1897—also in the Rhône—a thirteen-year-old boy shepherd. Although Vacher confessed to the murder and sexual violation of seven females and four males, the authorities, noting the unexplained hiatus in his attacks between September 1895 and September 1896, suspected him of being responsible for as many as sixteen other rural killings.

Shouting, "Glory to Jesus! Glory to Joan of Arc! To the greatest martyr of all time! And glory to the Great Savior!," Joseph Vacher on the 26 October 1898 entered the cour d'assises of the department of the Ain sitting at Bourg to face the charge of murder.[7] The trial took place between the 26 and 28 October under the presidency of M. le conseiller Coston. M. Charbonnier appeared for the defense; M. Ducher was the procureur. Forty-nine witnesses testified, including Vacher's shame-faced brothers and sisters. The accusation was that Vacher, driven by the overexcitation of a shameful passion, had mercilessly killed unsuspecting victims. He had showed his sanity, argued the prosecution, in picking on the weak and isolated, in never receiving as much as a scratch, and in hiding the bodies of his victims afterwards. The "sang-froid" he demonstrated excluded the notion of his being the victim of "aliénations mentales."

The question the court dealt with was not if Vacher had committed murder, but why. What sort of person was he? Vacher's simple response was that he was a madman. A multitude of witnesses concurred that Vacher had, in a brief twenty-nine years, lived a tragic and violent life. Born 16 November 1869 at Beaufort (Isère), he came from a poor family of eleven brothers and sisters. At fourteen he had been sent out to work as a shepherd for M. Declerieux at St-Genis-Laval. The boy's peculiar nature was noted early on. If he cried like a dog, Vacher repeatedly insisted, it was because of the bite he had received as a child from a rabid animal. But some neighbors claimed that he had from the first been a brutal, violent, and crafty character. At the early age of twelve, according to François Bouvier, a landowner from Beaufort, Vacher had tried to strangle a brother.

Many of Vacher's difficulties with others were attributed to the sexual conflicts he experienced in dealing with males. He did learn to read and write and at eighteen had entered the monastery of the frères Maristes as a postulant. He left two years later. Witnesses stated that he was expelled by the brothers because he subjected some of his comrades to odious and infamous acts. At the very least, he had shown "his celery" to others and, according to a friend, "il avait masturbé ses camarades" and attempted an act "contre nature" with twelve-year-old Marcelin Bourde.[8] On a later occasion he attempted to climb into bed with a man whose room he was sharing. The latter reported he had threatened Vacher with a chair, "adding that we were not in Africa."[9] Contracting a venereal disease, he sought cures in Lyon and Grenoble. He claimed in court that he had, thanks to Drs. Gailleton and Désiré at the "hospice de l'Antiquaille," been miraculously cured of his "secret disease." In Lyon he took up the trade of papermaker. Here he again manifested an abnormally violent temper, reportedly menacing a fellow worker with a knife. Ex-employers claimed that he spouted anarchist ideas, and a colleague recalled that "we used to say that he had a screw loose."[10]

In November 1890 Vacher began his military service at Besançon with the Sixtieth Artillery Regiment. Plunged once more into an all-male environment, Vacher found that his "inversion tendencies" elicited his comrades' hostility. Unlike them he did not drink or go to the brothels. His mess mates regarded him as a bigot and brownnoser. As a "blue" or rookie, he was accordingly subjected to much rough hazing that reached such levels that even his officers protested. Vacher's response, true to form, was more deadly; on one occasion he replied to the barrack room bullies' attempt to trip him up by firing his rifle at them. Enraged when not named corporal, he threatened to bayonet a roommate. He attacked a noncommissioned officer with a razor. His fellow recruits became so terrified of the one whom they called the "bear" or the "madman" that they slept with bayonets unsheathed. Captain Greilsammer, Vacher's lieutenant when he was in the Sixtieth Regiment, later recalled having to report him as a bad character who was always looking for victims.

But Vacher was as much a menace to himself. He was known to cry out in his sleep and strike his head against the barracks's walls and on one occasion try to cut his own throat. In October 1891 his paranoid delusions led to him being put under medical observation. In 1893 his incoherence was such that he was first hospitalized and then allowed to go on convalescent leave. In this confused state, Vacher found himself not only taunted by men but rejected by a woman. At Beau-les-Dames he asked Louise Barrant, whom he had met in Besançon, to marry him. For the short time that he had known her, he had proven himself insanely jealous of rivals, threatening her and others with a knife. When she refused his offer of marriage he shot her and then turned the gun on himself. She was slightly wounded, and Vacher only succeeded in lodging a bullet in his own skull. The slug, which could not be removed from his right ear, caused deafness and facial paralysis. The attack was treated by the authorities as a simple "crime passionel," and in July 1893 Vacher was sent to the asylum at Dole, from which he reportedly twice escaped. He was arrested in Besançon, judged by the authorities to be irresponsible and sent to the asylum of St. Robert in his home department. There he was treated by Dr. Dufour, who, after a mere five months, optimistically declared Vacher, who still had a bullet lodged in his skull, to have been restored to mental health. He was released in April 1894 and then began, in Vacher's words, his horrible "pilgrimage," which in three years resulted in the loss of at least eleven lives.

In court the overarching argument of Vacher's melodramatic defense was that he was only responsible to God, of whom he was an instrument. He was happy to be photographed with his bible and staff, on which he had inscribed words of praise for Mary of Lourdes. Raising his voice to a shout, he concluded his court address with the words: "To be able to resist my particular passion for so long required Providence to keep special watch over me."[11] Vacher's second tack was to claim that as a child he had been bitten by a rabid dog and his blood poisoned by the medicine he was later given. The "guilty" were therefore the empirics who sold cures for rabies. Having a bullet in his head due to his attempted suicide he described as a third extenuating circumstance. And finally Vacher accused Dr. Dufour of the asylum of St. Robert for incompetently letting loose a dangerous man.

When the court applauded Plantier, the stonecutter of Champuis who had apprehended him, Vacher wailed "too late, too late" and hit out at the gendarmes, saying that they should have arrested him much earlier. Why had so much blood been shed? The asylum doctors were guilty: "Because of the faults of the asylums which succeeded in having the innocent turn on each other, alas." [12] Indeed, Vacher went on to present his crimes as a sort of providential mission against psychiatry. Why had murders been committed? "In order to provide a warning of what happens in the lunatic asylums." [13] He compared himself to Joan of Arc, "une martyr comme moi." "Yes, in reading a book, I understood my mission; Joan of Arc is like me; she was locked up in an iron cage; she had to defend herself against the doctors." [14] And Joan like him—and his victims—had been a shepherd.

The public, though calling for Vacher's death—"À l'eau! À l'eau!"—assumed that he was insane. [15] Journalists covering the trial were mesmerized by his curious behavior. He was a physical and mental oddity. He listened impatiently to the testimony of witnesses, raising his hands to the heavens, covering his face. He was calm at some moments, menacing the next. He, whom the spectators presumed would look like the personification of evil, was, with his nervous tics and outbursts, unexpectedly more like a comic monkey. [16] He had a magpie-like memory and included odd passages of what he had read in his defense statement. He expected responses from the audience to his hodgepodge of assertions and was not disappointed. The correspondent of *Le Matin* reported that "ce sinistre mélo," with the accused's eccentric language, caused hilarity. His comparing himself to Joan of Arc and other preposterous comments, led to repeated outbursts of laughter. But reporters were also awed by the accused's incredible strength; he had long avoided capture by walking amazing distances of sixty to eighty kilometers a day.

Vacher never denied any of his crimes; his basic argument was that they were not premeditated. He insisted that the doctors who claimed he was sane were liars. How did they know what he felt or thought? He invoked the very number of his attacks as the final confirmation of his self-proclaimed madness: "Do you believe that a man who did what I did is not mad? To say that I am responsible, is to be more criminal than me." [17] But the court was not impressed by Vacher's railings. The president chided Vacher for not being a good liar. The accused, warned the judge, had to give up his meandering arguments and decide whether his dog bite or his providential mission were responsible for his deeds. The medical experts declared him to be sane. In the end he was found guilty, and on 31 December 1898 on the Champs de Mars at Bourg before an immense clamorous crowd, which bayed for his blood, he was publicly guillotined.[18]

Vacher's fearful reputation entered the canon of peasant folklore in songs such as "La grande complainte sur Vacher le tueur de bergers."

> Petits bergers pleine de peines
> Le soir, prenez garde à vous
> Il est des bêtes humaines,
> Inhumaines, inhumaines;
> Lâches assassins ou fous
> Plus terribles que les loups.[19]

But the bourgeois reading public quickly lost interest in the case. The same week that he was tried, the French newspapers were filled with accounts of the attempted revision of the Dreyfus affair. Then came reports of Marchand's alarming clash with the British at Fashoda in the Sudan and Kaiser Wilhelm II's provocative visit to Jerusalem. Yet if public attention was turned away from the provinces and back to Paris, the medical community was far from finished with Vacher and the lessons that could be drawn from his case.[20]

ONE MIGHT HAVE EXPECTED THE DOCTORS TO HAVE BEEN RECEPTIVE TO Vacher's claims to be a madman. A good deal has recently been written about the way in which psychiatrists in late-nineteenth-century trials, for both humanitarian reasons and in order to exalt their profession's expertise, advanced the concept of mental irresponsibility.[21] Patrizia Guarnieri, for example, in *A Case of Child Murder: Law and Science in Nineteenth-century Tuscany* provides a careful analysis of such medical involvement in the 1876 trial of the Italian multiple murderer Callisto (Carlino) Grandi. His trial, like Vacher's, was a scientific spectacle; not Grandi's guilt but his sanity became the issue. The defense stated that he was an imbecile who lacked the cunning of the criminal and behaved like a child.[22] He must, the doctors argued, have internal lesions; they cited his physical deformities and atavisms, including his extra toe and immature sex organs as evidence of his degenerate state. "The appearance of the accused," argues Guarnieri, "provided a perfect opportunity to prove how modern, objective psychiatry could alone provide superior expertise to the advantage of society in general."[23] The members of the positivist criminological school did not really explain the accused's motive—indeed they were more interested in the criminal than the act—but still enjoyed a good deal of public support.

"Not only was it [crimonolgy] popular despite its theoretical weaknesses, but that popularity actually depended on them. It was rooted in the ability or refusal to collect and explain the meaning of sickness and violence within a living context. By depicting a dangerous type, either criminal or mad, with an aberration which was unavoidable and motiveless, it removed all responsibility for these tragedies from the deprivations of poverty and suffering."[24] Such analyses reflected the general tendency among nineteenth-century social and medical scientists to exploit the findings of phrenology, physiognomy, and cranial capacity to provide a physical basis for character traits and racial differences.

In France psychiatrists adopted similar tactics to increase their professional power. After P——, convicted of murder and necrophilia, was executed at Beauvais on 13 November 1879, doctors at the autopsy revealed his pronounced brain lesions. A madman had been put to death. V. A. Cornil and M. V. Galippe sarcastically commented, "If guillotining has to be included in the treatment of mental illness, let it be so stated."[25] Dr. Madeuf, who appeared for Vacher's defense, reminded the court that similarly after Menesclou was guillotined in 1880 evidence of his damaged brain—in particular the degeneration of his frontal lobes—had been discovered. "Previously Menesclou, although a victim of such a softening of the brain that after his execution it was impossible to make a mold of his brain, had nevertheless been guillotined; such a thing should never happen again."[26] But in 1898 the leading French psychiatrists chose, despite all the evidence to the contrary, to regard Vacher as sane.[27] This reflected in part that in the criminological world of the 1890s the Italian stress on biological determinism was being usurped by the French focus on pathological social forces.[28] Nevertheless, the medical witnesses' stance in the Vacher trial was still rather curious inasmuch as psychiatrists were saying that a man who had been twice institutionalized and who after the repeated assaults in his regiment and the events of Baume-les-Dames was described by doctors as crazy was actually sane. The three medical experts called by the court insisted that Vacher was neither an epileptic nor an "impulsif" but an "immoral violent" occasionally plagued by melancholy delirium, paranoia, and thoughts of suicide. What made the diagnosis of Vacher's mental state all the more important was that it was chiefly established by France's leading expert in criminology, Professor Alexandre Lacassagne.[29]

Lacassagne is best known today as the leader of late-nineteenth-century French legal medicine who fought against Cesare Lombroso and the positivist school of criminal anthropology, which held that treatment rather than punishment was needed for the "born criminals" who could not help themselves.[30] Lacassagne, a staunch defender of the death penalty, sought to shift the emphasis in criminal psychiatry from the biological to the social determinants of crime. Two of his epigrams were to become famous: "The social milieu is the mother culture of criminality; the microbe is the criminal, an element which gains significance only at the moment when it finds the broth which makes it ferment" and "Societies have the criminals they deserve."[31] The French school attributed most criminal behavior to pathological social influences such as poverty, alcoholism, poor housing, and bad companions. They advanced a positivistic message, but one sufficiently close to jurists' orthodox stress on individual responsibility to be welcomed by the courts.[32]

Lacassagne followed such a tack in the Vacher case. While Vacher screamed that the doctors were lying, Lacassagne argued that the accused was sane, that he had always been playing a role and was in fact a rather maladroit simulator. To make his case, Lacassagne asserted that Vacher had a "system." Vacher had told some witnesses, including a "mouton" placed in his cell that he only played the fool to get around the doctors. Realizing early on that he might pass as a madman, he only admitted to crimes that appeared to be motiveless and claimed to act without thinking. But in fact, Lacassagne argued, proof that Vacher was not pushed solely by perverted sexual passions was indicated by evidence that he rationally took precautions, hid his bodies, robbed his victims, and successfully eluded capture. Though offering no evidence, Lacassagne further asserted that Vacher worked with a band of "chemineaux" and attributed to him up to twenty-eight other murders. And finally Lacassagne asked how Vacher could claim to be mad when he had been promoted by the army to the rank of sergeant?[33] Here Lacassagne blundered; no military witnesses imagined that madness might disqualify one from promotion.

Why had Vacher committed his crimes? Vacher's argument was that the enormity of his crimes proved that he was a madman. This claim was accepted by some. Dr. Maxime de Fleury declared:

> Vacher, the killer of shepherds, a conscious impulsive, is really a sort of madman, though about the day to day things of life he reasons without too much difficulty. The very excesses of his heinous crimes should save him from the hand of the executioner; if he was charged with only one murder one would condemn him to death without even subjecting him to a medico-legal examination; but he so many times sated his dreadful craving, and for no possible motive, for nothing, for pleasure, that it is really necessary to deal with him as with a brute lacking full consciousness.[34]

Enrico Ferri, the Italian criminologist, agreed that Vacher was clearly mad and that the French experts simply lacked the courage to defend him. "Vacher, they say, pretended to be mad. Now, it is well known that the feigning of madness is always a psychopathological symptom."[35] Magnus Hirschfeld, the pioneering German sex reformer, concurred that true sadists were psychopaths who did not know what they were doing and that, as horrible as were the crimes of lust murderers, only severe psychopathic cases were capable of committing them. The court had declared that Vacher's crimes were "those of an antisocial, bloodthirsty, and sadistic person who believes that because of his earlier madness and the fact that he was not then punished, he has a permit for the perpetration of his horrible deeds." Hirschfeld's responses was that "this report, as so many others, is based more upon moralistic than upon psychological and psychiatric principles."[36]

The question of whether Vacher was insane or not cannot be answered here. What we can try to trace are the social, cultural, and political preoccupations that colored the findings of Lacassagne and his followers. In the first place, professional solidarity no doubt played a role in the doctors' refutation of Vacher's claim to be mad. Vacher had been declared sane by an esteemed colleague, Dr. Dufour of the asylum at St. Robert. Vacher was now arguing that the psychiatrists, in releasing a madman, were responsible for his atrocious deeds.[37] The experts may have felt some minor embarrassment in noting that the military doctors had been wrong in thinking Vacher crazy, but the psychiatrists saw that to support the accused's claim that he was insane would put them in the impossible position of attacking their own profession and admitting to being accomplices to murder. Drs. Lacassagne, Rebatel, and Pierret accordingly concurred that Vacher was not mad; he only pretended to be.[38]

The second motive that the French professors of legal medicine had in demolishing Vacher's claim was that in doing so they could demonstrate how sophisticated the science of criminology had become. Anthropometric measurements were taken of all of Vacher's limbs; his scars, weight, height, and eye coloring were noted and a radiographic analysis made of his head. Investigations were carried out to determine that he bore no signs of physical degeneration, that he suffered from no debilitating childhood sickness, that his family contained no mad, epileptic, or idiotic members. The experts conceded that the bullet in Vacher's head—the wound still suppurating—did cause facial paralysis on the right side of his face and deafness in one ear, but they cheerfully noted that Vacher had no history of hallucinations.[39] Thanks to the autopsy carried out after Vacher's execution, the voyeuristic public further learned that he had a large penis and an atrophied left testicle but a normal anus and therefore had not been a passive pederast. His brain, which weighed fifteen hundred grams, was sliced open by the doctors, who declared it to be normal. It was photographed and a mold taken of it. No one found it ironic that the medical experts, who condemned Vacher for mutilating his victims, proceeded after his execution to subject his body to such a meticulous dissection.[40] In short all the sorts of efforts by criminal anthropologists—in particular the Italians—to detect the stigmata of the born criminal were made and the findings declared by the French to be of no great importance. Lacassagne authoritatively asserted that those who might claim that a bloodthirsty killer like Vacher would have to have been suffering from some major physical or psychological handicap were proven wrong; there was nothing irresistible or impulsive in Vacher's acts.[41]

The third and, for the purposes of this chapter, most important preoccupation that colored Lacassagne's view of the Vacher case was his interest in the new concept of sadism. Vacher's trial was not responsible for spawning the concept, but it provided the occasion for nineteenth-century French psychiatrists' most extensive discussion of the term. Why did Vacher commit his bloody deeds? Lacassagne quoted extensively from the psychiatric report on Menesclou, the 1880 murderer, which helpfully contrasted "imbéciles de l'intelligence" to "débiles du sentiment." The latter, though reasoning beings, claimed Lacassagne, did not have the moral repugnances of the normal.[42] Vacher manifested just such failings by his dabbling in anarchism, vagabondism, and homosexuality.[43] Lacassagne's point was that Vacher was not insane but an antisocial sadist. His acts were the work of a "monstrous criminal" not those of a madman.[44] And as horrific as sadists might be, many were completely sane. Vacher was a sadist who was aroused by the sight of flesh but that did not make him irresponsible.[45]

What did Lacassagne mean by sadism? Dr. Marciat, who contributed a discussion of sadism to Lacassagne's volume on Vacher, began with Thoinot's definition.[46]

> The perversion of the genital instinct that is known today by the name of sadism consists in finding suffering in a human being a condition always necessary and at times sufficient for sexual enjoyment; this suffering is of a very variable degree,—at times slight, at times severe or of a degree of atrocious refinement,—and the subject either causes it to be inflicted, or sees it inflicted, or finally inflicts it himself on some human being.[47]

Yet what sadism was from the point of view of legal medicine was left rather vague; no specific act was required. Lacassagne and his colleagues used the term as a sort of moral label to designate those who were monsters but not mad.

The term "sadism" had first been used on rare occasions by critics in the 1850s to describe the decadent themes found in the writings of Flaubert and Baudelaire.[48] The word only began to be widely employed in the 1880s. De Sade, who had been almost forgotten for much of the nineteenth century, was simultaneously rediscovered in the 1880s by both psychiatrists and novelists. Isidore Liseux republished *Justine, Juliette* and *La Philosophie dans le boudoir,* and several biographies of the marquis soon followed.[49] Few may have actually read de Sade's works very closely, but an interest in his ideas quickly mushroomed. They drew the attention in England of Swinburne and Wilde and in Germany of Herbst, Eulenberg, Rutter, and Blaubert, but his first and greatest appeal was in France.[50] Those decadents who dabbled in sadistic themes of black masses, the occult, demonic pederasty, and flagellation, who declared self-conscious evil better than ignorance, and who envisaged society culminating in sacrifice and death, included the Goncourts, Guillaume Apollinaire, Barbey d'Aurevilly, Léon Bloy, Paul Bourget, Villiers de l'Isle-Adam, Rachilde (Marguérite Vallette), Jean Lorraine, and Pierre Louys.[51] Most of the literary acolytes of de Sade, though they paraded their irreverence and atheism, were on the political right, avowed enemies of mass society.[52]

J. K. Huysmans's *À Rebours* (1884) was the decadents' key work, full of references to erotic experiments and celebrations of "demoniac erotomania." The author toyed self-consciously with subjects such as abortion and homosexuality, transgressing powerful taboos in the search for forbidden fruit. In *Là-bas* (1891) he demonstrated the same striving for effect in lovingly devoting an entire chapter to horrific scenes of the fifteenth-century nobleman Gilles de Rais's disemboweling children and masturbating on their intestines, exactly the outrages of which Vacher would later be accused.[53] Huysmans so strained to shock by overturning all contemporary views that his works quickly dated. Like Barbey d'Aurevilly, he never freed himself from his preoccupation with Catholicism and the focus of his form of sadism lay not so much in sexual cruelty as in sacrilege.[54] Armand de Pontmartin referred to such writers as thinking like de Maistre and writing like de Sade.[55] A similar anticlericalism was reflected in the sadistic tableaux of priests flagellating women produced by writers on the left, such as Léo Taxil and Octave Mirbeau.[56] Mirbeau, in castigating the anti-Dreyfusards as "sadists," provides a useful reminder that, though writers who harbored sadistic fantasies were drawn from the political left as well as the right, both factions shared a penchant for pronounced misogynistic themes.[57]

The birth of the literary cult of sadism was in part precipitated by the conservative social reaction to the defeat of France by Germany in 1870 and the Paris Commune of 1871.[58] Pessimists, disgusted by the encroachments of mass society, retreated into elitist daydreams.[59] Such novelists pandered to and exploited the middle class's fear of disorder and chaos associated with a purportedly revolutionary working class. And by the 1890s a new threat emerged with the appearance of the "nouvelle femme." Decadence offered "imaginary solutions to real problems" inasmuch as it played with the possibility of finding freedom from the fetters of mass society by losing ones' self in sadistic fantasies.[60] Fictional and medical portrayals of sadism fed off each other. Lacassagne noted that Dostoievski remarked on the well-known correlation between beatings and sexual arousal and went on to say of Zola's La Bête humaine—inspired in part by accounts of Jack the Ripper's murders—that it "is a wonderful confirmation of the notion of the relations which link sex and violence."[61] Alfred Binet similarly drew many of his references to fetishes from fiction. And the sexually troubled learned to be as much influenced by literature as were doctors. Serge Paul reported that patients by the 1890s were already citing in their defense the works of de Sade, Jean-Jacques Rousseau, and Sacher-Masoch.[62]

The literary notion of sadism popularized in the 1880s and 1890s was primarily a manifestation of an elitist disdain for the conventions of middle class and mass society. The perverse was personified by libertine noblemen like Gilles de Rais, de Sade, and Des Esseintes. But ironically the real men of the fin-de-siècle whose actual acts led psychiatrists to label them as sadists were for the most part, like Vacher, crude and violent members of the very lower classes, whom the decadent novelists most feared. The "real" sadists, far from being powerful, sexual supermen, were slaves to their own compulsive behavior.[63]

Yet when one turns from the literary world to the sexological writings of the late nineteenth century, one discovers much the same morbid fascination with perversions. The tabloids, police files, decadent novels, and psychiatric journals shared similar vocabularies and concerns. The European presses churned out popular bestiaries of sadists or lust murderers, both the medical accounts and literary chronicles of behavioral aberrations producing the same sort of fetishistic literature that blended biography and clinical case histories of exemplary perverts.[64] The work of one of Lacassagne's colleagues, Dr. Alexis Lepaulard's *Vampirisme: Nécrophilie, nécrosadisme, nécrophage* (Lyon: Stock, 1901), was a typical compilation. Such medical studies contained much moralizing and little analysis. Their authors usually adopted a scatter-gun approach, beginning with Gilles de Rais, the fourteenth-century killer of children, and then hopping four centuries to the marquis de Sade himself. For the nineteenth century, they could be counted on to include Leger, Menesclou, Jack the Ripper, and a host of lesser villains.[65]

What most strikes the historian is how scientifically uninformative these catalogues of sex murders and sadists were. The sadists ranged in social class from aristocrats to vagrants; their crimes ran from Gilles de Rais' purported hundreds of murders and Leger's cannibalism and vampirism to Charles Bertle, who pricked or stabbed women's bottoms or breasts, to those who cut boys' ears. Some never masturbated (Bertle); others were compulsive self-abusers (Xavier); some were excited by flagellations; others were epileptic; some suffered from general paralysis (Leger); others carried the stigmata of degeneration; some had brains that were obviously damaged (P. executed at Beauvais 1879, Menesclou); some bore hereditary taints (Menesclou), or had alcoholic or neuropathic parents (Garayo). Some were bizarre; others were apparently normal. This motley collection was rounded up by the classifiers and labeled sadists. The groupings proceeded not from a classification of the perpetrators but from the similarity of their crimes. These medical dystopias provided no guidance on how to catch or cure the criminal. Their chief function was to serve as a cautionary literature that could be brandished against what were regarded as the social or psychic vices that threatened society.[66]

What sorts of threats precipitated the construction of sadism? One might imagine that the sadist represented the danger posed by a hypermasculinity. Certainly the creation of the concept of "sadism" spoke to a contemporary concern for gender relations. Sadism, like all the perversions catalogued in the late nineteenth century, was a gendered notion that could only be fully understood in the context of what contemporaries saw as appropriate male or female behavior; that men were supposed to be aggressive and women passive.[67] Aggressiveness had both its costs and benefits. Because males were supposed to be the sexually aggressive and adventurous sex, doctors assumed that only males could be perverts. As the male was more cerebral than the female, his mind was more likely to overcome his body. His desires could be degraded and decline from the active to the passive, from the genital to the oral, from the masculine to the effeminate. Much if not all homosexuality, for example, was said to result from sexual excesses and exhaustion.[68] Impotency was presented by physicians such as Tardieu as the revenge of the body that had given way to deviant desires. Nineteenth-century experts now presented a variety of corrupt practices—including masturbation and sodomy—which were once seen as choices, as symptoms of the entire personality of dangerous "others."[69] Male doctors disciplined other men in inventing and brandishing such labels as masochist, exhibitionist, and sadist; what previously had been regarded as momentary sexual preferences were increasingly taken as revelations of the whole of a person's being.[70]

Doctors claimed that females, despite evidence to the contrary, were largely inhibited by their innate passivity from actively indulging in such vices. Hence the assumption that if a man stood naked in a window and was observed by a woman he was an exhibitionist; if a woman stood naked in a window and was observed by a man he was a voyeur. Alfred Binet's famous account of the fetishes accordingly described only men's fixations on lips, hair, hands, boots.[71] Given the general assumption of sexual asymmetry, it followed that Binet took a man's being attracted to an old, ugly woman as an indication of some fetishistic appeal, while he found nothing puzzling about a young woman's marriage to an old, ugly man. Money, despite what Marx had said, was not regarded by doctors as a fetish.

Sadism has to be understood as just such a gendered perversion, which French doctors employed for both descriptive and prescriptive purposes.[72] Richard von Krafft-Ebing, the German sexologist, has often been credited with coining the term, but as he himself made clear, it was already being employed in France when *Psychopathia Sexualis* appeared in 1886, and his boast was simply that he coined as sadism's analogue the concept of "masochism."[73] Doctors, in speaking of "sadism," were taking over a concept popularized by writers of fiction, and accordingly a historical analysis of the concept has to take into account why, in the cultural context of the 1880s and 1890s, such an idea was "good to think with."[74]

How did doctors employ the concept? Sadism was first turned to by sexologists not to curb, but to incite male aggressiveness. Krafft-Ebing, whom Lacassagne frequently cited, stated there were wide gradations of sadism. At the most innocent level stood the husband who, in asking for sex in unusual locales or in employing force in the conjugal act, exhibited sadistic tendencies.

It seems probable that this sadistic force is developed by the natural shyness and modesty of woman towards the aggressive manners of the male, especially during the earlier periods of married life and particularly when the husband is hypersexual. Woman no doubt derives pleasure from her innate coyness and the final victory of the man affords her intense and refined gratification. Hence the frequent recurrence of these little love comedies.[75]

The atavistic notion—that in times past sex followed assault—was carried on by the aptly named André Lamoureux, who saw sadism as a hereditary trait of the male seizing the female.[76] Such atavisms resurfaced occasionally. Krafft-Ebing cited the case of a man who could only make love to his wife after having made himself angry, and Moll that of a boy who could only get an erection when resisted.[77] Even in "normal" sexual relations, sexologists detected in the desire to tease or mock a loved one a remnant of cruelty.

In England Havelock Ellis in his discussion of "Love and Pain" followed the same line in presenting wooing as a domesticated form of the earlier violent male pursuit of the female. Males delighted in displaying force and in the "simulacrum of pain"; their "arousal" depended on a degree of female resistance. Women delighted in submitting, and as they had to be penetrated the ideas of pain and pleasure were necessarily mingled in the female mind. Accordingly there existed a biological justification for a degree of male sexual violence.[78] Normal men had an impulse to give pain and normal women an impulse to receive it: "So that we need not unduly deprecate the 'cruelty' of men within these limits, nor unduly commiserate the women who are subjected to it."[79] In other words a normal man was in a sense "naturally" sadistic and a normal woman "naturally" masochistic.[80] At the same time, doctors were warning their male readers that masculinity was not the fundamental and unalterable element they might have imagined but rather something fragile. Without a conscious effort of the will to spurn vice, one could potentially spin off into the perversions.[81]

Some, like Dimitry Stefanowsky in an 1892 article in the *Archives d'anthropologie criminelle*, confusingly spoke of male "sadistic passivity"; what Krafft-Ebing more clearly called masochism.[82] But all commentators agreed that masochism, being an inherent female trait, was only a "true perversion" in a man; commentators specifically defined the syndrome as the sexual pleasure a man associated with the idea of being humiliated by a woman. The vice, according to Laurent, was a manifestation of a male's abdication of his legitimate domination.[83] For French readers the most famous description of a youth's discovery of his masochistic feelings was that which Rousseau confided to his *Confessions*. "To be on my knees before an imperious mistress, to obey her orders, to have to ask her forgiveness, were for me the sweetest pleasures; the more my lively imagination inflamed my blood, the more I felt like an overwhelmed lover."[84] Stefanowsky described the man who gave oral sex to a woman as a passivist who was subjecting himself to a "femme sadiste." Such passivity, if unchecked, could lead on to the victim's sexual inversion and the ultimate degradation—that of becoming a fellator of other men.

If men had a sadistic streak, women's masochism was, doctors agreed, so natural as not to count as a perversion. They thus followed the old idea posited by Michelet and Comte that women were more "alive to the chain of self-sacrifice."[85] Indeed Serge Paul noted that since a woman was meant to serve it was hard to notice a masochistic female. In Russia, he claimed, the blows a woman received were taken as proof of her spouse's love.[86] In America it was believed, wrote G. Stanley Hall in his classic text on adolescence, that there was something wrong with the young man who was not aggressive.[87] In short the concept of "sadism" was first employed by doctors to foster certain forms of male sexuality. They, like many other late-nineteenth-century commentators, believed that civilized men were most threatened not by excess passion but by the enervation spawned by urban life.

Sadism's second function was to censor certain forms of sexual behavior. Although the sexologists told men that they were supposed to be sexually aggressive, there were limits. According to Binet the line between healthy sexual excitation and perversion was crossed when the fetishistic act became more important than the heterosexual intercourse to which it was supposed to lead. When the pain inflicted became the chief source of a man's sexual pleasure, he became a pervert. Exactly the same practice, if it abetted heterosexual intercourse, could be deemed healthy. Doctors described the lust murder of the sadist not as an act that could be located at the aggressive extreme on the continuum of normal male violence but as an aberrant crime that had nothing to do with heterosexuality. Healthy masculinity emerged unscathed if not reinvigorated from such analyses, which began with the premise that sex crimes were individual deviant acts, not distorted reflections of normal gender relations. In creating the "sadist," doctors constructed a creature who roamed somewhere beyond the norms of masculine sexual aggressiveness.[88]

Was sadism a result of unleashed primitive passions or the product of overrefinement; a sign of hypermasculinity or an evidence of effeminacy and impotency? The most serious version of sadism—lust murder—Krafft-Ebing designated a "primitive anomaly." "It is a disturbance (a deviation) in the evolution of psychosexual processes sprouting from the soil of psychical degeneration."[89] Males, needing to win and conquer women, were necessarily aggressive, but under pathological conditions such a drive could "likewise be excessively developed, and express itself in an impulse to subdue absolutely the object of desire, even to destroy or kill it."[90] Lust awakened cruelty and cruelty awakened lust. Lust and anger were often linked, and in the abnormal the customary inhibitory checks were absent. Yet some in whom the sadistic instinct existed from birth managed, according to Krafft-Ebing, to fight off such urges.

In France the more common view was that perversions were not simply inherited but acquired as a result of being overcivilized. According to Serge Paul and Valentin Magnan, civilization needed boundaries.[91] But the luxurious, feverish life of the city led to excesses, alcoholism, menstrual problems, tuberculosis, and psychiatric troubles. Sexual perversions followed. Once their senses were jaded, the blasé turned to sadism.[92] Krafft-Ebing declared sadism to be congenital; the French, though they conceded that the degenerate were particularly susceptible, asserted it to be an acquired vice. Sadism accordingly was presented by French psychiatrists as a product of insufficient rather than excessive masculinity. Lacassagne envisaged the brain having special organs that presided over the functioning of the two instincts of reproduction and destruction. The genital instinct was, aside from the instinct for self-preservation, the strongest and should normally predominate.[93] Signs of effeminacy or homosexuality provided evidence that the reproductive drive was incapacitated; if that happened the instinct for destruction could take over and sadism result.

The third way in which doctors employed the concept of sadism was to alert the public to the dangers of a male manifesting feminine traits. To understand why a man's effeminacy would be considered dangerous, it has to be remembered that nineteenth-century medical scientists were in the process of drawing a sharp line between what were called the "opposite" sexes. The fact of sexual incommensurability and the demands of reproduction, they asserted, governed all aspects of life and any blurring of the gender roles smacked of the perverse. Accordingly, the term *féminisme* first came into common usage in France about the same time as the term sadisme and for related reasons. Féminisme was originally used by doctors in the 1870s in the pathological sense to describe the physical and psychological ways in which a man might manifest certain female characteristics.[94] Pierre Garnier, for example, referred to homosexuality and neuras-thenia as being engendered by a man's feminism. Charles Féré asserted that feminine characteristics (féminisme, gynécomstie) were manifested by the man who suffered the "sexual death" of losing his genitals.[95] Women writ-ers were only to appropriate the term and employ it in a positive sense from the 1890s onward. Doctors who employed féminisme in the pathological sense were not so much attacking the "nouvelle femme" as the possibility of the emergence of a "nouvel homme." Both sadism and feminism, they asserted, were manifestations of a dangerous lack of virility. Lacassagne argued that the sexual passions of the sadist were not masculine but essen-tially feminine. According to his captors, Vacher, was always in search of flesh, was always like a woman in rut. "The sadist," declared Lacassagne, "has something of the cerebral licentiousness of the woman."[96] Such asser-tions linked up with the old idea that the woman was preoccupied by sex all the time; the normal man only occasionally.

The fourth function of the concept of sadism was its use by medical men as a stick with which to beat back the threat of inversion (as homosexuality was called in the late nineteenth century). If normal women were preoccu-pied by sex all the time, so too, according to the psychiatrists, were some abnormal men—homosexuals. Accordingly, at Vacher's trial great stress was placed on the accused's inversion tendencies. Fourquet, the investi-gating magistrate, expressed surprise that Vacher, who among his fellow tramps had the reputation of being a pederast, should have wooed Louise Barrant. "Until his arrival in the army, Vacher appeared to have never been attracted to any woman. No romantic adventures were found in his past. Besides, he was a pederast and no one had ever noticed him looking for women until his induction into the 60th artillery regiment."[97] The presiding judge reminded Vacher of the disparaging reports that his comrades made of his passions.[98] Lacassagne, in describing Vacher's murdering and sod-omizing of Pierre Massot-Pellet, Victor Portalier, and the shepherds at Courzieu and Tassin-La Demi Lune, concluded that these young herdsmen inflamed Vacher with a lubricious passion. When women in the audience expressed their shock at hearing such accounts, the judge took obvious pleasure in retorting, "Too bad for you ladies, you were warned; you should not be here."[99] The doctor, in further reporting that in one of the interrogations Vacher admitted that young men had a power of attraction over him, concluded: "Yes, there is the truth; Vacher had always been a pederast, later he became a murderer and sadist."[100] Such linkages were even made by those who tried to avoid tarring all homosexuals with the same brush; André Raffalovich, for example, asserted that in Europe sodomy was the delight of only "the ignorant, the violent, the criminal, the cruel, the masochistic, the sadistic."[101]

The term homosexual, coined in 1869 by the Swiss doctor Karoly Maria Benkert, was not in common use until the 1890s. Invert, which originally was utilized as a verb meaning to turn upside down was employed by doctors in the latter decades of the nineteenth century as a noun to refer to a man who was attracted to other men. The term *pervert* went through a similar transformation. Whereas it once meant to turn from correct to erroneous religious beliefs, in the nineteenth century it took on a new sexual and psychological coloring. Lacassagne, in an earlier study devoted to pederasty, had followed Brouardel and Tardieu in attributing "sexual inversion" to a poorly balanced nervous system marked by infantilism and lack of masculine energy.[102] Some were "native," or congenital homosexuals; others drifted into the vice as a result of impotence, onanism, or a fear of women. Whether homosexuality was innate or acquired, Lacassagne insisted on referring to it as a "school for crime" and listed a string of murders with which the perversion was associated. Henri Joly and Benjamin Ball provided similar lurid accounts of the dangers posed by perverts who raped and killed children.[103] Octave Uzanne noted with some surprise that by 1900 sadism, which fifteen years previously had been very much in vogue among the advanced literary set, had become a central preoccupation of those who studied male prostitution and sexual inversion.[104]

In the early twentieth century, this line of argument associating sadism with effeminacy was pursued in England, the United States, and Germany. Havelock Ellis recognized that something like the love bite could slip off into the "region of the morbid" and artificial excesses.[105] When such practices reached the pathological stage, they no longer could be viewed as simply an extension of normal masculine aggressiveness. What was wrong with the sadistic man, claimed Ellis, was that he was not masculine enough.[106]

> It [sadism] is not, as we might infer, both from the definition usually given and from its probable biological heredity from primitive times, a perversion due to excessive masculinity. The strong man is more apt to be tender than cruel, or at all events knows how to restrain within bounds any impulse to cruelty; the most extreme and elaborate forms of sadism (putting aside such as are associated with a considerable degree of imbecility) are more apt to be allied with a somewhat feminine organization.[107]

As evidence Ellis claimed that a St. Louis man who stabbed women had a boyish appearance and a high pitched voice; while Reidel, the murderer, was "timid, modest and delicate."[108] Ellis was arguing that such men were trying to prove a masculinity they lacked with the penetrating phallic instrument of the knife.

In the United States, G. Frank Lydston claimed that in a city like Chicago male sex perverts had by the 1890s "so increased in numbers that they form large colonies with well-known resorts."[109] Their degeneracy was made obvious by their effeminate traits, though Lydston was did not make it clear whether their tainted passions were acquired or inherited. Whatever the case it was in such milieus that one expected to find sex murderers. Arthur MacDonald, who spent years trying to obtain funds from the United States Congress to establish a laboratory for the study of the "criminal, pauper and defective classes," predictably reported that the typical serial killer he interviewed was "effeminate" inasmuch as he used the "effeminate method" of poisoning.[110]

Among the psychoanalysts Wilhelm Stekel provided the fullest early twentieth-century account of sadism or what he called the "need to hate."[111] Stekel, following Ellis and Krafft-Ebing, agreed that the "normal sex impulse is always bound with a more or less prominent brutal element."[112] Sadism was an atavism, a reversion to the infantile stage in which the sadist sought to overcome resistance; killing was the ultimate way to obliterate all resistance.[113] For Stekel real sadists by definition could not be normal heterosexual males. They had to be onanists since masturbation, like killing, excluded all resistance. Homosexual urges were also related to sadism but in particular to masochism, as the suppression of a natural disposition to homosexuality could lead to aberrations in one's later sexual life.[114] Masochists found it easier to confess their urges; sadists were more likely to repress them. Among his patients Stekel had some who admitted to fantasies of killing prostitutes; others who screamed, "Die, you canaille!" during coitus; an officer who purposely infected a dozen women with gonorrhea as "revenge" for his own illness; and a patient who used weapons to impose himself on women.[115] In lust-murder, Stekel argued, "the act of murder became the symbol of possession. It is also sexual union; the revolver or the dagger represents the phallus, the blood the semen. Murder is therefore the sexual act of the impotent man. There is not a fully potent man in my gallery of imaginary 'Jack the Rippers.'"[116] In short Stekel, for all his sophistication, brought his study to an end, like Ellis, by exculpating full-blooded heterosexuality.

To conclude this chapter, let us return to nineteenth-century France. We began this investigation to see how the concept of sadism was first employed. What we found was that it was used, not to describe simply the deviant, but to shore up certain preconceived notions of manliness. The question remains why such concerns were so strongly felt. Why were French doctors preoccupied by male sexual deviancy? Why did the press at the turn of the century assert that the family was threatened and traditional gender roles under attack? One answer is that the French, with the lowest birth rate in nineteenth-century Europe, were particularly preoccupied by the notion of incapacitated reproductive drives. From 1850 onward biological fears of degeneration were extended by alarmists to explain both family and social problems. After France's defeat by Germany in 1870, a full-blown depopulation hysteria developed, only to be followed in neighboring countries in the 1890s. There too the mood of somber despair deepened in the century's last decades as doctors brandished the threats that drugs, alcohol, and syphilis also posed the family.

The fall in fertility—attributed to short-sighted egoism—and the pronatalist rhetoric to which it gave rise played a central role in the "discovery" in France of male sexual perversions. The nation's sense of guilt, precipitated by the drop in the birth rate, obviously led to the hunt for scapegoats on whom anxieties could be projected.[117] Psychiatry exploited such fears; although the science was perceived by many as being anticlerical, if anything it outstripped the Catholic church in its condemnations of the moral egoism that was supposedly weakening the nation.[118] Thus we find Étienne Martin, professor of legal medicine at Lyon, attributing Vacher's sadism to the fact that as an isolated individual he had no natural curb on his insatiable needs. The normal man had the "duties and charms of family" to act as brake on his sex drive, but rules of love were missing for the violent and brutal. Vacher's sadistic assaults, the doctors warned, represented merely the ultimate manifestation of unbridled egoism.[119]

Gabriel Tarde, the conservative jurist and crowd psychologist known for his development of the concept of criminal suggestion, followed a similar line in the chapter he contributed to Lacassagne's volume on Vacher. Tarde pessimistically argued that advances of civilization led to increases in criminality. In particular he held the press responsible for exploiting sensational crime stories and so contributing to a contagion of murder, blackmail, and pornography.[120] The fall in fertility rates he also attributed to the force of "imitation."[121] What the rise of the new, nervous, suggestible society represented in his eyes was the decline of the patriarchal family with its "serenity" and "majestic particularism." Given the intemperance and temptations fin-de-siècle society dangled before free-floating individuals, one did not have to attribute killing to the peculiarities of the "born" criminal. All men were placed at risk and only the strong could resist. "The psychology of the murderer," Tarde declared gloomily, "is the psychology of everybody."[122]

Sadism was a versatile concept that could be turned to a variety of purposes. In the literary world, novelists, who remained true to the stalest misogynistic clichés, used it to parade a fresh irreverence. In the psychiatric world its discussion began with what appeared to be a critique of masculinity but concluded with its defense. Sexual aggressiveness was part of the normal masculine psyche; only when pushed beyond the limits of the "normal" was it described by doctors as a sign of impotency rather than potency, of femininity rather than of masculinity. More sharply demarcated notions of active masculinity and passive femininity accordingly emerged from the first discussions of sadism. The new biomedical models of masculinity and femininity served ideological functions. Doctors claimed that it was "natural" or a "timeless" practice for men to use force to subdue females, yet we know that the notion of the passionless female was in fact a new nineteenth-century creation. Traditionally women were seen to be as much interested in sex as males and indeed as potentially insatiable. Late-nineteenth-century doctors, in advancing complementary psychological models of the aggressive male and the passive female, were responding to a demand. There existed a reading public that wanted to be reassured that despite the host of social changes that appeared to blur gender divisions, deep psychic cleavages necessarily separated the sexes. In locating the emergence of the concept of sadism in the context of this reordering of gender roles, it becomes clear that doctors were reflecting society's belief that the threats modern life posed the virility of the mass of ordinary men was far more worrying than the violence of the isolated pervert.[123]

In the early twentieth century, Émile Laurent, a disciple of Lacassagne, began his account of criminality by acknowledging the public's enormous interest in the stories of infamous criminals like Vacher, "le sinistre trimardeur." Laurent went on to state that crime stories—like the fabliaux of the middle ages—appealed to more than society's need to know about villainy and protect itself from it. Though the prudish might think such accounts spawned crime, in fact, by eliciting the reading public's revulsion, they played an important role in forging the social solidarity of the law abiding.[124] The discussion of sadism was likewise supposedly about monstrous criminals, but was as much about what psychiatrists believed should constitute normalcy, or normal maleness, which the above analysis suggests was not stable or fixed but a historically constructed social category. The product, along with the other sexual perversions, of an era of confusion about appropriate male behavior, sadism in its creation and exploitation helped give both positive and negative definition to fin-de-siècle masculinity. It was one of a cluster of defining concepts, its unsavory aspects fostered by the morbid sexual obsessions that permeated decadent fiction and criminal psychiatry in the closing decades of the century.

EIGHT

EXHIBITIONISTS

THE LAST THIRD OF THE NINETEENTH CENTURY WITNESSED, if one is to judge by the legal and medical writings of the time, an epidemic of male exhibitionism. The first reports came from France. Soldiers, it was said, waved their penises at women through windows. One fellow exposed himself on city streets, saying to his victims, "Je vous presente Mlle Cocodette, elle est à votre disposition." The countryside was not spared such outrages. A farm laborer referred proudly to his "inexpressible." In the first decade of the twentieth century, older peasants reported, "il m'a montré sa nature," the younger stated, "il m'a montré sa flamme."[1] Germany experienced a similar phenomenon. Herr L——, aged thirty-seven, Krafft-Ebing reported, rapped on public house windows with his penis so that children and servant girls would see it, while Dr. S——, a neuropathic sleepwalker, ran around the Berlin Zoological Gardens exposing himself.[2] To draw attention to his act and produce the maximum shock, a Strasbourg man was in the habit at night of throwing off his cloak and exposing himself under a street lamp or in the glow of an ignited match.[3]

English exhibitionists, though somewhat less dramatic, were more methodical. They included a recently married businessman who regularly left his office at mid-day wearing a long mackintosh. In a public lavatory he would remove his trousers and place them in an attaché case. With his ankles covered by his gaiters and his legs by his mac he gave the impression of still being fully dressed. So meticulously prepared, he went forth to expose himself to women on trains because, as he explained, "he felt like it." English exhibitionists included the "park pests" who offered sweets or money to children, the delusional who said they were only following the orders of the Almighty, and the obsessed who, as one claimed, had to carry out such an objectionable act as it "eased his nature." Doctors found there was little they could do with most of them. Dr. East, medical officer at Brixton prison, exasperatedly noted that a forty-eight-year-old inmate, arrested for exposing himself on a tube train, even took the opportunity while awaiting a medical examination, to expose himself to thirty other prisoners.[4]

There were few crimes that one can imagine that were more contrary to the mores of respectable, nineteenth-century, middle-class society than exhibitionism: yet what is the historian to make of it? At the turn of the century, one French doctor stated that his patient's exhibitionistic performances raised both laughs and indignation.[5] These two views, which dominated the initial discussions of such displays, likely as not hold true today. The first, the one that most deters scholars from investigating such acts, is that they were, unlike more serious forms of male perversity, silly and insignificant. The records of masochism and sadism, Lantéri-Laura has shrewdly pointed out, "conserve the dignity accruing to a narrative of pain," whereas accounts of fetishism and exhibitionism often seem little more than either sad or funny. "To risk so much for so little seems grotesque and pitiful; fetishistic clients give off the impression of being had, of paying too much for a paltry illusion."[6] Who was most harmed by such compulsive acts, if not the exhibitionist himself, who in a self-lacerating fashion rendered himself ridiculous? The second view is that exhibitionism is not a laughing matter. Such acts were "naked" demonstrations of male power. At the very least they were crude insults directed at women and children, and such assaults were moreover dangerous inasmuch as they could lead on to more serious crimes like rape.

There is some truth in both arguments, yet each misses the essential point that exhibitionism was "discovered" or "invented" at a particular time and place—in late nineteenth-century Europe. This is not to say that in other times and places men's exposing of their genitals was not censored, but in the Victorian age there emerged a new sensitivity to male nudity that was carried on into the twentieth century. Two symptoms of this new view were the creation and elaboration of the psychiatric syndrome that doctors termed "exhibitionism" and the increased levying of charges against "indecent exposure" whereby nineteenth-century medicine and law placed unprecedented restraints on the freedom of males to expose their bodies.[7] The body, anthropologists tell us, "has an iconography of signs and symbols." The regulation of the body in Victorian times, a process that Foucault linked in a slightly simplistic fashion to the growth of social scientists' knowledge and surveillance, is usually associated by scholars with restrictions applied by males to females.[8] What has not received attention and what an analysis of exhibitionism promises is some understanding of the restrictions placed by society on the male body.

At the most abstract level, the problem that this chapter wrestles with is as follows. Most males enjoyed a position of dominance vis-à-vis females in nineteenth-century western Europe and North America, not because of any ascribed status as had been the case under the old regime, but because of biological difference. Gender, Joan Scott has pointed out, had become a "primary way of signifying relationships of power."[9] A wide range of political and cultural rights were literally embodied and only enjoyed by members of the male sex. Yet a man who revealed his genitals in public was condemned by other men as a pervert or criminal. Why? Who was threatened by his actions? Contemporaries asserted that obviously women and children were endangered, but one suspects that those most involved in the discussion of exhibitionism had other preoccupations. This chapter will attempt to determine what these were. We will largely follow Foucault in arguing that those who gained most from an elaboration of the concept of "exhibitionism" were clearly not victimized women and children but the legal and medical experts who thereby widened their terrain of surveillance, albeit at the price of other men's freedom. Such an approach requires asking additional questions. Who would be labeled an exhibitionist? To what extent did the time and place and person count? Was the law employed to protect anyone or rather to set standards?

To place exhibitionism in its historical perspective, we will begin by recalling that what is considered "indecent" is a relative concept related to time and class. Even apparently naked tribes usually employ scars or tattoos as a social cover.[10] Exhibitionism was said by nineteenth-century doctors to be contrary to law, culture, and rationality, but male nudity was not repressed in all societies. In some "primitive" cultures, boys were encouraged to flaunt their genitals and engage in an exhibitionism forbidden to sisters.[11] Until the Periclean age, the Greeks employed representations of the erect phallus as the dominant symbol of power. The Cynic Peregrinus Proteus supposedly masturbated before others in the town square. Ordinary Greek men, to the amazement of foreigners, openly displayed their genitals; their male children were always depicted with their penises exposed so there would be no confusion as to their sex.[12] In Rome, as in Greece, enormous phalli were borne by women in Dionysiac processions.[13] The forceful removal of one's clothing, however, was in the ancient world as in the modern a shaming technique employed in degradation ceremonies.

There was a great gap between the Jewish and Greek views regarding nakedness; the biblical fall turned what was a symbol of innocence into a sign of evil. Moreover, nakedness was in the Jewish tradition related to the orgies of the pagans and to the poverty, vulnerability, and shame of unbelievers.[14] At the same time, the Jewish rite of circumcision focused the community's attention on the great symbolic importance of the male genitalia. Christianity, based on the credo that its God had taken on human flesh, necessarily adopted a dualistic view of the body. Representations of female nakedness were used by the church to symbolize sin, sex, and death.[15] Yet a new respect for the flesh was also embraced by Christianity. Indeed representations of Christ's nakedness were central to the Christian mystery. Leo Steinberg has perceptively revealed that "in many hundreds of pious, religious works, from before 1400 to past the mid-16th century, the ostensive unveiling of the Child's sex, or the touching, protecting or presentation of it, is the main action."[16] The Christ child's genitals had to be seen to show that he was both man and God. Social pressures and intellectual concerns in short always influenced the ways in which the naked male body was both represented and seen.[17]

Unlike the Greeks, Europeans did not have the festivals in which the magic of the exhibitionist rite was used to break taboos. The medieval period does offer us in Lady Godiva's ride one legendary act of female nudity—the story of which some scholars relate to an earlier fertility cult—but in early modern times there were many more documented male acts of ritualized nudity.[18] For example, in fifteenth-century Venice four Franciscan friars, for the purpose of demonstrating Franciscan poverty, walked nude through the streets of the city with crosses in their hands. Likewise, on Good Friday in 1438, a group of Venetian nobles belonging to a confraternity stripped off and were whipped in public by their fellow members. We know of such nude marches because they were beginning to be considered scandalous and their participants were apprehended and jailed. The new crackdown was a sign of changing preoccupations as the authorities had previously permitted other male nude processions.[19] During the Middle Ages and the Reformation, many millenarian sects that described themselves as Adamites continued to practice ritual nudity in imitation of the original man, usually in the privacy of their meeting places.[20]

In early-modern Europe, exposure of the nude body was used to signify religious humility; it was also employed for offensive purposes. Martin Luther, who claimed to have mooned the devil, maintained at least on the symbolic level the link between religion and exposure. Eric Erickson attributed to Luther an anal fixation, pointing out that he swore at the devil, "I have shit in the pants and you can hang them around your neck and wipe your mouth with it" and had prints made showing the church giving rectal birth to hordes of devils, but "mooning" or exposing one's ass to shame an enemy, far from being an individual quirk of Luther's, had a long pedigree in peasant culture.[21] Mikhail Bakhtin refers to mooning, which was incorporated in the charivaris, as "one of the most common uncrowning gestures throughout the world," though the naked buttocks, as revealed in a public thrashing, could also be a sign of humiliation.[22] To bare one's ass at another was a provocative insult; to be caught with one's pants down was shameful. In the Middle Ages, adulterers were occasionally condemned to appear nude in public. Popular woodcuts of witches frequently showed women kissing the devil's ass as a sign of their subjection. Albanian women lifted their skirts at their Montenegrin enemies, the buttocks being shown as a mark of contempt.[23] The south Slav peasants lifted their skirts with the left hand and slapped the nates with the right saying, "This is for you." In Cornwall and Wales, "Kiss my ass" was an old insult as it was in France, where Diderot included the term "baisser le cul" in *Le Nevue de Rameau* and Émile Zola had Mouquette mooning her neighbors in *Germinal.* Even local priests employed the same gestures of contempt as their congregations. In the 1830s a curé, who had been booed during mass, lifted his soutane and mooned his entire congregation.[24] The bare ass insult was clearly not restricted to the peasantry. The motif was repeatedly exploited in the eighteenth-century cartoons produced by such English artists as George Cruikshank, James Gillray, and Thomas Rowlandson; in the popular prints of Revolutionary France it enjoyed a surge in popularity. Depictions of mooning disappeared from British publications by the 1830s, but were retained by the more daring nineteenth-century French journals.[25]

Though there is obviously a difference between a man exposing his ass and his penis, the fact that a man had exhibited his genitals was in early modern Europe not taken all that seriously. European men of fashion, it has to be recalled, though not actual exhibitionists, for centuries dressed in such a way as to accentuate if not exaggerate the size of their penises. The codpiece acted as a sort of sartorial flying buttress.[26] Montaigne argued in the mid sixteenth century that the flaunting of the loins was an obvious continuation of the phallic ceremonies of the Greeks.

> And I know not whether I have not in my time seen some air of like devotion. What was the meaning of that ridiculous thing our forefathers wore on the forepart of their breeches, and that is still worn by the Swiss? To what end do we make a show of our implements in figure under our gaskins, and often, which is worse, above

their natural size, by falsehood and imposture? I have half a mind
to believe that this sort of vestment was invented in the better and
more conscientious ages, that the world might not be deceived, and
that every one should give a public account of his proportions: the
simple nations wear them yet, and near about the real size.[27]

Even when the "public account" involved the actual exposure of the penis,
the act seems not to have been regarded by the authorities as too worrying.
In Renaissance Venice, for example, morality laws focused rather on such
issues as fornication, marriage, rape, and adultery. Since the concern of the
community was with marriage and its accompanying property arrangements, little attention was paid to obscene acts that did not put them at
risk. In 1474 a Venetian noble, Andrea Coppo, was accused "of agitating
his virile member most evilly in the presence of Marino, a goldworker."
Since there was no contact, but only exhibitionism no charge was laid.[28]
Masturbation was tolerated by Venetians; sodomy they punished by death.
A man convicted of this crime in the excessively moralistic city state of
Siena was hanged by his testicles in public for an entire day.

Women ran the greater risk of having men expose themselves to them.
"Master Thomas Ysakyr," reported a London church official in 1476,
"showed his private parts to many women in the parish." One milk maid
in early-seventeenth-century England reported being called to by a man
over the hedge: "Agnes, my prick doth stand and hath a great whiles for
thee."[29] These cases were regarded as indecent by the ecclesiastical courts
that reprimanded the culprits, yet some genital exhibitions were, as late
as the nineteenth century in areas such as North Wales, apparently part of
a courtship ritual by which a man sought to prove his virility. Taking his
partner to an isolated spot he would ask: "'Do you wish to . . . (rhythu)'" If
she said 'yes,' he would hold the brim of her hat between his teeth, then
open the front part of his trousers and urinate on her dress. By exposing
himself, he was proving his virility to the woman."[30] In the early twentieth
century a French sexologist reported that amongst peasants and workers,
where there was less "sexual censorship" it was still not uncommon for a
young man to jokingly expose himself to a group of young women.[31]

More serious public displays of virility also took place on the continent.
Men in sixteenth-century Italy, as in seventeenth-and eighteenth-century
France, might formally counter rumors of impotency that could lead to the
annulment of their marriages, by demonstrating before assemblies of
priests, physicians, and jurists their erections and on occasion even proof
of ejaculation.[32] In the early modern period, the purposeful exposure of
the genitals in and of itself, though not considered an "innocent" act, was

in short not one that the community felt warranted undue attention. Such a deed could be located within a familiar repertoire of obscene gestures; the sense of shame that was to become associated with this action in modern times had yet to be instilled.[33] The usual assumption was that a man exposed himself for a reason—to either insult or seduce his victim.

In the eighteenth century, a new notion began to emerge, the idea that the genital display could, in providing sexual pleasure to the exhibitionist, be an "irrational" end in itself. Though such a syndrome might well have existed earlier, it appears to have been first reported by Jean-Jacques Rousseau. The young Rousseau, timid but sexually aroused, admitted to having exposed himself to some women in 1728; he was apprehended but let loose. He was not trying to insult or seduce the women; in his *Confessions* he spoke with his customary candor of simply the foolish pleasure he experienced in displaying his "ridiculous object."[34] It was fitting that the man most associated with popularizing new notions of chaste romantic love based on a rigid demarcation of male and female gender roles should also chronicle the birth of a new perversion. One could not exist without the other.

The titillation a man might have experienced in exposing the body could only have been heightened as a greater stress was placed by society on covering it. From the sixteenth century onward, all forms of exposing the male body came to be regarded by the social elite as in increasingly bad taste. Norbert Elias has charted this "civilizing process" by which the issue of how one appropriately expressed oneself was worked out.[35] He attributes the growing constraint and repugnance for old uncouth manners and the stress on new forms of socially acceptable behavior in eating, speaking, and attending to natural functions to new social elites' desire to mark the distance that separated their culture from that of ignorant rustics. Well-off men were taught by Erasmus and others to be embarrassed if they manifested the indifference of peasants to bodily propriety.

> A well-bred person should always avoid exposing without necessity the parts to which nature has attached modesty. If necessity compels this, it should be done with decency and reserve, even if no witness is present. For angels are always present, and nothing is more welcome to them in a boy than modesty, the companion and guardian of decency. If it arouses shame to show them to the eyes of others, still less should they be exposed to their touch.[36]

To the question "Which is the more shameful part: the part in front or the hole in the arse?" the Spanish humanist educator Luis Vives replied, "Both parts are extremely improper, the behind because of its unpleasantness, and the other part because of lechery and dishonor."[37] Richard Weste, in *The Book of Demeanor and the Allowance and Disallowance of Certaine Misdemeanors in Companie* (1619), advised his readers:

> Let not thy privy members be
> layd open to be view'd
> it is most shameful and abhorred,
> detestable and rude.[38]

Accordingly German Court regulations forbad gentlemen to relieve themselves in front of ladies or on stairs.

By the late eighteenth century, it was not necessary for writers of books on manners to go on at length about the bad taste of scratching and touching oneself. Stricter controls on the impulses and emotions had been largely ingrained in the upper classes, yet the status of the observer and the observed still determined whether shame was experienced or not. It was commonly acknowledged that there were people—one's equals or superiors—before whom one was ashamed to expose one's nakedness, but that before one's inferiors one was not. Voltaire's mistress, the Marquise de Châtelet, it was reported, "shows herself naked to her servant while bathing in a way that casts him into confusion, and then with a total unconcern scolds him because he is not pouring in the hot water properly."[39] Male and female members of the upper classes who continued well on into the nineteenth century to disrobe in front of their domestics were accordingly never to be labeled exhibitionists.

Nevertheless, in general, new, higher standards of body coverage—sustained by such technological changes as the water closet and the belts, buttons, buckles, lighter textiles and underclothing accessible to the middle class—were established by the nineteenth century. In a few short years, well-brought-up Victorian children went through the evolution—from nakedness first eliciting their curiosity and then their shame—that had taken their society centuries to complete. Moreover, as the Western world became more democratic, argues Elias, such bodily taboos were equalized. Though exposure of the body was initially associated with the poverty of the lower orders, the social references of the taboos against the disclosure of the natural functions were slowly forgotten.[40] By the nineteenth century, the bourgeoisie could only take the inability to control oneself and keep one's privates covered as evidence of either mental illness or criminality.

The living conditions of the great mass of the nineteenth-century population were such that they could not have been as prudish as once was claimed, but for the middle class at least most forms of public exposure of the body became shameful. For example, a French woman could no longer seek to have her marriage ended by recourse to the "impotence trials," which required her husband's genitals to be examined. "If private interests must suffer," declared an 1858 decree, "it is justifiable to impose such a sacrifice in the broader interests of public order and morals."[41] For some nakedness, even in the privacy of the marital bed, was no longer acceptable. The nightdress for both men and women emerged in the Victorian world; and then for men the more socially presentable pajamas.[42] Sleep itself became a more private affair, with servants and children banished from the master bedroom. Indeed even public references to the bed were considered by the prudish to be shameful; in the nineteenth century the respectable "retired" for the night.

Daytime male dress also changed. Nineteenth-century women's fashions, dominated by the corset and bustle, accentuated the female's bosom and backside. In short her sexuality was magnified, but at the same time men's sexuality was hidden. Male fashions no longer drew attention to the legs and thighs. The tight breeches and stockings were replaced by the 1830s in England by looser fitting trousers. And the "full fall" of the breeches was replaced by the 1860s with the more discreet buttoned fly front. For formal occasions the middle-class male donned a black three-piece suit. For every day dress, drab grays, blues, and browns replaced lighter colors and coarser wools the finer fabrics. Recourse by men to corsets and cosmetics became a laughing matter. Swords were replaced by walking sticks; ostentatious jewelry by utilitarian watches and fobs. By the twentieth century, the only hints of color were found in the tie or cravat, which led the eye away from the genitals up to the man's head.[43] A glance at a portrait of Marx or Engels reminds us that even political radicals donned the new uniform of the bourgeoisie. The tone had been set by the American revolutionaries' contempt for "Yankee Doodle Dandy" and the French sans-culottes of 1789, who attacked as reactionary and pretentious fops men who affected too much attention to their dress. In response the pose of the dandy was taken up by such decadent artists and bohemians as Baudelaire, Barbey d'Aurevilly, Wilde, Swinburne, and Beardsley who wished to parade their disdain for middle-class proprieties.[44] The extent to which Western society sought to hide the male body was perhaps best evidenced in nineteenth-century artistic representations. Female nudes were found in libraries and town halls, representing everything from "Liberty" and "Electricity" to "Slavery" and "Morphine." The nude male virtually disappeared from the painter's canvas. Visitors to galleries could imagine a no more shocking idea than that of a naked man as a subject for artistic representation.[45]

An examination of the English case law on indecent exposure demonstrates how the new restrictions on male nudity were imposed. Rex versus Sedley (1663) first established the principle that at common law it was a misdemeanor to commit an outraging of public decency in such a way that more than one person sees the act.[46] Sir Charles Sedley, a friend of Charles II, was indicted for exposing himself naked with two drunken friends on the balcony of the aptly named Cock Tavern in Covent Garden and urinating on the large crowd below. All three stripped off, and Sedley preached a mock sermon before over one thousand spectators. Sedley, Pepys noted in his diary for 1 July 1663, acted out all the postures of "lust and buggery," gave a Mountebank sermon, and while ridiculing doctors claimed to have a powder "as should make all the cunts in town run after him. . . . And that being done, he took a glass of wine and washed his prick in it and then drank it off; and then took another and drank the King's health."[47]

It appears to have been not uncommon for seventeenth-century revelers, when deep in their cups, to strip naked, but Sedley with his mock sermon had gone too far. He was apprehended by the outraged crowd and forced to appear in court, where the question was posed as to what law he had broken. The Star Chamber, which previously had been responsible for moral charges (which it in turn had taken over from the ecclesiastical courts) had been abolished as a result of the English Civil War. There was accordingly no specific law against what Sedley had done, and being a gentleman, he was merely fined two thousand marks and bound to keep the peace.[48] Sedley's blasphemy was what appears to have most preoccupied the seventeenth-century authorities; his two friends who had merely stripped off were not charged. But by the next century, it was Sedley's indecency, not his irreligion, that was remembered. Henry Fielding referred to the case as typical of an "open act of lewdness and indecency in public, to the scandal of good manners."[49] Pornography was likewise initially regarded by the respectable as dangerous inasmuch as it critiqued religion and politics. Decency only became a central concern in the late eighteenth and early nineteenth centuries.[50]

The clash between new standards of propriety and the traditional rights of males was first played out in nineteenth-century court cases over bans on male nude bathing. In 1809 a Mr. Crunden attempted to counter such restrictions by arguing that nude male swimming was not indecent. Whole regiments of men had traditionally swum naked near Brighton. They had no criminal intent and sought only to improve their health; if such nudity was a "nuisance," he argued, it was one to which the new home builders had come. Mr. Justice McDonald tersely replied that this appeal to traditional liberties was pointless because such acts were now obviously indecent and outrageous.

> Nor is it any justification that bathing at this spot might a few years ago be innocent. For anything that I know, a man might a few years ago have harmlessly danced naked in the fields beyond Montague House; but it will scarcely be said by the learned counsel for the defendant, that anyone might now do so with impunity in Russell Square. Whatever place becomes the habitation of civilized men, there the laws of decency must be enforced.[51]

Similarly the Sussex Spring Assizes meeting at Lewes on 25 March 1871 heard the case of Regina versus Reed and Others, in which a Mr. Stamford, a man apparently gifted with remarkable eyesight, claimed he could see stark naked men swimming half a mile from his house on the outskirts of Chichester. The men replied once again that there was a long tradition of bathing at that particular spot. The prosecution countered that it was unjust that females had to shun a pleasant walk, and the court took the side of the ladies, concluding that concerns for indecency overrode any "usage to so bathe, however long it might have existed."[52]

Despite the fact that some gentlemen came into conflict with the law over their right to swim in the nude, English law primarily associated indecency with lower-class males. Section Four of the Vagrancy Act of 1824 held as liable "every Person willfully, openly, lewdly and obscenely exposing his person in any Street, Road or public Highway, or in the View thereof, or in any Place of public Resort, with Intent to insult any Female." The crime could only be committed by a man exposing his penis, presumably a poor man, as the indecency provision was lumped in with references to the idle and disorderly, including fortune tellers, readers of palms, wanderers and those sleeping in barns and outhouses without obvious means of subsistence, those exposing wounds or deformities to gather alms, men who ran away and left a wife and children on the parish, those betting in the street, anyone having burglary tools or a gun or cutlass with intent, and any suspect person loitering on dock, wharf, canal, or street. Those found guilty of such crimes could be committed as rogues and vagabonds to the House of Correction for three months hard labor.[53] Men were also specifically targeted by the Police of Towns Act of 1847, which held to be committing an offense "Every person who willfully and indecently exposes his Person."[54]

English common law held that for an act to be indecent it had to be made in public; that is, more than one person had to see it occur.[55] Early-nineteenth-century judges were fairly cautious in defining what was "public," even if it meant morality was on occasion outraged. In the 1840s one judge stoically opined that although the law could not be applied to cases where a man exposed himself to one woman, there were in any event many offenses against morality that the law could not hope to reach.[56] Thus James Webb, who on 2 October 1848 exposed himself to Mary Ann Cherrill, who was tending the bar at a victualing house, had his conviction overturned on the grounds that more than one person had to witness the act.[57] However, George Thallman, a servant, failed when employing the same defense. On the night of 31 July 1863, he exposed himself for twenty minutes from the roof of a house on Albermarle Street, Hanover Square, to the female servants across the way. He repeated his performance the subsequent evening and was apprehended. His ingenious argument that, since he could not be seen from the street below he had not exposed himself in a "public" place, was rejected. All that was necessary to make an act public, concluded the judges, was that several people could see it.[58]

Equally unsuccessful was Frederick Wellard, an ex-convict who, in the summer of 1884 in a marsh near Maidstone, Kent, paid seven or eight girls between the ages of eight and eleven a few pennies to observe him exposing himself. Some boys swimming in the nude nearby, wondering what the girls were up to, dressed and followed them. The boys—whose nudity was passed over by the court in silence—reported what they saw, and Wellard was tried and convicted for having indecently exposed his person in a "public place." His appeal was based on the fact that he carried out his act on private property, but the court held that the "offence may be indictable if committed before divers subjects of the realm, even if the place be not public." Indeed Mr. Justice Huddleston argued that even indecencies committed in a private place should be punishable.[59]

An examination of the development of English case law reveals that the English authorities employed increasingly repressive interpretations of the statutes to ban male genital displays. Such interpretations were purportedly designed to protect women from men, but many were turned to the purposes of criminalizing homosexual acts. At the Westminster Sessions of 7 May 1842, Michael Rowed and a friend were charged with having met "for the purpose and with the intent of committing with each other, openly, lewdly and indecently, in the said public place, divers nasty, wicked, filthy, lewd, beastly, unnatural and sodomitical practices." Rowed was found guilty; his counsels appealed that no specific offense was charged with any certainty. Perhaps exposure and sodomy were involved in what the two men had been up to in Kensington Gardens, but only vague epithets had been employed by the prosecution. The judges agreed and held that the judgment had to be arrested.[60]

Similarly the Central Criminal Court in April 1848 heard that the previous February James Thurtle met James Orchard in the Farringdon Market urinal. There they "did exhibit and expose their persons and private parts to each other in indecent postures and situations, with intent then and there to stir up and excite in their own minds, and in the minds of each other filthy, wicked, lewd, beastly, unnatural and sodomitical desires and inclinations." Each, moreover, the charge read, "did lay his hands on the person and private parts" of the other. The defense argued that the urinal was not a public place and more importantly that no specific act had been charged. The judges again agreed that for indecent exposure to take place more than one person needed to see and that an act, rather than an intention, had to be specified in a charge.[61]

By 1870, however, a urinal, which was the central concern in Regina versus Samuel Harris and Henry Cocks, was declared by the appeal court to be a public place.[62] Two plain clothes officers, claiming they had received complaints, kept watch through an opening into the compartment of a urinal in Hyde Park. On 10 October 1870 they reported finding Harris and Cocks facing each other. "Cocks turned round, and the prisoners exposed their persons and committed acts of lewdness." The defense held that the acts did not take place in an open and public place but in a urinal fourteen feet from the footpath and past a gate. Moreover, a urinal, necessarily requiring exposure of the person, was by definition not public. The appeal judges in this instance held that a urinal was a public place and sustained the convictions of the accused.

In Victorian England indecent exposure was treated by the courts more and more severely, the authorities regarding it as a legal rather than a medical problem. Magistrates rarely called on doctors to throw light on the mental condition of the accused. The few prisoners examined were, the unsympathetic Alfred Swain Taylor informed the readers of his classic text on legal medicine, "almost invariably found to be lunatics."[63] And if exposing oneself was not attributed to madness, it was taken as a symptom of working-class immorality. Havelock Ellis stated that some ignorant males actually thought exposing oneself was a good way to attract the attention of females. Dr. East gave the example of a youth of eighteen whose room overlooked an orphan school. After several fourteen-year-old girls lifted their skirts at him, he exposed himself, was seen and arrested. Another sixteen-year-old boy exposed himself three times from his own window as friends had told him that it was "an efficient means of exciting a girl." Such repellent cases conjured up in the imagination of observers like Dr. East the "courtships of the farmyard."[64] Dr. Booth, in describing a patient who exposed himself so frequently that the newspapers reported his activities and the police hunted him down, was one of the first English doctors to use the term exhibitionist. His patient claimed to feel a "wave" passing over him and to remember neither the deed nor any feelings of sexual desire. Indeed he carried out the act with a "silly grin" on his face. The accused, whom Booth thought was suffering from overwork, was acquitted on grounds of insanity.[65]

This idea that a certain sort of otherwise sane man—the exhibitionist—might have an overwhelming need to expose himself, which was only taken up in England at the turn of the century, had been first advanced by French psychiatrists. According to Paul Garnier, a medical expert attached to the Paris prefecture of police, cases of such men exposing themselves became so common on the continent in the last third of the nineteenth century that magistrates finally turned for help to the doctors. The result was the elaboration by French physicians of a new psychiatric syndrome. A typical case was that of D——, a forty-five-year-old typographer arrested in 1893. Since 1877 D—— had been arrested five times for exposing himself. He was a dreamer whose unspecified hereditary weakness, which surfaced in childhood, led to his being released from the army. He claimed to have no knowledge of his acts, but little girls told their parents, "Cet homme m'a montré son devant." As he suffered on occasions from a mysterious "mal," something like epilepsy, the court agreed with the medical expert that D—— was sick and sent him to the asile of Sainte-Anne.[66]

A similar case requiring treatment was that of a young, married worker previously arrested twice for masturbating in front of a girls school. The doctors attributed the man's pernicious habit to his "bad heredity," his addiction to onanism, and his having been led astray at an early age by a young woman. Though married this small, weak, naive individual experienced the need to "se déboutonner et d'étaler ses organes génitales." It was clearly an obsession. He knew others did not do it, and he struggled against it.[67] A final example was that of E——, a timid thirty-two-year-old knife-grinder, who though illiterate and burdened with an asymmetrical head, had proven himself a good worker and soldier. An orphan, he had been first caught at the age of thirteen masturbating near some women. As an adult he exposed himself to women and children. Occasionally he paid the latter a few sous to touch his penis. The idea of exposing himself, sometimes inspired by the presence of little girls, would come to him while working. His wife could notice the change in his expression. He claimed not to know what he was doing but afterward experienced feelings of fear and guilt. Usually he did not have an erection and was always repentant. His punishments, which escalated from a twenty-five-franc fine to eight days in jail to three months in prison, had no effect. In 1895 he was condemned to four months in prison for having shown his "verge" to some little girls on the main street of P——, a town of two thousand inhabitants. It was his fourth offense. He left prison on 14 January 1896; on 3 February he again exposed himself and was re-arrested.[68] Such manias, argued the doctors, proved the impotency of attempting to deal with perverts via the Criminal Code. These men were not criminals; they were victims of an exhibitionistic obsession.[69]

What did the experts mean by the term *exhibitionisme*? Paul Garnier defined it as "a sexual pervert obsession and impulse characterized by an irresistible tendency to exhibit in public, generally with a sort of fixity of hours and place, the genitalia in a state of flaccidity without any lascivious provocation; an act in which the sexual appetite expresses itself, and the accomplishment of which, closing the agonizing struggle, finishes the attack."[70] Dr. Charles Lasègue (who in 1873 had also created the concept of the hysterical syndrome of anorexia nervosa) coined the term *exhibitioniste* in 1877.[71] The concept was quickly picked up.[72] Valentin Magnan stressed the importance to the patient of the particular time and place of the act, his struggle to fight against it, and his limited goal.[73]

Who was an exhibitionist? The first point that the doctors stressed was that only men were exhibitionists, an issue to which we will return. The second point was that the "true" exhibitionist could not help himself.[74] Krafft-Ebing, the leading German sexologist, labeled exhibitionists psychopaths, the majority of whom he claimed were senile, epileptic, and impotent. Modesty and decency were expected of the normal. He who violated decency was either an idiot incapable of moral feelings or a neurotic suffering a loss of consciousness.[75] On the contrary, most experts came to exclude the weak-minded and imbeciles including some who whistled to draw attention to themselves. Also excluded were general paralytics, the senile, and epileptics.[76] The doctors stressed that those who felt a compulsion to expose themselves and achieved sexual pleasure thereby were not just the old and the debauched, the drunk and the mad; they included the married and others who were otherwise "normal." The true exhibitionist was silent and repetitive. He was conscious and struggled against his desires but knew he would succumb despite his best intentions.

The third point noted by doctors was that the true exhibitionist was not seeking to seduce or insult his victim. Some of these men were married, and their deviancy proved—to the surprise of conservatives who often prescribed marriage as a cure for deviancy—that one sex act did not compensate for another. Such irresponsible perverts were usually timid and solitary and sought no direct contact with their prey. Sexual release came to them from the exhibitionistic display itself. Dr. East imaginatively described as "visionaries" the men in his sample who received pleasure, even complete orgasm from mere exposure.[77] Some doctors argued that exhibitionists' finer feelings must have been blunted for they often selected children as their victims.[78] Other experts pointed out that since the exhibitionist's intent was not to establish any sort of relationship his favored prey were children and young females, whom he could most count on to be repelled rather than attracted by genital displays. Exhibitionism followed a ritual character; the man sought a reaction, even signs of disgust rather than his victims' positive response.

Why did one become an exhibitionist? Exhibitionism was attributed by most French physicians in the first instance to the taint of degeneration. Paul Garnier traced the power of exhibitionist obsessions and impulses, like the other sexual perversions, back to the degenerate state of the patient, who carried "stigmates moraux." Paul Moreau (de Tours), concurred, listing as contributing causes the patient's age, constitution, physical and psychological problems, and weakness for liquor and debauchery.[79] Alfred Binet stressed the more modern notion that early shocks and unhealthy associations were responsible for planting the seeds of an exhibitionist passion. Perhaps the patient's first sexual experience occurred when he was caught naked; he later sought to recapture the experience and was seduced into the habit.[80] But Garnier countered that only those already degenerate would be susceptible to such a vice.[81]

The doctors argued, in a circular fashion, that the proof that an exhibitionist was a degenerate was that he did not behave in a mature sexual manner and the proof of his degeneracy was his exhibitionism. The fetishist, argued Garnier, focused unhealthily on a part of a person, not the whole. Exhibitionism was a similar type of incompleted courtship—a "sorte d'ectopie amoureuse"—or psychic onanism. In England Havelock Ellis agreed that exhibitionists were congenitally abnormal and suffered from a "pseudo-atavism" due to a paralysis of "higher feelings." Exhibitionists were feeble, usually degenerate, and often alcoholic. In the early twentieth century, Dr. East, who likened exhibitionism to other infantile habits such as sticking out one's tongue, claimed he was unhappy using the term degenerate since, as he perceptively pointed out, it denoted no precise clinical entity and tended "to thwart clear thinking or psychological investigation." Yet East in general also attributed sexual offenses to "pathological heredity."[82] He actually found mental abnormality in only nineteen of 150 cases of exhibitionism but insisted on attributing this "disappointing result" to criminals' ignorance of their families and their reluctance to admit defects.[83]

We know who, according to the doctors, exposed themselves and why. Where did they expose themselves and to whom? Such questions are important because, as Goffman has pointed out, even profane acts that seem to be driven by "blind impulse" have symbolic meaning. Dr. Serge Paul perceptively noted that the exhibitionist followed an unconscious script. He did not flash other men but targeted women and children. Some saw exhibitionism as similar to masochism inasmuch as the man sought humiliation—not coitus—as the source of his pleasure. But the exhibitionist moreover sought the humiliation of the child or women, especially the elegant female. This fastidiousness was manifested by one of Dr. Paul's patients haughtily reporting that he never went to the Bois de Boulogne on Sunday because that was "workers day." It followed as well that the exhibitionist shunned prostitutes, who were subjected to the attention of so many other perverts, knowing they would be the least likely to be shocked.[84]

Churches, with their darkened naves and opportunities for one-on-one confrontations, seem to have held a particular appeal for the French exhibitionist.[85] Magnan cited the cases of a twenty-nine-year-old waiter who flashed from under a church portal, a twenty-seven-year-old ex-soldier who shifted his locale from street urinals to chapels, and a man who exhibited himself to girls in a churchyard.[86] Those deviants who entered churches usually sought only one or two victims and carefully avoided the busy hours. Garnier provided the 1900 Congress of Medicine in Paris with an extensive report of a patient who was in the habit of exposing himself in the church of Saint-Roche in Paris. "I know what repulsion my conduct must inspire," he confessed, yet if he had to carry out his act in a church he did not see it as an act of profanation.[87] A woman in church, he imagined, would appreciate the gravity of the act and not take it as a joke. The doctor concluded that some exhibitionism was not lubricious or provocative but indeed "platonic"![88] He wondered if the vice was not linked to some phallic cult tradition. The French preferences in locales can be interestingly contrasted with those of the English. In England exhibitionists were reportedly found in the streets, on trains, and in trams, but the archetypal flasher was the "park pest" found lurking near the local public green or common. Churches were rarely the site of their activities, which leads one to speculate that the park was chosen not simply due to convenience but because it enjoyed in late-nineteenth-century English culture a sacrosanct quality equivalent to that of the church in France.

The fact that the men whom the experts labeled exhibitionists were mainly drawn from the lower classes appeared to sustain the degeneration hypothesis. Yet Hôpital noted that there was no predicting who might become an exhibitionist; some were intelligent.[89] If little was known of the deviant sexual behavior of the social elite, it was because their foibles were rarely brought to the attention of police or magistrates. The middle-class man who flashed his servants, for example, would not be arrested because they would not complain. Doctors obviously knew more about exhibitionism than did the police. Havelock Ellis gave the case of a London actor of high standing who went through such an exhibitionist stage, yet "the attention of the police was never attracted to the matter, and so far as possible he was quietly supervised by his friends."[90] Dr. Voisin reported that he had similar cases, including a composer who "s'est déculotté" several times in good company and a painter who "baissait aussi son pantalon."[91] Such "eccentrics" could be found at the highest levels of society. Lewis Harcourt, the one-time British colonial secretary, was in the habit of exposing himself at his estate to children, including one whose cousin later recalled: "He asked her if she would like to see the grotto, took her there and said, 'I'll show you my stalactite.' The poor girl got such a shock she became deaf."[92] The girl did not inform the police; an Eton school boy did complain to his mother, and Harcourt, who had made the mistake of preying on his social equals, only avoided a public scandal by committing suicide.

Doctors appeared to feel duty bound to cover up the moral failings of the propertied. At the very least, they acknowledged that care had to be taken that innocent middle-class men not be carelessly branded as exhibitionists.[93] Dr. Laugier asserted that respectable gentlemen plagued with urinary problems, having failed to reach the nearest vespasienne or lavatory, were sometimes mistakenly arrested while urinating in public.[94] And every small town, Dr. Hôpital noted, had some old, rich bachelor who sooner or later would be attacked as an exhibitionist. The authorities had to be alert in such cases, as in all sex crimes, that an attempt at blackmail did not lie behind a trumped up charge.[95] When there was irrefutable evidence that otherwise upstanding members of the community were exposing themselves, doctors could not hide their astonishment that for a ridiculous pleasure well-placed men would risk their reputation, honor, and interests.[96] Observers noted that they afterward necessarily felt like fools.[97] Such indignant doctors expressed a curiosity bordering on sympathy for compulsive middle-class deviants whose monomanias, in alternating sexual excitations and oppressive fears, pushed them to the edge of insanity.

The doctors attributed the exhibitionism of the otherwise respectable to a variety of extenuating circumstances. First was stress. Middle-class men, it was argued, "overworked and brain worn," could become victims of such obsessions. Lasègue attributed exhibitionism to a morbid anxiety associated with the pressures of modern life. From America Hughes gave the case of an "over-brain-strained minister of the gospel," whose automatic acts were ended by rest, restoratives, and a vacation. Less fortunate was Charles K. Cannon, a wealthy Jersey City lawyer, who was sentenced to fifteen years in prison after seventeen girls between the ages of eight and fourteen testified against him. Hughes argued that mental decay not moral guilt was the issue in such cases. Doctors had to use psychopathology to separate the acts of the moral and well-ordered from those of the "voluntarily vulgar and depraved sensualist."[98] It should be recalled that Lasègue, who coined the term exhibitionist, to explain the irrational acts of otherwise virile and honorable men also popularized the concept of kleptomania to explain the department store thefts of well-off women. These women, he argued, fell victim to the calculated provocation, the seduction, the solicitation of modern merchandising. And just as their thefts were absurd and uncalculating, so too were the actions of exhibitionists. In both cases, he asserted, the acts were carried out "not because of the powerfulness of the excitation, but because of the insufficiency of the resistance to a temptation."[99]

A second attenuating circumstance was sexual frustration. Dr. East provided two such cases. The first was that of a thirty-two-year-old man who had served in the army in India. East clearly thought it significant that the man had indulged in sexual relations with native women but when married in England was forced by economic necessity to practice coitus interruptus with his wife. Walking across a common, he picked up a "continental book," which excited him, and so he exposed himself to children.[100] The doctor's second case was that of a neurotic middle-aged man whose wife refused him all sexual relations. He was found guilty of exposing himself on three occasions, despite the fact that, as East sadly noted, "an enormous pendulous abdomen must have partially, if not entirely, concealed his genitals."[101]

Presented with middle-class exhibitionist patients, doctors at the turn of century shifted from a degeneration to a more psychodynamic explanation of the malady. Exhibitionistic temptations, researchers admitted, were not restricted simply to the degenerate. Even the dour Krafft-Ebing spoke of graffiti artists who drew genitals as practicing a sort of "ideal exhibitionism."[102] The telling of off-color stories, Ellis pointed out, was a sort of "psychic exhibitionism" in which the enjoyment came from the confusion caused. To the list of "verbal exhibitionists," who make obscene remarks, and "ideal exhibitionists," who looked at smutty pictures, George Jacoby added peepers and voyeurs who simply stared at clothed women and undressed them in their mind, to obtain "illusionary cohabitation."[103] Dreams about being "insufficiently dressed," J. J. Putnam asserted, revealed the fact that nearly everyone at some time had exhibitionist preoccupations.[104] Sex reformers such as Paolo Mantegazza and Iwan Bloch adopted a relativist, ethnographic approach in calling for a greater understanding of variations in sexual practices.[105] The word exhibitionism was new to the nineteenth century, but, Dr. Hôpital noted in 1905, the obscene relics of the classical world found in repositories such as the museum at Naples revealed that the act was not.[106]

Exhibitionism was recognized in the early twentieth century by the progressive as part of the normal "exploratory behavior" of the young. The problem with the adult exhibitionist, according to such experts, was that he had not moved on to complete his pursuit of the female. Havelock Ellis declared that the exhibitionist was prevented from physically taking the female and only provided a symbolic declaration of love, a "psychical defloration." "We may probably best approach exhibitionism by regarding it as fundamentally a symbolic act based on a perversion of courtship. The exhibitionist displays the organ of sex to a feminine witness, and in the shock of modest sexual shame by which she reacts to that spectacle, he finds a gratifying similitude of the normal emotions of coitus. He feels he has effected a psychic defloration."[107] East suggested that onanism led to such exhibitionism; both were products of fantasy; one impulsive habit led to the next.[108]

Freud made the curious assertion that "the genitals themselves have not taken part in the development of the human body in the direction of beauty."[109] Beauty here was very much in the eye of the beholder. Freud, in implying that elbows, toes, ears and noses had somehow over the millennia gained an attractiveness that penises and vaginas had mysteriously failed to attain, was simply falling back on popular notions of Darwinian evolution to justify common prudery. More insightful was his observation that every exhibitionist was also a voyeur; in both cases the eye corresponded to an "erotogenic zone." Touching and looking, according to Freud, were not perversions, "provided that in the long run the sexual act is carried further."[110] Just as children's interest in genitals was repressed with the development of a sense of shame, so Freud argued, for the purpose of keeping sexual curiosity alive adults had practiced, as civilization advanced, a progressive concealment of the body. The normal process of repression was in the case of the exhibitionist either exaggerated or incomplete. He exhibited his own genitals in hopes of reciprocation and thereby provided evidence of his psychosexual infantilism. The Spanish biologist Gregorio Marañon made much the same point in arguing that Casanova, in exposing himself, was manifesting his sexual deficiencies. According to the old proverb, "la bonne marchandise n'a pas besoin d'être étalée."[111]

Wilhelm Stekel similarly regarded exhibitionism as a childlike tendency to show rather than to communicate; he curiously likened the compulsion, which he related to the oral stage of development, to a desire for "eternal suckling."[112] Some psychoanalysts believe exhibitionism expressed the patient's fear of castration; the self-exposure found in the victim's shock proved that the genitals were alive and well. Others blamed the syndrome on the patient attempting to break from his narcissistic, penis-envying mother.[113] How helpful all these theories were is a moot point. East reported that at least one subject blamed his psychoanalyst rather than his mother for failing to cure him of his exhibitionist tendencies. These turn-of-the-century views of exhibitionism were liberal inasmuch as they acknowledged that everyone was prone to exhibitionistic temptations, but they still damned the patient as infantile who did not have the will power to fight off his desires. The voice of the patient is rarely heard in such accounts. Possibly the exhibitionist was not an infantile slave to but actually a "friend" of his instinct, something he could never admit in court.[114] The magistrates and doctors insisted on either a "cure" or a punishment; the accused who sought to avoid jail necessarily had to say that he was a victim of an irresistible urge or compulsion.

By way of concluding this examination of exhibitionism, let us return to Michel Foucault, who cites the arrest in 1867 in the village of Lapcourt of a simple-minded farm hand who had exposed himself to a little girl. The parents complained to the mayor, who in turn called in the gendarmes. The accused was examined by doctors and eventually locked up in the asylum at Maréville.[115] Foucault's exasperated reading of the case was that a simpleton who had "obtained a few caresses from a little girl" for a penny or two had been made the subject of a medical discourse. "The pettiness of it all; the fact that this everyday occurrence in the life of village sexuality, these inconsequential bucolic pleasures, could become from a certain time, the object not only of collective intolerance but of a judicial action, a medical intervention, a careful clinical examination, and an entire theoretical elaboration."[116] Foucault's main point is well taken. Sexologists and psychologists advanced their professions' fortunes by medicalizing variations in sexual practices. It would be wrong, however, to imagine that nineteenth-century experts were free, for the purposes of increasing their professional power, to "invent" perversions at will. The experts, we might paraphrase, made the pervert but not under conditions of their own choosing. These conditions in the nineteenth century were dominated by shifting gender relationships that focused the attention of all members of society on relatively new notions of sexual incommensurability. It is possible, though we can never really know, that this new stress on males being biologically the "opposite" of females led to an actual rise in the number of men who exposed themselves. At the very least, the new range of "body techniques" employed by some men in the last century to cloak their physicality in a decent way presumably incited and taught others how to expose theirs in an indecent fashion.[117] In addition, worries about lower-class sexual predators, greater concerns about juvenile sexuality, and a fear of actions that in an urban milieu were not given the innocent gloss they might have been awarded in a rural setting forced a timeless practice onto the attention of legal and medical authorities. Our chief interest has been in the demonstrable increase in the "reportage" of exhibitionism. Males had no doubt long exposed themselves, but doctors in discovering and diagnosing such acts as psychotic compulsions granted them an unprecedented significance.[118]

The notion that the surveillance of sexuality should be entrusted to doctors benefited the medical profession; what of the exhibitionists? Typically shy, impulsive, and obsessional, they were "eccentric" rather than psychopathic. They represented a broad cross-section of the population by age and profession, though they were more timid and inhibited than most. One commentator has likened their vice to stammering, not communicating but making oneself conspicuous.[119] Though they were rarely violent or otherwise criminal, exhibitionists were treated severely.[120] In the twentieth century, more men were jailed for exhibitionism than any other sex crime. Why was their form of erotic enjoyment regarded as so dangerous? A common argument was that exhibitionists might go on to rape their victims. This on occasion did happened, but it was most unusual for a minor offense to progress to a more serious one. In any event the rapist was regarded by doctors as being a more healthy heterosexual than the exhibitionist. The actions of the former made sense; those of the latter did not. Indeed the fact that such men did not seek complete intercourse called all men's virility into question and was what led the experts to label exhibitionism a "silly" act. Accordingly the man who exposed himself was labeled a pervert; the rapist was not. In England exhibitionists, along with pimps and transvestites, were flogged as being less than men. Those who sexually assaulted women, though they were subjected to longer jail terms, were spared such humiliating punishments.

Which brings us finally to the gender question raised by the doctors' discussion of exhibitionism, an issue that Foucault in his insistence on the innocence of "bucolic pleasures" completely overlooks. Doctors and magistrates asserted that only men could be legitimately labeled exhibitionists. Erich Wulffen, the German expert in sex crimes, stated in the 1930s that he had never found a case of a woman being tried for such a crime.[121] But this did not mean that the experts believed that women were inherently more modest than men. On the contrary, as Alfred Swain Taylor complained in his recounting of the English law on indecent exposure, the legislation only targeted males. "It is strange that the law should have confined the offense to persons of the male sex only, for there are plenty of women so depraved that they could easily be capable of committing this offense."[122] Some doctors also grumbled that it was not fair that only men were labeled as voyeurs and exhibitionists. Émile Laurent asserted that it was well known that menopausal women pursued priests and bachelor doctors.[123] Maids and other female domestics, reported Hôpital, traditionally tried to excite young boys.[124] Voisin informed his colleagues that he even had a patient, a "dame du meilleur monde," who in epileptic fits showed her breasts to passersby.[125]

If doctors did not label such women as exhibitionists, it was because females, compared to males, were regarded as having lower rather than higher standards of modesty. Women, argued the psychoanalysts of the

1920s, had in their revealing fashions "acceptable social channels" by which they could sublimated their exhibitionistic urges.[126] Make-up, according to other experts, was yet another tolerated means by which women's narcissistic and egocentric desires to flaunt their bodies was manifested.

> By a mechanism of transference known to psychoanalysts as a shift of behavior from "below to above," our exhibitionistic females, incorrigibly infantile emotionally (the better to serve Nature's divine purposes), have carried the painting of the lips and the red adornment of the mouth to a point of advertising attractiveness that is a revealing study in oral eroticism, the visible counterpart of a conventionally concealed sexuality. If nice girls understood the true meaning of their exhibitionism! Nudity were, forsooth, more sane and sweet—and moral. The genitalizing of the lips tells us eloquently what we need to know about woman's *natural* modesty![127]

When it came to applying the term exhibitionism in the pathological sense, doctors reserved the label for men. Exhibitionism by a man was viewed by sexologists as a perversion inasmuch as the man—who was supposed to be sexually active—was thereby rendering himself a passive spectacle for the female gaze. Women's exhibitionism, however, posed no challenge to gender norms. They were supposed to be sexually passive and make themselves accessible to the male gaze. Like children they were "naturally" but not perversely exhibitionistic. For example, in revealing their breasts, argued Paul, women were being true to their role of innocently offering themselves to males. Such exposure was not perverse since it was what women were supposed to do.[128] Ironically this gendering of the perversions resulted in doctors declaring that a man who exposed his penis—presumably the most masculine of acts—was behaving like a woman. In citing the case of the exhibitionism of an American minister suffering from mental decay, a consulting physician could accordingly conclude with a straight face that the vice was to be taken as evidence of the man's "feminine morbid erotism."[129] What such commentators were unconsciously admitting was that the purpose of clothing was to accentuate rather than hide sexual differentiation. As Balzac noted, in relating a story of children who could not tell the sex of the characters in a painting because they had no clothes on, nudity could blur rather than clarify gender boundaries.[130]

New notions of civilized and restrained masculinity placed new restrictions on men's freedom to expose their bodies. By the end of the nineteenth century, a man who swam in the nude or urinated from the open door of a moving train risked being charged with outraging public decency.[131] Yet this chapter's attempt to understand obsessional exhibitionism was not fueled by any great sympathy for exhibitionists. Such men undoubtedly posed a danger to many, chief of whom were the women and children they frightened and terrorized. These men's acts could only be regarded by their victims as threatening and aggressive. However, as can be seen by the way in which doctors drew similarities between exhibitionists and women, the danger to which the medical experts were most sensitive was the way in which exhibitionism jeopardized notions of male virility. Women were expected to be preoccupied by their bodies whereas modern men were supposed to pride themselves on their well-regulated minds.[132] Those who exposed themselves demonstrated that there were males who were so sexually timid, inhibited, and uncertain of their masculinity that they had to prove to themselves and others in the crudest possible way that they were men. In castigating exhibitionists doctors seized yet another opportunity to shore up the dominant discourse that held that the parading of one's sexuality was an infantile preoccupation embraced by women, children, and perverts, but spurned by mature males.[133] The threat exhibitionists posed was in unintentionally devaluing masculinity, or rather the notion that masculinity could only be manifested by aggressive, heterosexual deeds.

NINE

TRANSVESTITES

"CLOTHES MAKE THE MAN" RUNS THE OLD PROVERB, WHICH could be taken to imply that masculinity can be as easily appropriated or discarded as any costume or disguise. Such a subversive notion ran completely counter to the late-nineteenth-century commonplace assumption that sex and gender—the biological apparatus and the appropriate social behavior—were in effect inseparable. Men were masculine and women were feminine.[1] Yet those who were most strenuous in their claims that these "natural" couplings were powerful and predetermined often expressed in the same breath the contradictory fear that the linkages were so fragile that they had to be closely policed and enforced. The occasional observation made by adventurous thinkers that cultural, biological, and psychological evidence indicated that such relations were inherently unstable led the anxious to be even more vehement in asserting that there had to be a clear polarity in sex roles. Oscar Wilde's tragic fate dramatically demonstrated that those who failed to conform to sexual norms, if caught out, faced persecution and social ostracism.

It was hardly surprising that a society that had invested heavily in a clear division between sex roles felt the necessity to counter the threats of confusion and disorder posed by the "transgressive" bodies of masculine women and feminine men who did not embrace appropriate gender roles.[2] First among these were the countless homosexual males, who were harassed by the police. But after the First World War, important segments of the public began to accept the claims of sexologists such as Havelock Ellis that psychiatrists were better qualified than policemen to deal with cases of sexual deviancy. A number of sensational court cases in the 1920s and 1930s, in revealing the plasticity and instability of sex and gender roles, provided such sex reformers with the occasion to call for a reappraisal of the "threat" posed by the deviant. Such interventions, according to one observer, represented a shift in experts' responses to sexual offenses from "disgust to compassion."[3] However, more was at play here than a simple quest for understanding. In the following analysis, we are stretching our time frame somewhat to analyze the trial of a male transvestite in what was regarded as perhaps the most sensational British sex trial of the interwar period. A retelling of the story serves several purposes. First, the case provides a "hook" on which we can hang a history of cross-dressing, an understanding of which is essential to any account of gender. Second, an examination of the debate both in and outside of the court reveals the extent to which those who argued over the proper treatment of transvestites advanced self-serving claims that only with the emergence of sex experts could both "normal" and "abnormal" sexuality be efficiently policed. The third and most important purpose of looking at transvestism is that no other form of sexual deviancy so challenged the defenders of the notion that masculinity had a natural, biological basis. The question still has to be asked, however, if transvestism, even while it demonstrated the extent to which gender roles were socially defined and impermanent, mocked or simply mirrored the power of stereotypical notions of masculinity and femininity. The fact that increasing numbers of men felt that to be "true" to their natures they had to dress as women was, it will be suggested, not due to any serious undermining of the masculine ideal; on the contrary such men were acknowledging, though in an unanticipated fashion, the unprecedented importance attributed by society at the turn of the century to the notion that only a narrowly defined, aggressive form of masculinity was the mark of a real man.

ON SATURDAY, 14 NOVEMBER 1931, GEORGE BURROWS, AN UNEMPLOYED laborer of Sutton Manor gave the following testimony at the Liverpool Assizes. Ten months previously on the night of 6 January he had met, when bicycling to a dance, a young woman dressed in black; striking up a conversation, they went off together to the pictures. The evening went so well they arranged to meet to go out walking again the next night. The young woman, who called herself Norma Jackson, confessed to having led an unhappy life. Her parents were dead, and she lived with a married sister who treated her "like a dog." On a subsequent evening outing, after she said she was only allowed five shillings a week, Burrows gave her money with which to buy food, and following this conversation "certain acts took place."[4]

Later Norma complained she was tired of living with her sister and suggested that she and Burrows run off and marry. When Burrows responded that, being unemployed and having been through a number of operations on his nose and head, he was not in a position to take a wife, the high-strung Norma threatened suicide. In mid-February the infatuated Burrows finally agreed to go away with her. A week later, having told his mother he had married, he moved into a bedsitting room in St. Helens with Norma, where they lived happily as "man and wife." They appeared to others to be a not untypical working-class couple. Burrows, obtaining a job at the brewery opposite their rented accommodations, handed over his weekly pay packet to Norma, who shared his bed and carried out the household duties. They led others to believe that they were married; Norma called herself Mrs. Burrows and wore a wedding ring. They began to save money for a real wedding, but Norma soon informed Burrows that as she was going to come into an inheritance of five thousand pounds when she turned twenty-five, they should hold off marrying until then.

So life proceeded for a few months until June, when Norma, shortly after reporting her sister's suicide drowning, suddenly announced to Burrows that, as her furious uncle had found out that they were not married, they would have to leave town. They set off for London, where they arrived apparently penniless. Burrows stayed at the Church Army Hostel and Norma at the Ladies' Church Army Headquarters. The move to London was not a success. To Burrow's disappointment, Norma's assertion that she might obtain an advance on her inheritance proved unfounded. A more troubling confrontation followed. Norma claimed that she had found a position as a lady's companion, but Burrows, discovering that she was simply scrubbing floors for ten shillings a week (most of which she handed over to him), coldly called her a liar. "What happened?—We stood in Trafalgar Square and she nearly broke her heart. I told her I was going straight back to St. Helens. She replied: 'Let's get friendly. It's the first lie I have ever told you.' Witness—We made it up and decided to come north again the next morning at nine o'clock." But Norma, having agreed to return to St. Helens to marry, disappeared. Burrows, after spending two days looking for her in London, returned home.

Norma went north to Edinburgh, from where, during a remorseful moment, she wrote Burrows in late August care of his St. Helens friends.

> Dear Love,—I am sorry about how we left each other, but George, love, you thought I was not playing you straight and, dear, if you only could see me now at in my digs with nobody to talk to but only your photograph. I am killing myself. I am seven stone four pounds now. Next week I am going to Belgium to Ostend, then from there, love I am going to Spain. Further and further on. I don't

care what becomes of me, love, for I deserve it. I hope your head
is keeping fit, dear, and you are well. George, dear, just think of me
a little, dear. I have a broken ankle, and I just picture to myself
what you must be going through. That is all, love, now. Good-bye
dear. Keep smiling. With heaps of love,—Norma XXX.[5]

Even the somewhat slow-witted Burrows must have been made aware by
this self-dramatizing correspondence that he was dealing with a difficult
person. His inquiries in St. Helens led to a number of unexpected and startling discoveries. They jolted him into realizing that Norma had lied repeatedly to him. To his consternation he found that Norma's purportedly
deceased parents were alive, that her sister had not drowned, and—most
shattering of all—that Norma Jackson, with whom he had lived as a
spouse for six months, was in fact not a woman but a male transvestite by
the name of Austin Hull. Burrows took his incredible story to the police
with the result that Hull was tracked down and arrested in Blackpool on 24
September and now in November stood in the dock charged with inducing
another to commit a "gross indecency."

The trial was a media sensation, receiving much newspaper coverage
under such headlines as "Man with a Feminine Mind," "Masqueraded as
Girl," "Posing as a Woman," "Astonishing Deception of a 'Husband,'" and
"Man-Woman Sentenced."[6] The case, unusual to say the least, was further
sensationalized by the actions of the presiding judge. Mr. Justice Talbot,
despite the defense's protests, and after ordering that all women spectators
be removed from the court, cruelly insisted that the distraught twenty-one-
year-old Augustine Joseph Hull appear in court dressed in women's
clothes.[7] The press had a field day in meticulously noting the accused's
ankle length black lace frock, imitation leopard skin coat, blue silk under-
slip, pink knickers, gun metal stockings, ladies-size three high-heeled shoes,
black felt hat, and handbag containing rouge and powder puff.[8] Prison
regulations clearly stipulated that the accused be allowed to appear in his
or her own clothes. Mr. Justice Talbot agreed that it was "unseemly" to
produce a man in court in women's clothes yet claimed he did not think his
insistence on Hull wearing his "disguise" would prejudice the case. The
judge only relented to the extent of agreeing to the defense's request that
Hull be allowed to change into male attire once the case for the prosecution
had been made.

Hull was charged not with cross-dressing per se, but with procuring
another to commit a "gross indecency"—that is, to engage in a homosexual act. The prosecution's chief witness was Burrows, whose account has

been given above. The most amazing aspect of the case was that he claimed that though he had committed certain sexual acts with Hull over the course of several months, he never doubted he was with a woman. Burrows was a depressed not terribly intelligent young man. In the police court, he had admitted, "I cannot remember things very well, because of trouble in my head."[9] Asked repeatedly by the judge and defense counsel if he had truly believed that Hull was a woman, he doggedly insisted that he had. One such response, precipitating an outburst of laughter among the male spectators, led the judge to threaten to clear the court. It is only fair to note that Burrows was not alone in being confused by Hull's cross-dressing; even the crown counsels continued to refer to Hull as "she." And none of the landlords from whom Burrows and Hull rented—including one who boasted of thirty-five years' experience in the theatrical business—ever suspected that Hull was not a woman. The newspaper reporters covering the case were equally prone to mix their pronouns. The *Liverpool Echo*, for example, provided the following confused account. "Burrows made certain suggestions. She acquiesced. After that they met on about five other occasions, and prisoner kept saying he wanted Burrows and her to go away together."[10]

Hull, once the case for the prosecution was made, was permitted to slip into male attire of pink shirt, dark gray suit, and dark tie. He rebutted the crown's accusations of indecency in a cool and emphatic manner. He stated that until the age of six, though he never dressed as a girl, he did play with "girlish" toys. At home his parents treated him up to the age of sixteen very much as a daughter. He did the housework and took girls' parts in theatricals.[11] He began cross-dressing sometime in his teens. At the time of his arrest, his long hair was trimmed and "marcel" waved; he spoke in a light, feminine voice.

When asked why he dressed as a woman, Hull replied that even when dressed as a man he was often taken for a woman. When attired in male clothes people followed and stared at him.[12] "I have no peace in St. Helens with the police whichever way I dress. I was taken to the Town Hall when dressed as a man because they thought I was a woman and when I was in a convalescent home at Grange over Sands, the nurses became suspicious, thought I was a woman and took me to the doctors."[13] But Hull admitted that he enjoyed wearing women's clothes and that he wanted to pass as a woman. In response to his counsel's query, he agreed that he had the desires of a woman, "to be passive and not active" in affection. Hull accordingly asserted that it was the aggressive Burrows who was the one who made the initial advances, wanted to marry, and threatened suicide if they did not go off together.

The testimony of medical experts tended to support the defense's claims. Dr. McLaren Ferris, the local police surgeon, having examined Hull, declared: "To all external appearances, Hull is a normally made male person, and there is no evidence to show that this man had recently been an addict to certain indecent acts." Dr. W. D. Higson, the resident medical officer of the Walton Prison, concurred that Hull was an asexual "living in a state of make belief or fantasy." "It was not Hull's intentions in posing as a woman to perpetrate beastliness. If such indecent acts as Burrows had described to the court had occurred, then he could hardly see how Burrows had not discovered he was a man."[14]

Dr. Charles Rankin, visiting psychiatrist to the Walton Hospital, described Hull as a "medical curiosity. He was a man with a feminine mind. This condition was a congenital one, recognized in medical law and practice." Rankin went on to assert that Hull was only a man in appearance, but someone who was feminine in outlook and mentality seeking an idealized Platonic sort of love. "He is not a degenerate. He is carried away entirely by his emotions. Hull, in my opinion, is an invert and not a pervert."[15] The term pervert was used at the time by doctors to refer to those who willfully and for commercial gain—like male and female prostitutes—engaged in deviant sexual practices. By describing Hull as an invert, the doctors were supporting his claim that he could not help his outlook.

Hull's defense counsel, in his concluding statement, expressed a willingness to admit that Hull, in masquerading as a woman, had acted in a foolish and unseemly way, but insisted that the charge of gross indecency against him had not been proven. The only evidence came from the confused Burrows, who would have had to have been aware of Hull's true sex if the purported indecent acts had occurred. The prosecution skirted this logical difficulty by countering that Hull admitted that it gratified him to dress as a woman. The court had been satisfied as to the accused's guilt not just by Burrows's testimony but by the "corroboration from the prisoner and the witnesses, as to the prisoner's desires and wants." In other words, the crown was arguing that Hull's desires rather than his actions were being judged; to want to be a woman meant to want to be used sexually as a woman. "It had," the prosecutor concluded, "been a most disgusting case and it was the duty of the jury to simply apply the medicine of the law."

The judge, in his summation, made it clear to the jury that to his mind the charge had been clearly proven. "You may think," he informed them, "that evidence so palpably true is not often heard." [16] Nevertheless it was only after three-quarters of an hour that the jury returned with a guilty verdict. The judge in passing upon Hull almost the harshest sentence available for gross indecency—eighteen months' imprisonment with hard labor—rationalized the court's severe actions by expressions of sympathy for the bewildered Burrows. "You have done a cruel wrong to this young man," he informed Hull, "and you made it worse by telling lies in the witness box against him."

What exactly did the judge mean in referring to a "cruel wrong" committed by Hull? Presumably it was some sex act that the judge believed Hull had duped the gullible Burrows into committing. But Burrows never thought that anything they did together was disgusting. His complaint was that Hull had left him. This may have been the main reason he went to the police. It was the ending of the relationship, not its maintenance, that he objected to. "I always said I would stick to her, no matter what happened. I was devoted to her and still would be if she hadn't turned out to be a man. I would have done anything for her, and she knows it." [17] Hull made similar assertions concerning his devotion to Burrows. The unexpectedly harsh sentence he received was traumatic. "On hearing the sentence, Hull burst into tears and then fainted. He had to be assisted from the dock." [18]

Much of the public must have been confused by the outcome of the trial. Hull's offense, one commentator noted, "seems to have been simply the gratification of a phantasy that he desired, and he ran away when it threatened to become real. There is no definite evidence of homosexuality. The charge was 'indecency,' but the judge based his sentence on cruelty. Which was it?" [19] Nevertheless on 14 December 1931, Hull's appeal was dismissed after a few minutes' discussion by the Court of Criminal Appeal. Mr. Justice Avory went so far as to declare that he "did not consider the sentence a day too much." [20]

$$\int$$

FOR CONTEMPORARIES THE HULL CASE WAS A REMARKABLE STORY. TODAY the chief importance of the trial and its aftermath is that they provide a vantage point from which to view some key aspects of the early-twentieth-century public discussion of sex and gender. Why was cross-dressing viewed by some as so alarming? Why were others beginning to discount its import? By examining the response made to the case by magistrates, medical scientists, and sexologists, one is provided with first an insight into the complexities of transvestism and secondly some sense of how the discus-

sion of sexual abnormality in the interwar period served particular professional interests. The third and most important aspect of the case is that it
reveals the enormous importance of the notion that the sexes were "opposite"—that if one was not masculine one was necessarily feminine.

To understand the ramifications of the Hull case, it is necessary to place
it in context. Beginning with the legal side, the first question to be asked is
what was Hull found guilty of? Much of the public assumed that his crime
was cross-dressing, since that was the focus of the news reports and headlines. In a later, similar case, a London tabloid reported that "a young man
in red dance dress and silver shoes accosted two police officers who were
patrolling in a motor car on the Great West Road." The press let it be
understood that the man in question was charged with "masquerading,"
when in fact he, like most transvestites, was actually charged with committing a homosexual offense. Such confusions were due to the reluctance of
newspapers to discuss openly homosexuality.

Trials involving transvestism were always given more coverage than simple cases of homosexuality, but few readers understood the legal status of
cross-dressing. Hull's trial judge described the case as "exceedingly peculiar" and told the jury that they would have to search long and hard to find
a parallel.[21] This was obviously true, though one should not forget that in
western Europe there was a long tradition of cross-dressing for purposes of
disguises, masquerades, rituals, and theater.[22] English priests, like shamans
elsewhere, customarily wore gowns. In earlier centuries cross-dressing was
employed at the Feast of Fools, by mummers, and frequently by male pro-
testers in skimmingtons, enclosure protests, and large-scale confrontations
with the authorities, as in the Rebecca riots of the 1840s. In Shakespeare's
plays the female roles were first played by men, and by the nineteenth century comic drag artists emerged and female impersonators had become a
popular staple at naval and military celebrations.[23] Indeed the same newspapers that reported the shocking and puzzling events of the Hull case carried the reviews of the traditional English Christmas pantomimes in which
Peter Pan was played by a woman and Cinderella's ugly sisters by men.[24]
Dame Edna Everage and Danny Larue in the late twentieth century would
embody, each in their own way, long drag queen traditions. Such socially
accepted forms of cross-dressing were legitimated because—by being dra-
matized, ritualized, and controlled—they provided the community with
safe entertainment free of sexual involvement or danger.[25]

But cross-dressing had an equally long subversive tradition, particularly
when employed by women. People disguised themselves to play roles other-

wise forbidden to them. In the religious realm, in addition to the acceptable "manly" female saints, there were popular memories of the mythical usurper Pope Joan.[26] The most famous female cross-dresser, Joan of Arc, was burned as a witch. Most women, however, had practical, "external" reasons for donning men's garb, the pursuit of employment opportunities. In eighty-three of the ninety-three cases of female transvestism traced in seventeenth-and eighteenth-century Holland, the woman had passed as a soldier or sailor.[27] The idea that women would seek male powers by donning male attire made sufficient sense to be usually viewed by the public as presumptuous rather than perverse. Cross-dressing women were sometimes punished, but on occasion the valiant Nancys and Pollys who were discovered serving as soldiers or sailors were feted as heroines.[28] In eighteenth-century popular ballads, such masquerades were portrayed as momentarily subverting gender order, a theme that was to resurface in twentieth-century films.[29] In nineteenth-century France and Germany, the law forbad women to wear male clothing, yet permits could be acquired to circumvent such restrictions.[30] In the Victorian age, a number of famous women writers assumed men's names—including George Eliot, George Sand, Daniel Stern—for reasons of professional benefit.[31] Female transvestism among the lower classes declined, it has been suggested, because the new medical inspections of the army and navy made passing more difficult. It may have been also related to clothes becoming less bulky and form-concealing. Cross-dressing presumably permitted the expression of lesbian sexual feelings. Some have advanced the unlikely idea that such feelings were more easily expressed in the nineteenth century and therefore female cross-dressing became less necessary.

In the twentieth century, the most notorious female transvestite was "Colonel Barker"—actually an English woman by the name of Valerie Arkell-Smith—who passed for many years as a retired military officer. Not only did she successfully pass herself off as a blimpish military hero and sometime member of the British Fascist party, she married an unsuspecting woman whom she abandoned three years later. Only the colonel's bankruptcy in 1929 brought the scandal to light.[32] Radclyffe Hall, author of the classic lesbian novel *The Well of Loneliness,* which came out the previous year, was appalled by the revelations of Barker's activities, which Hall believed would set back the movement for homosexual rights. She wrote that she would like to see the colonel drawn and quartered. "A mad pervert of the most undesirable type, with her mock war medals, wounds, etc.; and then after having married the woman if she doesn't go and desert her! Her exposure at the moment is unfortunate indeed and will give a handle to endless people—the more so as what I long for is some sort of marriage for the invert."[33] Hall, seeing herself as having a masculine psyche, wore male attire and called herself John. Colonel Barker offended her not for cross-dressing but for only having "pretended" to be a male.[34] Magnus Hirschfeld, the Weimar sex reformer, described the similar case of a German painter charged with adultery. The painter, a determined and intelligent woman, had run away from home at the age of fourteen, passed as a man, and finally settled down and "married." The painter's wanderlust led to the charge of adultery being pressed against "him," which in turn led to the wife's discovery that her painter "husband" was a woman.[35]

Observers such as Lombroso fretted that there were some young women who began in their school years by showing an excessive interest in mathematics and chemistry and ended up by opting for short hair and male clothes. Many more men, he lamented, as males potentially more excitable, variable and perverse than females, were led to don female apparel.[36] Women's cross-dressing could be rationalized as a practical matter, but most commentators assumed that cases of male transvestism could not because it made no sense for a man to dress like a woman. Only the mentally unbalanced would embrace a role that offered no practical advantages. Nevertheless cases of male transvestism, regarded by doctors as precipitated by irrational "inner" drives, were increasingly reported after the 1850s.[37] The few cases of male transvestism that came to light in the nineteenth century were regarded by doctors as morbidly dangerous and necessarily linked to homosexuality. Taylor's *Principles and Practices of Medical Jurisprudence* contained one report of an "Eliza Edwards," whose unclaimed dead body was sent to Guy's Hospital. Edwards, to the surprise of all, including her personal physician, turned out to be a man. Since the age of fourteen, he had played the role of an actress. His male organs were perfect, but, noted the doctors with apparent satisfaction, "The State of his rectum left no doubt of the abominable practices to which this individual had been addicted."[38]

Sodomy and soliciting by male prostitutes were associated in the public mind with transvestism, but the point that cross-dressing was not in itself a crime was made clear in the most famous nineteenth-century exposé of male transvestites, the trial of Boulton and Park.[39] Ernest Boulton, the twenty-two-year-old son of a stockbroker, and Frederick William Park, son of a Master in the Court of Common Pleas, played women's roles in amateur theatricals and often went about in public in female attire. They were arrested outside the Strand Theater in April 1870 and charged with intent to commit a felony. The felony in question was buggery. The crown produced as evidence many letters in which Boulton and Park announced their affections for male friends but failed to provide any evidence of sexual relations. The defense reiterated that in England going about dressed as a member of the opposite sex was not a crime.[40] The judge summed up in the accused's favor and the jury found them not guilty. Nevertheless the popular belief that homosexuality and transvestism were inseparable was captured in a contemporary limerick.

> There was an old person of Sark
> Who buggered a pig in the dark;
> The swine in surprise
> Murmured: "God blast your eyes
> Do you take me for Boulton or Park?"[41]

Such suspicions were apparently confirmed by occasional trial accounts of individuals who cross-dressed to entrap homosexual clients. Julius Walters, an Austrian (also known as Klara Myer), was on 13 November 1908, sentenced to five months in jail for "masquerading as a female." Walters had been similarly convicted in 1896, 1899, 1900, 1904, 1906, and 1907.[42] Walters was, according to the police, a well-known associate of blackmailers who regularly accosted gentlemen in Bloomsbury. At his 1904 trial, the judge castigated him as an incorrigible rogue and sentenced him to twelve months of hard labor and twelve strokes of the cat.[43] Masquerading was not a crime as long as no criminal deception was involved, but by law any disguise could be cited as evidence of an intention to commit a crime.[44] The crime in the case of a man dressed as a woman would usually be soliciting. Transvestites were most likely to be charged with importuning for immoral purposes under section one of the Vagrancy Act of 1898, a law applied exclusively to homosexual men.[45]

Aside from female impersonators and male prostitutes, men rarely ever cross-dressed, as women did, to gain employment, but a 1930s case reads remarkably like a cross between the scripts of the American films *Some Like It Hot* and *Tootsie*. A Birmingham male saxophonist, unable to get work in an orchestra as a man, thought he might have better luck if, dressed as a woman, he applied to a "ladies orchestra." He accordingly borrowed an outfit from his wife, but before he could audition was arrested and charged under section four of the Vagrancy Act of 1824 with being an "idle and disorderly person found in female attire at the —— hotel for an unlawful purpose." Since he had not committed a larceny, he was acquitted. A legal expert observed that the situation would have been different if the position in the orchestra had been obtained. "Had the Birmingham saxophonist succeeded in getting money for playing in a 'ladies orchestra' and done nothing except wear his frock and blow his instrument, he would presumably have been convicted of obtaining his wages or salary by false pretences."[46] In a similar case, an ex-officer who obtained work in the 1930s as a parlor maid was jailed though not for cross-dressing; having provided a false character, he was convicted under the Servants Character Act of 1792.

Since cross-dressing was not a crime, to what was the crown counsel in the Hull case referring when speaking of the "disgusting story" that the jury had heard? Presumably it was Hull's purported homosexuality. Hull was charged with "procuring a man to do an act of gross indecency with him." The exact act that Hull had committed, which constituted a "gross indecency," was never made clear to the newspaper reading public because the press felt it could not report Burrows's description of "the intimate acts that had taken place."[47] The defense insisted that nothing indecent had occurred. Hull cogently pointed out that since he and Burrows had slept together for over six months, "if anything had happened he would have found out my sex." Despite his plea and the medical expert's evidence, which tended to support him, Hull was found guilty.

When it came to the prosecution of homosexuals, such apparent injustices were the rule rather than the exception. In the Boulton and Park case, Lord Chief Justice Cockburn noted that while the crown argued that the crime was "conspiracy to commit a felony"—the felony being buggery—it could only prove it by labeling the accuseds' friendship a "conspiracy." Moreover the conspiracy charge allowed the prosecutor to use the evidence of each of the accused against the other. How was one to prove that one did not so conspire? Under this law—on the books until 1967, when homosexual offenses between consenting adults in private were abolished—many homosexuals were ensnared.

Certain sexual acts associated with homosexuality such as sodomy had, of course, always been prosecuted, but after 1885 homosexuality itself was criminalized. The Labouchère Amendment to the Criminal Law Amendment Act of 1885 (48 and 49 Vict. c.69, s.11) made acts of gross indecency between men misdemeanors punishable by up to two years of hard labor. The law, in not defining a "gross indecency," provided the police with enormous powers of discretion. For example, in 1896 Jones and Bowerbank were both charged under the act, but at the trial Bowerbank acted as the crown's only witness and Jones was found guilty and sentenced to nine months of hard labor. On appeal the defense asked two obvious questions: how could Jones be alone guilty of an act that both he and Bowerbank committed and how could Jones procure the commission of a crime in which he participated?[48] The judges remained indifferent to such logic, and the conviction stood.

Why at the turn of the century was it felt necessary to criminalize a type of person—the homosexual—rather than specific acts that anyone might commit? In part because a host of commentators, fearful of the social changes associated with an increasingly urbanized, bureaucratized world, had raised the cry that masculinity was at risk. Viewing their overcivilized, increasingly "feminized" world as unhealthy, such observers viewed men with "feminine tendencies" with unprecedented loathing.[49] Self-doubts rather than confidence in short fueled the strident Victorian claims that there existed clear-cut male and female roles. To be male was to be assertive; to be female, passive. Inversion was determined to consist of a reversal of such roles. Therefore the homosexual, it was believed, would necessarily be effeminate and given to wearing women's clothes; the lesbian would be mannish.

The rising concern about the purported threat posed by homosexuality was also partly a reaction to changing women's roles. With declining fertility rates and women's demands for access to male educational and professional preserves being read as signs of a repudiation of motherhood, social commentators felt obliged to reassert what sexuality was all about. Doctors in the last decades of the nineteenth century accordingly insisted with unprecedented vigor that healthy individuals demonstrate their heterosexuality by cleaving to an appropriate gender role. Those who failed were deemed to be sick. The sexologist Richard von Krafft-Ebing accordingly first fell back on degeneration theory to explain the spread of homosexuality, and most late-nineteenth-century commentators agreed that it was a sort of insanity.

Even the first defenders of homosexuality who appeared at the turn of the century felt compelled, given the prestige of biology, to base their arguments on theories of physical and psychic hermaphroditism. Edward Carpenter and Magnus Hirschfeld presented the homosexual as an "intermediate sex" carrying specific somatic or psychological anomalies. Havelock Ellis believed inversion had, like color-blindness, some congenital basis but was a harmless anomaly. Freud's originality lay in dispensing with organic arguments and in suggesting that the hope of attaining a full understanding of heterosexuality was just as problematical as deciphering the causes of homosexuality. Heterosexuality was according to him something that had to be attained, and in such a context he viewed homosexuality simply as developmental failure.[50]

The central thrust of the new sexual analyses of the early twentieth century was to split sexual aims and objects. Experts increasingly accepted that there was no necessary link between appearance and desire and there existed a multiplicity of roles, including the masculine type who was homosexual and the transvestite who was heterosexual.[51] Though doctors might still describe homosexuality as "abnormal," they now tended to view it as a medical rather than a moral problem. Medical hegemony was accepted and the "sickness" explanation embraced by many homosexuals including Oscar Wilde, Sir Roger Casement, and Goldsworthy Lowes Dickinson. The "cures" doctors trotted out ranged from hypnotism to aversion therapy.[52]

The discussion of transvestism followed a similar pattern. The classic account of transvestism and the coining of the term was provided by the pioneering German sex reformer Magnus Hirschfeld (1868–1935) in *Die Transvestiten* (1910). In the late nineteenth century, his fellow countryman Carl Westphal and Krafft-Ebing had presented the first scientific descriptions of cross-dressing. The pessimistic Krafft-Ebing viewed it as the first stage on the road to insanity. The ever curious and optimistic Hirschfeld became interested in transvestism when assisting two army men who had been arrested for dressing as women.[53] Cross-dressers, he found, were overrepresented in the ranks of the military.

Hirschfeld, a homosexual himself, countered the claims of both pioneering sexologists such as Krafft-Ebing and the Freudians such as Wilhelm Stekel that transvestism was necessarily linked to homosexuality. Only about 35 percent of Hirschfeld's sample were homosexual, as many were heterosexual, 15 percent were bisexual, and the rest were "auto-monosexual." Of the fourteen female impersonators Hirschfeld interviewed, eight were married, and of these five were heterosexual. Transvestism was, according to Hirschfeld, a sexual variation in itself that demanded proper investigation. He viewed the transvestite as a sort of androgyne who in cross-dressing displayed his "true" personality. Effeminacy did not mean homosexuality. Hirschfeld suggested that male clothing had simply lost much of the individualism and expressiveness that it once possessed. Female clothing offered some males a longed-for form of expression. Their mothers and wives tended to be understanding.[54]

Hirschfeld also gave examples of individuals who, like Hull, were almost forced by society into cross-dressing. On the one hand, a Polish man who lived in Berlin was constantly stared at when he wore men's clothing. On the other, the police arrested a masculine woman on seven different occasions on suspicion of her being a cross-dressed man. Such harassment occurred despite the fact that police on occasion actually provided permits to allow cross dressing (which technically violated the law in Germany).[55] Since we inherited traits from both male and female parents, Hirschfeld felt it hardly surprising that the boundaries between the sexes were not as firm as respectable society imagined. Transvestism was for him simply a vivid demonstration that in each individual "there rests the sex that does not belong to it."[56] This was a sympathetic though obviously not a full-hearted endorsement of such a persona. Hirschfeld, as liberal as he was, harbored the fear that transvestites would produce "degenerate" offspring.[57]

The French did very little work on the subject of transvestism.[58] The first short though sympathetic account of cross-dressing in English was written by Edward Carpenter, while in the process of defending homosexuals as normal and healthy.[59] In "Intermediate Types among Primitive Folk," which first appeared in the *American Journal of Religious Psychology* in July 1911, Carpenter drew on anthropological accounts of priests and witches adopting the clothing of the opposite sex. He went on to note that the "enormous delight" that many people experienced through cross-dressing was due to more than either religious inspiration or homosexuality. "It must also not be overlooked, in dealing with this complex and difficult subject, that the mere fact of a person delighting to adopt the garb of the opposite sex does not in itself prove that his or her love-tendency is abnormal—i.e. cross-dressing does not *prove* homosexuality."[60]

Havelock Ellis, the British sexologist who devoted his life to the collecting and classifying of variants of sexual behavior, only got around to dealing with transvestism in the late 1920s.[61] Ellis, like others, began by assuming that transvestism was an annex of homosexuality; he concluded that it was not necessarily an aspect of sexual inversion nor a fetish or replacement of the sexual object. Though he noted that Hirschfeld was of the same opinion, Ellis went on to critique the German's stress on the significance of the subject's dress or as Hirschfeld called it, his "disguise." Clothing was only part of the syndrome, argued Ellis, and the term "disguise" was hardly appropriate because it was only when wearing the attire of the opposite sex that the subject really felt *not* disguised. As an example Ellis provided, among his many first-person accounts, that of "R. L." who poignantly described the unpleasant sensations of returning to male attire. "I slipped out into a world that was particularly distasteful to me, my collar choked me, my trousers oppressed me like bandages, my boots felt clumsy, and I missed the clasp of corsets, and the beautiful feel of underwear." [62] Ellis did not like either the terms cross-dressing or transvestism, both of which he felt paid too much attention to external trappings. In their place Ellis preferred to use the term eonism after the remarkable eighteenth-century French diplomat, the chevalier d'Eon, an intellectually gifted man who though not an invert desired to wear women's clothing. [63]

Ellis devoted the long opening chapter of the seventh and final volume of *Studies in the Psychology of Sex* to a discussion of "eonism." All perversions were, for Ellis, simple distortions of healthy feelings. Sadism, for example, he viewed as an exaggeration of the enjoyment of the element of pain inherent in the sexual act. Transvestism he similarly presented as due to an exaggerated identification of the young male with his first object of attraction—the mother. Ellis, in seeking to win the public's understanding for the transvestite shrewdly made the mother—England's icon of respectability—central to his explanation. The subject was presented as motivated not by some base instinct but by an inflated sympathy for and identification with his mother, whom he in effect was "courting." "It is normal for a man to identify himself with the women he loves. The eonist carries that identification too far, stimulated by a sensitive and feminine element in himself which is associated with a rather defective virile sexuality on what may be a neurotic basis." [64] Ellis noted that the Freudians also viewed cross-dressing as an aspect of the "persistence of infantile traits." Wilhelm Stekel in particular attacked Hirschfeld's notion that there was any biological basis to the syndrome. But Ellis observed that the blanket claim of the Freudians that all transvestites—even the heterosexual—were latent homosexuals was not very helpful. [65]

Freud in *Three Essays* (1905) had given a partial account of transvestism according to which the urge was located in infancy. The child fixated at a certain stage of development on the mother. Fearing her loss the child refused to move on. [66] Transvestites like homosexuals, according to the English psychoanalysts, suffered from a "lack of development." Bernard Hollander opposed jailing homosexuals except for those "culprits" who had led others astray. But he declared that no punishment would cure either passive or active homosexuals, both of whom were neurotics. [67] Theodore J. Faithful agreed that only therapy would bring a "final surrender to normality." [68]

In addition to childhood experiences Ellis believed hormonal influences or what he called "secretions" were important. Cross-dressing's basis could be due to both acquired and innate causes. The transvestite might have an "erotic empathy" for members of his own sex, but that was not the same as a homosexual passion. Indeed Ellis pointed out that some transvestites found homosexuality as distasteful as any other aspect of masculinity.[69] Although Ellis regarded the syndrome as shaded by tones of masochism and autoeroticism he found his subjects to be usually highly moral individuals who identified with others. "It [transvestism] tends to occur among people who are often educated, refined, sensitive and reserved."[70] They were, he claimed, of "high character and distinguished ability and normal in other respects."[71]

Such new views of sexual deviancy formed the backdrop for the campaign precipitated by the Hull case, a campaign in favor not so much for changes in the law, as for changes in the ways in which sexual delinquents were treated. The key notion advanced by the reformers was that abnormalities like transvestism were better dealt with by medicine than by the law. It was in the context of such appeals in the legal and medical worlds for a better understanding of sexual deviancy that demands were voiced for Hull's release. The campaign for a review of his case was led by the *Week-End Review,* a progressive publication that had devoted many of its columns to demands for sex reform. In the fall of 1931, when the Hull case burst onto the scene, it was carrying discussions of the legitimacy of abortion and birth control by such stalwarts of the sex-reform movement as Stella Browne, Norman Haire, Winifred Holtby, and John Haldane Blackie. The first to comment on the Hull trial was John Connell, a journalist working for the *Evening News,* whose letter to the editor of 21 November 1931 was headlined "Psycho-Analysis or Hard Labour?" In this squalid trial, according to Connell, "the pathetic, puzzled victim of an abnormality which he cannot control is treated as a reasonable moral being, and has to suffer for transgressing a code he cannot recognize. . . . The boy needed a trained psycho-pathologist, and prolonged clinical treatment: he got eighteen months' hard labor."[72]

The following weeks brought a supportive flood of letters. Hull's legal defenders included E. Roy Calvert, an active opponent of capital punishment, and J. Whitely Nance, who declared that most lawyers would agree that cases like Hull's "are altogether outside the realm of the criminal code, and are rather for treatment in hospitals than in prisons." Herbert Chorley, drawing on his experience of years at the bar to note that eighteen months of hard labor was a ferocious sentence calculated to destroy the health of even the hardened criminal, referred to Hull as "one of Nature's mistakes."[73] An Association for the Scientific Treatment of Offenders had just been created, wrote another correspondent, sparked by a Home Office report by Dr. G. W. Pailthorpe that asserted that many cases of criminality were due to an "underlying pathological state of mind."[74] The case for psychoanalysis was made by Grace Bristow, who wrote "as one who at present is undergoing psychological treatment" to endorse the need for more clinics.[75] Claire Madden provided perhaps the best interpretation of such therapy. "Inversion is neither a mental disease nor something that can be cured. But such treatment would have given him a little self-knowledge, helped him to grow into a useful citizen, if not a happy one."[76] Thomas F. Lindsay, editor of *The Isis,* agreed completely with Madden's views of the limits of therapy.[77]

Havelock Ellis, having a few years before produced the fullest account in English of transvestism or "eonism," now entered the lists in defense of Hull in both a letter to the *Week-End Review* and an article destined for an American journal. He noted that on the continent cross-dressing was not regarded as a threat as long as no public disturbance resulted. The United Kingdom and the United States were the most backward nations in this regard. Ellis's main concern, however, was that the medical evidence offered at the trial had been ignored. He concluded by presenting Hull as victim of his body. "Sex depends on the balance of the hormone-producing glands, and that balance sometimes results in states that are naturally intersexual."[78] Someday old prejudices would be swept away. "These cases do not call for the psycho-analyst, or, indeed, for any form of psycho-therapeutics, and medical art cannot at present deal with them. They no doubt present an inter-sexual state based on an unusual hormonic balance."[79] The social side of the issue was touched on by the libertarian E. S. P. Haynes, who, in noting that Hull would not have been in legal trouble if he had not been impoverished, claimed that if all the "well-to-do antitypes" were convicted huge numbers of prisons would have to be built. Haynes gloomily assumed that even if Hull were pardoned his miseries would not end. "He will almost certainly (by reason of his poverty) endure further police trouble unless and until he commits another criminal offence, to wit, suicide."[80]

The Hull case was discussed at the British Sexological Society on 15 December 1931 and again on 5 January 1932, when its members collected money for Mrs. Hull.[81] Stella Browne, one of the society's most active propagandists, though believing that much sexual deviancy—including homosexuality—was due to the restrictions society placed on the free expression of heterosexual desires, conceded that there were "real" or congenital homosexuals. "We are learning to recognize congenital inversion as a vital and very often valuable factor in civilization, subject of course, to the same restraints as to public order and propriety, freedom of consent, and the protection of the immature, as normal heterosexual desire."[82] She returned to this theme in speaking to a Manchester audience in February 1932 on the topic "Some Mental Types." Arguing that the Hull case demonstrated the impact of endocrines on temperament, she concluded that it was "one of the problems of a civilization based on science and freedom, to develop a sense of social responsibility in abnormal persons as well as to cease systematic persecution of such people."[83]

Claire Madden noted that it was imperative that a petition be got up to show that there was an important section of public opinion opposed to such cruel injustices, and the lawyer John Stevenson undertook the campaign in defense of Hull. Stevenson protested that he was no "mollycoddler" and believed that on occasion certain crimes even warranted corporal punishment. But in cases such as Hull's, he saw the need for legislation that would allow judges to send the accused to a "State medical home for observation and treatment."[84] Stevenson contacted the British Sexological Society and the Howard League for Penal Reform and personally approached Sir Herbert Samuel.[85] He also oversaw the drawing up of a petition by the solicitor hired with the funds raised from the readers of the *Week-End Review,* who also exerted pressure through individual M.P.s.[86] The petition was submitted in February, but no formal response was made, and Stevenson himself was rebuffed in his attempts to see Hull in prison.[87] Yet the public outcry finally did have some effect. In April Hull was transferred to Wormwood Scrubs and arrangements made for him to attend the Tavistock Clinic for treatment.[88]

We can only speculate about the sort of treatment Hull was given. The Tavistock Clinic had been established by Hugh Crichton-Miller in 1920 to provide outpatient psychotherapy. The clinic's goal, according to Crichton-Miller, was "the work of creating harmony in the unharmonized, adjustment in the maladjusted, independence in the dependent, and social worth in the socially worthless; and when we speak of the 'socially worthless' we are thinking of our average patient not as he is but as he may become if he is allowed to drift."[89] Crichton-Miller, who had worked with shell-shock victims, introduced a generation of psychologists to Freudian forms of therapy. The clinic though psychodynamically oriented was open minded about techniques. The sort of therapies offered ranged from full psychoanalysis to suggestion and persuasion. Between 1920 and 1936, the Tavistock dealt with 496 cases of delinquency, including one case of transvestism, Hull's. The staff found that sexual cases seemed to be especially suitable for treatment by psychotherapy. After three years, out of the seventy-three sexual cases, twenty-five "remained free of symptoms."[90] We are not, however, told if the latter included Austin Hull. Having slipped from public view, one can only assume that he finally succeeded in escaping the clutches of both the police and the doctors.

Having disentangled the various sexual, medical, and legal threads that were entwined in the story of Austin Hull, what, in conclusion, are we to make of this case? First and foremost it casts a revealing light on the medicalization of deviancy. Hull's journey from Wormwood Scrubs to the Tavistock Clinic represented a victory for psychiatry. The doctors by convincing the public that Hull's syndrome—an involuntary compulsion—was a medical problem had turned him from a prisoner into a "patient" and so rescued him from the police. And what of Hull? Though he must have benefited from being saved from forced labor, he was far from being free. Once declared guilty of a crime, he was now diagnosed as victimized by a delusion. Hull was subjected to treatment, yet the discomfort caused by his cross-dressing was experienced by the community not by him. His transvestism, though not a "disease," had been medicalized, the intervention of doctors had been legitimated, and gender norms strengthened.

The inherent conservativism of such approaches was noted by the French sex radical René Guyon, who attacked those who like Freud talked of "illnesses" and "aberrations" for which "cures" could be provided when what was often required were practical solutions for social problems. Why, Guyon wondered, did a relativist like Freud refer to the "normal" and the "abnormal" and the ideal "reasonable man" when he knew how subjective such views, often a mere matter of taste, were.[91] With Hull's case problematized as a pathological condition, the therapist's task was simply to determine why he was "sick." Sexologists and psychologists, while calling for a greater understanding of sexual deviancy, were in practice adopting a pathological approach that held that the tragedies resulting from sexual confusions were the responsibility of the persecuted individual not an intolerant society. Accordingly Hull's well-meaning defenders in the *Week-End Review* referred to him patronizingly as a "boy" and "one of nature's mistakes." The fact that one reader went so far as to equate Hull's case with that of Sylvestre Matuschka, an Austrian madman whose 1931 train derailment caused twenty-two deaths, suggests how dangerous deviancy was regarded even by progressives.

Some of Hull's defenders, like Stella Browne, were motivated by a fervent desire for sexual diversity. But the second reason that the Hull case warrants investigation is that it reminds us that many sex reformers were often as preoccupied by the pursuit of efficient social control as by considerations for individual happiness. Everyone, they believed, was deserving of "scientific treatment," and they were accordingly attracted to anomalies out of a desire to collect research material. They hoped a "cure" would result in socially stabilizing, marital heterosexuality. The idea that sex reform would result in a healthier, more efficient citizenry was perhaps best captured in a book published in 1934 by the British Sexological Society. Intercourse, according to the author, was something that signaled its necessity to the male by bouts of sleeplessness and forgetfulness. After indulging, the man happily discovers that "all sexual obsessions vanish," his health and well-being is renewed, and he emerges from the bedroom "stronger and jollier, and more keen on his work." "A woman the day after a successful coitus will be happy and jolly, with sparkling eyes and inclined to sing over her work." [92]

As regards deviant sexual behavior, more knowledge was needed, wrote Havelock Ellis, to "save patients much persecution and the police much bewilderment." The concern for order ran throughout such discussions. John Stevenson, for example, who got up Hull's petition, was the sort of maverick magistrate who also rushed to the defense of nude bathers and those seeking noise abatement [93] Sex crimes, Stevenson asserted, were clogging up the courts. He claimed to know, as a lawyer and magistrate, that some outrages like incest were due not so much to unnatural desires as to "unnatural housing conditions." He shared the views of Mr. Justice McCardie, who, at the Leeds Assizes in December 1931, refused to imprison two women who had procured their own abortions and protested that many judges also opposed the existing laws on eugenic sterilization, abortion, and bigamy. "When the entire set of laws relating to sex are not only generally disregarded by large numbers of otherwise good citizens, but cannot be conscientiously enforced by a growing number of judges appointed to administer them, it is surely time for a Commission with full powers to find a code more acceptable to responsible contemporary opinion." [94] Stevenson, like McCardie, harbored the eugenic notion that it would have been better if some criminals had never been allowed to be born. [95] He shared the views of the hereditarians that prisons and asylums could be emptied by the employment of rational scientific reforms and happily noted that Mr. Justice McCardie had also "awoken the public conscience to the results of breeding unchecked and leaving at large thousands of mental defectives."[96] Such troubling enthusiasms for rationalization and efficiency underpinned much of the interwar sex reformers' discussions. Sexuality was to be better understood in order to be better controlled.[97]

The third interesting aspect of the Hull case stems from the insights it offers into the public's response to homosexuality in the 1930s. We have already observed the lack of understanding which even experts demonstrated when dealing with deviancy. The press coverage of transvestite trials seems to have reinforced suspicion of sexual experimentation. Why then did Hull succeeded in garnering so much public sympathy while hundreds of jailed homosexuals did not? The answer would appear to be because of the way in which his case was covered by journalists. Ellis noted that, although transvestism was hard to define, "it is, strange as that may seem, the commonest of all sexual anomalies to attain prominence in the public newspapers." Not only because it was so striking and intriguing. "There is the further consideration that since in its simple uncomplicated form it constitutes no violation of our moral feelings and laws, it is entirely possible to discuss it plainly in the most reputable public papers."[98] Hull won support, as Ellis suggests, because he was presented by his supporters as in fact not a homosexual. Cross-dressing had a nonsexual history and could be presented without indecent connotations. Effeminacy had been part of the cliché of the nineteenth-century homosexual, but sympathy for Hull was based firmly on the argument that he was not sexually active. He was presented as a "true" transvestite. "They are apt," reported Max Hodann, a German sex reformer, "to be very shy and diffident in their general and social attitude, quite apart from sexual matters. Another complexity in their natures is this: they are by no means always homosexuals."[99]

Any hedonistic desires that Hull may have actually harbored had to be denied by his defenders if they were to succeed. Curiously enough they defended this transvestite's reputation in much the same chivalrous fashion that gentlemen were expected to accord to ladies. Hull could attract the public attention of the sex reformers because their sympathy went out to a fragile young man whom they viewed as victimized first by his own psyche and then by the authorities. The image presented of Hull in the press was that of a trapped being. He was quoted as saying, "If I wear male clothes I am frightened I shall be taken to the police station and charged with posing as a man."[100] Ellis played up the same episode. "So much is he like a girl that at the age of sixteen, when returning from church one Sunday morning in ordinary male attire, he was arrested by the police, taken to the station and stripped, because he was supposed to be a girl masquerading as a man." [101] One might have first expected the public to have shown less toleration for a transvestite—even a not terribly flamboyant one—than for a discreet homosexual. But the homosexual who willingly sought deviant pleasures was regarded by the public as a threat whereas Hull won support by allowing himself to be portrayed as a "victim" of uncontrolled desires. What Hull's true feeling were we cannot know. The sex reformers in defining Hull as an asexual transvestite created a role by which he was both protected and controlled.

The fourth interest that the Hull case holds results from what it tells us about heterosexuality. Such cases, far from undermining sex and gender roles, actually appear to have reinforced them. Hull fulfilled the fantasy of the compliant female; he successfully "passed" as a woman. Today this would make him a likely candidate for a sex-change operation.[102] It is a moot point if such operations erode sex-role stereotyping. Surgeons in the last years of the twentieth century provide operations only to those who act in an appropriately "feminine" way. Such operations, it has been argued, actually empower doctors by allowing them to "create" women and the power of real women is correspondingly diminished.[103]

Why did male transvestism appear to be on the rise in the late nineteenth century? Foucault has reminded us that the demand to know one's "true" sex is a recent phenomenon. Hermaphrodites were for centuries accepted in the Western world as marvelous beings. By the nineteenth century, biology, law, and administration insisted that one was either male or female. Medicine and the state not only restricted choices but, intent on making sure that sex and gender matched, set about tearing off disguises, detecting errors, and enforcing "legitimate" sexual constitutions. Sex, once a hidden attribute, was in the twentieth century proclaimed by the experts to be the most profound aspect of an individual's identity.[104] Ironically, the rise of male cross-dressing was probably precipitated by the unprecedented attention paid to the importance of knowing one's "true" sex. The unintended consequence of experts' insistence on sexual polarity was the driving of men, who felt feminine, into wearing women's clothing.

Hull's transvestism was not timeless; it was created by the sex role stereotyping of the 1920s and 1930s. The usefulness of looking at such a case is that it directs our attention to what early twentieth-century people did when they performed gender roles. Transvestism provided evidence for the social construction of gender roles and demonstrated the relative ease with which they may be convincingly adopted. Such findings should have countered any claim for the natural, biological basis of sexual difference and separate spheres and led to a fresh appreciation of how people "worked"—often in a conservative, conformist fashion—at presenting themselves as men or women. To pass as a man, one had to be sexually aggressive; to pass as a woman, one had to be sexually acquiescent. If some cross-dressing women like "Colonel Barker" were successful in maintaining marriages with unsuspecting women, it was because while acting as a "man" they could dictate the sorts of sexual activities that would or would not take place.

In the case of Burrows and Hull, the confused Burrows did not press his demands; hence the male spectators' hilarity.[105] And yet it was repeatedly stated that Burrows and Hull "lived as man and wife." How did one work at being a working-class man and wife? It meant, witnesses told the court, that they shared the same bed and, more importantly, that they apportioned their economic duties according to an understood gendered division of labor. Burrows worked outside the home and brought back to Hull his pay packet; Hull was responsible for finances and household chores. "When you were sharing the room with Burrows," Hull was asked by the crown counsel, "did he give you his wages?—Yes" "In fact he treated you in the same way as a wife?—Yes."[106] Heterosexuality was in the eyes of the community, we are reminded, as much an economic as a sexual relationship.

We are left knowing a good deal about the society that created Austin Hull though little of Hull himself. In the official account of the Tavistock Clinic's early days, we catch a last fleeting glimpse of Hull the patient.

> A modest beginning [by 1931] had been made in our treatment, not only of neurotics, but also of behavior disorders, including some criminals. Among the more sensational events of the week for some months was the arrival three times weekly of a prisoner serving sentence for homosexual offenses, with two uniformed warders, to one of whom he was always handcuffed. In the course of these visits the handcuffs came to be left off.[107]

What does the Hull trial tell us about the policing of masculinity? According to the sexual double-standard, men were expected to enjoy greater sexual liberties than women. Yet this was not to be the case when it came to cross-dressing. A woman who dressed as a man was not viewed as particularly threatening; her "disguise," which could be regarded as functional or provocative or erotic, did not necessarily undermine her femininity. Sarah Bernhardt and Marlene Dietrich would be lauded for cross-dressing; any man who dared do the same would have been derided.[108] At worst doctors recoiled from transvestites with disbelief or disgust; at best physicians presented the male transvestite as "sick." Yet those who confessed to being made nervous or nauseous by cross-dressing were the self-proclaimed "normal." The image of masculinity that emerged from such discussions was that of a surprisingly fragile entity that had to be carefully cosseted and protected.[109] The experts were on the lookout for sissified men; a good deal of masculine self-policing also took place. In America males were afraid that if they appeared too sophisticated it could reflect adversely on their manhood. Similarly in Britain, as Quentin Crisp recalled, "The men of the twenties searched themselves for vestiges of effeminacy as though for lice."[110]

Western society appeared to remain as shackled by stereotyped sex roles as Hull was by his handcuffs. The sensational transvestite trials of the 1920s and 1930s may, simply by the publicity they produced, have led some to sympathize to an extent with those portrayed as suffering from their sexual deviancy. The general impression given by the newspaper reports of the Hull trial and the responses made to it, however, is that once again the authorities had succeeded in turning apparent violations of sex and gender roles to the purposes of reinforcing heterosexual order. Such cases, far from shaking the public out of its social complacency, reinforced suspicions of any straying from the hegemonic model of masculinity.

CONCLUSION

IN 1920 THE EMINENT AUSTRIAN PSYCHIATRIST DR. JULIUS von Wagner-Jauregg—later to be winner of the 1928 Nobel prize for his malaria cure for general paralysis of the insane—had to submit himself to a public investigation. During the recently concluded world war, he was reported to have harshly treated the shell-shock victims delivered into his care. The Austrian socialists were particularly incensed by his use of electric shock treatments on working-class soldiers, which the deputies described as little more than "torture." In fact French, English, American, and German doctors had also responded to patients who failed to "act like men" with the same sorts of punitive therapies. The debate over the treatment of shell-shocked soldiers precipitated both professional and public discussions across Europe and North America of how military doctors should respond to masses of male invalids who manifested the hysterical behavior usually attributed to females.

The war had been initially welcomed on all sides, in particular by those men who hankered after an all-male environment "uncomplicated by women."[1] But the nostalgic notion that modern war might consist of daring acts of individual heroism was soon displaced by factual accounts of the barbarity, anonymity, and technological horrors of actual trench warfare.[2] Some asserted that the war, in killing off the "fittest" males, was clearly dysgenic.[3] Even the manhood of the survivors appeared to be undermined. Thousands of men in regiments across the western front, after being subjected to weeks of terrifying bombardments, broke down and were wracked by the bouts of weeping, depression, nightmares, and nervous fits commonly associated with hysterical women. "The effeminate homosexual is decidedly unfit for the army," wrote an American psychiatrist, "being unable to stand war stress."[4] To the horror of the high command, thousands of "normal" men appeared to demonstrate a similar lack of "will and character." Many feared not so much the gas and shrapnel but the fear itself that would expose their cowardice. Soldiers who had volunteered actually surpassed ordinary conscripts in manifesting higher levels of incapacitating distress. Although not physically incapacitated, masses of men found they could not function in battle and had to be relieved of their duties.

The military high command, unprepared to deal with a surge of psychological casualties, was panicked by the nightmarish scenario of a contagion of cowardice and indiscipline resulting in the complete collapse of whole armies.[5] Accordingly the first wave of shell-shock victims was treated in a harsh and humiliating fashion. Doctors divided those who had "real" cerebral damage from those with only psychological or emotional problems. The care-givers castigated the latter as cowards, "moral invalids," and "poltroons." Experts in the field advised their colleagues not to mollycoddle such patients, but to respond quickly, briskly, and authoritatively. Electrical shocks, for example, supposedly calibrated so as not to be so painful that the patient could make himself out to be a "martyr," were to be used to "snap" the soldier out of his lethargy.[6] The English employed the "quick cure" and "Queen's square"; the French the "manière forte" and "torpillage" (electric shocks). The same sorts of people who had called for flogging to deal with pimps and Apaches in civilian life believed that similarly brutal methods could cure cowardice in the military. Armies on both sides of the line responded to the specter of malingering with a constant barrage of hectoring appeals for men to demonstrate their pluck and manliness.

The short, sharp treatments did not work. In the course of the war, the psychological experts increasingly came to the realization that punishing men for their lack of manliness was in fact counterproductive.[7] Sigmund Freud, who was called as an expert witness in the trial of Dr. von Wagner-Jauregg, reported that in his experience there were among the shell-shocked very few malingerers; most patients were unconscious of their feelings. Nevertheless many doctors felt it was their duty to make therapy so painful that it would drive the patient back into health. "The physicians had to play a role somewhat like that of a machine gun behind the front line," Freud noted in retrospect, "that of driving back those who fled."[8] Such doctors, he was forced to conclude, had betrayed medicine.

The history of the shell-shock debate, which has been so well told elsewhere, does not have to be reviewed in its entirety here.[9] We only touch on it in concluding this study because Freud's appearance at the trial of von Wagner-Jauregg could well serve as an appropriate way in which to turn the last page of a chapter in the history of masculinity. It will be recalled that Freud and Sandor Ferenczi on the continent and W. H. Rivers in Britain found they had a higher success rate in dealing with the shell-shocked patient if, instead of belittling him with old-fashioned challenges to forget his troubles, show a stiff upper lip, and act like a man, they allowed him to "talk out" his problem. In short such therapists have been seen as moving away from a nineteenth-century model of masculinity that emphasized the centrality of self-control and will power and toward a twentieth-century model that took into account the forces of emotion and unconscious motivations.

World War I has been represented as leading to a reappraisal of traditional views on sex and gender in other ways as well.[10] The war, in gathering together huge masses of young men, forced upon the public and military authorities the extensive discussion of such heretofore tabooed subjects as the treatment of venereal disease, the policing of brothels, and the distribution of prophylactics. The demands of the wartime economy necessitated the recruitment of thousands of women to take up tasks heretofore called "men's work."[11] Intellectually the conflict, which had been entered into with much macho talk of "playing the game," gave birth to a culture of resignation and introspection.[12] The bloodletting was taken by many as a sign of the end of an age of reason. Those male cultural rebels of the prewar period, such as Wilde, Proust, and Gide, who had embraced hedonism and castigated the repressive morality of the Victorians, were hailed by the progressives of the 1920s as prophets. And sophisticated readers living in a time in which repression seemed out of fashion and sexual experimentation in vogue necessarily turned for advice to seasoned explorers of the unconscious such as Freud.[13]

Even before the war broke out, reappraisals of gender had been begun. The German feminist Rose Mayreder asserted that if one took aggressiveness as the standard, the savage was the most masculine of men. Unfortunately, noted Mayreder, many European men's continued fascination with dueling and warfare revealed that they still worshipped the idol of primitive masculinity.[14] "The fear of appearing unmanly, of displaying any lack of that virility attributed to the primitive ideal of the sex, serves to maintain all the preposterous atavistic prejudices, all the senseless, incompatible tendencies of which the life of the modern man is so full."[15] The older ideal masculine type was out of step with modern social conditions, concluded Mayreder; men would soon have to recognize the pointlessness of arguments based on physical strength and come to terms with living in an intellectualized, urbanized world.

Ending our survey of the male perversions, as we did, with an analysis of transvestitism and a tracing of the shift in the attitudes of the experts toward it from "disgust to compassion," tempts one to conclude that World War I did mark a sharp relaxation of the constraints associated with the older model of aggressive masculinity.[16] Such a conclusion would moreover complement the work of a number of other historians who have sketched out changes in appropriate male role models between the eighteenth and twentieth centuries. They have traced the subduing of the drinking and gambling aristocrat and the stress on male sensibility espoused by Burke and Rousseau and manifested in the American War of Independence and the French Revolution. This, they suggest, led on to the Victorians' ideal of self-restrained, moral manliness, which gave way in the latter nineteenth century to the aggressive, sexualized model of masculinity. In the early twentieth century, the trend was away from rugged masculinity and toward "masculine domesticity."[17]

Less linear, less optimistic, and more complex trajectories can also be traced. If the war blurred gender lines, the authorities were upon its conclusion all the more insistent that women be relegated to their "traditional" tasks.[18] If a few creative writers embraced modernism, there were many more who trotted out old jingoistic arguments.[19] If the military finally accepted the diagnosis of "war neurosis" and allowed less punitive treatments of shell-shocked men, it was not a symptom of a softer attitude toward malingering or the embracing of a new view of true masculinity: the military accepted a psychological diagnosis primarily to individualize the problem and thereby prevent mass mutinies.[20] And if Freud was associated with the subversive notion that each individual was originally bisexual in nature, his postwar popularity is better attributed to psychoanalysis's usefulness in reinvigorating rather than in undermining what were now seen as traditional male and female roles.

The power held in the postwar world by appeals to conservative models of gender that stressed the primacy of masculine virility was most dramatically demonstrated in the writings of another product of Viennese culture, Adolf Hitler. In Mein Kampf (1923) one finds not only the assertion that Aryans are "men" and Jews are not, but a rehash of familiar late-nineteenth-century ideas: those tainted with venereal disease should not be allowed to reproduce; early marriages are needed to combat prostitution; birth control is a danger because it limits genetic choice and so leads to degeneration; too much study is unhealthy; the sexual excitation proffered by films, plays, paintings, and posters undermines the morals of youth; young men have to be rendered hard by gymnastics and sport.[21] Having examined the ways in which attempts were made in the nineteenth century to define and defend healthy masculinity, it should come as no surprise that in the twentieth many in the West were impressed by the ruddy masculine vigor of the Hitler Youth and few protested the Nazis' passing laws for the castration of male "sex criminals" and homosexuals diagnosed as "sick."[22] To suggest therefore that one progressive twentieth-century model of masculinity displaced its repressive nineteenth-century counterpart is simplistic. Perhaps the best that can be said is that in the early twentieth century determining what were the boundaries of appropriate masculine behavior was rendered more complicated than it had been when male sexuality was first problematized a century earlier.

This study had as its goal to show how concepts of masculinity were created, policed, and maintained by men. Males, it should be clear by now, measured their masculinity against that of other men not women. Communities always had a variety of formal and informal means by which to police gender. Dominant forms of masculinity in the nineteenth and early twentieth centuries, we have argued, were largely constituted out of a set of negative varieties that appeared in everyday discourse and practice. "A curious feature of our patriarchal society," notes one author, in making much the same point, "is the lack of sympathy given to the fate of men in certain contexts, particularly in areas of failure."[23] We set out to show how a series of key trials, often by making scapegoats or "examples" of male violators who came to the attention of the press or public, set normative boundaries for turn-of-the-century masculinity. Gauging the impact of such cases on the mass of men poses obvious difficulties. The verdicts in sensational trials did not always provide an accurate reflection of the extent of either the public or the professionals' intent to enforce ruthlessly such boundaries. Muddled or debated messages—as in the case of what was expected of a gentleman when in conflict with a lady, for example—were often the result of these contests. Gender disputes were moreover made endlessly complicated by social class, cultural setting, and—as in the case of Mr. Justice Day—individual perspective.

Here it is worth recalling Robert Connell's point that femininity and masculinity refer not to essences but to ways of living that are historical. Femininities and masculinities change; their meanings shift. Connell identifies an "emphasized femininity" and a "hegemonic masculinity" as currently powerful, public ideologies in Western culture.[24] He also argues, as we have, that such models do not necessarily correspond to actual femininities and masculinities as they are lived, and such dominant forms are always contested. "Ascendant definitions of reality," to use the cumbersome terminology of the sociologist, are always partial and always to some extent contested accomplishments. In theory no one countered the bourgeois argument that the man who committed bigamy was a scoundrel; in practice many working-class men and women appreciated the social conditions that might lead to such a marriage.

As we demonstrated, especially in part two of this study, the dominant ideology of masculinity did not totally obliterate alternative readings. Men selected, used, and appropriated elements of the ideology; they "took it up" when necessary to rationalize or make sense of their actions. We do not have to imagine them as all passively internalizing the ideology of "hegemonic masculinity" in a simple cause and effect or coerced way. This ideology created linguistic and social positions that it "invited" men to assume. Nor are we suggesting that the legal and medical professions formed some homogenous mass that conspired to wield power over the sex lives of their fellow citizens. Their members were often no doubt moved by genuine scientific curiosity, by understandable concerns for order, by philanthropy. What we argue is that the notion that there was one essential form of masculinity was simply assumed by judges, journalists, and doctors. What they did not realize themselves is that the model of masculinity that they took as a given was one that they were actually helping to construct.

In short, although the public rhetoric of what it meant "to be a man" was dominated by a male elite, masculinity necessarily had different meanings depending on men's individual experiences and on their class, race, and sexual orientation. Unfortunately we could not hope to reveal all the ways in which to talk or act like a man varied by class, industry, region, locality, or ethnic group. Nor, in taking a highly selective choice of trial cases, did we propose to show a clear process of change in men's behavior over time. Consequently we are wary of making any grand claims about evolving models of masculinity. What a reading of the sort of evidence unearthed by this study does allow us to appreciate is how and why nineteenth- and early-twentieth-century doctors, lawyers, and laymen, in condemning the "unmanly," helped to construct and sought to impose on their societies what for decades to come were to be heralded as natural and timeless norms of masculinity.

NOTES

INTRODUCTION

1. The historical analysis of masculinity and femininity is a relatively recent phenomenon; there is no discussion of gendered terms in a classic text such as Raymond Williams, *Keywords: A Vocabulary of Culture and Society* (New York: Oxford University Press, 1976).

2. Pierre Bourdieu, *Outline of a Theory of Practice*, trans. Richard Nice (Cambridge: Cambridge University Press, 1977), 94.

3. As was made clear in Ruddiman's 1749 passing reference to the term—"Besides the Prerogative of his Sex, or Masculinity (as the French call it)"—"masculinity" had only recently entered the English language. In France it was used from the sixteenth century onward to describe the legal privileges of males; in both languages it began in the nineteenth century to be employed to refer to what were taken to be male physiological and psychological traits. *Oxford English Dictionary; Dictionnaire de la langue française du 16e siècle* (Paris: Didier, 1961).

4. See, for example, Edward Shorter, *The Making of the Modern Family* (New York: Basic Books, 1976); Paul Robinson, *The Modernization of Sex: Havelock Ellis, Alfred Kinsey, William Masters and Virginia Johnson* (New York: Harper and Row, 1976).

5. Michel Foucault, *The History of Sexuality: Introduction*, trans. Robert Hurley (London: Allen Lane, 1978); and see also Rosalind Coward, *Patriarchal Precedents, Sexuality and Social Relations* (London: Routledge and Kegan Paul, 1983).

6. Thomas Laqueur, *Making Sex: Body and Gender from the Greeks to Freud* (Cambridge: Harvard University Press, 1990); Lawrence Birken, *Consuming Desires: Sexual Science and the Emergence of a Culture of Abundance, 1871–1914* (Ithaca: Cornell University Press, 1989); Cynthia Eagle Russett, *Sexual Science: The Victorian Construction of Womanhood* (Cambridge: Harvard University Press, 1989); Robert A. Nye, *Masculinity and Male Codes of Honor in Modern France* (New York: Oxford University Press 1993); E. Anthony Rotundo, *American Manhood* (New York: Basic Books, 1993); Lesley A. Hall, *Hidden Anxieties: Male Sexuality, 1900–1950* (Oxford: Polity Press, 1991); Kevin White, *The First Sexual Revolution: The Emergence of Male Heterosexuality in Modern America* (New York: New York University Press, 1993); Judith Walkowitz, *The City of Dreadful Delight* (Chicago: University of Chicago Press, 1992); Caroll Smith-Rosenberg, *Disorderly Conduct: Visions of Gender in Victorian America* (New York: Oxford University Press, 1985); Ruth Harris, *Murderers and Madness: Medicine, Law and Society in the Fin de Siècle* (Oxford: Clarendon Press, 1989). On the relationship of progressive political views and attitudes toward sexuality in Eastern Europe, see Laura Engelstein, *The Keys to Happiness: Sex and the Search for Modernity in Fin-de-siècle Russia* (Ithaca: Cornell University Press, 1992).

7. Studies that focus on "respectable" models of masculinity include Steven Seidman, *Romantic Longings: Love in America, 1830–1930* (New York: Routledge, 1991); Peter G. Filene, *Him/Her/Self: Sex Roles in Modern America* (Baltimore: Johns Hopkins University

Press, 1974); and Joe L. Dubbert, "Progressivism and the Masculinity Crisis," in *The American Man,* ed. E. Pleck and J. Pleck (New York: Prentice Hall, 1980), 303–19; Michael S. Kimmel, "The contemporary 'Crisis' of Masculinity in Historical Perspective," in *The Making of Masculinities: The New Men's Studies,* ed. Harry Brod (Boston: Unwin Hyman, 1987): Peter N. Stearns, *Be a Man! Males in Modern Society* (New York: Holmes and Meier, 1979); J. A. Mangan and James Walvin, *Manliness and Morality: Middle Class Masculinity in Britain and America, 1800–1940* (New York: St. Martin's Press, 1987); Michael Roper and John Tosh, eds. *Manful Assertions: Masculinities in Britain since 1800* (London: Routledge, 1991); Mark C. Carnes and Clyde Griffen, *Meanings for Manhood* (Chicago: University of Chicago Press, 1990); Elisabeth Badinter, *X Y: De l'Identité masculine* (Paris: Odile Jacob, 1992); Martin A. Danahay, *A Community of One: Masculine Autobiography and Autonomy in Nineteenth-Century Britain* (Albany: SUNY Press, 1993); Herbert Sussman, *Victorian Masculinities: Manhood and Masculine Poetics in Early Victorian Literature and Art* (Cambridge: Cambridge University Press, 1995); Claudia Nelson, *Invisible Men: Fatherhood in Victorian Periodicals, 1850–1910* (Athens: University of Georgia Press, 1995).

8. For suggestive insights on historicizing and sociologizing masculinity, see R. W. Connell, *Which Way Is Up? Essays on Sex, Class and Culture* (London: Allen and Unwin, 1983); John Tosh, "What Should Historians Do with Masculinity? Reflections on Nineteenth-Century Britain," *History Workshop Journal* 38 (1994): 179–202.

9. Harris, *Murderers and Madness,* 327.

10. Joan Scott, "Statistical Representations of Work: The Politics of the Chamber of Commerce's Statitique de l'industrie à Paris, 1847–48," in *Work in France: Representations, Meaning, Organization and Practice,* ed. Steven Lawrence Kaplan and Cynthia J. Koepp (Ithaca: Cornell University Press, 1986), 361n83.

11. Theodore Zeldin, "Les Français et l'amour," in *Amour et sexualité en l'occident,* ed. Georges Duby (Paris: Points, 1991), 317–23.

12. For an introduction to this issue see Gail Bederman, *Manliness and Civilization: A Cultural History of Gender and Race in the United States, 1880–1917* (Chicago: University of Chicago Press, 1995); Anne McClintock, *Imperial Leather: Race, Gender and Sexuality in Colonial Conquest* (New York: Routledge, 1995); Mrinalini Sinha, *Colonial Masculinity: The "Manly Englishman" and the "Effeminate Bengali" in the Late Nineteenth Century* (Manchester: Manchester University Press, 1995); Antoinette Burton, *Burdens of History: British Feminists, Indian Women and Imperial Culture, 1865–1915* (Chapel Hill: University of North Carolina Press, 1994).

13. So much has been written about the construction of nineteenth-century homosexuality that one is often left with the misleading impression that the only form of "sexual dissidence" that preoccupied the sexologists was inversion. See, for example, Jonathan Dollimore, *Sexual Dissidence: Augustine to Wilde, Freud to Foucault* (Oxford: Clarendon Press, 1991).

14. Leonore Davidoff and Catherine Hall, *Family Fortunes: Men and Women of the English Middle Class, 1780–1850* (London: Hutchinson, 1987), 33.

15. Ed Cohen, *Talk on the Wilde Side: Toward a Genealogy of a Discourse on Male Sexualities* (London: Routledge, 1993), 129.

16. Guido Ruggiero, *The Boundaries of Eros* (New York: Oxford University Press, 1985).

17. Sander Gilman, *Difference and Pathology: Stereotypes of Sexuality, Race and Madness* (Ithaca: Cornell University Press, 1985).

18. James W. Messerschmidt, *Masculinities and Crime: Critique and Reconceptualization of Theory* (Lanham, Md.: Rowman and Littlefield, 1993).

19. Rotundo, for example, in *American Manhood* completely skirts the linkages of violence and masculinity.

20. Marie-Elisabeth Handman, *La Violence et la ruse: Hommes et femmes dans un village grec* (Paris: Edisud, 1983), 154–59.

21. Georges Lanteri-Laura, *Lecture des perversions: Histoire de leur appropriation médicale* (Paris: Masson, 1979).

22. Katherine Fischer Taylor, *In the Theater of Criminal Justice: The Palais de Justice in Second Empire Paris* (Princeton: Princeton University Press, 1993).

23. André Gide, *Souvenirs de la cour d'assises* (Paris: Nouvelle revue française, 1913); and on the crucial role of popular prejudice as reflected by juries in the United States, see Samuel Walker, *Popular Justice: A History of American Criminal Justice* (New York: Oxford University Press, 1980), 111.

24. Joan Wallach Scott, *Gender and the Politics of History* (New York: Columbia University Press, 1988), 42.

25. Robert A. Nye, *Masculinity and Male Codes of Honor in Modern France* (New York: Oxford University Press, 1993).

26. On the role of film and television in the shoring up of gender roles in twentieth-century America, see Susan Jeffords, *The Remasculinization of America: Gender and the Vietnam War* (Bloomington: Indiana University Press, 1989).

27. Arnold Davidson, "Sex and the Emergence of Sexuality," *Critical Inquiry* 14 (1987): 16–48; Jeffrey Weeks, *Sex, Politics and Society: The Regulation of Sexuality since 1800* (London: Longman, 1981).

28. Karen Dubinsky, *Improper Advances: Rape and Heterosexual Conflict in Ontario* (Chicago: University of Chicago Press, 1993).

29. Maurice Godelier, *New Left Review* 127 (1987): 17, cited in Scott, *Gender and the Politics of History*, 45. On the long history of such preoccupations, see David Cohen, *Law, Sexuality and Society: The Enforcement of Morals in Classical Athens* (Cambridge: Cambridge University Press, 1991).

INTRODUCTION TO PART ONE

1. Brian Dippie, *The Vanishing American: White Attitudes and United States Indian Policy* (Middletown, Conn.: Wesleyan University Press, 1982).

2. William James, *Collected Essays and Reviews* (London: Longman, 1920), 404 5.

CHAPTER 1: DEVIANTS

1. *Parliamentary Debates, House of Commons* 43 (14 Nov. 1912), cols. 2084–86; Leon Radzinowicz and Roger Hood, *A History of English Criminal Law and its Administration from 1750* (London: Stevens, 1986), 5:711.

2. Pieter Spierenburg, *The Spectacle of Suffering: Executions and the Evolution of Repression from a Preindustrial Metropolis to the European Experience* (Cambridge: Cambridge University Press, 1984), 68–9; Michael Ignatieff, *A Just Measure of Pain: The Penitentiary in the Industrial Revolution, 1750–1850* (London: Macmillan, 1978).

3. Martin J. Wiener, *Reconstructing the Criminal: Culture, Law and Policy in England, 1830–1914* (Cambridge: Cambridge University Press, 1990). For a less optimistic view of the widening scope of criminal law and the accompanying growth of police powers, see V. A. C. Gatrell et al., eds., *Crime and the Law: The Social History of Crime in Western Europe since 1500* (London: Europa Press, 1980).

4. Radzinowicz and Hood, *English Criminal Law,* 5:690.

5. On the continued subjection into the twentieth century of males under the age of sixteen to birchings, see Geoffrey Pearson, *Hooligan: A History of Respectable Fears* (London: Macmillan, 1983), 261n92.

6. Jennifer Davis, "The London Garroting Panic of 1862: A Moral Panic and the Creation of a Criminal Class in Mid-Victorian England," in *Crime and the Law,* ed. Gatrell et al., 190–213.

7. On the numbers flogged, see *Parliamentary Papers* 54 (1882): 137; "Report of the

Departmental Committee on Corporal Punishment," *Parliamentary Papers* 9 (1937–1938): 461–619; Radzinowicz and Hood, *English Criminal Law,* 5:707.

8. The wave of garrotings was actually over before flogging was employed. See George Benson, M. P., *Flogging: The Law and Practice in England* (London: Howard League, 1931).

9. Radzinowicz and Hood, *English Criminal Law,* 5:694.

10. Maeve E. Doggett, *Marriage, Wife-Beating and the Law in Victorian England* (London: Weidenfeld and Nicolson, 1992), 106–33.

11. Elizabeth Pleck, *Domestic Tyranny: The Making of American Social Policy against Family Violence from Colonial Times to the Present* (New York: Oxford University Press, 1987), 108–24

12. Simeon Baldwin, *The American Judiciary* (New York: Century, 1905), 245.

13. Simeon Baldwin, "Whipping and Castration as Punishments for Crime," *Yale Law Journal* 8 (1899): 377.

14. Pleck, *Domestic Tyranny,* 111; Linda Gordon, *Heroes of Their Own Lives: The Politics and History of Family Violence, Boston 1880–1960* (New York: Viking, 1988), 255.

15. Radzinowicz and Hood, *English Criminal Law,* 695. See also *Parliamentary Debates, House of Lords* 300 (31 July 1885), cols. 722–51.

16. *Parliamentary Papers* 82 (1888): 33–35; 72 (1898): 569–71.

17. Floggings were used to enforce discipline in the army and navy until 1881; see Alan Ramsay Skelley, *The Victorian Army at Home* (London: Croom Helm, 1977), 147–52. For a first-person account of the horrors of being flogged, see Alexander Somerville, *The Autobiography of a Working Man* (London: Turnstile Press, 1951), 188–89.

18. T. B. L. Baker, "On Vagrants and Tramps" (pamphlet, Manchester Statistical Society, 1869).

19. "1898 Vagrancy Act Amendment Bill," *Parliamentary Debates, House of Commons* 62 (1898), col. 426ff.

20. Rev. Frank Charles Laubach, *Why There are Vagrants: A Study Based upon an Examination of One Hundred Men* (New York: Columbia University, 1916), 36; and on the "wolf" or "jocker," see also Josiah Flynt, *Tramping with Tramps* (New York: Century, 1899), 7. According to the *Oxford English Dictionary,* North Americans also employed the term *gunsel* (from the Yiddish "little goose") to refer to a tramp's companion and/or the young homosexual.

21. "A Bill to Amend the Vagrancy Act, 1824," *Parliamentary Papers* 7 (1898): 607–8; Henry S. Salt, *The Flogging Craze: A Statement of the Case against Corporal Punishment* (London: George Allen, 1916), 72.

22. Salt, *Flogging Craze,* 71.

23. Ibid., 73.

24. See letter to London *Times,* 28 Feb. 1899, 7f.

25. In 1895 only one person of 1,265 convicted of exposing himself had actually had been whipped; see Radzinowicz and Hood, *English Criminal Law,* 5:707.

26. Joseph Collinson, *The Flogging of Vagrants* (London: Humanitarian League, 1909), 9.

27. On the birching of four young male prostitutes for what the newspapers discretely referred to as the "annoying" of gentlemen in the West End, see London *Times,* 6 Nov. 1912, 4e. On the flogging of men for sex offenses in Canada, see Pierre Hurteau, "L'Homosexualité masculine et les discours sur le sexe en contexte montréalais de la fin du XIXe siècle à la revolution tranquille," *Histoire sociale/Social History* 26 (1993): 47.

28. Edward J. Bristow, *Prostitution and Prejudice: The Jewish Fight against White Slavery, 1870–1939* (New York: Schocken Books, 1983), 37. The highly charged image of British girls being held captive in Belgian brothels had been launched in 1879 by the moral purity advocate, Alfred Dyer. William Stead and William Coote subsequently carried on the campaign.

29. Edward J. Bristow, *Vice and Vigilance: Purity Movements in Britain since 1700* (London: Gill and Macmillan, 1977).

30. *Parliamentary Papers* 7 (1898): 607.

31. *Parliamentary Debates, House of Lords* 12 (1912), cols. 1193, 1198.

32. See also *Parliamentary Papers* 1 (1912–13): 599–614; *Parliamentary Debates, House of Commons* 43 (1912), cols. 725–806; cols 1842–1950; *House of Lords* 13 (1912), cols. 106–36; *House of Commons* 45 (1912), cols. 699–34; 696ff.

33. In prisons the last floggings took place in 1962 but were not actually abolished until 1967. Ian Gibson, *The English Vice: Beating, Sex and Shame in Victorian England and After* (London: Duckworth, 1978), 167. See also Arthur Griffiths, *Memorials of Millbank and Chapters in Prison History* (London: Chapman and Hall, 1884), 129–32.

34. E. Roy Calvert and Theodora Calvert, *The Law Breakers* (London: Routledge, 1933), 254.

35. *Daily Sketch*, 13 Feb. 1913. Mormons, because of their association with polygamy, played the stock role of sexual villains in literary works ranging from Arthur Conan Doyle's *A Study in Scarlet* (1887) to Zane Grey's *Riders of the Purple Sage* (1912).

36. William Tallack, *Penological and Preventive Principles* (London: Wertheimer, 1896), 414

37. Bristow, *Vice and Vigilance*, 193. But for Major Paget's 1924 attempt to extend whipping to males over sixteen who commit sexual offense against girls under thirteen, see *Lancet* 1 (1924): 1344.

38. Radzinowicz and Hood, *English Criminal Law*, 5:697.

39. M. St. J. Packe, *Life of John Stuart Mill* (1954), 482–3.

40. Tallack, *Penological and Preventive Principles*, 11.

41. Richard Maxwell Brown, *Strain of Violence* (New York: Oxford University Press, 1975), 177–79.

42. Tallack, *Penological and Preventive Principles*, 413.

43. Labouchère cited in ibid., 111–12.

44. Tallack, *Penological and Preventive Principles*, 117.

45. Ibid., 391.

46. Baldwin, "Whipping and Castration," 383. On views of childhood sexuality see, Sander Gilman, *Difference and Pathology: Stereotypes of Sexuality, Race, and Madness* (Ithaca: Cornell University Press, 1985).

47. Tallack, *Penological and Preventive Principles*, 414. On the press's support for Tallack's call to get tough with tramps, see the book of press cuttings on W. Tallack's *Penological and Preventive Principles* (British Library, 6057 ee 25).

48. *Parliamentary Debates, House of Parliament* 43 (1912), cols. 1900–1902. Jews had been accused of pimping by the popular journalist Arnold White, *The Modern Jew* (London: Heinemann, 1899). On the portrayal of Jews as effeminate and hysterical, see John M. Efron, *Defenders of the Race: Jewish Doctors and Race Science in Fin-de-Siècle Europe* (New Haven: Yale University Press, 1994), 7. On the association of black men with the drugging and seduction of English women, see Marek Kohn, *Dope Girls: The Birth of the British Drug Underground* (London: Lawrence and Wishart, 1992).

49. *Parliamentary Debates, House of Commons* 43 (1912), col. 1901.; col. 1892–1938; and see also the statements of Reginald McKenna, the Liberal home secretary, *Parliamentary Debates, House of Commons* 43 (1912), col. 767; and see also London *Times*, 2 Nov. 1912, 7f.

50. Baldwin, "Whipping and Castration," 380.

51. Simeon Baldwin, *The American Judiciary* (New York: Century, 1905), 246.

52. Pleck, *Domestic Tyranny*, 108–24. Virginia reverted to whipping in 1898 for under-sixteens as an alternative to a fine or jail sentence if the father consented. Theodore Roosevelt

threw his support behind the corporal punishment campaign in 1904, but the United States Congress rejected flogging legislation in 1906.

53. On opposition to whipping in India, see Thomas Babington Macaulay, *Works,* 4:196, cited in Gibson, *English Vice,* 154.

54. Baldwin, "Whipping and Castration," 382.

55. William Harbutt Dawson, *The Vagrancy Problem* (London: P. S. King, 1910), 3.

56. Hippolyte Laurent, *Les Châtiments corporels* (Lyon: Phily, 1912), 122, 348–50.

57. *Parliamentary Debates, House of Commons* 81 (1900), col. 555.

58. *Parliamentary Debates, House of Commons* 43 (1912), cols. 1874, 1877. The same argument had been made in 1898; see *Parliamentary Debates, House of Commons* 62 (1898 Vagrancy Act Amendment Bill), col. 429.

59. *Parliamentary Debates, House of Commons* 43 (1912), col. 728–30. The government was at this time seeking by way of a bill for feeble-mindedness to have placed under detention single pregnant women receiving relief; see London *Times,* 8 Nov. 1912, 4a.

60. Joseph Collinson, *Facts about Flogging* (London: Fifield, 1905), 17.

61. On the women's movement and sexual panics, see Lucy Bland, *Banishing the Beast: English Feminism and Sexual Morality, 1885–1914* (London: Penguin, 1995).

62. For the observation that, though men were beaten while women were not, women did not have higher status and indeed the pimp, in becoming the focus of criminal law, was given "the privilege of agency," which was denied women, see Laura Engelstein, *The Keys to Happiness: Sex and the Search for Modernity in Fin de Siècle Russia* (Ithaca: Cornell University Press, 1992), 74; 90–93.

63. *The Humanitarian* (December 1912): 90–91. The Humanitarian League was supported by feminists such as Lady Florence Dixie, who wrote one of its pamphlets, "The Mercilessness of Sport."

64. Between 1883 and 1899, Day had included in his sentencing 4,061 strokes; see *Parliamentary Debates, House of Commons* 81 (1900), col. 560; Salt, *Flogging Craze,* 134.

65. London *Times,* 13 Nov. 1912, 16d.

66. Teresa Billington-Greig, "The Truth about White Slavery," *English Review* 14 (1913): 434–35. Frances Power Cobbe had been an earlier vocal feminist opponent of flogging.

67. London *Times,* 13 Nov. 1912, 16d.

68. *Parliamentary Papers, House of Commons* 43 (1912), col. 1861.

69. *Parliamentary Papers, House of Commons* 43 (1912), col. 1930.

70. Elaine Showalter, *Sexual Anarchy: Gender and Culture at the Fin de Siècle* (London: Penguin, 1990).

71. Colin Watson, *Snobbery with Violence: English Crime Stories and Their Audience* (London: Eyre Methuen, 1971).

72. Predictably enough the defenders of flogging characterized their opponents as being not real men but "enthusiastic old women in trousers." Skelley, *Victorian Army,* 152.

73. Edward Carpenter provided some positive, remedial examples of caning but concluded that it was the lowest form of punishment and should only be used in reformatories by those who knew and cared for their charges, but never for adults. Edward Carpenter, *Prisons, Police and Punishment* (London: Fifield, 1905); and see also Dan Weinbren, "Against All Cruelty: The Humanitarian League, 1891–1919," *History Workshop Journal* (1995): 86–105.

74. On Oscar Wilde's revulsion at the floggings he witnessed in prison, see "The Case of Warder Martin: Some Cruelties of Prison Life," a letter to the editor of the *Daily Chronicle* published 28 May 1897, in *The Annotated Oscar Wilde,* ed. H. Montgomery Hyde (London: Orbis, 1982), 470.

75. See also H. G. Wells, *The Island of Dr. Moreau* (London: Heinemann, 1896).

76. Thomas de Quincey, "On Suicide," in *Collected Writings* (Edinburgh: Black, 1890), 8:400; and see also "Flogging in Schools," in *Collected Writings,* 1:291–95.

77. James Fitzjames Stephen, *A History of the Criminal Law* (London: Macmillan, 1883), 2:91.

78. Reported by Arthur Greenwood, M. P., in the introduction to Salt, *Flogging Craze*.

79. Mr. L. Williams, *Parliamentary Debates, House of Commons* 43 (1912), col. 1900.

80. Salt, *Flogging Craze*, 80.

81. *News of the World*, 22 June 1913, 1. The sexologists like Krafft-Ebing, Moll, and Ellis provided similar reports.

82. George Bernard Shaw, *The Awakener*, 16 Nov. 1912, 7–8; and see also *Humanity*, April 1898, 26–27; *Misalliance* in *Collected Works* (London: Constable, 1930), 13:56, in which he declared the 1912 act was "not a legislative phenomenon but a psychopathic one."

83. Salt, *Flogging Craze*, 87

84. *Parliamentary Debates, House of Commons* 43 (1912), cols. 1948–49.

85. A useful review of other countries' views on flogging was provided in the "Report of the Departmental Committee on Corporal Punishment," *Parliamentary Papers* 9 (1937–1938): 610ff. Canada stood out as a nation especially prone to using the whip; on average, in each year between 1932 and 1936, 130 adults were so punished.

86. Thanks to the work of the International Abolitionist Federation, first organized by Josephine Butler, international agreements of 1902 and 1910 had the use of fraud or force to move females under age twenty abroad recognized in international law as a crime. The Dutch in 1911 raised the age of consent to twenty-one. In the United States, in addition to the Mann Act, forty-two states passed similar legislation, though only 7.5 percent of women stated that they were coerced into the trade. Bristow, *Prostitution and Prejudice*; David J. Pivar, *Purity Crusade: Sexual Morality and Social Control, 1868–1900* (Westport, Conn.: Greenwood Press, 1973); Ruth Rosen, *Lost Sisterhood: Prostitution in America, 1900–1918* (Baltimore: Johns Hopkins University Press, 1982), 112–19, 134; David J. Langum, *Crossing over the Line: Legislating Morality and the Mann Act* (Chicago: University of Chicago Press, 1994).

87. Indeed on the continent a visit to a brothel remained a male rite of passage and the procurer could even be made the subject of a novel. See Charles-Louis Philippe, *Bubu of Montparnasse* (1905; Paris: Crosby, 1932), Richard J. Evans, *The Feminist Movement in Germany, 1894–1933* (London: Sage, 1976), 17.

88. On regulated prostitution, see Léo Taxil, *La Corruption fin-de-siècle* (Paris: Noirot, 1904), 66–169; Louis Fiaux, *La Police des moeurs en France et dans les principaux pays de l'Europe* (Paris: Dentu, 1888), 3 vols.; Alain Corbin, *Les Filles de noce: Misère sexuelle et prostitution, 19e et 20e siècles* (Paris: Aubier Montaigne, 1978); Jacques Termeau, *Maisons closes de province* (Paris: Editions cénomane, 1986); Jean-Marc Berlière, *La Police des moeurs sous la IIIe république* (Paris: Seuil, 1992).

89. Robert A. Nye, *Crime, Madness, and Politics in Modern France: The medical Concept of National Decline* (Princeton: Princeton University Press, 1984), 196–202.

90. They were also reported in Lille, Marseilles, and Lyon.

91. Dr. Lejeune, *Faut-il fouetter les Apaches?* (Paris: Librairie du Temple, 1910), 23; see also Hippolyte Laurent, *Les Châtiments corporels: La Peine capitale, le fouet aux apaches* (Lyon: Phily, 1912); *Le Fouet contre le crime* (Lyon: Phily, 1913). Edmond Locard, *Le Crime et les criminels* (Paris: Le Renaissance du livre, 1927).

92. For the observation that most young men in such gangs were in reality simply going through a pre-adulthood rite of passage, see Michelle Perrot, "Dans la France de la Belle Époque, les 'Apaches', premières bandes de jeunes," in *Les Marginaux et les exclus dans l'histoire*, ed. Bernard Vincent (Paris: Union générale d'éditions, 1979), 387–408.

93. Alexandre Lacassagne, *Peine de mort et criminalité* (Paris: Maloine, 1908), 96–7, 144, 164–65; A. Lacassagne, "Les chatiments corporels en Angleterre," *Archives de l'anthropologie criminelle* 26 (1911): 35–46.

94. Cesare Lombroso, *L'Uomo delinquente* (Milano: Hoepli, 1876); and see also Eu-

genio Florian and Guido Cavaglieri, *I Vagabondi: Studio sociologico-giuridico* (Torino: Bocca, 1900).

95. Flynt, *Tramping with Tramps*. "Josiah Flynt," who also contributed "Homosexuality among Tramps," to appendix A of Havelock Ellis's "Sexual Inversion," was actually F. Willard, a nephew of Miss Frances Willard, president of the WCTU. See Havelock Ellis, *Studies in the Psychology of Sexuality* (New York: Random House, 1942), 1:359–67.

96. Frank Charles Laubach, *Why There Are Vagrants: A Study Based upon an Examination of One Hundred Men* (New York: Columbia University Press, 1916). See also, Allan Pinkerton, *Strikers, Communists, Tramps and Detectives* (New York: Carleton, 1877).

97. Hubert du Puy, *Vagabondage et mendicité* (Paris: Larose, 1899), 2.

98. Pierre Boue, *Vagabondage et mendicité: Moyens de défense* (Pithiviers: A. Gibier, 1906), 39.

99. Boue, *Vagabondage et mendicité*, 9–11; Jean Berry and Georges Berry, *Le Vagabondage et la mendicité* (Paris: Figuière, 1913).

100. Émile Fourquet, "Les Vagabonds criminels," *Revue des deux mondes* 2 (1899): 399–437.

101. On tramps and sex crimes, see also Benjamin Ball, *La Folie érotique* (Paris: Baillière, 1888), 116, 147. The fifth Congrès pénitentiare international, which was held in Paris in 1895, focused its attention on the issue of vagabondage.

102. A. R. Diefendorf, ed., *Kraeplin's Clinical Psychiatry* (New York: Macmillan, 1912), 529.

103. Defenders of flogging maintained that "single-handed rape"—the ability of one man to assault a conscious woman—was impossible; see *Parliamentary Debates, House of Commons* 81 (1900), col. 554.

104. Paolo Mantegazza, *Physiologie de l'amour* (Paris: Kolb, 1886).

105. Henry Maudsley, *Body and Will* (London: Kegan Paul, Trench, 1883), 241. Charles Kingsley also spoke of a "process of degradation" that led to "effeminate barbarism." Charles Kingsley, *Health and Education* (Daldy: Isbister, 1875), 10–11.

106. Marie-Jo Bonnet, *Un Choix sans equivoque: Recherches sur les relations amoureuses entre les femmes XVIe–XXe siècle* (Paris: Denoel, 1981), 180; Jonathan Katz, *The Invention of Heterosexuality* (New York: Basic Books, 1994).

107. Pierre Hahn, *Nos ancestres les pervers: La Vie des homosexuels sous le Second Empire* (Paris: Olivier Orban, 1979), 20.

108. For more traditional views of deviant sexual behavior, see Marie-Véronique Gauthier, *Chanson, Sociabilité et Grivoiserie au XIXe siècle* (Paris: Aubier, 1992), 239–45.

109. Hahn, *Nos ancestres les pervers*, 125.

110. Joachim S. Hohmann, ed., *Der unterdruckte Sexus* (Lollar: Achenbach, 1977), 25 cited in George Mosse, "Masculinity and the Decadence," in *Sexual Knowledge: Sexual Science: The History of Attitudes to Sexuality*, ed. Roy Porter and Mikulas Teich (Cambridge: Cambridge University Press, 1994), 257.

111. Joseph Bristow, ed., *Sexual Sameness: Textual Differences in Lesbian and Gay Writing* (New York: Routledge, 1992).

112. *Review of Reviews* (1895), cited in H. Montgomery Hyde, ed., *Trials of Oscar Wilde* (London: London, Hodge, 1948)

113. Derek S. Linton, *"Who Has the Youth, Has the Future": The Campaign to Save Young Workers in Imperial Germany* (Cambridge: Cambridge University Press, 1991); Harry Hendrick, *Images of Youth: Age, Class, and the Male Youth Problem, 1880–1920* (Oxford: Clarendon Press, 1990); J. Robert Wegs, *Growing Up Working Class: Continuity and Change among Viennese Youth, 1890–1938* (University Park: Penn State University Press, 1989).

114. Gail Bederman, *Manliness and Civilization: A Cultural History of Gender and Race in the United States, 1880–1917* (Chicago: University of Chicago Press, 1995), 101–10.

115. Émile Pourésy, *La Gangrène pornographique* (Roubaix: Foyer Solidariste, 1908).

116. Annie Stora-Lamarre, *L'Enfer de la IIIe République: Censeurs et pornographes 1881–1914* (Paris: Imago, 1990), 21; Heywood Broun and Margaret Leech, *Anthony Comstock: Roundsman of the Lord* (New York: Albert and Boni, 1927).

117. On the notion that pornography's enemies first saw it as posing religious and political dangers and that the question of its threat to "decency" was a new nineteenth-century preoccupation, see Lynn Hunt, ed., *The Invention of Pornography: Obscenity and the Origins of Modernity, 1500–1800* (New York: Zone Books, 1993).

118. Pourésy, *La Gangrène pornographique*, 214–237.

119. Ibid., 293, 419.

120. Annelise Mauge, *L'Identité masculine en crise au tournant du siècle, 1871–1914* (Paris: Rivages, 1987), 242.

121. Sigmund Freud, "The Universal Tendency to Debasement in Love," (1912), *The Standard Edition of the Complete Psychological Works,* trans. James Strachey (London: Hogarth Press, 1966) 11: 185.

122. Henry Maudsley, *Life in Mind and Conduct* (London: Macmillan, 1902), 302.

123. Jacques Le Rider, *Modernity and Crises of Identity: Culture and Society in Fin-de-Siècle Vienna* (Cambridge: Polity Press, 1993).

124. Dr. P. J. Moebius, *De la debilité mentale physiologique chez la femme,* trans. Nicole et Simone Roche, (1900; Paris: Solin, 1991).

125. Caroll Smith-Rosenberg, *Disorderly Conduct: Visions of Gender in Victorian America* (New York: Oxford University Press, 1985); see also Bonnet, *Un Choix sans equivoque;* Martha Vicinus, *Independent Women: Work and Community for Single Women, 1850–1920* (London: Virago, 1985).

126. Smith-Rosenberg, *Disorderly Conduct,* 265.

127. G. J. Barker-Benfield, *The Horrors of the Half-Known Life: Male Attitudes toward Women and Sexuality in Nineteenth-century America* (New York: Harper and Row, 1976), 212.

128. Geneviève Fraisse, *Musée de la raison: La Démocratie exclusive et la différence des sexes* (Paris: Alinéa, 1989); Olwen H. Hufton, *Women and the Limits of Citizenship in the French Revolution* (Toronto: University of Toronto Press, 1992), 49.

129. On the development in France of male clubs from which women were excluded, see Maurice Agulhon, *Le Cercle dans la France bourgeoise, 1810–1848* (Paris: Colin, 1977); Jean-Luc Marais, *Les Sociétés d'hommes: Histoire d'une sociabilité du 18e siècle à nos jours: Anjou, Maine, Touraine* (Vauchetien: La Botellerie, 1986). On Germany, where laws prevented women from participating in clubs and politics, see Vernon L. Lidtke, *The Alternative Culture: Socialist Labor in Imperial Germany* (New York: Oxford University Press, 1982), 37.

130. On the emergence of new models of masculinity, see G. J. Barker-Benfield, *The Culture of Sensibility: Sex and Society in Eighteenth-Century Britain* (Chicago: University of Chicago Press, 1992), 247–48; Leonore Davidoff and Catherine Hall, *Family Fortunes: Men and Women of the English Middle Class, 1780–1850* (London: Hutchinson, 1987), 110, 250; Catherine Hall, *White, Male and Middle Class: Explorations in Feminism and History* (Cambridge: Polity Press, 1992); Robert L. Griswold, *Fatherhood in America: A History* (New York: Basic Books, 1993).

131. C. Davidson, *A Woman's Work Is Never Done* (London: Chatto and Windus, 1986), cited in Wally Seccombe, *Weathering the Storm: Working-class Families from the Industrial Revolution to the Fertility Decline* (London: Verso, 1993), 187–88; and see also Ava Baron, *Work Engendered: Toward a New History of American Labor* (Ithaca: Cornell University Press, 1991); Anna Clark, *The Struggle for the Breaches: Gender and the Making of the British Working Class* (Berkeley: University of California Press, 1995); Jean H. Quataert,

Reluctant Feminists in German Social Democracy, 1885–1917 (Princeton: Princeton University Press, 1979), 153–60, 199–200.

132. Bruce Haley, *The Healthy Body and Victorian Culture* (Cambridge: Harvard University Press, 1978), 206–14; Donald E. Hall, ed., *Muscular Christianity: Embodying the Victorian Age* (Cambridge: Cambridge University Press, 1994).

133. David D. Gilmor, *Manhood in the Making: Cultural Concepts of Masculinity* (New Haven: Yale University Press, 1990). Yet a woman who demanded political rights or engaged in a range of unacceptable behaviors would be described as having sacrificed her "womanhood."

134. David Lockwood, *The Blackcoated Worker: A Study in Class Consciousness* (London: Allen and Unwin, 1966). In the United States, the term squaw man was used to deride the individual who hoped to live on his Indian wife's land.

135. Eugen Weber, *France: Fin de siècle* (Cambridge, Mass.: Belknap Press, 1986), 42. Marie-Thérèse Eyquem, *Pierre de Coubertin: L'Époque olympique* (Paris; Calman-Levy, 1966).

136. Theodore Roosevelt, "The Manly Virtues and Practical Politics," *The Forum*, July 1894, 32.

137. Robert Ernst, *Weakness Is a Crime: The Life of Bernarr MacFadden* (Syracuse: Syracuse University Press, 1991); Bernarr A. MacFadden, *Méthode d'éducation physique* (Paris: n. p., 1899); Kathryn Grover, *Fitness in American Culture: Images of Health, Sport, and the Body, 1830–1940* (Amhurst: University of Massachusetts Press, 1989); Michael Oriard, *Reading Football: How the Popular Press Created an American Spectacle* (Chapel Hill: University of North Carolina Press, 1993), 188ff.

138. The quote is from C. F. G. Masterman cited in Michael Rosenthal, *The Character Factory: Baden-Powell's Boy Scouts and the Imperatives of Empire* (New York: Pantheon, 1986), 131–32.; and see also John Springhall, *Youth, Empire and Society: British Youth Movements, 1883–1940* (London: Croom Helm, 1977), and John Gillis, *Youth and History: Tradition and Change in European Age Relations, 1770–Present* (New York: Academic Press, 1974), 111–13; David I. Macleod, *Building Character in the American Boy: The Boy Scouts, YMCA, and Their Forerunners, 1870–1920* (Madison: University of Wisconsin Press, 1983). On Baden-Powell's desire to provide boys with a safe haven from women and the question of his homosexuality, see also Tim Jeal, *The Boy-Man: The Life of Lord Baden-Powell* (New York: William Morrow, 1990). Thorstein Veblen's opinion of grown men's involvement in "boys brigades" and sports was that it was a sign of "arrested spiritual development," which "may express itself not only in direct participation by adults in youthful exploits of ferocity, but also indirectly in aiding and abetting disturbances of this kind on the part of younger persons." Thorstein Veblen, *The Theory of the Leisure Class: An Economic Study of Institutions* (1899; London: Allen and Unwin, 1924), 254

139. Ann Douglas, *The Feminization of American Culture* (New York: Knopf, 1977), 327.

140. F. A. Vuillermet, *Soyez des hommes: À la conquête de la virilité* (Paris: Lethielleux, 1909).

141. Arthur Lautrec, *La Fin du monde prochainement* (Paris: Côte, 1901); see also for a religious gloss, Jean Rocroy, *La Fin du monde en 1921* (Paris: Vic, 1904).

142. Jean Philippe and G. Paul-Boncour, *Les Anomalies mentales chez les écoliers* (Paris: Alcan, 1905).

143. Previously magistrates, in order to try such cases summarily, had to reduce them to common assault. See E. Roy Calvert and Theodora Calvert, *The Law Breakers* (London: Routledge, 1933), 32–33.

144. Isabel V. Hull, *The Entourage of Kaiser Wilhelm II, 1888–1918* (Cambridge Cambridge University Press, 1982), 133.

145. On the cowboy myth, see Richard Slotkin, *Regeneration through Violence* (Middletown, Conn: Wesleyan University Press, 1973) and *Gunfighter Nation: The Myth of the Frontier in Twentieth-century America* (New York: Atheneum, 1992). And on the theme of America as nature's "good bad boy," violent but sexually pure, see Leslie Fielder, *Love and Death in the American Novel* (New York: Stein and Day, 1966).

146. The concern for gender that pervaded much of the literature meant purposefully for boys has yet to be fully analyzed. Horatio Alger, Jr., who beginning with *Ragged Dick* (1867) wrote more than a hundred classic boy stories on the rag to riches theme, made a point of always scorning the character of the effeminate young fop. He did so, it has been suggested, because he feared that the fact that he lost his first post as minister in Brewster, Massachusetts, in 1866 because of "unnatural familiarity with boys" might be discovered. Gary Schnarnhorst, *Horatio Alger, Jr.* (Boston: Twayne, 1980), 29. But Owen Wister, author of *The Virginian* (1902), had no reluctance in having the male narrator, mesmerized by the hero whom he first sees at a wedding, exclaim: "Had I been the bride, I should have taken the giant, dust and all" and "Had I been a woman, it would have made me his to do what he pleased with on the spot." Slotkin, *Gunfighter Nation*, 177.

147. Burroughs, whose *Tarzan of the Apes* first appeared in 1912, was influenced by the eugenic notions of Madison Grant and T. L. Stoddard; see Erling B. Holtsmark, *Edgar Rice Burroughs* (Boston: Twayne, 1986).

INTRODUCTION TO PART TWO

1. On the depiction in working-class melodramas of capitalists as "vampires" and "fiend-begotten monsters," see Patrick Joyce, *Visions of the People: Industrial England and the Question of Class, 1848–1914* (Cambridge: Cambridge Unversity Press, 1991), 34.

2. Paul Ginisty, *Le Mélodrame* (Paris: Louis Michaud, 1910), Peter Brooks, *The Melodramatic Imagination: Balzac, Henry James, Melodrama, and the Mode of Excess* (New Haven: Yale University Press, 1976); Pierre Gascar, *Le Boulevard du crime* (Paris: Hachette, 1980); Judith R. Walkowitz, *City of Dreadful Delight: Narratives of Sexual Danger in Late-Victorian London* (Chicago: University of Chicago Press, 1992).

3. On the ways in which trials inspired sensationalist novels, and fiction in turn influenced the roles individuals played in court, see Thomas Boyle, *Black Swine in the Sewers of Hampstead* (New York: Viking Books, 1989).

CHAPTER 2: FOOLS

1. Peter Gay, *The Bourgeois Experience, Victoria to Freud: The Tender Passion* (New York: Oxford University Press, 1986), 103; and see also Ellen K. Rothman, *Hands and Hearts: A History of Courtship in America* (New York: Basic, 1984), 105; Karen Lystra, *Searching the Heart: Women, Men and Romantic Love in Nineteenth-century America* (New York: Oxford University Press, 1989).

2. For both attacks on mercenary marriages—which included Marie Corelli's anti-Semitic slur that they saw the "Christian virgin sacrificed on the altar of matrimony to a money-lending, money grubbing son of Israel"—and the response that, although there would always be some "designing women" and some "unpleasant and repulsive" men, most who entered society with the intention of making advantageous marriages were acting in a rational—not despicable—fashion, see Marie Corelli, Lady Jeune, Flora Annie Steel, and Susanna, Countess of Malmsbury, *The Modern Marriage Market* (London: Hutchinson, 1898); and see also "The Marriage Market," *Spectator* 78 (24 April 1897): 622–24.

3. On the effect of increasing employment opportunities on working women's marriage options, see "The Matrimonial Market," *The Forum* 21 (1896): 747–52.

4. On the use of go-betweens, matchmakers, and marriage brokers, see Alan Macfarlane, *Marriage and Love in England: Modes of Reproduction, 1300–1840* (Oxford: Blackwell,

1986), 247, 294–95; Peter Borsheid, "Romantic Love or Material Interest: Choosing Partners in Nineteenth-century Germany," *Journal of Family History* 11 (1986): 166–67. In France matchmakers, used well into the twentieth century, included as their clients the parents of Simone de Beauvoir; see Michelle Perrot and Anne Martin-Fugier, "Bourgeois Rituals," in *A History of Private Life,* ed. Michelle Perrot (Cambridge, Mass.: Belknap Press, 1990), 310.

5. *Matrimonial Herald and Fashionable Marriage Gazette* [hereafter *Herald*], 4 Jan. 1890, 1.

6. Among the more infamous advertisers was William Corder, who, having murdered his pregnant sweetheart, placed an marriage advertisement in the *Sunday Times* that elicited more than one hundred responses. See *The Trial of William Corder at the Assizes, Bury St. Edmonds for the Murder of Maria Marten, in the red barn, at Polstead including the matrimonial advertisement. . .* (London: Knight and Lacey, 1828). An anonymous author almost immediately turned the case into a popular melodrama.

7. Sonia Orwell and Ian Angus, eds., *The Collected Essays, Journalism and Letters of George Orwell* (New York: Harcourt Brace, 1968), 139–40. See also Lincoln Springfield, "The Matrimonial Agency," *The Idler* 6 (1894–95): 173–81.

8. In court the agency only claimed to have assisted in fifteen hundred marriages between 1890 and 1895.

9. London *Times,* 12 Nov. 1895, 14.

10. There was mention in court of the association having previously weathered a private prosecution brought against it by a firm of solicitors. Ibid., 9 Jan. 1896, 14.

11. Warwick, one of the original complainants, because of ill health did not testify at the preliminary hearing. Robert Matthews of Birmingham came forward after he "found he was bit." Ibid., 31 Dec. 1895, 9.

12. *Penny Illustrated Paper,* 7 Mar. 1896, 150.

13. The World's Great Marriage Association was registered as a limited company in January 1893 with a nominal capital of £25,000. Its premises at New Oxford Street were imposing, but no business was done there; the clerks worked out of 5 Mecklenburgh Square. Forty Lamb's Conduit Street, where clients' mail was received, was simply a stationery shop.

14. London *Times,* 3 Dec. 1895, 12.

15. Ibid., 14 Jan. 1896, 14.

16. Ibid., 8 Jan. 1896, 15.

17. Ibid., 29 Feb. 1896, 14; 4 Mar. 1896, 4.

18. Girls stories also propounded the idea that an attractive male, though he should be economically active and successful, did not have to be handsome. Judith Rowbotham, *Good Girls Make Good Wives: Guidance for Girls in Victorian Fiction* (Oxford: Basil Blackwell, 1989). But, as the following advertisement makes clear, some women readers of the *Matrimonial Herald* did have very precise requirements: "A young lady, passionately fond of horse-racing, well connected, and with possibility of means, wishes to correspond with a light-weight jockey, occupying good position and of unimpeachable character, age eighteen to twenty-five with view to matrimony. Young trainer not objected to."

19. For accounts of the paper's advertisements, see also *Illustrated Police News,* 7 Mar. 1896, 3.

20. Such stereotypes enjoyed a long life. In the 1930s such advertisements in *Le Chasseur français,* a Parisian journal, inevitably characterized women as "affecteuses, caressantes, portant bien la toilette, de physique agréable," while men were always "beaux, vigoreux, and loyaux" and if fifty "looked forty." Jean Galtier-Boissière, "Les Petites announces," *Le Crapouillot,* November 1937, 46–50

21. *Matrimonial Herald,* 2 Nov. 1895. Much the same sort of male readership perused the *Illustrated Police News,* where they saw, next to the reports of the Association's trial, advertisements for Holloway Pills; "Brou's Injection" for disorders of the urinary organs; cures for deafness, baldness, and nervous and physical debility; Holywell Street pornographic

publications; and pamphlets with such titles as *A Boon to Weak Men, Vigour of Youth* and *Marriage and Its Consequences.*

22. London *Times,* 24 Dec. 1895, 3.

23. Ibid., 8 Jan. 1896, 3; 11 Jan. 1896, 14. This ruling was upheld by the Recorder at the trial; Ibid., 5 Mar. 1896, 12.

24. Ibid., 29 Jan. 1896, 14.

25. Ibid., 14 Jan. 1896, 14.

26. Jordan, in possessing a business, was an untypical complainant. Although no doubt exaggerating, he estimated the value of his tobacconist and hairdressing business at £2,000 and gave his yearly income as £400.

27. London *Times,* 29 Feb. 1896, 14.

28. *Illustrated Police News,* 7 Mar. 1896, 3.

29. London *Times,* 18 Dec. 1895, 4.

30. Ibid., 19 Nov. 1895, 13–14.

31. Ibid., 23 Dec. 1895, 14.

32. Ibid., 3 Mar. 1896, 14.

33. Ibid., 26 Nov. 1895, 12.

34. Ibid., 18 Dec. 1895, 4.

35. Ibid., 24 Dec. 1895, 3.

36. Ibid., 23 Dec. 1895, 14. At the preliminary hearing of 22 Dec. 1895, Joseph Avery's name, despite the protests of the defense, though written down, was not initially divulged to the public.

37. Sutton was particularly incautious. He had a friend who had been bilked of five pounds by a similar scheme. The defense also suggested that Mr. Avery had employed the International Matrimonial Agency.

38. London *Times,* 3 Dec. 1895, 12; 3 Mar. 1896, 13.

39. He came forward after the police raid. The defense counsels were advised by Mr. Justice Hawkins that a magistrate did have the right within his discretionary powers to prevent the disclosure of the names of witnesses. Ibid., 1 Jan. 1896, 4.

40. Ibid., 1 Jan. 1896, 14.

41. Ibid., 1 Jan. 1896, 14. On 31 Dec. 1895, the witness was described by the *Times* as having the appearance of a "fairly well-to-do artisan." He had replied to an advertisement in the *Glasgow Herald.*

42. London *Times,* 3 Dec. 1895, 12.

43. Ibid., 18 Dec. 1895, 4; 2 Mar. 1896, 13.

44. Ibid., 23 Dec. 1895, 14.

45. Ibid., 26 Nov. 1895, 12.

46. *Illustrated Police News,* 7 Mar. 1896, 3.

47. Ibid., 7 Mar. 1896, 3.

48. London *Times,* 6 Mar. 1896, 12.

49. George Orwell, "Boy's Weeklies" (1940), in *Collected Essays,* ed. S. Orwell and Angus, 461.

50. Robert Darnton, *The Great Cat Massacre and Other Episodes in French Cultural History* (New York: Basic Books, 1984), 77–78.

51. Stead was also, as he made clear in "If Christ Came to Chicago" (1894), a vocal opponent of the modern "marriage market." See Ruth Brandon, *The Dollar Princesses* (London: Weidenfeld and Nicolson, 1980), 48; and on his involvement in child prostitution, see John Stokes, *In the Nineties* (London: Harvester Wheatsheaf, 1989), 20.

52. On such agencies see J. Ronchet, *Crime Social: Les Bureaux de placement et leurs funestes conséquences* (Paris: Wattier, 1897); Theresa McBride, *The Domestic Revolution* (London: Croom-Helm, 1976), 77–78.

53. See Alfred C. Hills, *Matrimonial Brokerage in the Metropolis; being the True Narra-*

tives of the Strange Adventures in New York and the Startling Facts in City Life by a Reporter of the New York Press (New York: Thatcher and Hutchinson, 1859).

54. See Horace Wyndham, *Dramas of the Law* (London: Hutchinson, 1936), 170–93; London *Times*, 13 Aug. 1890, 8.

55. Miris, *Moderne Heiratsfchwindler und ihre Opfer* (Argus: Verlag Gokau, 1912).

56. *Gazette des tribunaux*, 24 Mar. 1886, 281.

57. Auguste Bebel, *La Femme dans le passé, le present et l'avenir* (Genève: Slatkine, 1979 [first translation 1891]), 74–75.

58. The British Library's newspaper depository at Colindale has runs of the *Matrimonial Chronicle* (1890–93), *Matrimonial Circle* (1914–15, 1931–32), *Matrimonial Courier* (1891), *Matrimonial Gazette* (1884), *International Matrimonial Gazette* of the International Bureau du Mariage (1909–44), *Matrimonial Gazette and Correspondence* (1913), *Matrimonial Intelligencer and Marriage Correspondent* (1896), *Matrimonial Journal and High Class Marriage Medium* (1895), *Matrimonial Mascot* (1910), *Matrimonial News and Special Advertiser* (1870–95), *Matrimonial Post and Fashionable Advertiser* (1885–1955), *Matrimonial World* (1882–90), *Matrimonial Standard* (1914–15), *Matrimonial Times* (1904–61), *Matrimonial Times and General Advertiser* (1874–75), *Matrimonial World and Universal Marriage Advertiser* (1891), *Matrimony* (1891), and *Matrimonial Gazette* (1883), which became *Nuptials* (1883–84), which in turn became *Matrimonial Herald and Fashionable Marriage Gazette* (1884–95). On this press see E. S. Turner, *A History of Courting* (New York: Dutton, 1955), 269–70.

59. François Barret-Ducrocq, *L'Amour sous Victoria: Sexualité et classes populaires à Londres au XIXe siècle* (Paris: Plon, 1989), 125, 227. It might be noted that Lushington was an expert on courtships that went awry, being the author of *The Law of Affiliation and Bastardy* (London: Shaw, 1897).

60. John Gillis, *For Better, for Worse: British Marriages, 1600 to the Present* (New York: Oxford University Press, 1985), 183; Martine Segalen, *Mari et femme dans la société paysanne* (Paris: Flammarion, 1980), 20.

61. Jules Noriac [Cairon] *Dictionnaire des amoureux* (Paris: Michel Levy, 1875), 101; and see also Drs. Jaf and Saldo, *L'École de la séduction: L'Art de plaire* (Paris: Denans, 1908), 141; Dr. Surbled, *La Vie à deux: Hygiène du mariage* (Paris: Maloine, 1890), 10.

62. Léon Blum, *Du Mariage* (Paris: Albin Michel, 1937 [1906]); Henry Maudsley, *Life in Mind and Conduct* (London: Macmillan, 1902); Paulo Mantegazza, *Comment se marier? L'art de prendre femme et du choix d'un mari* (Paris: Librairie illustrée, 1895).

63. Gillis, *For Better, for Worse*, 264.

64. London *Times*, 8 Jan. 1896, 15.

65. Ibid., 14 Jan. 1896, 14.

66. Ibid., 3 Dec. 1895, 12. It was claimed that the police found a letter from an ex-cabinet minister thanking the association for arranging his marriage. Ibid., 5 Mar. 1896, 12.

67. Bob Mullan, *The Mating Trade* (London: Routledge and Kegan Paul, 1984), 48; Maryse Lapeyre, *Dossier A comme agences matrimoniales* (Paris: Alain Moreaui, 1980).

68. Marie-Véronique Gauthier, *Chanson, Sociabilité et Grivoiserie au XIXe siècle* (Paris: Aubier, 1992), 179, 214–19; E. Anthony Rotundo, *American Manhood: Transformations in Masculinity from the Revolution to the Modern Era* (New York: Basic Books, 1993), 115; Judith F. Stone, "The Republican Brotherhood: Gender and Ideology" in *Gender and Politics of Social Reform in France, 1870–1914*, ed. Elinor Accampo, Rachel Fuchs, and Mary-Lynn Stewart (Baltimore: Johns Hopkins University Press, 1995), 35.

69. The bachelor was an equivocal figure, probably more suspect in the lower-middle-class than in the bourgeoisie, where in the late nineteenth century there was a certain idealization of the self-sufficient, manly individual typified by Holmes and Watson. On unmarried women, see Sheila Jeffreys, *The Spinster and her Enemies: Feminism and Sexuality, 1880–1930* (London: Pandora, 1985).

70. Jean Borie, *Le Célibataire française* (Paris: Le Sagittaire, 1976), 85. For the argument that bachelors were the cause of illegitimacy, adultery, and abortion, see Roger Debury [Georges Rossignol], *Un Pays de célibataires et de fils uniques* (Paris: Dentu, 1913), 29–31; Dr. Lavergne, "Mariage et psychopathes," *Archives de l'anthropologie criminelle* 27 (1912): 616–19; and for a defense, see Roger Gibb, "A Bachelor's Complaint," *Nation*, 29 Jan. 1916, 637–38.

71. Émile Durkheim, *Le Suicide: Étude de sociologie* (Paris: Alcan, 1897), 175.

72. Ginisty, *Le Mélodrame*, 14. The classic melodrama would have focused more on the threats of physicality rather than those of fraud and would not have evidenced as this trial did such a nice balance of greed.

73. Similarly in the United States, the basis of black-face minstrel humor was the purported preposterousness of African-Americans aspiring to act and talk like white men. Laughter was employed by Americans to shore up race divisions, by the English to reinforce class divisions. But for the insight that white working-class male audiences also enjoyed the caricatured upper-class type being shown up by the "plantation darkie," see Robert C. Allen, *Horrible Prettiness: Burlesque and American Culture* (Chapel Hill: University of North Carolina, 1991), 170–73; David D. Roediger, *The Wages of Whiteness: Race and the Making of the American Working Class* (London: Verso, 1991), 115–32.

74. Peter Bailey, "Champagne Charley: Performance and Ideology in the Music Hall Swell Song," in *Music Hall: Performance and Style*, ed. J. S. Bratten (Milton Keynes: Open University Press, 1986), 135–59; "Conspiracies of Meaning: Music Hall and the Knowingness of Popular Culture," *Past and Present* 144 (1994): 138–70; and see also Richard Hoggart, *The Uses of Literacy* (London: Penguin, 1958); Peter Bailey, *Leisure and Class in Victorian Society: Rational Recreation and the Contest for Control* (London: Routledge and Kegan Paul, 1978); Martha Vicinus, *The Industrial Muse: A Study of Nineteenth-century British Working Class Literature* (London: Croom Helm, 1974), 258–61; Wally Seccombe, *Weathering the Storm: Working-class Families from the Industrial Revolution to the Fertility Decline* (London: Verso, 1993), 141.

75. Judith Walkowitz, *City of Dreadful Delight: Narratives of Sexual Danger in Late-Victorian London* (Chicago: University of Chicago Press, 1992), 80.

76. Keith McClelland, "Masculinity and the 'Representative Artisan' in Britain, 1850–80," in *Manful Assertions: Masculinities in Britain since 1800*, ed. Michael Roper and John Tosh (London: Routledge, 1991), 81–84.

77. In fact working class mothers continued to supplement the family income and expected their children, having finished their schooling by age fourteen, to also contribute. See, Ellen Ross, *Love and Toil: Motherhood in Outcast London, 1870–1918* (New York: Oxford University Press, 1993). The response of radical, middle-class feminists to the call for a new sexual division of labor was to liken the idle woman who regarded "marriage as a trade" as a "kept woman" or "parasite." See Carol Dyehouse, *Feminism and the Family in England, 1880–1939* (Oxford: Blackwell, 1989), 155–56.

78. See, for example, Bebel, *La Femme*, 63.

79. The song "The City Toff" cited in Bailey, "Champagne Charlie," 151.

80. Steven Mintz, *A Prison of Expectations: The Family in Victorian Culture* (New York: New York University Press, 1983), 46.

CHAPTER 3: CADS

1. *Oxford English Dictionary*; Peter Bailey, "Conspiracies of Meaning: Music-Hall and the Knowingness of Popular Culture," *Past and Present* 144 (1994): 144.

2. *Gazette des Tribunaux*, 29 Jan. 1886, 93–4.

3. Ibid., 21 Sept. 1892, 926.

4. Ibid., 15 Nov. 1889, 1097.

5. Ibid., 9 June 1864, 562.

6. Ibid., 24 March 1886, 281.
7. Ibid., 26 Jan. 1886, 95.
8. Ibid., 23 June 1864, 611.
9. Ibid., 8–9 Jan. 1894, 29.
10. Ibid., 24 May 1866, 495.
11. Ibid., 8 Feb. 1877, 130.
12. Ibid., 9 Dec. 1896, 1224.
13. Ibid., 14 Jan. 1898, 45.
14. Ibid., 9–10 Aug. 1886, 752.
15. Ibid., 22 Feb. 1890, 178.
16. Ibid., 3 June 1892, 550.
17. Ibid., 11 Mar. 1886, 234.
18. Ibid., 21 Sept. 1892, 926.
19. Ernest Glasson, *Le Mariage civil et le divorce* (Paris: Durand and Pédone-Lauriel, 1880), 470.
20. *Gazette des Tribunaux,* 3 Oct. 1894, 969; *Le Petit Parisien,* 3 Oct. 1894.
21. Canadian investigations similarly revealed that when petitioning for divorce women were far more concerned by the question of nonsupport than men. James G. Snell, *In the Shadow of the Law: Divorce in Canada, 1900–1939* (Toronto: Toronto University Press, 1991), 154–55.
22. *Le Petit Parisien,* 12 Apr. 1897; 19 July 1897; *Gazette des Tribunaux,* 18 July 1897, 700.
23. Jessie L. Embry, *Mormon Polygamous Families: Life in Principle* (Salt Lake City: University of Utah Press, 1987), 8–10; F. Scarlett Potter, "The Most Successful Bigamist on Record," *Cornhill Magazine,* July 1899, 95–102.
24. *Gazette des Tribunaux,* 20 May 1864, 491. For similar scenarios acted out in English courts, see Walker Firth, "Circuit Notes," *Cornhill Magazine* 14 (1890): 36–37.
25. *Gazette des Tribunaux,* 12–13 Feb. 1894, 150.
26. Paul Masson, *Étude sur la bigamie* (Paris: Jouve, 1917).
27. *Gazette des Tribunaux,* 12 Apr. 1896, 367–8.
28. Ibid., 30–31 May 1892, 538.
29. Paul Parsy, *Une Affaire de bigamie* (Paris: Dodiviers, 1920).
30. But the term bigamist was sometimes used to describe a man who simply remarried after his wife's death. See Stephen Willm, *De la Bigamie en droit criminel* (Bordeaux: Cadoret, 1898).
31. Natalie Zemon Davis, *The Return of Martin Guerre* (Cambridge: Harvard University Press, 1983), 8, 46–47.
32. Paul-Auguste Brohan, *Étude sur le crime de bigamie* (Paris: Rousseau, 1898), 28.
33. Lawrence Stone, *Road to Divorce: England, 1530–1987* (Oxford: Oxford University Press, 1990), 142. Richard Boyer has, thanks to the sources provide by the Spanish Inquisition, been able to produce a fascinating account of multiple marriages in the early modern period; see *Lives of the Bigamists: Marriage, Family and Community in Colonial Mexico* (Albuquerque: University of New Mexico Press, 1995).
34. Roderick Phillips, *Putting Asunder: A History of Divorce in Western Society* (Cambridge: Cambridge University Press, 1988), 296–302.
35. *Gazette des Tribunaux,* 20 May 1864, 491.
36. Ibid., 3 June 1892, 550.
37. It is impossible to say how common bigamy was. On cases in Rouen in 1798–99, see Roderick Phillips, *Family Breakdown in Late Eighteenth-century France* (Oxford: Clarendon Press, 1980), 163–65. On the law see Max Rheinstein, "The Code and the Family," in *The Code Napoleon and the Common Law World,* ed. Bernard Schwartz (New York: New York University Press, 1956), 142–43.

38. Bigamy continues in the twentieth century to be regarded as a serious crime; see Law Reform Commisssion of Canada, *Bigamy* (Ottawa: Queen's Printer, 1985).

39. Administering the law proved difficult. Good faith was one defense that could be employed. Public officials who celebrated a second marriage were liable as accomplices. The newspaper press noted that Israel Bernard might get off since the mayor of Montrouge had in 1888 carried out a number of irregular marriage ceremonies. Great hopes were held out by the opponents of bigamy for the Michelin law of 1897—named after the deputy much preoccupied by France's low fertility rate—which required a record of each marriage to be inscribed on one's birth certificate. *Gazette des Tribunaux*, 5 Feb. 1886, 119; *Le Petit Parisien*, 12 Apr. 1897, 1; Brohan, *Étude*, 150.

40. According to a British commentator, marriage had to be made easier if society seriously intended to counter the "designs of criminal fraud or perfidious passion in entrapping the young, the ignorant and the inexperienced." W. O. C. Morris, "The Marriage Law of Great Britain," *British Quarterly Review* 34 (1862): 128.

41. John Gillis has suggested that in early-nineteenth-century Britain up to one-fifth of the population lived at some time in a common-law union; *For Better, for Worse: British Marriages, 1600 to the Present* (New York: Oxford University Press, 1985), 219.

42. For a Belgian who made the same claim, see *Gazette des Tribunaux*, 15 Nov. 1889, 1097.

43. Lenard Berlanstein, "Illegitimacy, Concubinage and Proletarianization in a French Town, 1760–1914," *Journal of Family History* 5 (1980): 368; Katherine A. Lynch, *Family, Class, and Ideology in Early Industrial France: Social Policy and the Working-Class Family, 1825–1848* (Madison: University of Wisconsin Press, 1988), 87–100.

44. Anna Clark, *The Struggle for the Breeches: Gender and the Making of the British Working Class* (Berkeley: University of California Press, 1995), 82–3.

45. John Skinner, *Journal of a Somerset Rector, 1803–1834*, ed. Howard and Peter Coombs (Oxford: Oxford University Press, 1984), 35. English law did in fact accept a seven-year separation as a sign that a marriage had been terminated. See Earl of Halsbury, *The Laws of England* (London: Butterworth, 1955), 10:663.

46. J. P. Menefee, *Wives for Sale: An Ethnographic Study of British Popular Divorce* (Oxford: Blackwell, 1981); E. P. Thompson, "The Sale of Wives," in *Customs in Common: Studies in Traditional Popular Culture* (New York: New Press, 1991), 404–66.

47. *Gazette des Tribunaux*, 17 June 1886, 480; 9 Sept. 1886. 856.

48. Francis Ronsin, *Les Divorciaires* (Paris: Aubier, 1992); William Reddy, "Marriage, Honor and the Public Sphere in Post-Revolutionary France: Séparations de corps, 1815–1848," *Journal of Modern History* 65 (1993): 437–72; Theresa McBride, "Divorce and the Republican Family," in *Gender and the Politics of Social Reform in France, 1870–1914*, ed. Elinor Accampo, Rachel Fuchs, and Mary-Lynn Stewart (Baltimore: Johns Hopkins University Press, 1995), 79.

49. Brohan, *Étude* , 63–64.

50. Ibid., 72–73.

51. *Gazette des Tribunaux*, 12 Feb. 1874, 148–9.

52. Ibid., 14 Jan. 1898, 45.

53. Ibid., 9 Sept. 1886,856.

54. Patricia Knight, "Women and Abortion in Victorian and Edwardian England," *History Workshop* 4 (1977): 57–68; Angus McLaren, "Women's Work and the Regulation of Family Size: The Question of Abortion in the Nineteenth Century," *History Workshop* 4 (1977): 70–81; Angus McLaren, *Birth Control in Nineteenth Century England* (London: Croom Helm, 1978), 231–53; Barbara Brookes, *Abortion in England, 1900–1967* (London: Croom Helm, 1988), 3–48. On North America, see James Mohr, *Abortion in America: The Origins and Evolution of National Policy* (New York: Oxfords University Press, 1978); Leslie J. Reagan, "'About to Meet Her Maker': Women, Doctors and Dying Declarations, and the

State's Investigation of Abortion, Chicago, 1867–1940," *Journal of American History* 77 (1991): 1240–64; Angus McLaren, "Illegal Operations: Women, Doctors, and Abortion, 1886–1939," *Journal of Social History* 26 (1993): 797–816.

55. *Birmingham Daily Mail,* 10 Mar. 1896, unpaginated here and hereafter; *Illustrated Police News,* 21 Mar. 1896, 7.

56. *Warwick, Leamington and Warwickshire Times,* 14 Dec. 1895, 5.

57. On 8 Nov. 1895, Hindson wrote Isabella Pirie that news of the Mabel Gordon affair had led to his being sacked. *Yorkshire Evening Post,* 10 Mar. 1896, 4; *Illustrated Police News,* 21 Mar. 1896, 7.

58. Mr. Justice Day insisted that this made no legal difference; she still had died. *Birmingham Daily Post,* 10 Dec. 1895, 7.

59. *Yorkshire Evening Post,* 10 Dec. 1895, 4.

60. *Birmingham Daily Post,* 11 Dec. 1895, 5.

61. *Warwick, Leamington and Warwickshire Times,* 14 Dec. 1895, 5.

62. *Yorkshire Evening Post,* 11 Dec. 1895, 3.

63. Ibid., 10 Mar. 1896, 4; *Illustrated Police News,* 21 Dec. 1895, 2.

64. *Daily Chronicle,* 12 Dec. 1895, 6; see also *Illustrated Police News,* 21 Dec. 1895, 2.

65. London *Times,* 24 Dec. 1895, 7; *Yorkshire Evening Post,* 9 Mar. 1896, 3.

66. *Birmingham Daily Gazette,* 10 Mar. 1896, 8.

67. London *Times,* 11 Mar. 1896, 10.

68. *Birmingham Daily Gazette,* 10 Mar. 1896, 8.

69. *Warwick, Leamington, and Warwickshire Times,* 14 Mar. 1896, 5; London *Times,* 11 Mar. 1896, 10.

70. *Penny Illustrated Paper,* 30 Apr. 1892, 286.

71. *Birmingham Daily Gazette,* 10 Dec. 1895, 4.

72. *Warwick, Leamington and Warwickshire Times,* 14 Dec. 1895, 5.

73. *Birmingham Daily Gazette,* 10 Dec. 1895, 4.

74. See, for example, London *Times,* 9 Apr. 1836, 6.

75. London *Times,* 14 Dec. 1890, 14; *Lancet,* 21 Feb. 1891, 463–4; London *Times,* 26 Oct. 1891, 4; 28 Mar. 1892, 7; 9 Nov. 1893, 8; 3 May 1893, 13; 9 Feb. 1899, 3; 21 Nov. 1900, 14.

76. See, for example, London *Times,* 3 Aug. 1885, 5.; 4 Aug., 8; and see also McLaren, "Illegal Operations," 797–816.

77. *Warwick, Leamington, and Warwickshire Times,* 21 Mar. 1896, 5.

78. *Birmingham Daily Mail,* 10 Mar. 1896.

79. *Birmingham Daily Gazette,* 11 Mar. 1896, 4.

80. *Birmingham Daily Mail,* 11 Mar. 1896.

81. *Yorkshire Evening Post,* 11 Mar. 1896, 3. The defense counsel, at the trial of another married man implicated in the abortion death of a single woman, met such a challenge head on and vainly appealed to the jury that it "was not a court of morals. They were not to try the prisoner because he was an immoral man." Nevertheless his client was found guilty; his death sentence was commuted to a twelve-year prison term. London *Times,* 9 Dec. 1898, 6.

82. Peter Bailey, "Parasexuality and Glamour: The Victorian Barmaid as Cultural Prototype," *Gender and History* 2 (1990): 148–72; and on working women's negotiation of their sexual favors, see Kathy Peiss, *Cheap Amusements: Working Women and Leisure in Turn of the Century New York* (Philadelphia: Temple University Press, 1986), 108–10.

83. In 1892, for example, eighteen men and no women were executed; in 1893 fifteen men and no women. *British Sessional Papers* 103 (1893–94): 38; 108 (1895): 122.

84. *Birmingham Daily Gazette,* 10 Mar. 1896, 8.

85. *Birmingham Daily Mail,* 10 Mar. 1896.

86. London *Times*, 16 Dec. 1858, 10; Charles Meymott Tidy, *Legal Medicine* (London: Smith, Elder, 1882), 2:162.

87. Arthur Day, *John C. F. S. Day: His Forebears and Himself* (London: Heath, Cranton, 1916), 117; and see also *Dictionary of National Biography, 1901–1911*, 481–85.

88. *Birmingham Daily Gazette*, 10 Dec. 1895, 4.

89. Sir John William Nott-Bower, *Fifty-Two Years a Policeman* (London: Edward Arnold, 1926), 151.

90. Day, *John C. F. S. Day*, 120.

91. Robert Sindall, *Street Violence in the Nineteenth Century: Media Panic or Real Danger* (Leicester: Leicester University Press, 1990), 153; and see also 121–22, 152.

92. Day's sexual censoriousness did not prevent him in 1900 at the age of seventy-four, though having slid into senility that entailed the loss of the ability to write and partial paralysis, from marrying a second time. Day, *John C. F. S. Day*, 135–36.

93. *Daily News*, 17 Dec. 1895, 5.

94. *Daily Chronicle*, 16 Dec. 1895, 4.

95. *Birmingham Daily Gazette*, 11 Dec. 1895, 4.

96. *Dictionary of National Biography, 1901–1911*, 589–90.

97. *Daily News*, 17 Dec. 1895, 5.

98. *The Torch of Anarchy*, 18 Dec. 1895, 107; reprinted in the American journal *Rebel*, February 1896, 56. Originally entitled *The Torch*, from October 1895 the journal called itself the *Torch of Anarchy;* hereafter it will be simply referred to as *The Torch.*

99. Richard D. Sohn, *Anarchism and Cultural Politics in Fin de Siècle France* (Lincoln: University of Nebraska Press, 1989), 216. In a letter of 20 Nov. 1896, Cohen described how Paul Robin, the best-known defender of fertility control in France, congratulated him on his defense of Mrs. Eden; I owe this reference to Ronald Spoor. See also Angus McLaren, *Sexuality and Social Order: The Debate over the Fertility of Women and Workers in France, 1770–1920* (New York: Holmes and Meier, 1983), 136–54; Jacques Dupaquier, "Combien d'avortements en France avant 1914," *Communications* 44 (1986): 87–105.

100. On Cohen (1864–1961), see his autobiography, *Van Anarchist tot Monarchist*, 2 vols. (Amsterdam: G. A. Oorschot-Uitgeuer, 1961). For assistance on tracing Cohen, I am indebted to Paul Avrich and Ronald Spoor, who is editing Cohen's letters. On London anarchism, see Rudolf Rocker, *The London Years* (London: Robert Anscombe, 1936), 65–98.

101. Hermia Oliver, *The International Anarchist Movement in Late Victorian London* (London: Croom-Helm, 1983), 121–24.

102. *The Torch*, 31 Oct. 1894, 11.

103. Ibid., 18 July 1895, 20.

104. Ibid., 18 Nov. 1895, 85–86.

105. The Social Democratic Federation also exploited infanticide cases to embarrass the government. For its defense of Fanny Gane, a twenty-six-year-old servant, sentenced to death for the murder of her male child, see *Justice*, 11 Dec. 1891, 6. Only in 1922 was infanticide designated a special noncapital offense; Brookes, *Abortion*, 31.

106. *The Torch*, 31 Oct. 1894, 11; London *Times*, 26 Oct. 1894, 7.

107. *The Torch*, 18 Dec. 1895, 2; London *Times*, 28 Mar. 1895, 14. For a general account of infanticide, see Lionel Rose, *The Massacre of the Innocents: Infanticide in Britain, 1800–1939* (London: Routledge and Kegan Paul, 1986); Ann R. Higginbotham, "Sin of the Age: Infanticide and Illegitimacy in Victorian London," *Victorian Studies* 32 (1989): 319–37.

108. Even Engels used the language of chivalry in denouncing Edward Aveling as the worst villain in socialist Europe. George Bernard Shaw agreed that Aveling's record as a swindler and seducer was "unapproachable." Aveling, an active socialist, supported himself for a time by tutoring female students in science. According to Shaw, "the more fortunate ones got nothing worse for their money than letters of apology for breaking the lesson engagement.

The others were seduced and had their microscopes appropriated." Aveling lived for years with Eleanor Marx but could not marry her as his first wife was still alive. When the latter died he secretly wed another woman, so precipitating Eleanor's suicide. See Hesketh Pearson, *Bernard Shaw: His Life and Personality* (London: Collins, 1942), 124; Yvonne Kapp, *Eleanor: Chronique familiale des Marx* (Paris: Éditions sociales, 1980), 39.

109. In the early nineteenth century at the time of the Queen Caroline Affair, the English radicals presented themselves as chivalrous defenders of womanhood. Similarly the opponents of the New Poor Law portrayed themselves as defending poor women from libertine seducers. In France the manly courage of anarchists facing death was even reluctantly noted by their opponents. See Anna Clarke, *Women's Silence, Men's Violence: Sexual Assault in England, 1770–1845* (London: Pandora, 1987), 164, 194; L. Proal, *La Criminalité politique* (Paris: Alcan, 1895), 43, 64; Alexandre Berard, *Documents d'études sociales: Sur l'anarchie* (Lyon: Storck, 1897), 131–39; Ruth Harris, "Understanding the Terrorist: Anarchism, Medicine and Politics in Fin-de-Siècle France," in *Legal Medicine in History*, ed. C. Crawford and M. Young (Cambridge: Cambridge University Press, 1994), 202–3.

110. On defense of abortion elsewhere, see Martin Henry Blatt, *Free Love and Anarchism: The Biography of Ezra Heywood* (Urbana: University of Illinois Press, 1989), 149; Margaret S. Marsh, *Anarchist Women, 1870–1920* (Philadelphia: Temple University Press, 1981), 76, 93; Janet Farrell Brodie, *Contraception and Abortion in Nineteenth-century America* (Ithaca: Cornell University Press, 1994), 99, 128, 186–7, 324; C. Wickert, B. Hamburger and M. Lienau, "Helene Stöcker and the Bund fuer Mutterschutz: (The Society for the Protection of Motherhood)," *Women's Studies International Forum* 5 (1982): 613; James Woycke, *Birth Control in Germany, 1871–1933* (London: Routledge, 1988), 54–57. There is a reference to abortion in a feminist novel by Lady Florence Dixie, *Gloriana: or The Revolution of 1900* (London: Henry, 1890), 137, but the issue was too hot a topic for the English women's movement to handle. In "Cry of the Unborn" (*Shafts,* October 1894, 344), for example, Evelyn Hunt would only talk of the need of male purity and healthy marriages to ensure a sound heredity.

111. *The Torch,* 18 July 1895, 31. Henry Seymour was one of the few English Anarchists who interested himself in sex questions. He stated that "a woman could employ devices to prevent conception, to avoid altogether or the too frequent burdens of maternity. In fact, I regard these means as almost indispensable in connection with sexual freedom." *The Anarchy of Love* (London: Seymour, 1888), 15.

112. *The Torch,* 1 Apr. 1896, 141.

113. Angus McLaren, *Birth Control in Nineteenth-century England* (London: Croom Helm, 1978), 157–74.

114. See Angus McLaren, "Sex Radicalism in the Canadian Pacific Northwest, 1890–1920," *Journal of the History of Sexuality* 2 (1992): 529–33; and for the 1890s literary critiques of sexuality, see Elaine Showalter, *Sexual Anarchy: Gender and Culture at the Fin de Siècle* (New York: Viking, 1990).

115. London *Times,* 18 Dec. 1895, 10; *Birmingham Daily Gazette,* 18 Dec. 1895, 4.

116. *Daily News,* 18 Dec. 1895, 3.

117. *Warwick, Leamington and Warwickshire Times,* 21 Dec. 1895, 4.

118. *Birmingham Daily Gazette,* 11 Mar. 1896, 4.

119. *Birmingham Daily Mail,* 11 Mar. 1896.

120. London *Times,* 17 Mar. 1896, 8.

121. *Yorkshire Evening Post,* 16 Mar. 1896, 2.

122. "Judicial Statistics (for 1895)," *House of Commons: Sessional Papers* 49 (1897), C., 54, table 1. In 1895 there were twenty prosecutions of abortionists. Five of the accused were male; fifteen were female.

123. London *Times,* 5 Apr. 1875, 11; 20 Apr. 1875, 9.

124. On Wark, see London *Times*, 8 Dec. 1898, 10; 9 Dec., 6.

125. John Glaister, *A Textbook of Medical Jurisprudence and Toxicology* (Edinburgh: Livingstone, 1910), 397. Glaister mistakenly refers to this as the Whitmarsh case; John Whitmarsh was tried for the same offense by Mr. Justice Bigham. See London *Times*, 26 Oct. 1898, 9; 27 Oct., 13. For James Fitzjames Stephen's attack on the concept of "constructive murder," see Henry Warburton, *A Selection of Leading Cases in the Criminal Law* (London: Stevens, 1908), 180–83.

126. Leonard A. Parry, *Some Famous Criminal Trials* (London: Churchill, 1927), 40–54; *British Medical Journal* 2 (1898): 59, 122; 1 (1899): 448.

127. Camille Mauclair, *L'Amour tragique* (Paris: Calman-Levy, 1908); Betty Becker-Theye, *The Seducer as Mythic Figure in Richardson, Laclos and Kierkegaard* (New York: Garland, 1988); James Mandrell, *Don Juan and the Point of Honor: Seduction, Patriarchal Society, and the Literary Tradition* (University Park: Penn State University Press, 1992).

128. Tony Tanner, *Adultery in the Novel: Contract and Transgression* (Baltimore: Johns Hopkins University Press, 1979); and for bourgeois society's attempt to argue that contracts can overcome sex differences, see Carole Pateman, *The Sexual Contract* (Cambridge: Polity Press, 1988).

129. See, Véronique Demars-Sion, *Femmes séduites et abandonées au 18e siècle: L'Example du Cambrésis* (Paris: L'Espace juridique, 1992); Rachel G. Fuchs, *Poor and Pregnant in Paris: Strategies for Survival in the Nineteenth Century* (New Brunswick, N.J.: Rutgers University Press, 1992); Marie-Victoire Louis, *Le Droit de cuissage: France 1860–1930* (Paris: Les Éditions de l'atelier, 1994).

130. Katherine Sobba Green, *The Courtship Novel, 1740–1820: A Feminized Genre* (Lexington: University Press of Kentucky, 1991).

131. Gregorio Marañón, *Don Juan et don juanisme*, trans. M.-B. Lacombe (Paris: Gallimard, 1958), 15–29.

132. Jean Borie, *Le Célibataire français* (Paris: Le Sagittaire, 1976), 45.

133. Edward J. Bristow, *Vice and Vigilance: Purity Movements in Britain since 1700* (London: Gill and Macmillan, 1977), 104; Jacques Amblard, *De la seduction: Thèse pour le doctorat* (Paris: Rousseau, 1908). Yet at the same time the popular press still produced books like, "Calypso," *Method pratique pour attirer et séduire n'importe quelle personne* (Paris: Calypso, 1915).

134. For an American example of the way in which an abortion death was turned to the purposes of a cautionary, melodramatic literature, see Amy Gilman Srebnick, *The Mysterious Death of Mary Rogers: Sex and Culture in Nineteenth-Century New York* (New York: Oxford University Press, 1995).

CHAPTER 4: GENTLEMEN

1. Jean Borie, *Le Celibataire français* (Paris: Sagittaire, 1976), 181.

2. Alexis de Tocqueville, *The Ancien Regime and the French Revolution*, trans. S. Gilbert (London: Fontana, 1966), 109. For a fascinating account of the early modern English scientist's claim to be a gentleman—one who could be trusted to speak the truth—see Steven Shapin, *A Social History of Truth: Civility and Science in Seventeenth-century England* (Chicago: University of Chicago Press, 1994), 42–64, 66–67, 81–83, 107–24.

3. Edwin Harrison Cady, *The Gentleman in America: A Literary Study in American Culture* (Syracuse: Syracuse University Press, 1949); David Castronovo, *The American Gentleman: Social Prestige and the Modern Literary Mind* (New York: Continuum, 1991); Tim Mason, *The English Gentleman: The Rise and Fall of an Ideal* (London: Andre Deutsch, 1982).

4. Patrick Joyce, *Visions of the People: Industrial England and the Question of Class, 1848–1914* (Cambridge: Cambridge University Press, 1991), 44.

5. Dr. Playfair's grandson's account of the trial, based on "original source materials in his own possession" though unfortunately not footnoted, is still useful; see Giles Playfair, *Six Studies in Hypocrisy* (London: Secker and Warburg, 1969), 134–65. A shorter, garbled version is provided in Edgar Lustgarten, *The Judges and the Judged* (London: Odhams, 1961), 245–47.

6. *Dictionary of National Biography: The Twentieth Century (1901–1911)*, 404–5.

7. *British Medical Journal* 1 (1896): 815.

8. He is mistakenly identified as "Nunzio" Williams in Playfair, *Six Studies*.

9. *Dictionary of National Biography: The Twentieth Century (1901–1911)*, 120; *British Medical Journal* 2 (1903): 439; *Lancet* 2 (1903): 570–75. Playfair's works included (with T. C. Allbutt) *A System of Gynaecology* (New York: Macmillan, 1896) and *A Treatise of Midwifery* (Philadelphia: Lea, 1893).

10. *Lancet* 1 (1896): 897.

11. London *Times*, 24 Mar. 1891, 13; *Daily Chronicle*, 24 Mar. 1896, 9.

12. For a discussion of anesthesia bringing on women's "unfounded dreams" of sexual assault, see Frederick J. Smith, *Lectures on Medical Jurisprudence and Toxicology* (London: Churchill, 1900), 187–88.

13. *British Medical Journal* 1 (1896): 817.

14. Nineteenth-century public commentators in a variety of mediums addressed the tragic fate that necessarily awaited the woman who transgressed sexual norms. On the depiction of the adulteress in Victorian narrative painting, see Lynda Nead, *Myths of Sexuality: Representations of Women in Victorian Britain* (Oxford: Blackwell, 1988), 48–90; and in literature, see Tony Tanner, *Adultery in the Novel: Contract and Transgression* (Baltimore: Johns Hopkins University Press, 1979); Chantal Gleyses, *La Femme coupable: Petit histoire de l'épouse adultère au XIXè siècle* (Paris: Imago, 1994).

15. *Lancet* 1 (1896): 896.

16. Playfair, *Six Studies*, 164. An 1890 text directed at young medical men anticipated Playfair's actions in carrying the warning that for a doctor to gossip about his cases could be disastrous for his career. "Do not let your wife, or anyone else, know your professional secrets, or the private details of your cases, even though they are not secrets." Jukes de Styrap, *The Young Practitioner* (London: Lewis, 1890), 113.

17. Playfair, *Six Studies*, 143.

18. Still stalling for time, Linda Kitson in her last letter to Playfair had asked, "Am I too late to say yes?" *British Medical Journal* 1 (1896): 816.

19. See Linda Kitson to Emily Playfair, 19 Mar. 1894; Emily Playfair to Linda Kitson, 24 Mar. 1894, in the *Daily Chronicle*, 24 Mar. 1896, 9.

20. W. S. Playfair to Arthur Kitson, 22 Sept. 1894, in *Daily Chronicle*, 25 Mar. 1896, 8.

21. As a husband and wife were in law one person, the fact that a libel had been disclosed to a spouse was not accepted as evidence of its publication. The courts turned back the suggestion that the passage in 1882 of the Married Women's Property Act undermined such a concept. *Law Reports: Queen's Bench Division* 20 (1888): 635–40.

22. In fact, Playfair, at his wife's request, had informed Sir James; Mrs. Playfair was not called to testify.

23. He is misidentified as "James" Spencer in Playfair, *Six Studies*, 147.

24. *British Medical Journal* 1 (1896): 818.

25. The witnesses were implicitly following the line set by Thomas Percival who, at the beginning of the century, argued that when the issue of medical confidentiality arose one simply had to rely upon the doctor's discretion. Chauncey D. Leake, ed., *Percival's Medical Ethics* (Baltimore: Williams and Wilkins, 1927), 90. Secrecy certainly seems to be demanded by the Hippocratic oath—"Whatever, in connection with my professional practice or not in connection with it, I see or hear in the life of men which ought not to be spoken abroad I will

not divulge, as reckoning that all such should be kept secret"—but was rarely referred to in the nineteenth century. Francis Gurry, *Breach of Confidence* (Oxford: Clarendon Press, 1984), 148.

26. London *Times*, 26 Mar. 1896, 13; and see also Walter Broadbent, ed., *Selections from the Writings of Sir William Broadbent* (London: Froude, 1908).

27. See Arthur Kitson's letter to the *British Medical Journal* 1 (1896): 1236.

28. The press portrayed her as "a lady who once possessed considerable attractions and even now, in spite of ill-health and mental anxiety, her pale face beneath her dark brown hair is not without its charm." Playfair's countenance was less flatteringly depicted as dominated by "a determined jaw" and "close-cropped iron-grey hair." *Penny Illustrated Paper*, 14 Mar. 1896, 214.

29. *Daily Chronicle*, 24 Mar. 1896, 9.

30. *Lancet* 1 (1896): 896.

31. *British Medical Journal* 1 (1896): 816.

32. *Daily Chronicle*, 25 Mar. 1896, 8.

33. But no one suggested that Playfair's providing of treatment for his sister-in-law constituted a breach of propriety. Today's notion that doctors should give only minor or emergency care to members of their immediate family was obviously not widely shared at the turn of the century.

34. London *Times*, 25 Mar. 1896, 3.

35. On scientists' fears of being made to look foolish in court, see Christopher Hamlin, "Scientific Method and Expert Witnessing: Victorian Perspectives on a Modern Problem," *Social Studies of Science* 16 (1986): 485–513.

36. *Daily Chronicle*, 27 Mar. 1896, 7.

37. London *Times*, 27 Mar. 1896, 14.

38. Bowen Rowlands, *The Life in the Law of Sir Henry Hawkins* (London: Wyman and Sons, 1897), 44; A. W. B. Simpson, ed., *Biographical Dictionary of the Common Law* (London: Butterworths, 1984), 229–30.

39. London *Times*, 28 Mar. 1896, 5.

40. *British Medical Journal* 1 (1896): 883.

41. On appeal the award was reduced to £9,200, but the scandalous nature of the case cost Playfair much of his practice and all hopes of any further honors from the Queen. Gladstone wrote to express his indignation at the jury's verdict and to declare "you have done neither more nor less than your duty." *Lancet* 2 (1903): 574.

42. *Reynold's Newspaper*, 29 Mar. 1896, 5.

43. *Daily News*, 28 Mar. 1896, 6.

44. R. Vasher Rodgers, Jr., *The Law and Medical Men* (Toronto: Carswell, 1884), 93.

45. Ibid., 93. On the contemporary assumption that doctors and lawyers had the same duty to keep secrets, see "Professional Secrecy," *Spectator* 75 (1895): 364–65.

46. James Neal and Hugh Woods, *The Conduct of Medical Practice* (London: Lancet, 1927), 222–23.

47. Paul Brouardel, *Le Secret médical* (Paris: Baillière, 1880); Robert Tod, "Le Secret médical au XIX siècle dans les textes médicaux et juridiques," *Nouvelle presse médicale* 8 (1979): 2695–97.

48. *New York Times*, 6 Apr. 1896, 4; Clinton DeWitt, *Privileged Communications between Physician and Patient* (Pittsburgh: Clarence C. Thomas, 1958).

49. Charles Meymott Tidy, *Legal Medicine* (London: Smith, Elder, 1882), 1:20–21.

50. John Glaister, *A Textbook of Medical Jurisprudence* (Edinburgh: Livingstone, 1915), 56.

51. *British Medical Journal* 1 (1896): 1012.

52. London *Times*, 24 Mar. 1896, 14.

53. Ibid., 26 Mar. 1896, 13; *Lancet* 1 (1896): 962.

54. London *Times,* 7 Apr. 1896, 6.

55. *Daily News,* 28 Mar. 1896, 9.

56. Ibid., 6.

57. London *Times,* 28 Mar. 1896, 11.

58. Playfair, *Six Studies,* 159.

59. Samuel Haber, *The Quest for Authority and Honor in the American Professions, 1750–1900* (Chicago: University of Chicago Press, 1991), 345–46.

60. *Lancet* 1 (1896): 1292.

61. *British Medical Journal* 1 (1896): 861.

62. Ibid., 861–2.

63. Percy Clarke and Charles Meymott Tidy, *Medical Law for Medical Men* (London: Baillière Tindall, 1890), 39, 55. In France doctors were warned by one writer that "circonspection" was always required when dealing with patients who at best misconstrued what one said and at worse sought to entrap their practitioner. Dr. Peinard, *La Profession médicale en France* (Paris: Société d'éditions scientifiques, 1894), 149.

64. *British Medical Journal* 1 (1896): 929–30; and see also 1 (1896): 871. The various attempts made in Britain in the 1920s and 1930s to establish medical secrecy were all unsuccessful.

65. London *Times,* 9 Apr. 1896, 12.

66. Ibid., 3 Apr. 1896, 6; 6 Apr. 1896, 10.

67. Ibid., 3 Apr. 1896, 6.

68. Ibid., 4 Apr. 1896, 10.

69. Ibid., 6 Apr. 1896, 10.

70. The same writer pointed out that in 1889 Sir Morell Mackenzie had been censored by the Royal College of Surgeons for publishing revelations concerning the cancer death of Emperor Frederick III of Germany. Ibid., 7 Apr. 1896, 6.

71. Émile Worms, *Les Attentats à l'honneur: diffamation, injures, outrages, adultère, duel, lois sur la presse, etc.* (Paris: Perrin, 1890); Émile Beaussire, *Les Principes du droit* (Paris: Alcan, 1888), 372–78.

72. On doctors' reporting of malingerers among soldiers and miners, see Sir John Collie, *Fraud in Medico-Legal Practice* (London: Arnolds, 1932).

73. *Daily News,* 28 Mar. 1896, 6.

74. *British Medical Journal* 2 (1884): 328–29.

75. *British Medical Journal* 2 (1899): 60.

76. *Justice,* 4 Apr. 1896, 6; and see also 25 Apr. 1896, 4–5; E. Belfort Bax, *The Fraud of Feminism* (London: Grant Richards, 1913).

77. *Justice,* 18 Apr. 1896, 3; 9 May 1896, 3.

78. London *Times,* 7 Apr. 1896, 6.

79. Cora Lansbury, "Gynaecology, Pornography and the Antivivisection Movement," *Victorian Studies* 28 (1985): 413–38.

80. *Lancet* 1 (1896): 961. In any event the notion had been long accepted that women, not enjoying complete freedom of action, would on occasion of necessity toy with the truth. See Shapin, *Social History of Truth,* 87–91.

81. Playfair, *Six Studies,* 156.

82. Frank Mort, *Dangerous Sexualities: Medico-Moral Politics in England since 1830* (London: Routledge and Kegan Paul, 1987), 95–109.

83. On doctors opposed to the Acts, see Benjamin Scott, *A State Iniquity: Its Rise, Extension, and Overthrow* (London: Kegan Paul, 1890), 116, 119, 217.

84. Glaister, *Medical Jurisprudence,* 60.

85. *British Medical Journal* 1 (1896): 817.

86. Jill Harsin, "Syphilis, Wives, and Physicians: Medical Ethics and the Family in Late Nineteenth-century France," *French Historical Studies* 16 (1989): 72–95; Gail Savage, "The Willful Communication of a Loathsome Disease: Medical Conflict and Venereal Disease in Victorian England," *Victorian Studies* 34 (1990): 35–54.

87. George Ives, *A History of Penal Methods* (London: Stanley Paul, 1914), 353–56; Alexander Welsh, *George Eliot and Blackmail* (Cambridge: Harvard University Press, 1985).

88. DeWitt, *Privileged Communications,* 247. But for demands made in America that abortions be reported, see Norman Barnesby, *Medical Chaos and Crime* (London: Mitchell Kennerley, 1910), 213, 223–27.

89. A. S. Taylor, *A Manual of Medical Jurisprudence* (London: J. A. Churchill, 1891), 560.

90. *British Medical Journal* 1 (1896): 883.

91. *Lancet* 1 (1896): 962.

92. *Dictionary of National Biography: The Twentieth Century (1901–1911),* 607–8.

93. *Law Reports (Appeal Cases),* 1905, 482.

94. *British Medical Journal* 1 (1904): 1416; *Scottish Law Reporter,* 1904, 42:213–21; Glaister, *Medical Jurisprudence,* 60– 63.

95. But even in the mid twentieth century, British courts, in order to accept the validity of a legitimate conception, showed themselves willing to stretch the length of the gestation period. In the 1940s judges took seriously claims that sperm could remain viable in the vagina for as long as twenty-eight days and that births might occur as late as three hundred and sixty days after conception. J. D. Cantley, "Medical Evidence in Matrimonial Cases," *Medico-Legal Journal* 18 (1950): 26–30.

96. For a discussion of how some nineteenth-century women literally got away with murder by playing the appropriate role, see Mary Hartman, *Victorian Murderesses* (New York: Schoken, 1977); Ruth Harris, *Murders and Madness: Medicine, Law and Society in the Fin-de-siècle* (Oxford: Clarendon, 1989); Virginia B. Morris, *Double Jeopardy: Women Who Kill in Victorian Fiction* (Lexington: University Press of Kentucky, 1990).

97. Immediately following the trial, the Royal College of Physicians of London set up a committee "to define in a legal sense the proper conduct of a Practitioner when brought into relation with a case of acknowledged or suspected criminal abortion," but the debate over the doctor's duty continued on into the twentieth century. Sir George Clark, *A History of the Royal College of Physicians of London* (Oxford: Clarendon Press, 1964–72), 3:980–85.

98. S. Squire Sprigge, *Medicine and the Public* (London: Heinemann, 1905), 243. But for a discussion of confidentiality, which by its cautious tone indicates a lesson had been drawn from the Playfair fiasco, see Robert Saundby, *Medical Ethics: A Guide to Personal Conduct* (London: Simpkin, Marshall, Hamilton, Kent, 1902), 62–5.

99. London *Times,* 28 June 1920, 10.

100. In the age of AIDS, the whole question of medical disclosure is being debated once more. See, Robert Lee, "Disclosure of Medical Records: A Confidence Trick?" in *Confidentiality and the Law,* ed. Linda Clarke (London: Lloyd's, 1990) , 26; Irvine Loudon, "A Question of Confidence: How It Strikes the Historian," *British Medical Journal* 288 (1984): 125–26.

101. Maurice Keen, *Chivalry* (New Haven: Yale University Press, 1984), 1.

102. John Fraser, *America and the Patterns of Chivalry* (Cambridge: Cambridge University Press, 1982); Mark Girouard, *The Return to Camelot: Chivalry and the English Gentleman* (New Haven: Yale University Press, 1981).

103. Robert A. Nye, *Masculinity and Male Codes of Honor in Modern France* (New York: Oxford University Press, 1993); Ute Frevert, "Bourgeois Honour: Middle-Class Duelists in Germany from the Late Eighteenth Century to the Early Twentieth Century," in *The German Bourgeoisie,* ed. David Blackbourn and Richard J. Evans (London: Routledge, 1991), 254–92; Ute Frevert, *Men of Honour: A Social and Cultural History of the Duel,*

trans. Anthony Williams (Cambridge, Eng.: Polity Press, 1995); Kevin McAleer, *The Cult of Honor in Fin-de-Siècle Germany* (Princeton: Princeton University Press, 1994); Norman Vance, *The Sinews of the Spirit: The Ideal of Christian Manliness in Victorian Literature and Religious Thought* (Cambridge: Cambridge University Press, 1985).

104. James Hammerton, *Cruelty and Companionship: Conflict in Nineteenth-Century Married Life* (London: Routledge, 1992).

105. Harold J. Laski, *The Danger of Being a Gentleman and Other Essays* (London: Allen and Unwin, 1939), 13–31; Robin Gilmour, *The Idea of the Gentleman in the Victorian Novel* (London: Allen and Unwin, 1981).

CHAPTER 5: MURDERERS

1. Such community norms were as much created as defended by the courts. See Julia Epstein and Kristina Staub, eds., *Body Guards: The Cultural Politics of Gender Ambiguity* (London: Routledge, 1991), 1–4.

2. Nanaimo *Free Press,* 12 Oct. 1910, 1–2.

3. Such sources, dealing as they do with deadly conflicts, are unlikely to reveal the working-class male's penchant for "cooperation, fraternity and equality" found by others. See Bryan Palmer, *A Culture in Conflict: Skilled Workers and Industrial Capitalism in Hamilton, Ontario, 1860–1914* (Kingston: McGill-Queens University Press, 1979), 40.

4. For fine examples of the cultural analysis of murder cases in Europe, see Edward Berenson, *The Trial of Mme Caillaux* (Berkeley: University of California Press, 1992); Carolyn Conley, *The Unwritten Law: Criminal Justice in Victorian Kent* (New York: Oxford University Press, 1991); Joelle Guillais, *Crimes of Passion: Dramas of Private Life in Nineteenth-century France* (New York: Routledge, 1991); and for the United States, see Roger Lane, *Violent Death in the City: Suicide, Accident and Murder in Nineteenth-century Philadelphia* (Cambridge: Harvard University Press, 1979); Bertram Wyatt-Brown, *Southern Honor: Ethics and Behavior in the Old South* (New York: Oxford University Press, 1982)

5. Papers of the Attorney General of British Columbia [hereafter BC] GR 419, vol. 198, file 1915/50.

6. Letter dated 24 Apr. 1915, in Ibid.

7. Cranbrook *Herald,* 22 Sept. 1915, 1; 21 Oct. 1915, 1.

8. Sherwood Herchmer to J. P. McLeod, 23 Oct. 1923, BC GR 1323, reel 2121, file 7049-4-15.

9. Anon., "L'Homicide en France comparé à l'homicide à l'étranger." *Archives de l'anthroplogie criminelle* 13 (1898): 349–51.

10. These disparities were recognized at the time. See Dr. Henri Leale, "De la criminalité des sexes," *Archives de l'anthroplogie criminelle* 25 (1910): 401–30; and for a more recent account, see Judith A. Allen, *Sex and Secrets: Crimes Involving Australian Women since 1880* (Melbourne: Oxford University Press, 1990), 28–30.

11.   *Population of British Columbia*

	1901	1921
males	114,160	293,400
females	64,497	231,173
total	178,657	524,582

Source: *Census of Canada, 1931,* table 16. See also Adele Perry, "'Oh I'm Just Sick of the Faces of Men': Gender Imbalance, Race, Sexuality and Sociability in Nineteenth-Century British Columbia," *BC Studies* 105–6 (1995): 27–43.

12. Perhaps the most notorious escapee was William McLaughan, who in 1912 killed two men and a woman. Vancouver *Daily Province,* 14 Oct. 1912, 1.

13. See Rosemary Gartner and Bill McCarthy, "The Social Distribution of Femicide in Urban Canada, 1921–1988," *Law and Society Review* 25 (1991): 287–311; Pamela Haig,

"The 'Ill-use of a Wife': Patterns of Working-class Violence in Domestic and Public New York, 1860–1880," *Journal of Social History* 25 (1992): 447–77; Ellen Ross, "Fierce Questions and Taunts: Married Life in London, 1870–1914," *Feminist Studies* 8 (1982): 575–602. On Catholic Europe's view of spousal murders as "crimes of passion," see Paul Peyssonnie, *Le Meurtre excusable* (Orleans: Morand, 1897); Paul Escoffier, *Les Crimes passionels* (Paris: George Jacob, 1891); Ermanno Cavazzoni, ed., *Alberto Olivo: Fatal courroux: Autobiographie d'un uxoricide* (Paris: Verdier, 1992).

    14. BC GR 429, box 11, file 5, #3142/04.

    15. BC GR 419, vol. 135, file 1909/73.

    16. Ibid., vol. 97, file 1903/54.

    17. Ibid., vol. 160, file 1912/134.

    18. Compare to Miles Fairburn and Stephen Haslett, "Violent Crime in Old and New Societies—A Case Study Based on New Zealand, 1853–1940," *Journal of Social History* 20 (1986): 89–126. For a classic account of living conditions, see Edwin Bradwin, *The Bunkhouse Man: A Study of the Work and Pay in the Camps of Canada, 1903–1914* (New York: Columbia University Press, 1928).

    19. On a fight between German prisoners of war at the Vernon Internment Camp leading to murder, see BC GR 419, vol. 229, file 1919/127.

    20. Ibid., vol. 198, file 1915/42.

    21. Ibid., vol. 125, file 1908/27A.

    22. In October 1907 a poker game at Kirby's Hotel, Keremeos, led to a shooting death. Ibid., vol. 127, file 1908/52. This case was unusual in that the accused successfully escaped police custody.

    23. Ibid., vol. 161, file 1912/151.

    24. On the relationship of sociability to violence, see Noel Dyck, "Booze, Barrooms and Scrapping: Masculinity and Violence in a Western Canadian Town," *Canadian Journal of Anthropology* 1 (1980): 191–98; Stephen Wilson, *Feuding: Conflict and Banditry in Nineteenth-century Corsica* (Cambridge: Cambridge University Press, 1988), 94.

    25. BC GR 419, vol. 101, file 1904/52.

    26. Ibid., vol. 125, file 1908/27b.

    27. Ibid., vol. 147, file 1911/27.

    28. BC GR 429, box 14, file 2 #2181/07.

    29. BC GR 419, vol. 119, file 1907, 35.

    30. Ibid., vol. 135, file 1909/63.

    31. Ibid., vol. 152, file 1911/104.

    32. Ibid., vol. 162, file 1912/129.

    33. Ibid., vol. 148, file 1911/45.

    34. Ibid., vol. 190, file 1914/155.

    35. Ibid., vol. 87, file 1901/27

    36. Ibid., vol. 183, file 1914/13.

    37. Ibid., vol. 229, file 1919/120.

    38. Ibid., vol. 210, file 1917/59.

    39. Ibid., vol. 175, 1913/122.

    40. Ibid., vol. 201, file 1915/95; Ibid., vol. 203, file 1916/8. For the case of a deranged rancher who in 1922 killed a neighbor he believed was "murmuring" against him, see ibid., vol. 255, file 1922/73.

    41. BC GR 419, vol. 218, file 1918/99.

    42. Ibid., vol. 160, file 1912/138; Ibid., vol. 157, file 1912/77.

    43. Ibid., vol. 189, file 1914/144.

    44. Ibid., vol. 232, file 1920/25.

    45. Ibid., vol. 236, file 1920/99.

46. Ibid., vol. 255, file 1922/64.

47. Ibid., vol. 266, file 1923/29.

48. BC GR 1327, B 2384; BC GR 419, vol. 145, file 1910/91.

49. BC GR 419, vol. 162, file 1912/170; Ibid., vol. 163, file 1912/179; Vancouver *Daily Province,* 26 Mar. 1912, 1, 4.

50. BC GR 419, vol. 169, file 1913/46.

51. Ibid., vol. 184, file 1914/59.

52. Ibid., vol. 193, file 1914/191.

53. Ibid., vol. 197, file 1915–26.

54. Ibid., vol. 204, file 1916/43.

55. Ibid., vol. 208, file 1917/15.

56. Ibid., vol. 258, file 1922/113.

57. Ibid., vol. 129, file 1908/105.

58. Ibid., vol. 235, file 1920/69; Ibid., vol. 271, file 1923/74.

59. For a recent account of such motivations, see Kenneth Polk, "Masculinity, Honour and Confrontational Homicide," in *Just Boys Doing Business? Men, Masculinities and Crime,* ed. Tim Newburn and Elizabeth A. Stanko (London: Routledge, 1994), 166–88.

60. Donald MacDonald was in 1910 found not guilty of murdering Frank Savage, who, though sworn in as a special constable, was viewed by the community as a bully who used his temporary authority to terrorize an old rival. Nanaimo *Free Press,* 12 Oct. 1910, 1–2.

61. BC GR 419, vol. 196, file 1915/9.

62. Ibid., vol. 89, file 59.

63. Kamloops *Inland Sentinel,* 15 May 1913, 1.

64. BC GR 419, vol. 144, file 1910/63.

65. BC GR 1323, reel B2121, file 6515–4–15.

66. BC GR 1327, reel B2399, file 1917/54.

67. Prince Rupert *Daily News,* 10 Jan. 1921, 6.

68. Prince Rupert *Evening Empire,* 18 Jan. 1919, 2.

69. BC GR 419, vol. 101, file 1904/54.

70. Ibid., vol. 135, file 1909/63.

71. For American examples of this credo, see Elliott Gorn, "Bye Bye Boys, I Die a True American: Homicide, Nativism and Working-class Culture in Antebellum New York," *Journal of American History* 74 (1987):40; Gorn, *The Manly Art: Bare-knuckle Prize Fighting in America* (Ithaca: Cornell University Press, 1989).

72. BC GR 419, vol. 91, file 1902/6.

73. Ibid., vol. 147, file 1911/34.

74. These were typical prison sentences. Juries had the option of acquitting the accused or finding him guilty of either manslaughter (due to provocation or by criminal negligence) or murder. Fifty-eight of 125 men tried for murder went free because they were found not guilty or their cases were dropped or dismissed. Thirty-eight received prison sentences that ranged from one year to life, the average being between five and ten years. Twenty-nine men were sentenced to death.

75. Greenwood *Weekly Times,* 9 May 1901, 1.

76. BC GR 419, vol. 125, file 1908/29.

77. Ibid., vol. 176, file 1913/166.

78. Ibid., vol. 87, file 1901/27.

79. Ibid., vol. 129, file 1908/105.

80. Ibid., vol. 93, file 1902/61

81. For a French case of a murder committed by a man who believed that people were whispering about his being sodomized as a youth, see Drs. Reignier, Lagardelle, and Legrand du Saulle, "Sodomie et assassinat," *Annales médico-psychologiques* 17 (1877): 190–202.

82. For the argument that some homosexual relations were tolerated in working-class

milieus, see Steven Maynard, "Rough Work and Rugged Men: The Social Construction of Masculinity in Working-class History," *Labour/Le Travail* 23 (1989): 159–70. For the legal context, see Terry L. Chapman, "'An Oscar Wilde Type': 'The Abominable Crime of Buggery' in Western Canada, 1890–1920," *Criminal Justice History* 4 (1983): 97–118.

83. BC GR 419, vol. 89, file 1900/77; Victoria *Daily Colonist*, 29, 30 Oct. 1901.

84. BC GR 419, vol. 116, file 1906/79.

85. Ibid., vol. 124, file 1908/2.

86. Vancouver *Daily Province*, 9 May 1908, 1.

87. Of all the murders that took place between 1900 and 1923, the only one in which actual proof that a homosexual act (though perhaps best described as a pedophilic attack) occurred was reported in 1913. A simple-minded Clinton ranch hand was sentenced to death for buggering and then killing the four-and-a-half-year-old boy left in his care. BC GR 419, vol. 176, file 1913/164.

88. On the subject of "male sexual proprietariness," see Kenneth Polk, *When Men Kill: Scenarios of Masculine Violence* (Cambridge: Cambridge University Press, 1994), 58–61.

89. BC GR 419, vol. 87, file 1901/12.

90. Ibid., vol. 101, file 1904/55; Vancouver *Daily Province*, 21 May 1904, 2.

91. Ibid., vol. 108, file 1905/58.

92. Ibid., vol. 246, file 1921/43; Prince Rupert *Daily News*, 10 Jan. 1921, 6.

93. BC GR 1327 B3294, #122/14; BC GR 419, vol. 187, file 1914/86

94. I will be treating the option of the husband killing the wife in a forthcoming study of intersexual murders.

95. BC GR 419, vol. 92, file 1902/36.

96. Ibid., vol. 146, fil 1913/149.

97. Ibid., vol. 141, file 1910/28.

98. Ibid., vol. 167, file 1913/14; Vancouver *Daily Province*, 15 Oct. 1912, 30; 28 Mar. 1913, 22; 29 Mar. 1913, 3. Mary Henrietta McNaughton, the accused's mother, was a leading member of the WCTU and in January 1912 the first woman elected to the Vancouver City Council. On class and murder in England, see Conley, *Unwritten Law*, 56–59.

99. BC GR 419, vol. 113, file 1906/27.

100. Ibid., vol. 230, file 1919/135.

101. Ibid., vol. 272, file 1923/92.

102. *Kootenaian*, 19 Oct. 1922, 1; Nelson *Daily News*, 14 Oct. 1922, 1.

103. Prince Rupert *Daily News*, 6 June 1921, 4.

104. Fernie *Free Press*, 22 Oct. 1915, 1.

105. Peter N. Stearns, *Be a Man: Males in Modern Society* (New York: Holmes and Meier, 1984); Mark C. Carnes and Clyde Griffen, eds., *Meanings for Manhood: Constructions of Masculinity in Victorian America* (Chicago: University of Chicago Press, 1990); J. A. Mangan and James Walvin, eds., *Manliness and Morality: Middle-Class Masculinity in Britain and America, 1800–1940* (Manchester: Manchester University Press, 1987); Michael S. Kimmel, "The Contemporary 'Crisis' of Masculinity," in *The Making of Masculinities*, ed. Harry Brod (Boston: Allen and Unwin, 1987), 122–55; Marilyn Lake, "The Politics of Respectability: Identifying the Masculinist Context," *Historical Studies* 22 (1986): 116–31; Jock Phillips, *A Man's Country? The Image of the Pakeha Male* (Aukland: Penguin, 1987).

INTRODUCTION TO PART THREE

1. Jean Claude Bologne, *Histoire de la pudeur* (Paris: Olivier Orban, 1986); Anne Vincent-Buffault, *Histoire des larmes* (Marseille: Rivages, 1986).

2. Charles Darwin, *The Expression of the Emotions in Man and Animals*, in *The Works of Charles Darwin* (London: Pickering, 1989), 23:181–83; and see also Charles Féré, *Pathologie des émotions* (Paris: Alcan, 1892).

3. Henri Bergson, *Le Rire: Essai sur la signification du comique* (Paris: Alcan, 1900), 5.

4. Respectable women were contrariwise counseled that it was unbecoming a female to appear, in public at least, too intelligent.

5. Jean-Jacques Rousseau, *Émile,* (Paris: La Pléaide, Gallimard, 1969), book V, p. 697.

6. Lesley A. Hall, *Hidden Anxieties: Male Sexuality, 1900–1950* (Oxford: Polity Press, 1991).

7. M. L. Holbrook, *Parturition without Pain* (New York: 1882), p. 36 cited in Charles Rosenberg, *No Other Gods: On Science and American Social Thought* (Baltimore: Johns Hopkins University Press, 1976), 47.

8. On the role of the experts, starting with the German sexologists, see Vern L. Bullough, *Science in the Bedroom: A History of Sex Research* (New York: Basic Books, 1994).

CHAPTER 6: WEAKLINGS

1. For examples of such advertisements, see *Daily Telegraph,* 24 Oct. 1864, 2 ; *Illustrated Police News,* 12 Mar. 1870, 4.

2. London *Times,* 24 Oct. 1864, 9.

3. On the Henery case, see *Lancet* 2 (1864): 502–7, 529, 620, 640, 647, 648, 650; *Daily Telegraph,* 25 Nov. 1864, 2; and see also *Punch,* 30 Nov. 1864. The *Oxford Times* of 10 Dec. 1864 noted that such advertisements provided the struggling newspaper with a "ready but very questionable prop."

4. *Lancet* 2 (1864): 620, 640.

5. William Acton, *The Functions and Disorders of the Reproductive Organs,* 3d ed. (London: John Churchill, 1862),. appendix E, p. 211; and see also *Lancet* 2 (1857).

6. *British Medical Journal* 2 (1864): 632.

7. *Lancet* 1 (1865): 98–99

8. Ibid., 161.

9. *Lancet* 2 (1865): 391; and see also, *Lancet* 1 (1865): 277, 294; 2 (1865): 518.

10. On earlier attacks, see J. Corry, *Quack Doctors Dissected* (London: Whitrow, n.d.), and *The Detector of Quackery* (London: Crosby, 1802).

11. Lynn Hunt, ed., *The Invention of Pornography: Obscenity and the Origins of Modernity, 1500–1800* (New York: Zone Books, 1993), 41; Annie Stora-Lamarre, *L'Enfer de la IIIe République: Censeurs et pornographes 1881–1914* (Paris: Imago, 1990).

12. For the argument that in a new age of privacy the masturbation panic reflected a fear of the autonomous hedonism sponsored by the rise of capitalism, see Colin Campbell, *The Romantic Ethic and the Spirit of Modern Consumerism* (Oxford: Blackwell, 1987). For older interpretations, see E. H. Hare, "Masturbatory Insanity: The History of an Idea," *Journal of Mental Science* 108 (1962): 1–25; Jean Stengers and Anne van Eck, *Histoire d'une grande peur: La Masturbation* (Bruxelles: Éditions de l'Université de Bruxelles, 1984); Freddy Mortier, Willem Colen, and Frank Simon, "Inner-Scientific Reconstructions in the Discourse on Masturbation (1760–1950)," *Paedagogica Historica* 30, no. 3 (1994): 817–48.

13. Early works that exploited the fears of sexual abuse included W. Farrer, *A Short Treatise on Onanism or, the Detestable Vice of Self-Pollution* (London: 1767); Dr. James Graham, *A Lecture on the Generation, Increase and Improvement of the Human Species* (London: Smith, 1784); William Brodum, *A Guide to Old Age or a Cure for the Indiscretions of Youth,* 2 vols. (London: Myers, 1795), which publicized the author's "Nervous Cordial"; Samuel Solomon, *A Guide to Health* (London: Mathews, 1796), which puffed "Solomon's Cordial Balm of Gilead"; E. Senate, *The Medical Moniteur, Containing Observations on the Effects of Early Dissipation* (London: by the author, n.d.).

14. Samuel La'Mert, *Self-Preservation: A Popular Inquiry into the Concealed Causes of Those Obscure and Neglected Disorders of the Generative System* (Manchester: by the author, 1841), which appeared in France as *La Préservation personnelle* (Paris: Ledoyen and Laroque, 1847), and *The Science of Life* (London: Piper, Spence, 1858); J. L. Curtis, *Manhood: The Causes of Its Premature Decline with Directions for Its Perfect Restoration* (Lon-

don, 1840) and *Guide medical du mariage* (Paris: Brachet, 1868); Dr. Belliol, *Conseils aux hommes affaiblés* (Paris: Dentu, 1877), Dr. Brennus, *L'Acte bref* (Paris: Hall, 1907); Dr. Pouillet, *La Spermatorrhée* (Paris: Delahaye, 1877). Dr. O. Retau, *Das Büch uber die Ehe* (Luzern: Nedwig, s.d.).

15. *Lancet* 2 (1864): 529

16. *Lancet* 1 (1901): 493; and see also British Medical Association, *Secret Remedies, What They Cost and What They Contain* (London: B.M.A., 1909) and *More Secret Remedies* (London: B.M.A., 1912).

17. M. H. Utley, *Didactic Elucidations, Respecting the Original Sin, or the Sin of Imagination, and Its Consequences, Morally, Physically and Mentally* (Montreal, 1874).

18. For one doctor's assertion that he was attacked in the medical press for merely broaching sexual issues, see R. Dawson, *An Essay on Spermatorrhoea* (London: H. Hughes, 1847).

19. On the lack of unanimity among doctors, see Michael Mason, *The Making of Victorian Sexuality* (New York: Oxford University Press, 1994), 175–228; Lesley Hall and Roy Porter, *The Facts of Life: The Creation of Sexual Knowledge in Britain, 1650–1950* (New Haven: Yale University Press, 1995), 132–55.

20. Some discreetly wrote about tabooed subjects in Latin; see, for example, Henrico Kaan, *Psychopathia Sexualis* (Lipsiae: Apud Leopoldum, 1844).

21. Anti-Semitic slurs were frequently employed by doctors in their attacks on quacks. One medical journalist said of a salesman of "Dr. Jordan's Balsam Rakasir" that his "face was as Jewish as his conduct." *Monthly Gazette of Health* 9 (January 1824): 786. John L. Milton, who popularized the notion of "spermatorrhoea," claimed that the "most illustrious" of the "wretches of the Manly Vigor school and the spermatorrhoea quacks" belonged to "the stricken house of Judah." *Practical Remarks on the Treatment of Spermatorrhoea* (London: Highley, 1855), 5. Similarly the editor of the *Lancet,* in hailing the founding of a "Union for the Discouragement of Vicious Advertisements," described quacks as "hook-nosed, blacklocked, and overdone in jewelry and dress of the most extravagant fashion." *Lancet* 1 (1851): 73. Such statements suggest not that Jews were actually overrepresented within the ranks of unqualified practitioners but that non-Jews attributed to them—the exotic "other" arcane sexual knowledge. On the social context, see Bill Williams, *The Making of Manchester Jewry, 1740–1875* (Manchester: Manchester University Press, 1976).

22. See chapter 6, entitled "The Price of Repression," in Peter Gay, *The Tender Passion,* vol. 2 of *The Bourgeois Experience, Victoria to Freud* (New York: Oxford University Press, 1986).

23. William Acton, *The Functions and Disorders of the Reproductive Organs* (London: John Churchill, 1857); and for the context, see F. Barry Smith, "Sexuality in Britain, 1800–1900: Some Suggested Revisions," in *A Widening Sphere: Changing Roles of Victorian Women,* ed. Martha Vicinus (Bloomington: Indiana University Press, 1977), 18–98.

24. George Drysdale, in later life a sex radical, was so frightened of masturbating that he had himself cauterized seven or eight times. Other remedies included blistering, camphor rubs, infibulation, and physical restraints. J. Miriam Benn, *The Predicaments of Love* (London: Pluto Press, 1992), 37–46

25. On Beard see Charles Rosenberg, *No Other Gods: On Science and American Social Thought* (Baltimore: Johns Hopkins University Press, 1976), 98ff.

26. George M. Beard, *Sexual Neurasthenia* (New York: E. B. Treat, 1884).

27. On Beard's influence on France, see Maurice de Fleury, *Les Grands symptomes neurasthéniques: Pathogénie et traitement* (Paris: Alcan, 1901).

28. Beard, *Sexual Neurasthenia,* 103.

29. Report of Dr. Hammond in the *American Journal of Neurology and Psychiatry* (August 1882) cited in Beard, *Sexual Neurasthenia,* 100.

30. Beard, *Sexual Neurasthenia,* 91.

31. Ibid., 125; and see also G. Stanley Hall, *Adolescence* (New York: D. Appleton, 1904), 1:432–63; Tom Lutz, *American Nervousness, 1903: An Anecdotal History* (Ithaca: Cornell University Press, 1991).

32. Félix Roubaud, *Traité de l'impuissance et de sterilité chez l'homme et chez la femme,* 2 vols. (Paris: Baillière, 1855).

33. M. H. Utley, *Didactic Elucidations, Respecting the Original Sin, or the Sin of Imagination, and Its Consequences, Morally, Physically and Mentally* (Montreal, 1874).

34. Victor G. Vecki, *Pathologie und Therapie der mannlichen Impotenz* (Wien: Urban & Schwarzenberg, 1897).

35. Vecki cited in F. R. Sturgis, *Sexual Debility in Man* (London: Rebman, 1901), 86.

36. George Hy. Savage, "Insanity, Its Cause and Increase," *British Medical Journal* 1 (1907): 622–23. William Wynn Westcott, in discussing causes of death noted, "I must not omit to notice that simple fatal syncope may be due to muscular exhaustion, especially during or after sexual intercourse; among 1,100 inquests a year, I have about four such occurrences, always of males." "Sudden and Unexpected Deaths," *British Medical Journal* 1 (1908): 491.

37. Sigmund Freud, *An Autobiographical Study* (London, 1948), 42–46; and see also Hannah Decker, *Freud in Germany: Revolution and Reaction in Science, 1893–1907* (New York: International Universities Press, 1977), 134ff; Jeffrey Masson, ed., *The Complete Letters of Sigmund Freud to Wilhelm Fliess, 1877–1904* (Cambridge: Harvard University Press, 1985), 41, 43, 57–58, 61, 78–79.

38. "How Anxiety Originates," (1894), *Standard Edition of the Complete Psychological Works,* trans. J. Strachey (London: Hogarth Press, 1966), 1:189–90.

39. Ibid., 1:191; and see also 1: 214, 3: 251.

40. "Draft A" (1892), Ibid., 1:177.

41. "Draft B" (1893), Ibid., 1:181.

42. "The Anxiety Neurosis," (1893), Ibid., 3:101; and see also 16: 401–402.

43. "Draft B. Aetiology of the Neurosis," (1893), Ibid., 1:183.

44. "The Anxiety Neurosis" (1895), Ibid., 3:103.

45. "The Anxiety Neurosis" (1898), Ibid., 3:106. See also Sandor Ferenczi's 1905 assertion that neurasthenia was caused by a loss of semen "si riche en glycérophosphates." Sandor Ferenczi, *Les Écrits de Budapest,* trans. G. Kurcz and C. Lorin (Paris: E. P. E.L., 1994), 259.

46. Sander Gilman, *Difference and Pathology: Stereotypes of Sexuality, Race, and Madness* (Ithaca: Cornell University Press, 1985), 213–24.

47. "'Civilized' Sexual Morality" (1908), *Standard Edition,* 9:200.

48. *Introductory Lectures* (1915) in Ibid., 16: 316. In this passage Freud refers to both defecation and coitus interruputus as being as "perverse" in that both engender a form of sexual pleasure and yet are nonreproductive.

49. James Paget, *Clinical Lectures and Essays* (London: Longman Green, 1875), 268–92.

50. *Sexual Debility in Man,* 68.

51. For a poem on "Un Jean qui ne peut" and assorted jokes and anecdotes concerning impotency, all of which predated the nineteenth century, see *Grande Dictionnaire du XIXe siècle* (Paris: Larousse, 1866–1900) and see also Margaret Waller, *The Male Malady: Fictions of Impotence in the French Romantic Novel* (New Brunswick: Rutgers University Press, 1993).

52. Acton, *Functions,* 3d ed., 1862. appendix E, "Exposure of the Quack System," 30.

53. James Woycke, *Birth Control in Germany, 1871–1933* (New York: London, 1988), 12.

54. Rex versus Descôtes, *Rapports Judiciares de Québec: Cour Supérieure* 63 (1925), 52–56. Descôtes was entrapped by the police into selling a police constable one of the cited

texts. Such tactics were not unusual in such cases. In 1899 Dr. Villeneuve informed the Société médico-psychologique de Québec of the case of "H.C.," a Belgian patissier-décorateur, charged under article 179 of the Criminal Code for selling three pastry figures tending to corrupt morals.

Ces figures, d'un caractère obscène par la prédominance données aux organes génitaux, étaient en sucre colorié et représentaient une femme et un homme nus, avec un chien. Une image de l'Enfant Jésus portait une croix était collée sur la boite.

One of the pastry cook's creations had been discovered and reported to the authorities. The police sent along an agent to entrap "H.C." into selling him something similar. "H.C." stated that in Belgium he produced such wares when he needed the money but such undertakings were more dangerous in Quebec. He was finally talked into producing the confection and then arrested. His last line of defense was to claim to be an epileptic, which explains why Dr. Villeneuve of the asile Saint Jean de Dieu became involved in the case. *Annales médico-psychologiques* 11 (1900): 268.

55. Also cited was Jean Ernest-Charles, *La Possession criminelle: Drames d'amour et de jalousie* (Paris: Flammarion, 1923).

56. The Montreal press was at the same time reporting that the city's estimated eighty brothels posed the question of whether regulation was required. See *Le Devoir*, 23 Dec. 1924, 1; 26 Dec. 1924, 1; 29 Dec. 1924, 1; *Montreal Gazette*, 23 Dec. 1924, 10; 24 Dec. 1924, 2. On the discussion of sexual issues in Quebec, see Andrée Lévesque, *La Norme et les déviantes: Des femmes au Quebec pendant l'entre-deux-guerres* (Montreal: Les Éditions du remue-ménage, 1989).

57. Peter Gay, *Education of the Senses*, vol. 1 of *The Bourgeois Experience: Victoria to Freud* (New York: Oxford University Press, 1984), 318.

58. Some of the same material was repackaged in the series "Collection de psychologie populaire." A competitor who ran the "Institut Rabelais," which distributed books, nude photographs, contraceptives, and abortifacients, was in 1910 sentenced to six months in prison; see *Gazette des Tribunaux*, 23 July 1910, 662–23.

59. Dr. Caufeynon, *Bréviare de l'amour dans le marriage, d'après le Dr. Venette* (Paris: Fort, 1907); Drs. Caufeynon et Jaf, *Les Secrets merveilleux du grand et du petit Albert* (Paris, Librairie des ouvrages pratiques, 1905); Dr. Jaf, *Unisexual Love* (New York: New Era Press, 1954).

60. Dr. Caufeynon, *L'Eunuchisme: Histoire générale de la castration* (Paris: Charles Offenstadt, 1903).

61. Dr. Caufeynon, *L'Hermaphrodisme* (Paris: Charles Offenstadt, 1904).

62. Dr. Jaf, *Les Tatouages* (Paris: J. Fort, 1908), 73, 76.

63. Drs. Caufeynon and Jaf, *Les Secrets merveilleux du grand et petit Albert* (Paris: Librairie des ouvrages practiques, 1905); *Bréviare de l'amour dans le mariage, d'après le Dr. Venette* (Paris: Fort, 1907).

64. Dr. Caufeynon, *La Procréation à volonté des filles et des garçons, suivie de fécondation artificielle et de l'ami des jeunes femmes* (Paris: Fort, 1903).

65. Drs. Jaf and Caufeynon, *Sécurité de deux sexes en amour* (Paris: Georges-Anquetil, 1926), 425, 429, 437; and see also J. C. Bernard, "Fille ou garçon à volonté: Un Aspect du discours médical au XIXe siècle," *Ethnographie française* 11 (1981): 63–76.

66. Dr. Caufeynon, *Aberrations, folies et aberrations du sens génital* (Paris: Charles Offenstadt, 1903), 63; and see also on the dismissal of women's claims of being raped, Ambroise Tardieu, *Étude médico-légale sur les attentats aux moeurs* (Paris: Baillière, 1878), 101–2, 133–35.

67. On changing diagnoses, see Martha Noel Evans, *Fits and Starts: A Genealogy of Hysteria in Modern France* (Ithaca: Cornell University Press, 1992).

68. On such continuities, see Angus McLaren, *Reproductive Rituals: The Perception of Fertility in England from the Sixteenth Century to the Nineteenth Century* (London: Methuen, 1984).

69. Dr. Jaf, *Physiologie du vice* (Paris: Charles Offenstadt, 1904), 55.

70. Dr. Jaf, *L'Amour malade* (Paris: J. Fort, 1908), 86ff.

71. Dr. Caufeynon, *L'Hystérie* (Paris: Nouvelle librarie médicale, 1905); and see also Jan Goldstein, "The Hysteria Diagnosis and the Politics of Anti-clericalism in Late Nineteenth-century France," *Journal of Modern History* 54 (1982): 209–39, and *Console and Classify: The French Psychiatric Profession in the Nineteenth Century* (Cambridge: Cambridge University Press, 1987).

72. Dr. Caufeynon, *Aberrations, folies et aberrations du sens génital* (Paris: Charles Offenstadt, 1903), 46

73. Dr. Caufeynon, *The Vice of Woman* (Paris: Artistic Library, 1925), 170–75.

74. Dr. Caufeynon, *Les Vénus impudiques: La Grande prostitution à travers les âges* (Paris: Société parisienne d'édition, 1903).

75. For claims that contraception was physically and psychologically debilitating, see Dr. Michel Bourgas, *Le Droit à l'amour pour la femme* (Paris: Vigot frères, n.d.), 106–10.

76. Drs. Jaf and Caufeynon, *Sécurité de deux sexes en amour* (Paris: Georges-Anquetil, 1926), 399, 422; and compare to Doctor Saldo, *Love without Danger, followed with The Short Act* (Paris: Editions Modernes, 1927).

77. Dr. Forel's recommendations on a range of birth-control techniques including condoms and coitus interruptus was included in Drs. Jaf and Saldo, *Physiologie secrète de l'homme et de la femme* (Paris: Denans, 1908), 118–23.

78. Dr. Jaf, *Amour et mariage en Orient* (Paris: J. Fort, 1908). This text appeared in the "Collection de psychologie populaire." The even more extensive list that appeared in Doctor-Brennus, *Amour et sécurité* (Paris: Saint-Elme Guerin, 1906), included advertisements for pessaries, douches, sponges, bidets, contraceptive powders, diaphragms, aphrodisiacs, anti-spermatorrhea rings, chastity belts, injectors for artificial insemination, false breasts, vaginal protectors, ("L'Infallible"), *capuchons* ("bonnet fin-de-siècle"), *baudruches,* condoms in a variety of colors and imitation crocodile hide, and cigarette cases, hollow one franc pieces and "boutins de violettes" in which such condoms could be discretely hidden. For similar advertisements in a man's magazine, see *Le Sourire* 25 Aug. 1899.

79. Dr. Caufeynon, *L'Hystérie* (Paris: Nouvelle librarie médicale, 1905).

80. Dr. Caufeynon, *Aberrations, folies et aberrations du sens genital* (Paris: Charles Offenstadt, 1903), 26, 27, 61.

81. Dr. Caufeynon, *L'Onanisme chez l'homme* (Paris: Charles Offenstadt, 1902), 8, 9, 45, 107.

82. Dr. Jaf, *Le Commerce sexuel et le proxénètisme* (Paris: J. Fort, 1908), 53, 56, 98. See also Dr. Caufeynon, *La Prostitution — débauche — corruption* (Paris: Nouvelle librairie médicale, 1905).

83. For contemporary accounts of the dangers prostitution posed society, see Charles-Jérôme Lecour, *La Prostitution à Paris et à Londres* (Paris: Asselin, 1877); Louis Martineau, *La Prostitution clandestine* (Paris: Lecrosnier, 1885).

84. Dr. Jaf, *Physiologie du vice* (Paris: Charles Offenstadt, 1904), 235–36.

85. Dr. Caufeynon, *The Vice of Woman* (Paris: Artistic Library, 1925), 132.

86. Dr. Caufeynon, *Scènes d'amour morbide (Observations psycho-physiologiques* (Paris: P. Fort, 1902).

87. On the linkage of male and female prostitution, see F. Carlier, *Les Deux prostitutions* (Paris: E. Dentu, 1887).

88. Dr. Jaf, *Physiologie du vice* (Paris: Charles Offenstadt, 1904), 8, 205. On the argument that "compensatory" masturbation was permissible, but "essential Onanism" led on to homosexuality, see Auguste Forel, *The Sexual Question,* trans. C. F. Marshall (New York: Medical Art Agency, n.d. [first French edition 1905]), 228–31. The similar argument that cases of inversion that were mere school-boy flings could be cured by marriage was asserted by Pierre Garnier, *Anomalies sexuelles: Apparentes et cachées* (Paris: Garnier 1889), 490–502.

89. On homosexuality and degeneration fears see J. Aron and R. Kempf, *La bourgeoisie, le sexe et l'honneur* (Paris: Edition complèxe, 1984).

90. Dr. Caufeynon, *La Péderastie* (Paris: Charles Offenstadt, 1905), 17, 19. But Fauconney also noted that blackmailers exploited homosexuals' fears of being revealed.

91. On the construction of the medical image of the homosexual, see Robert A. Nye, "Sex Difference and Male Homosexuality in French Medical Discourse, 1830–1930," *Bulletin of the History of Medicine* 63 (1989): 32–52.

92. On the emergence in the nineteenth century of such views, see E. K. Sedgwick, *The Epistemology of the Closet* (Berkeley: University of California Press, 1990), 8.

93. Dr. Jaf, *L'Amour malade* (Paris: J. Fort, 1908), 18, 29, 31; Dr. Caufeynon, *La Folie érotique* (Paris: Charles Offenstadt, 1903).

94. Michel Foucault, *The History of Sexuality: An Introduction,* trans. Richard Howard (New York: Vintage, 1980).

95. See, for example, Stekel's assertion that "love inadequacy" increased as civilization advanced; Wilhelm Stekel, *Impotence in the Male* (New York: Liverwright, 1927), 1:11; and see also Martin J. Weiner, *Reconstructing the Criminal: Culture, Law and Policy in England, 1830–1914* (Cambridge: Cambridge University Press, 1990), 238–40.

96. Edward Shorter, *From Hysteria to Fatigue: A History of Psychosomatic Illness in the Modern Era* (New York: Free Press, 1992).

97. Karen Offen, "Depopulation, Nationalism, and Feminism in Fin-de-Siècle France," *American Historical Review* 89 (1984): 648–76; and on fears of declining virility, see Robert A. Nye, "Honor, Impotence, and Male Sexuality in Nineteenth-century French Medicine," *French Historical Studies* 16 (1989): 48–71.

98. William Schneider, *Quality and Quantity: The Quest for Biological Regeneration in Twentieth-century France* (Cambridge: Cambridge University Press, 1990); Ian Dowbiggen, *Inheriting Madness: Professionalization and Psychiatric Knowledge in Nineteenth-century France* (Berkeley: University of California Press, 1991).

99. Sander Gilman, *Difference and Pathology: Stereotypes of Sexuality, Race, and Madness* (Ithaca: Cornell University Press, 1985), 213–24.

100. On the biological preoccupations of the late nineteenth century, see Alain Corbin, *Le Temps, le désir et l'horreur* (Paris: Aubier, 1991)

101. On the popularity of the treatments offered by Drs. Brown-Sequard, Steinach, and Voronoff, see "Impuissance," in *La Grande Encyclopédie* (Paris: Lamirault, 1887–1902), 647–48; Naomi Pfeffer, *The Stork and the Syringe: A Political History of Reproductive Medicine* (Oxford: Polity, 1993), 51ff.

102. On changing therapies see, Kevin J. Mumford, "'Lost Manhood' Found: Male Sexual Impotence in Victorian Culture in the United States," *Journal of the History of Sexuality* 3 (1992): 33–57.

103. Sheila Faith Weiss, *Race Hygiene and National Efficiency: The Eugenics of Wilhelm Schallmayer* (Berkeley: University of California Press, 1987), 23.

104. Eugene Terraillon, *L'Honneur, sentiment et principe moral* (Paris: Alcan, 1912), 171–76.

105. See, for example, the argument that African-American students were exhausted in trying to keep up with their white counterparts in C. K. Mills, *Mental Overwork and Prema-*

ture Disease among Public and Professional Men (Washington: Smithsonian Misc. Collections, 1885) 15.

106. Henri Martin, "La Dépopulation," *Semaine Sociale du Canada: Compte Rendu des cours et conférences* (Montréal: Bibliothèque de l'Action française, 1924), 152.

CHAPTER 7: SADISTS

1. Alexandre Lacassagne, *Vacher l'éventreur et les crimes sadiques* (Lyon: Storck, 1899), 288.

2. Jeffrey Weeks, "Questions of Identity," in *The Cultural Construction of Sexuality*, ed. Pat Caplan (New York: Tavistock, 1987), 31–51; and see also Georges Lanteri-Laura, *Lecture des perversions: Histoire de leur appropriation médicale* (Paris: Masson, 1979).

3. Ian Hacking, "Making Up People," in *Reconstructing Individualism: Autonomy, Individuality and the Self in Western Thought*, ed. T. C. Heller et al. (Stanford: Stanford University Press, 1986), 228. On twentieth-century views of sadism, see Vern Bullough, Dwight Dixon, and Joan Dixon, "Sadism, Masochism and History, or When Is Behavior Sado-Masochistic?" in *Sexual Knowledge, Sexual Science: The History of Attitudes to Sexuality*, ed. Roy Porter and Michael Teich (Cambridge: Cambridge University Press, 1994), 47–62; Martin S. Weinberg, Colin J. Williams, and Charles Moser, "The Social Constituents of Sado-masochism," *Social Problems* 31 (1984): 379–89.

4. Which explains why sadomasochistic practices became more popular in the brothels of the 1890s; see Alain Corbin, *Women for Hire: Prostitution and Sexuality in France after 1850* (Cambridge: Harvard University Press, 1990), 81.

5. Three years earlier Victor's mother had handed him over to the Société lyonnaise pour le sauvetage de l'enfance, which had found him work with a local landowner.

6. Even before Vacher's trial concluded, a book had been devoted to his case, M. Laurent-Martin, *Le Roi des assassins* (Paris: Librairie universelle, 1897). The fullest account of his career was produced by the investigating magistrate, Émile Fourquet, *Vacher* (Paris: Gallimard, 1931). Fourquet's conservative social views were made evident by the titles of his other works: *Les Vagabonds; Les Faux témoins; Les meneurs de grèves*. See also René Tavernier et Henri Garet, *Le Juge et l'assassin* (Paris: France Loisirs, 1976), on which was based Bertrand Tavernier's excellent film of the same name.

7. *Gazette de Tribunaux,* 27 Oct. 1898, 987. Joan, whose beatification took place in 1909 and canonization in 1920, was in the 1890s vociferously claimed as a martyr by both the republican nationalists and the Catholic monarchists. Marina Warner, *Joan of Arc: The Image of Female Heroism* (London: Weidenfeld and Nicolson, 1981), 255–64. Thérèse of Lisieux, whose remarkably speedy advancement to sainthood also occurred in the early twentieth century, recorded as her first triumph, by the power of prayer alone, of having the impenitent murderer Pranzini convert before his execution on 31 Aug. 1887. *Histoire d'une âme* (Lisieux: O.L.L., 1946), 77–78.

8. Alexandre Lacassagne, "Vacher l'Éventreur," *Archives de l'anthropologie criminelle* 13 (1898): 641.

9. Fourquet, *Vacher,* 235.

10. Lacassagne, "Vacher," 641.

11. *Gazette de Tribunaux,* 31 October–1 Nov. 1898, 1004.

12. Ibid.

13. Ibid.

14. Ibid. No one noted at the time that Vacher identified with Joan of Arc rather than with her companion in arms, the notorious Gilles de Rais, who helped liberate Orleans in 1429 but in 1440 was turned over by the inquisition to the bishop of Nantes, accused of the evocation of the devil and the murder and sodomy of hundreds of children. In 1885 the original court documents of the man whose memory had become confused with the Bluebeard

story were published in Abbé Eugène Bossard, *Gilles de Rais, maréchal de France, dit Barbe-Bleue* (Paris: Champion, 1886). The account was challenged by the dreyfusard Salomon Reinach in "Gilles de Rais," *Cultes, mythes et religion* (Paris: Ernest Leroux, 1912), 4:267–99, who—following Voltaire—argued that Gilles, like Joan and Dreyfus, had been disposed of for political reasons. Gilles's lands, a tempting prize for his suzerain, the duke of Brittany, were indeed seized, and his confession, in which he attributed his murder of hundreds of boys to idleness and irreligion, rang hollow.

> He urged the fathers of families, moreover, to guard against dressing their children daintily and permitting them to live in idleness; and he noted and claimed that very many evils are generated from idleness and overeating and declared most expressly about himself that idleness and excessive, frequent consumption of savory foods and warm wines had supplied him chiefly with the incentives from which he perpetrated so many sins and misdeeds.

Reginald Hyatte, ed., *Laughter for the Devil: The Trials of Gilles de Rais, Companion in Arms of Joan of Arc (1440)* (Cranbury, N.J.: Associated University Presses, 1984), 120; and see also Fernand Fleuret, *De Gilles de Rais à Guillaume Apollinaire* (Paris: Mercure de France, 1933).

15. *L'Intransigeant,* 26 October 1898, 2.

16. Ibid.; *Le Matin,* 27 Oct. 1898, 2. For the claim that some in France boasted that Vacher had bested the record set in England by Jack the Ripper, see *L'Illustration,* 6 Nov. 1897, 897–98. Vacher himself supposedly wrote a special column for *Le Petit Journal.*

17. *Gazette de Tribunaux,* 31 Oct.–1 Nov. 1898, 1004.

18. On the debate over the morality of public executions, see Alexandre Berard, *La Publicité des exécutions capitales* (Lyon: Storck, 1894).

19. Fourquet, *Vacher,* 312.

20. *Le Figaro,* 28, 29 Oct. 1898.

21. Ruth Harris, *Murders and Madness: Medicine, Law, and Society in the Fin-de-Siècle* (Oxford: Oxford University Press, 1989); Jan Goldstein, *Console and Classify: The French Psychiatric Profession in the Nineteenth Century* (Cambridge: Cambridge University Press, 1987); Robert A. Nye, *Crime, Madness and Politics in Modern France: The Medical Concept of National Decline* (Princeton University Press, 1984).

22. Patrizia Guarnieri, *A Case of Child Murder: Law and Science in Nineteenth-century Tuscany* (Cambridge: Polity, 1993), 121.

23. Guarnieri, *Child Murder,* 139.

24. Ibid., 167–68.

25. Cited in Paul Moreau de Tours, *Aberration du sens génésiques* (Paris: Asselin, 1880), 243. Sexual aberrations, according to Moreau de Tours, could like epilepsy override the powers of reason.

26. *Gazette de Tribunaux,* 31 Oct.–1 Nov. 1898, 1004.

27. Dr. Bozonnet, doctor of the prison at Belley, stated that Vacher was not completely responsible. Dr. François Madeuf concurred, pointing out the importance of the bullet in Vacher's skull. Madeuf, author of *L'Art de éviter et de guérir les maladies intimes spéciales à l'homme et à la femme* (Paris: Port-Royal, s.d.) and other self-help medical guides, was very much an outsider, and his testimony was thus easily discounted by Lacassagne.

28. Ian R. Dowbiggin, *Inheriting Madness: Professionalization and Psychiatric Knowledge in Nineteenth-century France* (Berkeley: University of California Press, 1991).

29. On Lacassagne's traditional view of sex roles, see his *Précis d'hygiène privée et sociale* (Paris: Masson, 1876), 502–30.

30. On Lombroso's influence, see Rafael Huertas, "Madness and Degeneration, III. Degeneration and Criminality," *History of Psychiatry* 4 (1993): 141–58; on Lacassagne's early

deference to the Italians, see Alexandre Lacassagne, *L'Homme criminel comparé à l'homme primitif* (Lyon: Association typographique, 1882); and for the flowering of the French school, see Émile Laurent, *L'Anthropologie criminelle et les nouvelles théories du crime* (Paris: Société d'éditions scientifiques, 1893).

31. See Robert Nye, "Heredity or Milieu: The Foundations of Modern European Criminological Theory," *Isis* 67 (1976): 339; Nye, *Madness*, 103–6, 191–92, 221–24; Henri Souchon, "Alexandre Lacassagne et l'école de Lyon," *Revue de science criminelle* 35 (1974): 533–59.

32. See Alexande Berard, *La Responsibilité morale* (Lyon: Storck, 1892).

33. Lacassagne, *Vacher*, 286.

34. Maxime de Fleury, *L'Âme du criminel* (Paris: Alcan, 1898), 87.

35. *La Scuola positiva* (January 1899), cited in Lacassagne, *Vacher*, 289; and see also Raffaele Garofalo, *Criminology* (Boston: Little Brown, 1914), 133.

36. Magnus Hirschfeld, *Sexual Pathology* (New York: Emerson, 1947), 221.

37. Patients' attacks on asylum keepers were in the news; for an account written to expose conditions at the Salpêtrière by a woman committed by her parents for fourteen years see, Hersilie Rouy, *Mémoires d'une aliénée* (Paris: Ollendorf, 1883), cited in Martha Noel Evans, *Fits and Starts: A Genealogy of Hysteria in Modern France* (Ithaca: Cornell University Press, 1991).

38. Paul Garnier, "Des Perversions sexuelles obsédantes et impulsives," *Archives de l'anthropologie criminelle* 15 (1900): 626–29.

39. Lacassagne, *Vacher*, 57–59. A. Pierret, médecin en chef de la maison de santé de Champvert at Lyon and expert on malingering, was responsible for reporting to the court on Vacher's heredity; Lacassagne provided an account of the accused's sadism, Dr. F. Rebatel reviewed the physical and anthropological evidence, and Dr. Lannois, an ear specialist, explained the effect of the bullet lodged in Vacher's skull.

40. Vacher's brain, like some sort of forensic football, was kicked around by competing teams of European psychiatrists, criminologists, and anthropologists. The Italians Lombroso and Roncoroni insisted it carried all the characteristics of the born criminal. The French anthropologists Laborde and Manouvrier followed Lacassagne in declaring it normal, indeed disturbingly similar to the republican politician Gambetta's beautiful gray matter. Madeuf, Klippel, Philippe, Rabaud, Marchand, and Toulouse more or less agreed, but Toulouse made the point that the brain's lack of lesions did not mean Vacher was sane. Édouard Toulouse, *Le Rapport des médicins expert sur Vacher* (Clermont: Daix frères, 1898); Alexandre Lacassagne, "Le Cerveau de Vacher," *Archives de l'anthropologie criminelle* 14 (1899): 653–62; M. J. V. Laborde avec la collaboration de MM. Manouvrier, Papillault & Gelle, *Étude psycho-physiologique, médico-légal & anatomique sur Vacher* (Paris: Schleicher frères, 1900); and see also *Chronique médicale* (1900): 208, cited in Pierre Darmon, *Médicins et assassins à la belle époque* (Paris: Seuil, 1989), 70.

41. Under Lacassagne's editorship the *Archives de l'anthropologie criminelle et des sciences pénales* published the first results of the sort of large-scale measurements of criminals called for by Adolphe Bertillon. "It was this circumstance that accelerated the French shift away from the atavism hypothesis and towards the degeneration approach—that is to say, away from physiognomy and craniology and towards psychopathology and psychodynamics." Jaap van Ginneken, *Crowds, Psychology, and Politics, 1871–1899* (Cambridge: Cambridge University Press, 1992), 112–13. But for evidence that biological determinism had its French defenders, see Charles Féré, *Dégénérescence et criminalité* (Paris: Alcan, 1888); Charles Féré, *La Famille nevropathique* (Paris: Alcan, 1898).

42. Three psychiatrists—Lasègue, Brouardel, and Motet—had held that Menesclou was sane. Lacassagne, *Vacher*, 253.

43. *Gazette de Tribunaux*, 31 Oct.–1 Nov. 1898, 1004.

44. Lacassagne, "Vacher," 636.

45. Lacassagne, *Vacher,* 288.

46. Marciat, "Le Marquis de Sade et le sadisme," in Lacassagne, *Vacher,* 185–238.

47. L. Thoinot, *Attentats aux moeurs et perversions du sens génital* (Paris: Doin, 1898); and see also L. Thoinot and A. W. Weysse, *Medicolegal Aspects of Moral Offenses* (Philadelphia: F. A. Davis, 1921), 417.

48. The term decadent was first taken up in the 1850s and was most associated with Baudelaire, author of *Fleurs du mal* (1857), of whom Paul Bourget said, "He is a libertine, and depraved visions amounting to Sadism disturb the very man who comes to worship the raised finger of his Madonna." Flaubert was called a "sadiste" in the 1850s and accused by Sainte-Beuve in the 1860s of having an "imagination sadique." *Le Grand Robert de la langue française* (Paris: Le Robert, 1985).

49. Octave Uzanne, *Idées sur les romans, par D.A.F. Sade* (Paris: Rouveyre, 1878); Charles Henry, *La Verité sur le marquis de Sade* (Paris: Dentu, 1887), H. d'Almeras, *Le Marquis de Sade* (Paris: Michel, 1906), Guillaume Apollinaire, *L'Oeuvre du marquis de Sade* (Paris: Bibliothèque des curieux, 1909); Dr. Salvatore Sarfati, *Essai médico-psychologique sur le marquis de Sade* (Lyon: Bosc and Riou, 1930); and on the literary cult of sadism, see the introduction by Octave Uzanne to Eugen Duehren [Iwan Bloch], *Le Marquis de Sade et son temps* (Paris: Michalon 1904); Maurice Heine, *Le Marquis de Sade* (Paris; Gallimard, 1950), Michel Delon, "Un type épatant pour les saloperies," in "Jean Lorrain: vices et écriture," *Revue des Sciences humaines* 230 (1993–94): 163–73.

50. Iwan Bloch, *Das Sexualleben unserer zeit* (Berlin: Marcuse, 1919), 586–626; Max Nordau, *Degeneration* (London: Heineman, 1913 [French edition 1895]); Mario Praz, *The Romantic Agony* (New York: Oxford University Press, 1970); Jean Pierrot, *The Decadent Imagination,* trans. Derek Coltman (Chicago: University of Chicago Press, 1981); Jennifer Birkett, *The Sins of the Fathers: Decadence in France, 1870–1914* (London: Quartet Books, 1986).

51. Emily Apter, *Feminizing the Fetish: Psychoanalysis and Narrative Obsession in Turn-of-the-Century France* (Ithaca: Cornell University Press, 1991), 128; Deborah L. Silverman, *Art Nouveau in Fin-de-Siècle France* (Berkeley: University of California Press, 1989); Wanda Bannour, *Édmond et Jules de Goncourt ou le génie androgyne* (Paris: Persona, 1985); and on England see Elaine Showalter, *Sexual Anarchy: Gender and Culture at the Fin de Siècle* (New York: Penguin, 1990), 8–18; Linda Gertner Zatlin, *Aubrey Beardsley and Victorian Sexual Politics* (Oxford: Clarendon Press, 1990).

52. Few were more bizarre than Jean Lorrain, who combed his hair over his forehead to make himself look like a murderer. A more serious interest in decadence was taken by Paul Bourget, who moving from positivism to conservative, social Catholicism, was attracted by de Sade's idea that there was an animalistic if not satanic side to love; see, Paul Bourget, *Nouveaux essais de psychologie contemporaine* (Paris; Lamerre, 1886) 2 vols; *Physiologie de l'amour moderne* (Paris: Lemmerre, 1891).

53. J.-K. Huysmans, *Là-Bas* in *Oeuvres complètes* (Paris: Cres, 1928), vol. 12, chap. 11.

54. Satanic sadism in fact offered many of the decadents like Huysmans a way back into Catholicism; see the introduction by Havelock Ellis to J. K. Huysmans, *Against the Grain (À Rebours)* trans. Arthur Zaidenberg (New York: Illustrated Editions, 1931).

55. Cited in Barbey d'Aurevilly, *Oeuvres* (Paris: Bibliothèque de la Pléaide, 1964), 1: 1295.

56. Octave Mirbeau, who in *Le Jardin des supplices* (1899) provided a seductive account of sadism, moved from Roman Catholicism to anarchism as a result of the Dreyfus affair. His *Le Journal d'une femme de chambre* (1901), which portrays a Vacher-like rape and killing of a child, presents the anti-Semitic, provincial bourgeoisie as the real sadists. He similarly critiqued the criminal psychiatry of period, presenting a doctor diagnosing poverty as a form of

cranial degeneration. Reg Carr, *Anarchism in France: The Case of Octave Mirbeau* (Montreal: McGill-Queens, 1977); Apter, *Fetish,* 157; and see also Germain Galerant, *Les Roses sadiques de Maupassant* (Paris: Bertot, 1992).

57. Duehren, *Sade,* 460; and on misogyny in painting see Bram Djkstra, *Idols of Perversity: Fantasies of Feminine Evil in Fin-de-Siècle Culture* (New York: Oxford University Press, 1986). See also footnote 80 below.

58. Paul Lidsky, *Les Écrivains contre la Commune* (Paris: Maspero, 1970); but for the argument that 1871 actually retarded until the 1880s the emergence of decadent literature, see Pierre Citti, *Contre la décadence: Histoire de l'imagination française dans le roman, 1890–1914* (Paris: PUF, 1987), 52–53.

59. Eugen Weber, *France, Fin-de-Siècle* (Cambridge: Harvard University Press, 1986), 13.

60. Birkett, *Sins of the Fathers,* 4. On De Sade's rehabilitation in the twentieth century, see Carolyn J. Dean, *The Self and Its Pleasures: Bataille, Lacan and the History of the Decentered Subject* (Ithaca: Cornell University Press, 1992), 127ff.

61. Lacassagne, *Vacher,* 276; and for similar praise, see Scipio Sighele, *Littérature et criminalité* (Paris: Giard et Brière, 1908), 132–34.

62. But for the argument that the decadent writers were themselves sick, see Dr. Émile Laurent, *La Poésie décadente devant la science psychiatrique* (Paris: Alexandre Maloine, 1897).

63. Paul Garnier, "Des Perversions sexuelles obsédantes et impulsives," *Archives de l'anthropologie criminelle* 15 (1900): 618.

64. See Cesare Lombroso, *L'Homme criminel* (Paris: Alcan, 1887); Arthur MacDonald, *Le Criminel-type dans quelque formes graves de la criminalité,* trans. Henry Coutagne (Lyon: Storck, 1894).

65. Dr. Georget, *Examen médical des procès criminals des nommés Leger, Feldtmann, Lecouffe, Jean-Pierre et Papavoine* (Paris: Migneret, 1825); Lacassagne, *Vacher,* 265–70; Arthur MacDonald, "Observations pour servir à l'étude de la sexualité pathologique et criminelle," *Archives de l'anthropologie criminelle* 7 (1892): 637–55; 8 (1893): 40–62; 277–98; Paul Garnier, "Pervertis et inverts sexuels," *Annales d'hygiène* (1893): 349, 385; Dr. Serge Paul, *Le Vice et l'amour* (Paris: Nouvelle librairie médicale, 1905),130.

66. Apter, *Fetish,* xi.

67. According to Dr. Toulouse, women asylum patients were not as inventive as men in their deliriums and more given to melancholy and sulkiness. Édouard Toulouse, *Les Conflits intersexuelles et sociaux* (Paris: Charpentier, 1904), 4; Féré cited women's fewer suicides as evidence of their weaker emotions; Charles Féré, *Pathologie des émotions* (Paris: Alcan, 1892), 479–80.

68. J. M. Charcot and V. Magnan, "Inversion du sens génital," *Archive de neurologie* 3–4 (1882): 53–60, 296–322.

69. Louis Martineau, driven by what he claimed to be a love of humanity, devoted a book to the delicate question of unnatural sex acts. He claimed that sodomy, both among homosexuals and heterosexuals, was increasing. He was particularly outraged that husbands forced it on their wives, but noted that some women did not understand that it was wrong and actually preferred it to genital intercourse. Louis Martineau, *Les Déformations vulvaires et anales produites par la masturbation, le saphisme, la défloration et la sodomie* (Paris: Vigot frères, 1905), 121–40; and see also A. Brierre de Boismont, *Manuel de médecine légale* (Paris: Baillière, 1835), 242–44.

70. Robert Nye, *Masculinity and Male Codes of Honor in Modern France* (New York: Oxford University Press, 1993).

71. Alfred Binet, "Le Fétichisme dans l'amour," *Revue philosophique* 24 (1887): 143–67, 252–77; and see also Paul Garnier, *Les Fétichistes pervertis et invertis sexuels: Observations médico-légales* (Paris: Baillière, 1896). Émile Laurent, *Fétichistes et érotomanes* (Paris: Vigot frères, 1903).

72. Some displacement can be detected in the French attributing a penchant for sadistic practices to the English and a taste for masochism to the Germans.

73. Richard von Krafft-Ebing, *Psychopathia Sexualis,* trans. Franklin S. Klaf (New York: Stein and Day, 1965), 87, 417 n12. Charles Féré in *Pathologie des émotions* (Paris: Alcan, 1892) noted Krafft-Ebing's creation of the term masochism, but made no mention of sadism. For the assertion that Krafft-Ebing coined *sadism,* see, for example, Frank J. Solloway, *Freud: Biologist of the Mind* (New York: Basic Books, 1979), 483; H. F. Ellenberger, *The Discovery of the Unconscious* (New York: Basic, 1970), 299.

74. A sense of how late the concept of sadism entered the medical vocabulary can be gauged from the fact that it was not mentioned by Ambroise Tardieu in his celebrated study of legal medicine *Étude médico-légal sur les attentats aux moeurs* (Paris: Baillière, 1865) nor in Paul Moreau (de Tours), *Aberration du sens génésiques* (Paris: Asselin, 1880). The Index-Catalogue of the Library of the Surgeon General's Office did not include sadism as a topic in its first series (1891), but the second (1910) listed nine books (four in German and five in French) and forty-two articles on the subject. On the use of ideas "good to think with" in cultural history, see Robert Darnton, *The Great Cat Massacre and Other Episodes in French Cultural History* (New York: Basic Books, 1984).

75. Krafft-Ebing, *Psychopathia Sexualis,* 53–54.

76. André Lamoureux, *De l'éventration au point de vue médico-légal* (Lyon: Storck, 1891).

77. Albert Moll, *Die Kontrare Sexualempfindung* (Berlin: Fischer, 1893), 186–87; see also the translation by Drs. Pactet and Romme, *Les perversions de l'instinct génital* (Paris: Carré, 1893), 172ff; and on similar ideas in Italy, see Dr. A. La Cara, *La Base organica dei pervertimenti sessuali e la loro profilassi sociale* (Torinto: Bocca, 1902).

78. Margaret Jackson, "'Facts of Life' or the Eroticization of Women's Oppression? Sexology and the Social Construction of Heterosexuality," in *Cultural Construction,* ed. Caplan, 52–66; and see also Jackson, "Sexual Liberation or Social Control," *Women's Studies International Forum* 6 (1983): 1–17; Jackson "Sex Research and the Construction of Sexuality: A Tool of Male Supremacy," *Women's Studies International Forum* 7 (1984), 43–51; Jackson, *The "Real" Facts of Life: Feminism and the Politics of Sexuality 1850–1940* (London: Taylor and Francis, 1994).

79. Havelock Ellis, *Studies in the Psychology of Sex* (New York: Random House, 1936), vol. 1, part 2, p. 164.

80. The pervasive misogyny of the 1890s manifested itself in numerous literary and artistic portrayals of feminine evil in the guises of the invalid, vamp, or vampire. Novelists like Mirbeau were fixated on the notion of the sadistic woman. Though the sexologists regarded sadism as primarily a male perversion, they dutifully noted that cruel, "masculine" women like Salome, Messalina, and Catherine de Médici warranted the titles of illustrious female sadists. Dr. Erich Wulffen, a German expert in legal medicine, labeled as sadistic such French women as Rose Lacomb, Théroigne de Méricourt, and Louise Michel, who by participating in radical politics had violated gender boundaries. *Woman as Sexual Criminal* (New York: Ethnological Press, 1934), 287. For a popular novel that ends happily with a simple peasant's mother delivering her son from his sadistic wife by murdering her, see Jean Richepin, *La Glu* (Paris: Tallandier, 1927).

81. E. Gley, "Les Aberations de l'instinct sexuel," *Revue philosophique* 17 (1884): 66–92.

82. Stefanowsky made the point that Krafft-Ebing had been heartless in coining masochism, a term that had no intrinsic meaning and covered both Sacher-Masoch and his children in shame. Indeed, years later the latter, in asking Lou Salome for letters of reference, claimed to be still suffering from their father's notoriety. Dimitry Stefanowsky, "Le Passivism," *Archives de l'anthropologie criminelle* 7 (1892): 294–98.

83. Émile Laurent, *Sadisme et masochisme* (Paris: Vigot frères, 1903).

84. Paul, *Le Vice,* 169.

85. Auguste Comte, *System of Positive Polity* (London: Longmans, Green, 1877), 4:100.

86. Paul, *Le Vice,* 146.

87. E. Anthony Rotundo, *American Manhood: Transformations from the Revolution to the Modern Era* (New York: Basic, 1993), 269.

88. On the ways in which the "sex fiend" motif is played up and "normal" male sexual assaults played down by the newspaper press in the twentieth century, see Keith Soothill and Sylvia Walby, *Sex Crimes in the News* (London: Routledge, 1991); Helen Benedict, *Virgin or Vamp: How the Press Covers Sex Crimes* (New York: Oxford University Press, 1992).

89. Krafft-Ebing, *Psychopathia Sexualis,* 54.

90. Ibid., 56.

91. Paul, *Le Vice;* for the argument that "morbid love" was usually related to anatomical anomalies, see Féré, *Pathologie,* 434.

92. Binet, "Fétichisme," 266.

93. Lacassagne followed MacDonald in stressing the notion that the sexual impulse was the strongest drive we have.

94. Paul-Émile Littré, *Dictionnaire de la langue française* (Paris: Hachette, 1878), makes no mention of féminisme. *Le Grand Robert de la langue française* (Paris: Le Robert, 1985) notes féminisme was used by Fourier (1837) and employed in a medical sense by 1877 and in a political sense by 1904. Proust, for example, spoke of the "psychological feminism" of Charlus in *Le temps retrouvé* (Paris: Gallimard, 1954), 3:991. For the strictly political uses of the term, see Karen Offen, "Sur les origines des mots 'féminisme' et 'feministe,'" *Revue d'histoire moderne et contemporaine* 34 (July–September 1987): 492–96. For Sir Richard Burton's use of the term "male *feminism*" to refer to homosexuality, see Elaine Showalter, *Sexual Anarchy: Gender and Culture at the Fin-de-Siècle* (Penguin: Harmondsworth, 1990), 82.

95. Pierre Garnier, *Anomalies sexuelles: Apparentes et cachées* (Paris: Garnier, 1889), 371; Féré, *Pathologie,* 495; and see also Jules Dallemagne, *Théories de la criminalité* (Paris: Masson, 1896), 175.

96. Lacassagne, *Vacher,* 288.

97. Fourquet, *Vacher,* 80; and see also 242.

98. *Le Figaro,* 27 Oct. 1898, 3–4.

99. Fourquet, *Vacher,* 323.

100. Lacassagne, *Vacher,* 33. In the 1890s a number of doctors, accepting the idea of innate homosexual instincts that the individual could not repress, came to view homosexuality as pathological rather than criminal in nature, yet contradicted themselves in continuing to speak about "cures." Émile Laurent, *L'Amour morbide* (Paris: Société d'éditions scientifiques, 1891), 275–76; Antoney Copley, *Sexual Moralities in France, 1780–1980* (London: Routledge, 1989), 135–54; Gert Hekma, "A Female Soul in a Male Body: Sexual Inversion as Gender Inversion in Nineteenth-century Sexology," in *Third Sex, Third Gender: Beyond Sexual Dimorphism in Culture and History,* ed. Gilbert Herdt (New York: Zone, 1994), 213–40.

101. The campaign in Germany against Article 175, which criminalized homosexuality, led to more open discussions of same-sex relationships east of the Rhine, but on the French debate, see André Raffalovich, "Unisexualité anglaise," *Archives de l'anthropologie criminelle* 11 (1896): 431; Raffalovich's exchange with Dr. Laupts, *Archives de l'anthropologie criminelle* 24 (1909): 353, 693–96; Paul-Louis Ladame, "Les travaux recents des auteurs allemands sur l'homosexualité," *Archives de l'anthropologie criminelle* 28 (1913): 827–61; Ladame, "Homosexualité originaire et homosexualité acquise," *Archives de l'anthropologie criminelle* 29 (1914): 262–86; and see also, Patrick Cardon, "A Homosexual Militant at the Beginning of the Century: Marc André Raffalovich," *Journal of Homosexuality* 25 (1993): 83–92;

Claude Courouve, "L'Uranisme entre la France et l'Angleterre," in *André Gide et l'Angleterre,* ed. Patrick Collard (London: Birkbeck College, 1986), 100–103; Courouve, *Vocabulaire de l'homosexualité masculine* (Paris: Payot, 1985).

102. Alexandre Lacassagne, "Péderastie," *Dictionnaire encyclopédique des sciences médicales,* 2d series (Paris: Masson and Asselin, 1886), 22:239–59. Lacassagne approvingly cited the work of his colleague Julian Chevalier, *Sur l'inversion de l'instinct sexuel au point de vue médico-légal* (Lyon: Storck, 1893); see also Julian Chevalier, "De l'inversion sexuelle aux points de vue clinique, anthropologique et médico-légal," *Archives de l'anthropologie criminelle* 5 (1890): 314–36; 6 (1891): 500–519.

103. Benjamin Ball, *La Folie érotique* (Paris: Baillière, 1888), 116, 147; Henri Joly, *Le Crime: Étude sociale* (Paris: Cerf, 1888), 124–25. Among writers of fiction, the first to broach the subject of homosexuality were decadents like Huysmans and Lorrain, who were drawn to sadism.

104. Uzanne in Duehren, *De Sade,* xv; Moll noted homosexual cases of sadism as did Ulrichs, who in *Incube* (1896) spoke of lovers' bites and scratches.

105. In England perhaps the earliest discussion of sadism was included in the anonymously authored 1897 obituary of police surgeon George Bagster Phillips, who had conducted necropsies on the victims of Jack the Ripper. The author described the sadist as an individual who aside from his murderous desires might be otherwise sane. Such individuals sprang from "neurotic stock" and had cranial defects; symptoms of insanity, hysteria, and other neuropathic conditions would be found in their families. Young people prone to cruelty to animals (to which the English were predictably more sensitive than the French) would have to be carefully watched. If as adults sadistic attacks were launched, the same horrific acts would be repeated until capture. *Lancet* 2 (1897): 1263.

106. Ellis described de Sade's gait, skull, and temperament as "feminine" and noted that aside from his whipping of Rosa Keller his actual offenses had been fairly mild. Ellis, *Studies,* vol. 1, part 2, p. 106.

107. Ibid., vol. 1, part 2, p. 109.

108. Ibid., vol. 1, part 2, p. 110.

109. G. Frank Lydston, *The Diseases of Society: The Vice and Crime Problem* (Philadelphia: J. B. Lippincott, 1904), 309.

110. Arthur MacDonald, *Hearing on the Bill (H.R. 14798) to Establish a Laboratory for the Study of the Criminal, Pauper and Defective Classes* (Washington, D.C.: Government Printing Office, 1902), 18–30.

111. Stekel labeled as "medical sadism" doctors' use of the "Paquelin cautery" (employed like a red hot poker to deal with hysteria), the extortion from patients of admissions of health by patriotic medical officers during the war, and psychoanalysis' own inquisition-like practices. Wilhelm Stekel, *Sadism and Masochism: The Psychology of Hatred and Cruelty,* trans. Louise Brink (New York: Liverwright, 1929), 453 n4. See also Marie Bonaparte's statement, "Lorsque parait sur la scene un de ces rares grands pervers, tel Vacher ou Kurten, qui tuent pour le simple plaisir, l'âme entière de la foule est soulevée. Non pas par l'horreur seule, mais par un étrange intérêt, qui est la réponse de notre profound sadisme au leur."

112. Stekel, *Sadism and Masochism,* 40. Freud also followed Ellis in noting that sadists were simultaneously masochists. A. A. Brill, ed., *The Basic Writings of Sigmund Freud* (New York: Modern Library, 1938), 569–71.

113. Stekel noted that for some sadism was equated to heightened masculinity and masochism to heightened femininity, but he stressed that both sexes could manifest such syndromes.

114. Stekel, *Sadism and Masochism,* 60, 146. Many conservatives attacked decadent literature and tabloid journalism for acting as a "school for sadism." Stekel noted that his patients who confessed to harboring sadistic desires were as children more likely to have been

influenced by fairy tale accounts of wolves and witches, parents' assertions that they would "eat them up," and fears of being whipped by their teachers. Ibid., 416, 425.

115. Ibid., 73, 76, 77.

116. Ibid., 154.

117. J. K. Huysmans provocatively defended abortion as consisting of "destroying an animal, less fully formed, less alive and certainly less intelligent and more ugly than a dog or a cat, which may be strangled at birth without penalty." *Against the Grain,* 279.

118. For claims that science was replacing religion, see Joanne Roux, *Psychologie de l'instinct sexuel* (Paris: Baillière, 1899).

119. Étienne Martin, "Vacher devant la cour d'assises de l'Ain," in Lacassagne, *Vacher,* 67.

120. Tarde, "Les transformations de l'impunité," in Lacassagne, *Vacher,* 167–84; and on suggestion, see also Sighele, *Littérature;* Dr. Haury, "Les faux témoins pathologiques," *Archives de l'anthropologie criminelle* 27 (1912): 637–53.

121. For the argument that the rise of "ripper" style killings was also due to imitation, see M.J.F.A. de St. Vincent de Paroism, *Du dépecage criminel* (Lyon: Storck, 1902).

122. Gabriel Tarde, "L'Amour morbide," *L'Archives de l'anthropologie criminelle* 5 (1890); Gabriel Tarde, *Penal Philosophy* (Boston: Little Brown, 1912), 256; and see also Tarde, *The Laws of Imitation* (New York: Henry Holt, 1903); Arsène Dumont, *Dépopulation et civilisation: Étude démographique,* ed. André Béjin (Paris: Economica, 1990), 402–10; Susannah Barrows, *Distorting Mirrors: Visions of the Crowd in Late Nineteenth-century France* (New Haven: Yale University Press, 1981), 137–45.

123. Annelise Mauge, *L'Identité masculine en crise au tournant du siècle, 1871–1914* (Paris: Rivages, 1987); Michelle Perrot, "The New Eve and the Old Adam; Changes in French Women's Condition at the Turn of the Century," in *Behind the Lines: Gender and the Two World Wars,* ed. M. R. Higonnet et al. (New Haven: Yale University Press, 1987), 51–60.

124. Émile Laurent, *Le Criminel aux points de vue anthropologique, psychologique et sociale* (Paris: Vigot, 1908), 2: 208–9.

CHAPTER 8: EXHIBITIONISTS

1. Dr. Hôpital, "Quelque mots sur les exhibitionistes," *Annales médico-psychologiques* 21 (1905): 220–28.

2. Richard von Krafft-Ebing, *Psychopathia Sexualis* (New York: Stein and Day, 1965), 341–42.

3. Cited in Havelock Ellis, *Studies in the Psychology of Sex* (New York: Random House, 1936), 3:89–104.

4. W. Norwood East, "Observations on Exhibitionism," *Lancet* 2 (1924): 370–75.

5. Hôpital, "Quelque mots sur les exhibitionistes," 222.

6. Georges Lantéri-Laura, *Lecture des perversions: Histoire de leur appropriation médicale* (Paris: Masson, 1979), 43.

7. Kinsey reported that almost all twentieth-century American children were exhibitionistic; boys' exhibitionism, which continued into late adolescence, often included demonstrations of masturbation. Exhibitionists ran a high chance of being caught since they performed their acts in public and before strangers. In the 1950s one-quarter to one-third of all sexual offenders in the United States and the United Kingdom were charged with exhibitionism. Paul H. Gebhard, John H. Gagnon, Wardell B. Pomeroy, and Cornelia V. Christenson, *Sex Offenders: An Analysis of Types* (New York: Harper and Row, 1965.) Ismond Rosen, "Exhibitionism, Scopophilia, and Voyeurism" in *Sexual Deviation,* ed. Ismond Rosen (Oxford: Oxford University Press, 1979), 139–94. Alfred C. Kinsey, Wardell B. Pomeroy, and Clyde E. Martin, *Sexual Behavior in the Human Male* (Philadelphia: W. B. Saunders, 1948), 169.

8. Michel Foucault, *The History of Sexuality,* trans. Robert Hurley (New York: Vintage,

1980), vol. 1; and see also Bryan S. Turner, *The Body and Society: Explorations in Social Theory* (Oxford: Basil Blackwell, 1984).

9. Joan Scott, *Gender and the Politics of History* (New York: Columbia University Press, 1988), 45.

10. France Borel, *Le Vêtement incarné* (Paris: Calmann-Levy, 1992).

11. Roger Goodland, ed., *A Bibliography of Sex Rites and Customs* (London: Routledge, 1931); Margaret Mead, *Male and Female: A Study of the Sexes in a Changing World* (New York: Morrow, 1949), 156–57; Daniel Rancour-Laferrière, *Signs of the Flesh: An Essay on the Evolution of Hominid Sexuality* (New York: Mouton de Gruyter, 1985), 299–300.

12. Eva C. Keuls, *The Reign of the Phallus* (New York: Harper and Row, 1985).

13. K. J. Dover, *Greek Homosexuality* (London: Duckworth, 1978), 125–35.

14. Leviticus 18:7–18.

15. Margaret Miles, *Carnal Knowing: Female Nakedness and Religious Meaning in the Christian West* (Boston: Beacon Press, 1989); Robin Lane Fox, *Pagans and Christians* (New York: Knopf, 1987).

16. Leo Steinberg, *The Sexuality of Christ in Renaissance Art and in Modern Oblivion* (New York: Pantheon, 1983).

17. Frank Bottomley, *Attitudes to the Body in Western Christendom* (London: Lepus, 1979).

18. The popular account of the ride held that the Earl of Mercia dared his wife that if she rode naked through the market place he would reduce his subject's taxes. Covering herself with her long tresses and accompanied by two soldiers she took up the challenge. In later seventeenth-century accounts, the soldiers disappeared and "Peeping Tom"—who looked at Godiva and was struck blind—emerged. *Encyclopedia Britannica* (1972), 10:515–16.

19. Guido Ruggiero, *The Boundaries of Eros: Sex Crime and Sexuality in Renaissance Venice* (New York: Oxford University Press, 1985), 141.

20. In the twentieth century, the Russian Doukhobors living in western Canada were led by the logic of spiritualism to employ nude marches in their struggles against the government. George Woodcock and Ivan Avakumovic, *The Doukhobors* (New York: Oxford University Press, 1968). See also Shirley Ardener, "Nudity, Vulgarity and Protest," *New Society* 27, no. 598 (1974): 704–5, and "Arson, Nudity and Bombs among the Canadian Doukhobors: A Question of Identity," in *Threatened Identities*, ed. Glynnis M. Breakwell (New York: Wiley, 1983), 239–66.

21. Erik H. Erikson, *Young Man Luther: A Study in Psychoanalysis and History* (London: Faber, 1958), 238–40.

22. Mikhail Bakhtin, *Rabelais and His World* (Cambridge: MIT Press, 1968), 373; and on pictorial representations of the wearing of breeches being equated with authority, see David Kunzle, *The Early Comic Strip*, vol. 1 of *History of the Comic Book* (Berkeley: University of California Press, 1973), 224–26, 236–40. For a cartoon portraying a group of artists stripping an old lecher as punishment for harassing a pretty woman, see *Gil blas*, 15 Nov. 1891, 4.

23. Ellis, *Psychology of Sex*, 3:100, cites Kleinpaul, *Sprache ohne worte*, 271–73.

24. Roger McGraw. "Popular Anticlericalism in Nineteenth-century Rural France," in *Disciplines of Faith: Studies in Religion, Politics and Patriarchy*, ed. J. Obelkevich, L. Roper, and R. Samuels (London: Routledge and Kegan Paul, 1987), 169.

25. Iain McCalman, *Radical Underworld: Prophets, Revolutionaries, and Pornographers in London, 1795–1840* (Oxford: Clarendon Press, 1993), 204–10; Vivian Cameron, "Political Exposures: Sexuality and Caricature in the French Revolution," in *Eroticism and the Body Politic*, ed. Lynn Hunt (Baltimore: Johns Hopkins University Press, 1991), 90–108; Joan B. Landes, "Representing the Body Politic: The Paradox of Gender in the Graphic Politics of the French Revolution," in *Rebel Daughters: Women and the French Revolution*, ed. Sara E. Melzer and Leslie W. Rabine (New York: Oxford University Press, 1992), 15–37; Robert

Justin Goldstein, "Censorship of Caricature in France, 1815–1914," *French History* (1993): 71–108.

26. Jean Claude Bologne, *Histoire de la pudeur* (Paris: Olivier Orban, 1986), 64.

27. Michel de Montaigne, "On Some Verses by Virgil," *The Complete Essays* (London: Bell, 1913), 3: 82.

28. Ruggiero, *Boundaries of Eros,* 114–15.

29. Paul Hair, *Before the Bawdy Courts* (London: Elek, 1972), 83; G. R. Quaife, *Wanton Wenches and Wayward Wives: Peasants and Illicit Sex in Early 17th Century England* (London: Croom Helm, 1979), 73.

30. Cited in John Gillis, *For Better, for Worse: British Marriages, 1600 to the Present* (New York: Oxford University Press, 1985), 126; but see 122 for evidence that such exposure was also used to humiliate a woman.

31. Angelo Hesnard, *Traité de sexologie normale et pathologique* (Paris: Payot, 1933), 611–12.

32. Pierre Darmon, *Trial by Impotence: Virility and Marriage in pre-Revolutionary France,* trans. Paul Keegan (London: Hogarth Press, 1985); Ruggiero, *Boundaries of Eros,* 146–47.

33. On the continued employment in contemporary Europe of genital gestures such as the "bras d'honneur" or forearm jerk as sexual insults, see Desmond Morris et al., *Gestures: Their Origin and Distribution* (London: Cape, 1979).

34. Jean-Jacques Rousseau, *Les Confessions* in *Oeuvres complètes* (Paris: Gallimard, 1959), 3:88–9.

35. For the argument that Elias, in failing to note the restraints of the classical world and the relaxed codes of the twentieth century, exaggerates the notion of an unlinear shift toward decorum, see Jan Bremmer and H. Roodenberg, eds., *A Cultural History of Gesture: From Antiquity to the Present Day* (Oxford: Polity Press, 1991).

36. Erasmus, *De Civiltae morum puerilium,* 1530 ed., cited in Norbert Elias, *The Civilizing Process: The History of Manners,* trans. Edmund Jephcott (New York: Urizen Books, 1978), 130.

37. Philippe Ariès, *Centuries of Childhood: A Social History of Family Life* (New York: Vintage Books, 1962), 109.

38. Elias, *Civilizing Process,* 131–32.

39. Ibid., 138.

40. Alfred Franklin, *La Civilité* (Paris: Émile Paul, 1908), 1:49; J. Frykman and O. Lofgren, *The Culture Builders: A Historical Anthropology of Middle-class Life* (New Brunswick, N.J.: Rutgers University Press, 1987).

41. Darmon, *Trial by Impotence,* 215; and see also Irving C. Rosse, "Sexual Incapacity in its Medico-Legal Relations," in *Medical Jurisprudence: Forensic Medicine and Toxocology,* ed. R. A. Witthaus and Tracy C. Becker (New York: William Wood, 1894), 2:393.

42. For a reference from *The People* of 26 July 1936 to a club of nightshirt wearers led by Dr. Davis of Ottawa, who opposed male pajamas as being effeminate while others attacked them as too masculine for women to wear, see Elias, *Civilizing Process,* 301 n80.

43. Octave Uzanne, *Sottisier des moeurs* (Paris: Paul, 1911), 32; Jennifer Craik, *The Face of Fashion: Cultural Studies in Fashion* (London: Routledge, 1994), 176–203; J. Finkelstein, *The Fashioned Self* (London: Polity, 1991); Richard Sennett, *The Fall of Public Man* (Cambridge: Cambridge University Press, 1974), 161, 163; Leonore Davidoff and Catherine Hall, *Family Fortunes: Men and Women of the English Middle Class, 1780–1850* (London: Hutchinson, 1987), 410–13; John Harvey, *Men in Black* (Chicago: University of Chicago Press, 1995).

44. Ellen Moers, *The Dandy: Brummell to Beerbohm* (London: Secker and Warburg, 1960); Françoise Coblence, *Le Dandysme, obligation d'incertitude* (Paris: Presses universitaires de France, 1988); Gilles Lipovetsky, *L'Empire de l'ephémère* (Paris: Gallimard, 1987);

Anne Martin-Fugier, *La Vie élégante ou la formation du Tout-Paris, 1815–1848* (Paris: Fayard, 1990); Mark M. Anderson, *Kafka's Clothes: Ornament and Aestheticism in the Hasburg Fin de Siècle* (Oxford: Clarendon Press, 1992).

45. Peter Gay, Education of the Senses, vol. 1 of *The Bourgeois Experience: Victoria to Freud* (New York: Oxford University Press, 1984), 338–39, 379–98; Edward Lucie-Smith, *The Male Nude: A Modern View* (London: Rizzoli, 1985); Tamar Garb, "The Forbidden Gaze: Women Artists and the Male Nude in Later Nineteenth-century France," in *The Body Imaged: The Human Form and Visual Culture since the Renaissance*, ed. Kathleen Adler and Marcia Pointon (Cambridge: Cambridge University Press, 1993); Joseph A. Kestner, *Masculinities in Victorian Painting* (Aldershot: Scolar Press, 1995). But on the male nude in fin-de-siècle northern Europe as the representation of the true ideals of both athletic and aesthetic beauty, see Patricia G. Berman, "Body and Body Politics in Edward Munsch's *Bathing Men*," in *Body Imaged*, ed. Adler and Pointon; George L. Mosse, *Nationalism and Sexuality: Middle-class Morality and Sexual Norms in Modern Europe* (Madison: University of Wisconsin Press, 1985), 50–57; Bram Dijkstra, *Idols of Perversity: Fantasies of Feminine Evil in Fin-de-Siècle Culture* (New York: Oxford University Press, 1986), 198–202.

46. Le Roy versus Sir Charles Sedley (1663) in 1 Sis 168 [*The English Reports: King's Bench Division*, 82:1036–37.]

47. Robert Latham and William Matthews, eds., *The Diary of Samuel Pepys* (London: Bell, 1971), 6:208–10.

48. V. de Sola Pinto, *Sir Charles Sedley, 1639–1701* (London: Constable, 1927), 60–64.

49. Henry Fielding, "A Charge to the Grand Jury," in *The Complete Works of Henry Fielding* (London: Heinemann, 1903), 13:211–12.

50. Lynn Hunt, ed., *The Invention of Pornography: Obscenity and the Origins of Modernity, 1500–1800* (New York: Zone Books, 1993).

51. Rex versus Crunden (1809) 2 Camp. 89.

52. 12 Cox's Criminal Cases 1. But young men and boys continued to swim naked in London parks in the late nineteenth century and a nude bathing place for men in Oxford called Parson's Pleasure was only closed in the 1990s. See J. J. Sexby, *The Municipal Parks, Gardens and Open Spaces of London* (London: Stock, 1898), 555; Leonora Collins, *London in the 1890s* (London: Saturn Press, 1950), 29. On the policing of swimming in the Seine, see J. P. Aron and R. Kempf, *La Bourgeoisie: Le Sexe et l'honneur* (Paris: Grasset, 1978).

53. 5 Geo. IV c.83: Vagrancy Act of 1824. Canada's Vagrancy Act of 1869 was based on the United Kingdom's 1822 act, not the 1824 act, which led to confusion inasmuch as it did not make clear what an "indecent act" was. It was finally amended in 1892. The Doukhobors were prosecuted under section 205 (a) which prohibited nude parades. Alexander K. Gigeroff, *Sexual Deviation in the Criminal Law* (Toronto: University of Toronto Press, 1968), 51–55.

54. 10 & 11 Vict. c.89, s.28; and see also Jeffrey S. Adler, "A Historical Analysis of the Laws of Vagrancy," *Criminology* 27 (1989): 209–29; M. J. D. Roberts, "Public and Private in Early Nineteenth-Century London: The Vagrant Act of 1822 and Its Enforcement," *Social History* 13 (1988): 273–94.

55. Regina versus the Justices of the Town and County Newcastle-upon-Tyne, in 1 B. & AD. 933 [English Reports, vol. 109, Kings Bench Division].

56. Regina versus Watson (1847), 2 Cox's Criminal Cases 376.

57. Regina versus Webb (1848), 3 Cox's Criminal Cases 183.

58. Regina versus George Thallman (1863), 9 Cox's Criminal Cases 388.

59. Regina versus Wellard (1884) 14 Q.B.D. 63.

60. Regina versus Michael Rowed and Another, 3 Q.B.D. 180.

61. 3 Cox's Criminal Cases 248; and see also 2 Cox's Criminal Cases 376 in which the Queen's Bench heard the case on 3 Dec. 1847 of John Watson, who had been indicted for exposing himself to a twelve-year-old girl in Paddington Churchyard, "to the great injury and corruption of the said Lydia Crickmore." The objection was raised that since only one person

was present it was in law no offense. The bench agreed that "a nuisance must be public," otherwise every man exposing himself to a woman would be indictable, and quashed the indictment.

62. Law Reports: Crown Cases Reserved, 1 (1872): 282–4.

63. Alfred Swain Taylor, *The Principles and Practices of Medical Jurisprudence* (London: J. A. Churchill, 1905), 2:367.

64. East, "Observations on Exhibitionism," 374.

65. David S. Booth, "Erotomania: A Case of Exhibitionism—A Medico-Legal Study," *Alienist and Neurologist* 26 (1905): 1–4. The term exhibitionist, according to the *Oxford English Dictionary,* was first employed in England to refer to the man who assisted the Anglican priest during church rituals. The term's modern psychiatric usage was made known to the English by C. G. Haddock's 1893 translation of Krafft-Ebing.

66. Paul Garnier, "Rapport médico-légal sur un exhibitioniste," *Annales médico-psychologiques* 19 (1894): 97–103.

67. A. Rousset, "Un Cas d'exhibitionisme," *Annales Médical-Psychologiques* 3 (1906): 394–401.

68. A. Vigoroux, "Un Exhibitioniste condamné par les tribunaux," *Annales médico-psychologiques* 3 (1896): 213–16.

69. But Tronchon warned that every man who exposed himself could not be simply let off as just "sick." A. Trochon, "Un Cas d'exhibitionisme," *Archives de l'anthropologie criminelle* 3 (1888): 256–64.

70. Garnier cited in Booth, "Erotomania," 2.

71. Charles Lasègue, "Les Exhibitionistes," *L'Union Médical* 3e serie, 23 (May 1877): 709; and on Lasègue's work on "l'anoréxie hysterique," see Joan Jacobs Brumberg, *Fasting Girls: The Emergence of Anorexia Nervosa as a Modern Disease* (Cambridge: Harvard University Press, 1988), 127–30.

72. Ambroise Tardieu, *Étude médico-légale sur les attentats aux moeurs* (Paris: Baillière, 1878), 5; "Exhibitionistes," *Dictionnaire des sciences médicales* (Paris: Lahure, 1887), 36: 427–29; Alfred Binet, "Le Fétishisme dans l'amour," *Revue philosophique* 24 (1887): 256.

73. Valentin Magnan, "Les Exhibitionistes," *Archives de l'anthropologie criminelle* 5 (1890): 436.

74. The author of the *Dictionnaire des sciences médicales* article on the subject also labeled as exhibitionists men who stalked their loved one and thus "exhibited" themselves.

75. Krafft-Ebing, *Psychopathia Sexualis,* 338–41.

76. On epileptics, who were often played up in the nineteenth century as exhibitionists and vagabonds, see Cesare Lombroso, *L'Homme criminel* (Paris: Alcan, 1895), 2:96–97. In the twentieth century, Ellis stated that epileptics should be excluded, and East found no cases of epilepsy in his sample. East did believe alcoholism played a role: in 1913 in England and Wales 866 men were convicted of indecent exposure, but in twelve months of 1922–23, after restrictions on sale of drinks were imposed, only 548. East, "Observations on Exhibitionism," 374.

77. Moll (as cited in Ellis, *Psychology of Sex,* 3: 90) even argued that if one masturbated during the act one was not a true exhibitionist.

78. For the assertion that most of the "attentats à la pudeur" were carried out by old men on children because bad stomachs needed "green fruit," see Émile Laurent, *L'Amour morbide* (Paris: Société d'éditions scientifiques, 1891), 195.

79. Paul Moreau (de Tours), *Des Aberrations du sens génésiques* (Paris: Asselin, 1880), 61–2.

80. Binet, "Le Fétishisme dans l'amour," 256.

81. Paul Garnier, "Des Perversions sexuelles obsédantes et impulsives," *Archives de l'anthropologie criminelle* 15 (1900): 612.

82. Dr. Hamblin Smith of Birmingham Prison classed about half of the exhibitionists he saw as insane, senile, or defective. See Smith, "The Mental Conditions Found in Certain Sexual Offenders," *Lancet* 1 (29 Mar. 1924), 643–46, and see also W. Norwood East, *An Introduction to Forensic Psychiatry in the Criminal Courts* (London: Churchill, 1927), 308.

83. East was medical inspector of Her Majesty's Prisons in England and Wales and had been senior medical officer of Brixton Prison. His paper was based on 150 cases received on remand at Brixton Prison. He assumed that since most had not been convicted before, prison terms did serve as a deterrent. See East, "Observations on Exhibitionism," 372.

84. Dr. Serge Paul, *Le Vice et l'amour* (Paris: Nouvelle librairie médicale, 1905), 257, 267.

85. Ibid., 262.

86. Krafft-Ebing, *Psychopathia Sexualis*, 344–46.

87. Ellis, *Psychology of Sex*, 3:92.

88. Garnier, "Des Perversions sexuelles obsédantes et impulsives," 604–43. See also Émile Laurent, *Fétichistes et érotomanes* (Paris: Vigot frères, 1903), 253.

89. For the interesting question of why the satisfaction of some vices was viewed as a sickness, see Hôpital, "Quelque mots sur les exhibitionistes."

90. Ellis, *Psychology of Sex*, 3:93.

91. Paul Garnier, "Rapport médico-légal sur un exhibitioniste," *Annales médico-psychologiques* 19 (1894): 97–103.

92. Edward James, *Swans Reflecting Elephants: My Early Years*, ed. George Melly, (London: Weidenfeld and Nicolson, 1982), 26; Ronald Hyam, *Empire and Sexuality: The British Experience* (Manchester: Manchester University Press), 27.

93. Even some doctors were accused of exhibitionism, though the only physician found to have been actually convicted of the offense in France prior to World War I was an Armenian; see Georges Vernet, "Un Médecin satyre," *Annales médico-psychologique* 1 (1912): 554–70.

94. Laugier's assertion from the *Annales de hygiène et de médecine* (1878) is cited in L. Thoinot and A. W. Weysse, *Medicolegal Aspects of Moral Offenses* (Philadelphia: F. A. Davis, 1911), 266.

95. Hôpital, "Quelque mots sur les exhibitionistes," 220–28.

96. Benjamin Ball, *La Folie érotique* (Paris: Baillière, 1888), 82–4.

97. Ellis, *Psychology of Sex*, 3:89–104.

98. C. H. Hughes, "Morbid Exhibitionism," *The Alienist and Neurologist* 25 (1904): 348–50.

99. Charles Lasègue, "Les exhibitionistes," in *Ecrits psychiatriques*, ed. J. Corraze (Paris: Privat, 1971), 118; and see also Michael Miller, *The Bon Marché* (Princeton: Princeton University Press, 1981), 197–201.

100. East, "Observations on Exhibitionism," 373.

101. Ibid.

102. Krafft-Ebing, *Psychopathia Sexualis*, 339.

103. George Jacoby, *The Unsound Mind and the Law* (New York: Funk and Wagnalls, 1918), 341.

104. Cited by East, "Observations on Exhibitionism," 375.

105. Paolo Mantegazza, *The Sexual Relations of Mankind* (1885; New York: Eugenics, 1935); Iwan Bloch, *The Sexual Life of Our Time* (New York: Allied, 1930).

106. Hôpital, "Quelque mots sur les exhibitionistes," 222.

107. Ellis, *Psychology of Sex*, 3:93–94.

108. Sir W. Norwood East, *Society and the Criminal* (Springfield, Ill.: Charles C. Thomas, 1949), 154.

109. Sigmund Freud, "On the Universal Tendency to Debasement in the Sphere of Love" (1912), *Standard Edition*, 11:189.

110. Sigmund Freud, "Three Essays on the Theory of Sexuality" (1905), Ibid., 7: 147.

111. Gregorio Marañón, *Don Juan et donjuanisme*, trans. M.-B. Lacombe (Paris: Gallimard, 1958), 183.

112. Benjamin Karpman, *The Sexual Offender and His Offenses* (New York: Julian Press, 1954), 199.

113. Rosen, "Exhibitionism, Scopophilia, and Voyeurism," 148.

114. Lars Ullerstam, *The Erotic Minorities,* trans. Anselm Hollo (New York: Grove Press, 1966), 60.

115. We know of this case thanks to H. Bonnet and J. Bulard, *Rapport médico-légal sur l'état mental de Ch. J. Jouy,* 4 Jan. 1868.

116. Foucault, *History of Sexuality,* 1:31.

117. Marcel Mauss, "Body Techniques" *Sociology and Psychology* (1950; London: Routledge and Kegan Paul, 1979), 95–123.

118. Exhibitionism was first discovered in Europe and North America. At the turn of the century, Bloch argued that perversions spread as a reaction to the constraints placed on the sexuality of civilized man by the forces of social coercion and sexual conventionality. Barrington Moore Jr. states that in "primitive" societies, where the boundaries between the private and the public are not firm, discretion is employed to prevent noticing that which should not be seen. See Bloch, *Sexual Life of Our Time,* 472; Barrington Moore Jr., *Privacy: Studies in Social and Cultural History* (London: M. E. Sharpe, 1984), 78; Graham Rooth, "Exhibitionism outside Europe and North America," *Archives of Sexual Behavior* 2 (1973): 351–63.

119. John M. MacDonald, *Indecent Exposure* (Springfield, Ill.: Charles C. Thomas, 1973), 43.

120. Karpman, *The Sexual Offender and His Offenses.*

121. Erich Wulffen, *Woman as Sexual Criminal* (New York: American Ethnological Press, 1934), 363.

122. Taylor, *Principles and Practices of Medical Jurisprudence,* 2:367.

123. Laurent, *Fétichistes et érotomanes,* 249.

124. Hôpital, "Quelque mots sur les exhibitionistes," 224.

125. Garnier, "Rapport médico-légal sur un exhibitioniste," 100.

126. J. C. Flugel, *The Psychology of Clothes* (London: Hogarth Press, 1930), 107–10.

127. Samuel D. Schmalhausen, "The Sexual Revolution" in V. F. Calverton and S. D. Schmalhausen, eds., *Sex in Civilization* (New York: Garden City, 1931), 433.

128. Paul, *Le Vice et l'amour,* 268.

129. Hughes, "Morbid Exhibitionism," 350.

130. See also Gregorio Marañón, *Psychologie du geste, du vêtement et de la parure,* trans. Roland Lauras (Paris: La Pensée universelle, 1971).

131. *Code intime* (Paris: Editions and Librairie, n.d), 17; and for protests against the 1882 law that in France treated writers and artists as if they were exhibitionists, see Lionel Autrec, *L'Outrage aux moeurs* (Paris: Cupidon, 1923).

132. Philippe Perrot, *Le Travail des appearances: Le Corps feminin, XVIII–XIXe siècle* (Paris: Seuil, 1984), 162.

133. For an analysis of how Cameroon women defend the dignity of their sex by flaunting that which is insulted, see Shirley Ardener, "A Note on Gender Iconography: the Vagina," in *The Cultural Construction of Sexuality,* ed. Pat Caplan (London: Tavistock, 1987), 113–42.

Chapter 9: Transvestites

1. Annie Woodhouse, *Fantastic Women: Sex, Gender and Transvestism* (New Brunswick, N.J.: Rutgers University Press, 1989).

2. Julia Epstein and Kristina Straub, eds., *Body Guards: The Cultural Politics of Gender Ambiguity* (New York: Routledge and Kegan Paul, 1991), 4.

3. W. Norwood East, "Observations on Exhibitionism," *Lancet* 2 (1924): 375.

4. *St. Helens Newspaper and Advertiser*, 20 Nov. 1931, 4.

5. Ibid.

6. Such cases are unusual but continue to be reported. For the trial of a Utah man who in the 1990s posed as a woman during a three-and-a-half-year marriage, see *Vancouver Sun*, 7 Sept. 1995, A20; and for an English woman who passed as a man over the space of a seventeen-year marriage, see *Manchester Guardian*, 10 Feb. 1996.

7. *Manchester Guardian*, 16 Nov. 1931, 11.

8. *Illustrated Police News*, 19 Nov. 1931, 3.

9. *St. Helens Newspaper and Advertiser*, 20 Nov. 1931, 4.

10. *Liverpool Echo*, 14 Nov. 1931, 6.

11. Mrs. Hull, according to press reports, was the mother of six children and expecting a seventh. *Week-End Review*, 19 Dec. 1931, 794.

12. *Glasgow Herald*, 16 Nov. 1931, 13.

13. Hull attended school until the age of fourteen and then obtained work as a haulage hand at the local collieries. From about age sixteen, he began to change from his work clothes into female attire for which behavior he received cautions from the St. Helens police and thrashings from his parents.

14. *St. Helens Newspaper and Advertiser*, 20 Nov. 1931, 5.

15. Ibid.

16. *Liverpool Post and Mercury*, 16 Nov. 1931, 9.

17. *St. Helens Newspaper and Advertiser*, 20 Nov. 1931, 4.

18. *Illustrated Police News*, 19 Nov. 1931, 3. Hull's father, apparently shaken by the trial, was taken to a mental hospital and his wife and children forced on relief. *Week-End Review*, 19 Dec. 1931, 794.

19. *Week-End Review*, 5 Dec. 1931, 712.

20. Ibid., 787, 794–95; Havelock Ellis, *Views and Reviews: A Selection of Uncollected Articles, 1884–1932* (London: Desmond Harmsworth, 1932), 2:220.

21. *Glasgow Herald*, 16 Nov. 1931, 13.

22. On evidence that many boys use Halloween parties to experiment with cross-dressing, see John T. Talamini, *Boys Will Be Girls: The Hidden World of the Heterosexual Male Transvestite* (Scranton, Pa.: University of Scranton Press, 1982), 20; Peter Ackroyd, *Dressing Up: Transvestism and Drag, the History of an Obsession* (London: Thames and Hudson, 1979).

23. On the popularity of female impersonators at American naval bases in the early twentieth century, see George Chauncey Jr., "Christian Brotherhood or Sexual Perversion: Homosexual Identities and the Construction of Sexual Boundaries in the World War One Era," *Journal of Social History* 19 (1985): 191, 207 n14.

24. On how cross-dressing allowed respectable male theater spectators to relax and with good conscience ogle the "principle boy's" legs or insult the horrid, old "dame," see Jane W. Stedman, "From Dame to Woman: W. S. Gilbert and Theatrical Transvestism," in *Suffer and Be Still: Women in the Victorian Era*, ed. Martha Vicinus (Bloomington: Indiana University Press, 1972), 20–37.

25. Sharon R. Ullman, "'The Twentieth Century Way': Female Impersonation and Sexual Practices in Turn of the Century America," *Journal of the History of Sexuality* 5 (1995): 573–600.

26. On the myth that to avoid electing a woman the cardinals inspect the papal candidate and must ritually declare "Habet duos testiculos et bene pendentes"—he has two testicles, well hung—see Alain Boureau, *La Papesse Jeanne* (Paris: Aubier, 1988), 16.

27. Rudolph M. Dekker and Lotte C. van de Pol, *The Tradition of Female Transvestism in Early Modern Europe* (New York: St. Martin's Press, 1989).

28. Randolph Trumbach, "London's Sapphists: From Three Sexes to Four Genders in the

Making of Modern Culture," in *Body Guards,* ed. Epstein and Straub, 122–23; Dianne Dugaw, *Warrior Women and Popular Balladry, 1650–1850* (Cambridge: Cambridge University Press, 1989); George S. Rousseau and Roy Porter, eds., *Sexual Underworlds of the Enlightenment* (Manchester: Manchester University Press, 1987).

29. Reinhold Schunze's play *Viktor und Viktoria* became the film *First a Girl* (1935) directed by Victor Saville and later *Victor Victoria* (1982) directed by Blake Edwards. See Patricia Petro, *Joyless Streets: Women and Melodramatic Representation in Weimar Germany* (Princeton: Princeton University Press, 1989), 153–55.

30. We know that in France the painter Rosa Bonheur and Napoleon III's mistress Marguerite Bellanger took advantage of such provisions, but it must have been a question of restricting bourgeois clothing since observers such as A. J. Munby noted that many working-class women in the mining and fishing industries necessarily dressed much like workmen; on the law of 16 brumaire year IX forbidding women to wear trousers or culottes without a medical certificate, see Anon., *Code de la femme* (Paris: Editions and Librairie, n.d.), 30–31; Arthur Boime, "Rosa Bonheur," *Art History* 4 (1981): 384–409; Jann Matlock, "Masquerading Women, Pathological Men: Cross-Dressing, Fetishism and the Theory of Perversion, 1882–1935," in *Fetishism as Cultural Discourse,* ed. Emily Apter and William Pietz (Ithaca: Cornell University Press, 1993), 31–61. On Germany, see Emil Gutheil, "Analysis of a Case of Transvestism," in Wilhelm Stekel, *Sexual Aberrations: The Phenomena of Fetishism in Relation to Sex* (New York: Liveright, 1930), 281–318; and on working women, see Michael Hiley, *Victorian Working Women: Portraits from Life* (London: G. Fraser, 1979), 41–43, 136n.21.

31. Susan Gubar, "Blessing in Disguise: Cross-Dressing for Female Modernists," *Massachusetts Review* 22 (1981): 477–508; Sandra M. Gilbert, "Costumes of the Mind: Transvestism as Metaphor in Modern Literature," *Critical Inquiry* 7 (1980): 394.

32. The trial reports filled the columns of the London *Times* during March and April of 1929. For the argument that the masquerade was employed so both women could deny their lesbianism, see Vern L. Bullough and Bonnie Bullough, *Cross Dressing, Sex, and Gender* (Philadelphia: University of Pennsylvania Press, 1993), 162–64.

33. Michael Baker, *Our Three Selves: The Life of Radclyffe Hall* (London: Hamish Hamilton, 1985), 254.

34. Hall's *The Well of Loneliness,* which seriously defended homosexuality, was seized by the police whereas Virginia Woolf's *Orlando* (1928), which played with ideas of transvestism and transsexualism, was a publishing triumph. "Different though the sexes are," wrote Woolf, "they intermix. In every human being a vacillation from one sex to the other takes place, and often it is only clothes that keep the male and female likeness, while underneath the sex is the very opposite of what is above." Quentin Bell, *Virginia Woolf: A Biography* (London: Hogarth Press, 1973), 138–39.

35. Magnus Hirschfeld, *Transvestites: The Erotic Desire to Cross Dress,* trans. Michael A. Lombardi-Nash (Buffalo: Prometheus Brooks, 1991), 95–100. In the eighteenth century, Henry Fielding reported that a woman, pretending to be a man, had duped a number of "wives." See *The Female Husband* (1746), ed. Claude E. Jones (Liverpool: Liverpool University Press, 1960).

36. Cesare Lombroso and G. Ferrero, *La Femme criminelle et la prostituée* (Paris: Alcan, 1896), 419–24.

37. On male transvestism in early modern Europe, see Guido Ruggiero, *The Boundaries of Eros: Sex Crime and Sexuality in Renaissance Venice* (New York: Oxford University Press, 1985), 136; Alan Bray, *Homosexuality in Renaissance England* (London: Gay Men's Press, 1982), 86–89.

38. A. S. Taylor, *The Principles and Practices of Medical Jurisprudence* (London: Churchill, 1894), 2:289, 470.

39. Jeffrey Weeks, *Sex, Politics and Society: The Regulation of Morality since 1800* (New York: Longman, 1981), 101; Michael Harris, "Social Diseases? Crime and Medicine in the Victorian Press," in *Medical Journals and Medical Knowledge: Historical Essays,* ed. W. F. Bynum, Stephen Lock, and Roy Porter (London: Routledge, 1992), 108–25.

40. William Roughead, *Bad Companions* (Edinburgh: W. Green, 1930), 149–83; and see also the London *Times* reports for 1870 and 1871.

41. H. Montgomery Hyde, *The Other Love* (London: Heinemann, 1970), 94.

42. Hirschfeld, *Transvestites,* 275.

43. London *Times,* 13 Apr. 1904, 3.

44. W. Norwood East, *Society and the Criminal* (Springfield, Ill.: Thomas, 1949), 165–66.

45. Weeks, *Sex, Politics and Society,* 102. On drag and travestititsm in the United States, see George Chauncey, *Gay New York: Gender, Urban Culture and the Making of the Gay Male World, 1890–1940* (New York: Basic Books, 1994).

46. Anon., "Masquerading," *Justice of the Peace and Local Government Review,* 26 Feb. 1938, 135.

47. *St. Helens Newspaper and Advertiser,* 20 Nov. 1931, 4.

48. Regina versus Jones (1896) 1 Q.B.4.

49. E. Anthony Rotundo, *American Manhood: Transformations in Masculinity from the Revolution to the Modern Era* (New York: Basic, 1993), 273–77; Sandra M. Gilbert and Susan Gubar, *Sex Changes,* vol. 2 of *No Man's Land: The Place of the Woman Writer in the Twentieth Century: Sexchanges* (New Haven: Yale University Press, 1989), 2:324–76.

50. Sigmund Freud, "Three Essays on Sexuality" (1905), *Standard Edition,* 7:136–38.

51. George Chauncy Jr., "From Sexual Inversion to Homosexuality: Medicine and the Changing Conceptualization of Female Deviance," *Salmagundi* 58–59 (1982–83): 120–30. For an ethnographic account of early-twentieth-century American homosexual communities, see Chauncey, *Gay New York.*

52. Weeks, *Sex, Politics and Society,* 105.

53. During the First World War call-up, reported Hirschfeld, there were several cases of men showing up in dresses at German recruiting offices. Magnus Hirschfeld, *Sexual Anomalies and Perversions,* ed. Norman Haire (London: Encyclopaedic Press, 1952), 198.

54. A 1960s study based on the Kinsey Institute files concluded that transvestites suffered at an early age from distorted and confused notions of gender, but it noted that such findings were drawn from a self-selected sample of sex offenders who ended up in jail. Little was known of the far larger number of "masqueraders" who avoided brushes with the law. Paul H. Gebhard, John H. Gagnon, Wardell B. Pomeroy, and Cornelia V. Christenson, *Sex Offenders: An Analysis of Types* (New York: Harper and Row, 1965), 410–11.

55. Hirschfeld, *Transvestites,* 267–73.

56. Ibid., 231.

57. Charlotte Wolff, *Magnus Hirschfeld: A Portrait of a Pioneer in Sexology* (London: Quartet, 1986), 107–9.

58. A twentieth-century overview of transvestism made it clear that the French had contributed little to its examination; see Dr. Agnes Masson, *Le Travestissement: Essai de psychopathologie sexuelle* (Paris: Editions Hippocrate, 1935); and see also H. Legludic, *Notes et observations de médecine légale: Attentats aux moeurs* (Paris Masson, 1896), 169–73; Eugène Wilhelm, "Publications allemandes sur les questions sexuelles," *Archives de l'anthropologie criminelle* 27 (1912): 301–9; Pierre Vachet, *Psychologie du vice* (Paris: Grasset, 1934).

59. Chushichi Tsuzuki, *Edward Carpenter, 1844–1929: Prophet of Human Fellowship* (Cambridge: Cambridge University Press, 1980), 131–34; 145–51.

60. Edward Carpenter, "Intermediate Types among Primitive Folk," *Sex,* vol. 1 of *Selected Writings* (London: GMP, 1984), 263; and on the Berdache, see Walter L. Williams,

The Spirit and the Flesh: Sexual Diversity in American Indian Culture (Boston: Beacon Press, 1986).

61. See Vincent Brome, *Havelock Ellis: Philosopher of Sex: A Biography* (London: Routledge and Kegan Paul, 1979); Phyllis Grosskurth, *Havelock Ellis: A Biography* (London: Allen Lane, 1980).

62. Havelock Ellis, "Eonism," *Studies in the Psychology of Sex* (Philadelphia: F. A. Davis, 1928), 7:87. For the similar argument that some women only feel at ease in male clothes and regard themselves as "transvestites" when forced to wear dresses, see Holly Devor, *Gender Blending: Confronting the Limits of Duality* (Bloomington: Indiana University Press, 1988), 129.

63. A further sign of the growing interest in the subject was the appearance of M. Coryn's *The Chevalier d'Eon* (1932), hailed as a "skillful biography of a pathological specimen" in *Week-End Review,* 20 Aug. 1932, 216. For a more recent account see Gary Kates, "D'Eon Returns to France: Gender and Power in 1777," in Epstein and Straub, *Body Guards,* 167; and Gary Kates, *Monsieur d'Eon Is a Woman: A Tale of Political Intrigue and Sexual Masquerade* (New York: Basic Books, 1995).

64. Ellis quoted in Max Hodann, *History of Modern Morals,* trans. Stella Browne (London: Heinemann, 1937), 49.

65. Ellis, "Eonism," 7:17, 102.

66. Freud, *Three Essays,* 56.

67. Bernard Hollander, *The Psychology of Misconduct, Vice and Crime* (London: Allen and Unwin, 1922), 142–43.

68. See the paper read to the British Sexological Society in May 1932 by Theodore J. Faithful, "The Re-Education of the Invert," *The Socialist Review* 4 (1932): 106–19.

69. For a similar claim that "true" transvestites were not homosexual, see East, *Society and the Criminal.*

70. Ellis, "Eonism," 7:29.

71. Ellis, *Views and Reviews,* 2:219.

72. *Week-End Review,* 21 Nov. 1931, 645.

73. See E. Roy Calvert's statement, "Four and a half centuries ago, in the city of Basle, a cock was solemnly tried and burnt alive for committing the unnatural crime of having laid an egg. It was not until later that it was discovered that there is such a thing as a crowing hen. Yet we still punish people to-day for acts which we do not understand." *Week-End Review,* 19 Dec. 1931, 794; and see also *Week-End Review,* 28 Nov. 1931, 678–79; E. Roy Calvert, *Capital Punishment in the Twentieth Century* (New York: Putnam, 1927); *The Law-breakers* (London: Routledge, 1931); *The Death Penalty Enquiry* (London: Gollancz, 1932). Herbert Chorley was author of *Cleave's End* (London: Sisley, 1908).

74. *Week-End Review,* 5 Dec. 1931, 712. See Grace Winnifred Pailthorpe, *What We Put in Prison* (London: Williams and Norgate, 1932); *Studies in the Psychology of Delinquency* (London: HMSO, 1932). On attempts to have psychoanalytic therapies offered to prisoners, see W. J. Forsythe, *Penal Discipline, Reformatory Projects and the English Prison Commission, 1895–1939* (Exeter: University of Exeter Press, 1990), 159–61.

75. *Week-End Review,* 28 Nov. 1931, 678–79.

76. Ibid., 679–80.

77. Ibid., 19 Dec. 1931, 795.

78. The unnamed American journal refused to print the article; Ellis, *Views and Reviews,* 2:221.

79. *Week-End Review,* 5 Dec. 1931, 712.

80. Ibid., 26 Dec. 1931, 822. Haynes, a lawyer, was the author of *Religious Persecution* (1904), *The Case for Liberty* (1919), and *A Lawyer's Notebook* (1932).

81. *Week-End Review,* 19 Dec. 1931, 787; 2 Jan. 1932, 10; and on the make up of the

Society, which went under a variety of names, see Lesley Hall, "'Disinterested Enthusiasm for Sexual Misconduct': The British Society for the Study of Sex Psychology, 1913–47," *Journal of Contemporary History* 30 (1995): 665–86; David C. Weigle, "Psychology and Homosexuality: The British Sexological Society," *Journal of the History of the Behavioral Sciences* 31 (1995): 136–48.

82. Stella Browne, "Sexual Variety and Variability among Women" (1915), in Sheila Rowbotham, *A New World for Women: Stella Browne, Socialist Feminist* (London: Pluto, 1977), 100.

83. *New Generation*, Feb. 1932, 29.

84. *Week-End Review*, 28 Nov. 1931, 679.

85. Ibid., 5 Dec. 1928, 711.

86. Ibid., 2 Jan. 1932, 10; 16 Jan. 1932, 68; and for the petition, see 6 Feb. 1932, 165.

87. Ibid., 9 Apr. 1932, 439, 446.

88. For the journal's expression of its appreciation for Sir Herbert Samuel "in mitigating by sympathy and science the rigours of the system which he finds himself responsible for administering," see *Week-End Review*, 16 Apr. 1932, 475.

89. H. V. Dicks, *Fifty Years of the Tavistock Clinic* (London: Routledge and Kegan Paul, 1970), 19.

90. Ibid., 78.

91. René Guyon, *Sex Life and Sex Ethics*, trans. J. C. Flugel and I. Flugel (London: Bodley Head, 1933), 246, 271.

92. F. B. Rockstro, *A Plain Talk on Sex Difficulties* (1934; London: British Sexological Society, 1947), 25, 27; and see also Laurie Taylor, "The Unfinished Sexual Revolution," *Journal of Biosocial Sciences* 3 (1971): 473–92.

93. Stevenson was the honorary secretary of the Noise Abatement Society; *Week-End Review*, 6 Aug. 1932, 156; 31 Dec. 1932, 797.

94. *Week-End Review*, 5 Dec. 1931, 703; and see also Barbara Brookes, *Abortion in England: 1900–1967* (London: Croom Helm, 1988), 37–40.

95. *Week-End Review*, 28 May 1932, 666.

96. Ibid., 24 Sept. 1932, 338.

97. Dave King, 'Gender Confusions: Psychological and Psychiatric Conceptions of Transvestism and Transsexualism,' in *The Making of the Modern Homosexual*, ed. Kenneth Plummer (London: Hutchinson, 1981), 55–83.

98. Ellis, "Eonism," 7:30.

99. Max Hodann, *A History of Modern Morals*, trans. Stella Browne (London: Heinemann, 1937), 48.

100. *Liverpool Post and Mercury*, 16 Nov. 1931, 9.

101. Ellis, *Views and Reviews*, 2:220.

102. For an an account of the Swedish sex-change operation of Einar Wegener, who called himself "Lili Elbe" and after surgery was known as Andreas Sparre (d. 1931), see Niels Hoyer [pseud. Ernst Harthern], *Man into Woman: An Authentic Record of a Change of Sex* (London; Jarrolds, 1933). In the introduction Norman Haire, a gynecologist and active member of the British Sexological Society, noted that Dr. Steinach had achieved some success in sex changes by employing hormone treatments on lower animals.

103. On the question of whether female transvestites can be feminists and by dressing like men are really opposing patriarchy, see Janice G. Raymond, *The Transsexual Empire* (London: Woman's Press, 1979).

104. Michel Foucault, *Herculine Barbin: Being the Recently Discovered Memoirs of a Nineteenth-century Female Hermaphrodite*, trans. Richard McDougall (New York: Pantheon, 1991), 4; Alice Domurat Dreger, "Doubtful Sex: The Fate of the Hermaphrodite in Victorian England," *Victorian Studies* 38 (1995): 335–71.

105. Burrows's sexual ignorance was not unique. A number of the letters received in the interwar period by Marie Stopes, the British birth-control propagandist, concerned nonconsummation. Stopes herself, a university educated woman, only realized after several months that her first marriage had not been consumated, and even in the 1990s a proportion of couples presenting at infertility clinics are unaware of how to have intercourse that will result in a conception. I owe this latter information to Lesley Hall.

106. *St. Helens Newspaper and Advertiser,* 20 Nov. 1931, 4.

107. Dicks, *Fifty Years of the Tavistock Clinic,* 45.

108. For a perceptive account of the popularity of female transvestite performances in French theater, see Lenard Berlanstein, "Breeches and Breaches: Cross-Dress Theater and the Culture of Gender Ambiguity in Modern France," *Comparative Studies in Society and History* (forthcoming). The question of why in the twentieth century several generations of heterosexual women who wished to appear mysteriously seductive adopted androgynous fashion styles deserves examination.

109. Marjorie Garber, *Vested Interests: Cross-dressing and Cultural Anxiety* (London: Routledge, 1992); Judith Butler, *Gender Trouble* (New York: Routledge, 1990).

110. Quentin Crisp, *The Naked Civil Servant* (New York: New American Library, 1983), 21.

CONCLUSION

1. On the trope of male camaraderie and war as a test of manliness, see Paul Fussell, *The Great War and Modern Memory* (New York: Oxford University Press, 1975); Michael C. C. Adams, *The Great Adventure: Male Desire and the Coming of World War I* (Bloomington: University of Indiana Press, 1990); George Mosse, *Fallen Soldiers: Reshaping the Memory of the World Wars* (New York: Oxford University Press, 1990).

2. The military also unintentionally unearthed unanticipated and disturbing evidence of male deviancy. Though officers were likely untroubled by a recruit's sadomasochistic tendencies, they were taken aback when transvestites in dresses appeared before recruiting boards and when more than one wife applied for a bigamous or common-law husband's dependence allowance. Stephen Parker, *Informal Marriage, Cohabitation and the Law, 1750–1989* (London: Macmillan, 1990).

3. Paul Crook, *Darwinism, War and History: The Debate over the Biology of War from the "Origin of the Species" to the First World War* (Cambridge; Cambridge University Press, 1994), 56–138.

4. E. E. Southard, *Shell-Shock and other Neuropsychiatric Problems* (Boston: Leonard, 1919), 257.

5. In the Boer and Cuban Wars, high levels of "inanity" had been noted; in the Russo-Japanese War of 1905, the Russians had used army specialists to deal with psychological problems. See Norman Fenton, *Shell Shock and its Aftermath* (London: Kimpton, 1926).

6. Even in peacetime many psychiatrists believed hysterics were simply craving sympathy and so dealt with them ruthlessly. Michael J. Clarke, "The Rejection of Psychological Approaches to Mental Disorder in Late Nineteenth-Century British Psychiatry," in *Madhouses, Mad-Doctors and Madmen: the Social History of Psychiatry in the Victorian Era,* ed. Andrew Scull (London; Athlone, 1981), 271–312.

7. André Leri, *Shell Shock: Commotional and Emotional Aspects* (London: University of London Press, 1919); Millais Culpin, *Psychoneuroses of War and Peace* (Cambridge: Cambridge University Press, 1920); and see also Joanna Bourke, *Dismembering the Male: Men's Bodies, Britain and the Great War* (London: Reaktion Books, 1996).

8. K. R. Eissler, *Freud as an Expert Witness: The Discussion of War Neuroses between Freud and Wagner-Jauregg,* trans. Christine Trollope (Madison, Conn.: International Universities Press, 1986), 60; and see also Sigmund Freud, "Memorandum on the Electrical Treat-

ment of War Neuroses" (1920), *Standard Edition of the Complete Psychological Works*, trans. J. Strachey (London: Hogarth Press, 1966), 17:211–15; Meyer S. Gunther, "Freud as Expert Witness: Wagner-Jauregg and the Problem of War Neuroses," *Annals of Psychoanalysis* 2 (1975): 3–23; Magda Whitrow, *Julius Wagner-Jauregg (1857–1940)* (London: Smith-Gordon, 1993), 101–7. Wagner-Jauregg later became a member of the Nazi party.

9. Martin Stone, "Shell Shock and the Psychologists," in *Anatomy of Madness*, ed. William F. Bynun (London: Tavistock, 1985), 2:242ff.

10. One symptom would be an old misogynist such as Belfort Bax lamenting the decline of male clubs and complaining that now men were being forced to regard their wives as intellectual companions. Ernest Belfort Bax, *Reminiscences and Reflections of a Mid and Late Victorian* (London: Allen and Unwin, 1918), 64–66, 174, 197–201.

11. Richard Wall and Jay Winter, eds., *The Upheaval of War: Family, Work and Welfare in Europe, 1914–1918* (Cambridge: Cambridge University Press, 1988); Mary Louise Roberts, *Civilization without Sexes: Reconstructing Gender in Postwar France, 1917–1927* (Chicago: University of Chicago Press, 1994).

12. Adrian Caesar, *Taking It Like a Man: Suffering, Sexuality and the War Poets: Brooke, Sassoon, Owen, Graves* (New York: Manchester University Press, 1993); Graham Dawson, *Soldier Heroes: British Adventure, Empire and the Imaginings of Masculinities* (New York: Routledge, 1994).

13. Modris Eksteins, *Rites of Spring: The Great War and the Birth of the Modern Age* (Toronto: Lester and Orpen Dennys, 1989), 292.

14. Doctors declared that sexual potency and military bravery were related. "A matter of fact bearing on this point is the experience of army officers, who have observed that a man of weak sexual instinct is always a poor soldier." Irving C. Rosse, "Sexual Incapacity in Its Medico-Legal Relations," in *Medical Jurisprudence: Forensic Medicine and Toxicology*, ed. R. A. Witthaus and Tracy C. Becker (New York: William Wood, 1894), 2:395.

15. Rosa Mayreder, *A Survey of the Woman Problem*, trans. Herman Scheffauer (London: Heinemann, 1913), 109.

16. Christina Simmons, "Modern Sexuality and the Myth of Victorian Repression," in Barbara Melosh, *Gender and American History since 1890* (London: Routledge, 1993), 24–27.

17. Claudia L. Johnston, *Politics, Gender and Sentimentality in the 1790's — Wollstonecraft, Radcliffe, Burney, Austen* (Chicago: Chicago University Press, 1995); Gail Bederman, *Manliness and Civilization: A Cultural History of Gender and Race in the United States* (Chicago: Chicago University Press, 1995).

18. Patrick Fridenson, ed., *1914–1918: L'Autre front* (Paris: Les Éditions ouvrières, 1977). Ann Higonnet, *Behind the Lines Gender and the Two World Wars* (New Haven: Yale University Press, 1987).

19. Rosa Maria Bracco, *Merchants of Hope: British Middlebrow Writers and the First World War, 1919–1939* (Oxford: Berg, 1993); Sandra M. Gilbert and Susan Gubar, *Sexchanges*, vol. 2 of *No Man's Land: The Place of the Woman Writer in the Twentieth Century* (New Haven: Yale University Press, 1989), 258–323.

20. For the argument that new therapies such as suggestion under hypnosis would be the quickest way whereby the shell-shocked could be cured and sent back into the lines, see M. D. Eder, *War-Shock: The Psychoneuroses in War Psychology and Treatment* (London: Heinemann, 1917), 128–33; and see also Eric J. Leed, *No Man's Land: Combat and Identity in World War One* (Cambridge: Cambridge University Press, 1979), 163ff.

21. Adolf Hitler, *Mein Kampf (Mon Combat)* (Paris: Librairie critique, 1930), 224–29; 370. On Adorno's statement that avowals of virility have to be regarded with suspicion, see Lynn Segal, *Slow Motion: Changing Masculinities, Changing Men* (New Brunswick, N.J.: Rutgers University Press, 1990), 45.

22. Paul Weindling, *Health, Race and German Politics: Between National Unification and Nazism, 1870–1945* (Oxford: Oxford University Press, 1989), 101–2. Sheila Faith Weiss, *Race Hygiene and National Efficiency: The Eugenics of Wilhem Schallmayer* (Berkeley: University of California Press, 1987); Robert Procter, *Racial Hygiene: Medicine under the Nazis* (Cambridge: Harvard University Press, 1988).

23. Alison Sinclair, *The Deceived Husband: A Kleinian Approach to the Literature of Infidelity* (Oxford: Clarendon Press, 1993), 24.

24. R. W. Connell, *Gender and Power: Society, the Person and Sexual Politics* (Stanford: Stanford University Press, 1987), 183–190.

Index